Catholic Peacemakers

GARLAND REFERENCE LIBRARY OF THE HUMANITIES
VOLUME 1372

CATHOLIC PEACEMAKERS
A DOCUMENTARY HISTORY

VOLUME II
FROM THE RENAISSANCE TO THE
TWENTIETH CENTURY, PART II

EDITED BY
RONALD G. MUSTO

GARLAND PUBLISHING, INC.
NEW YORK AND LONDON
1996

Library of Congress Cataloging-in-Publication Data

Musto, Ronald G.
    Catholic peacemakers : a documentary history / by Ronald G. Musto.
        p.   cm. — (Garland reference library of the humanities ;
    vol. 1372)
    Includes bibliographical references and index.
    Contents: v. 2. From the Renaissance to the twentieth century.
    ISBN 0-8153-0605-9 (v. 2: alk. paper)
    1. Peace—Religious aspects—Catholic Church.   2. Catholic Church—
Doctrines.   I. Title.   II. Series.
BX1795.P43M88   1996
261.8'73'08822—dc20   92–42658
                                                                            CIP

Cover photograph by Quentin Metsys. *Desiderius Erasmus at Age Fifty.*
Rome, Corsini Palace. (Alinari/Art Resource, New York)

Printed on acid-free, 250-year-life paper
Manufactured in the United States of America

To
Elizabeth Casey,
Matthew, and Margaret

"Your cities do not exist. Perhaps they have never existed. It is sure they will never exist again. Why do you amuse yourself with consolatory fables?..."
"This is the aim of my explorations: examining the traces of happiness still to be glimpsed, I gauge its short supply. If you want to know how much darkness there is around you, you must sharpen your eyes, peering at the faint lights in the distance."
— from Italo Calvino, *Invisible Cities*

Quentin Metsys. Desiderius Erasmus at Age Fifty. *Rome, Corsini Palace. (Alinari/Art Resource, New York)*

CONTENTS

VOLUME I: From the Bible to the Crusades

Contents: Volume 1

VOLUME 2: From the Renaissance to the Twentieth Century

Contents

Contents

Contents

*   *

*

ILLUSTRATIONS

NUMERICAL
LIST OF TEXTS

VOLUME 1

VOLUME 2

List of Texts: Volume 2

* *

*

Diego Rivera. Las Casas and Cortes. *Mexico City, National Palace. (SEF/Art Resource, New York)*

PREFACE

The following book is the final volume of a study of the peace tradition in the Catholic church from the Bible to the twentieth century. It examines the continuing, unbroken, and self-sustaining stream within Catholicism that spans the centuries between the peacemakers of the early church and the nonviolent movements for peace and justice in our own time. This series of studies addresses the teacher, student, or general reader who wants a basic introduction to the Catholic peace tradition, those who seek readings for a course on church or peace history, and specialists who want an introduction to the materials and issues involved in research on the various aspects of this tradition.

The first volume of this study, *The Catholic Peace Tradition* (Maryknoll, NY: Orbis Books, 1986) is a narrative history ranging from the biblical antecedents of our concepts of peace through the Gospels and early church, the peace movements of the Middle Ages, the Humanist tradition of peacemaking, and the problems and promise of peace in the early modern world, from the missionary peacemakers of Latin America to the papacy's work for international peace. In the twentieth century the book covers the issues of the world wars and the role of Catholics in furthering war or peace, the revolution in church life accomplished by Pope John XXIII and the Second Vatican Council, and peace movements today in Europe, the Third World, and the United States. This book was accompanied by extensive annotation and a complete bibliography, but the limits imposed by the size of the study and its purpose as an introductory survey precluded discursive notes and lengthy comments on citations.

The second volume, *The Peace Tradition in the Catholic Church: An Annotated Bibliography* (New York: Garland Publishing, 1987) served three purposes. The first was to update the research on the *Catholic Peace Tradition* from November 1984, when research for that book was completed, to November 1986, when research on the second volume was finished. Most of the entries in that work had already been cited in the first book, but there they were accompanied by extensive commentary. The second purpose, really an expansion of the first, was to provide the researcher with a detailed analysis of all these and more recent works as the basis both for detailed study of the first book and as a guide for further research in this field. While much work has appeared over the decade since it publication, it still offers a solid introduction to the basic materials. The third purpose was to arrange these materials by topic and period as a framework for study and reading. This was followed by a third volume closely tied by theme and intent to the present study: *Liberation Theologies: A Research Guide* (New York: Garland Publishing, 1991).

The fourth volume was the first part of this collection of readings, *Catholic Peacemakers: A Documentary History. From the Bible to the Era of the Crusades* (New York: Garland Publishing, 1993). This includes selections from the primary sources used in *The Catholic Peace Tradition* and cited in the *Annotated Bibliography* and stretches from the concepts of peace found in Greek and Roman antiquity and in the Hebrew Bible and New Testament into the early church, the collapse of the Roman Empire, the early Middle Ages, and through the Peace and Truce of God. It concludes with the peace movements and thought of the Crusade era, with papal peacemaking, and with a survey of medieval ideas on the rights of individual conscience.

The fifth and last volume of this study, the present book, begins with the Renaissance humanists, presents texts from the missionary peacemakers in Latin America into the eighteenth century and then delves into texts from the internationalists of early modern Europe. The last chapters then present materials describing the nature and broad scope of peacemaking in our own century. Chapter 4 covers the crisis of Christianity faced by the Holocaust and World War II; while Chapter 5 examines the rebirth of peacemaking in Europe during the era of Vatican II up to the Velvet Revolutions of 1989. A sixth chapter traces the new forms of nonviolent liberation in the Third World. The final chapter presents readings from the United States over the course of this century to the most recent Catholic peace thought and action during the Persian Gulf War of 1991, concluding with examples of some new forms of Catholic peacemaking. Thus each part of this documentary history can be read and used as a unique unit, yet each is also part of the larger whole of this tradition.

Preface

Research on this project has been an educational one for me, a process that has been full of surprises, and one whose richness of findings has deepened my own understanding of the issues involved and my own faith in the mysterious existence of this unique Catholic tradition. At the same time it has also convinced me of the high standards of research in, of the questions posed by, and of the controversies engendered within, the study of this peace tradition. While peace research courses and curricula have existed for decades on campuses and in schools across the United States, specifically Catholic and historical studies have only recently acquired a basic set of research materials, questions, and goals. I hope that this collection of studies has helped in this work.

One of the major inspirations for this collection has been the remarkable collection of Roman texts compiled by Naphtali Lewis and Meyer Reinhold in their sourcebook *Roman Civilization* (2 vols., New York: Columbia University Press, 1951; Harper & Row, 1966 and subsequent printings). That collection, used as the chief text for an undergraduate course in Roman history, opened to me the wonders and pleasures of reconstructing history from the primary written documents and convinced me that the study and writing of history was a noble task indeed.

I would like to thank those who helped make this work possible. The research facilities and staffs of the New York Public Library and of the Columbia and of Fordham University libraries have been indispensable resources. My editors at Garland over the long course of this project – Gary Kuris, Pamela Chergotis, Paula Ladenburg, Phyllis Korper, Chris Collins, David Estrin, Rita Quintas, Eunice Petrini, and Laurel Stegina – have all earned my thanks for their generous enthusiasm and professionalism.

As ever, the joy and unfolding mystery of my life with Eileen Gardiner has been, and remains for me, my truest vision of peace.

New York City
December 1995

INTRODUCTION

It is no coincidence – though it may surprise many – that over the last ten years six of the winners of the Nobel Peace Prize have been Roman Catholics (Mairead Corrigan, Betty Williams, Mother Teresa of Calcutta, Adolfo Pérez Esquivel, Lech Walesa, and Oscar Arias), while numerous others (including Oscar Romero, Dom Helder Camara, Danilo Dolci, Cesar Chavez, Dolores Huerta, and Paulo Cardinal Arns of São Paulo) have been nominated for the prize in recent years. All have demonstrated the indisputable truth that as never before religious motivations and personal faith are affecting and defining the most important issues of public policy and life facing us today: peace and justice. They have shown that their faith, *as Christians and Catholics*, is a living, active, and important element in the world today and that this faith is based on, and grows vitally from and within, a living Catholic tradition of peacemaking.

WHAT IS *CATHOLIC* PEACEMAKING?

Although the Catholic tradition must ultimately find its place within the Judeo-Christian tradition as a whole – and this must reach out to religious traditions and peoples all around the world – there are certain aspects of a particularly Catholic outlook and past that make singling it out a valid and worthwhile historical endeavor.

Only by reaching into their own past – as painful and misunderstood as that might sometimes be – can Catholics truly grasp their own positive contribution to building peace and thus helping to perfect God's creation. Only then can they reach out to others as equals in peacemaking and find a common ground on which to build a new world.

While its terms and limits are evolving and growing, this Catholic tradition has always defined peace as something active: not passive or acquiescent, not flattering to evil or retreating into indifference or silence, but activist, struggling for justice and motivated by Christian love. The Catholic tradition sees peace as a force that must confront evil, but at the same time must love the evildoer and convert that evil to good. For the Catholic "turning the other cheek" is not the answer to violence, but only the question that confronts violence at its roots with the reality of peace. It is a mysterious force offered to the violent to ponder, wrestle with, and finally, accept. From there it seeks to find new answers, to actively solve problems in new ways.

While the Catholic tradition has often been equated – unjustly – almost solely with the institutions of power and the intellectual construct of the just war, even this perversion of Christian principle has retained a kernel of this truth: that the Christian cannot passively acquiesce to evil, that he or she owes duty and service to the human community, and that this service must go beyond a simple "no" and involve self-sacrifice and struggle.

As the materials in this documentary history will show, many Catholics throughout the church's history have understood this truth; but only recently, in the twentieth century and in the wake of its holocausts, has the church seriously begun to question its own assumptions about the nature of this struggle and about this sacrifice and service. Thus in recent decades the term "pacifism" has begun to be replaced by "peacemaking" as the definition of Catholic action – not that "pacifism" has been rejected, but that our understanding of its meaning has taken on all the fullness and activism of the Christian meaning of "peace" as a force of love and justice in the world. At the same time, especially since Pope John XXIII, the church as a whole has begun to explicitly reject the just-war tradition as a theology and to see it as a secular ethical and legal system aimed at clarifying a human activity, one not essentially rooted in, or bound to, the revelation of the Gospels.

Today, therefore, we talk of "nonviolence" and active resistance instead of "passive resistance." We can describe nonviolent revolutions and "people's power" because we have actually seen them at work; and when we discuss resistance to war, we fully realize that this is only one part of an active and positive embrace of justice and love for the victims as well as the agents of violence and exploitation. The examples of the many individuals in the following selections will show, if nothing else, that there is certainly nothing "passive" about the life of the Christian peacemaker.

WHAT IS A *CHRISTIAN?*

One other question worth raising at this point is the very notion of what it is to be a Christian, both historically and in the present age. In the 1980s, in the United States at least, the term "Christian" seems almost inevitably to have been associated with the forces of reaction: with a life that is singularly repressed, repressive, and repressing on every level, from that of basic moral stances, the role of the individual in society, of the woman in the family, in work, and in the public arena, of a family life that is isolating of its members from society at large, authoritarian, and individualistic in all its definitions of daily life, leisure, work, economy, society, and religion.

This notion of the Christian was also frequently associated with political conservatism at home and support for repressive regimes around the world. It was also linked to forces that are culturally and artistically repressive, seeking to ban, censor, or ignore many forward-looking forms of expression in the visual arts, music, drama, and literature, all in the name of a hypothetically – and most often hypocritical – "Christian" morality. "Christian" in the United States, in the 1980s, was also most widely associated with a punitive God and a punitive sense of the place of religion in life: a set of laws and codes, of restrictions and punishments for behavior that seems to fall outside the narrow confines of certain "middle-class" norms. This outlook rewards the mundane and the commonplace, it speaks in terms of the unimaginative cliché and the tired ritual; it avoids – even condemns – risks and seeks instead what we would call the "peace" of quiet, of order, and of rigidity.

Such a definition of the Christian is a great tragedy of our times, a clear and present danger to the spiritual work at hand, and a stumbling block for the present discussion; for the Catholic Christians whom we shall be discussing below, whose thoughts and actions we will be documenting, have many things in common. They are risk-takers, they flourish on the margins and borders, the edges of "normal" society; they upset convention, moralities, and structures of influence and power. Their message is often anti-authoritarian; they are often egalitarian in their moral outlook and anti-establishment in their politics: their peace is that of justice, of movement, and of change. They are men and women, young and old who are tired of the status quo, who seek a new world, a new human society, a New Jerusalem. They have realized that

Christ's realm, being not of this world, is not tied to powerful men in established positions but finds its citizens among those for whom it came: the poor and restless, the disaffected, the outcasts and marginalized. These are more often than not the prime subjects of the documents that we have presented below.

But do not be misled: you will find among these pages many of the most important figures in history and in contemporary life. Yet they became so not by being forbidding figures of authority and repression, not by saying "No" to the world and its delights, but by answering a passionate "Yes" to challenges and to change, for seeking after the possibilities of the world with imagination and young eyes, realizing its potential for grace and for salvation both within themselves and within their neighbors, even within their enemies and within the enemies of change and growth.

THE SCOPE OF THIS WORK

Volume I of this documentary history presents selections from the Bible, writings of the early church, canon law and penitential texts, the lives and sayings of the saints, histories of popular peace movements, monastic texts on the meaning and practice of peace, missionary accounts and plans for nonviolent conversion, mystical and visionary tracts, accounts of individual witnesses for peace, episcopal and papal letters, and the decrees of church synods and councils.

Topics covered include all forms of Catholic peacemaking: pacifism in the traditional sense; key elements of the just-war tradition which still, unfortunately, characterizes the Catholic approach to peacemaking for so many, Catholic and non-Catholic alike. Here, however, I will focus on those elements of the just-war theory that attempt to limit war, to define the justness of conflicts, and to clarify the role and rights of conscience. This volume will also present texts demonstrating the place of international law in Catholic thought; theologies of peace, liberation, and social justice; as well as apocalyptic elements of Catholicism that have contributed to our understanding and practice of peace.

Volume I therefore describes a full circle of opposing currents in peace history. It traces the evolution of peace from concepts and structures of order and prosperity found in ancient agrarian societies to those of social justice and inner conversion described in both Jewish and Christian scripture. This cycle is repeated as the Romanized Christianity of the late Empire borrows notions of peace as the tranquility of order and builds these on top of Gospel roots. After a process of experimentation and reevaluation, Christian ideas of peace reemerge as active forces for justice and the conversion of individual hearts that take on the task of converting the new "barbarian" societies. At the end of the period covered in Volume I they blossom into newly active movements of prophecy and protest that flourished on a massive level during the Crusade era. Thus the Peace of God and the birth of the mendicant orders and their lay third orders touched hundreds of thousands with a world vision based on simplicity, compassion and nonviolence.

Volume II picks up the narrative with the Renaissance. It continues through the period of European expansionism to the end of the nineteenth century. But rather than tracing Christianity's triumphalist marriage to power during this era, the documents in Volume II tell a very different story. These sources illustrate movements that sought not conquest but the community of a heavenly city built slowly and patiently here on earth.

The last three chapters then present documents that describe the nature and broad scope of peacemaking in our own century, a century rocked by traumas to faith and community, yet one that has set about rebuilding the relationship of the individual to neighbor, society, and God's creation from the emptiness of ground zero up.

This second volume therefore adds the writings of pacifist missionaries, of humanists and Catholic internationalists, selections from church councils, including key texts in Latin American liberation theology, modern papal bulls, including *Pacem in Terris* and *Populorum Progressio,* and the writings of contemporary Catholic peacemakers around the world.

Since Catholic peace history is a relatively new field, and because my definition of peace follows contemporary Catholic practice, the works selected here are often not restricted simply to narrowly defined peace movements or statements but include materials on the work of the church for social justice. While the church's teaching on economic justice surely forms a part of this commitment to social justice, this is a topic that belongs to another field of research and is not included here.

THE TEXTS

The number and division of chapters in these two volumes has been designed to follow as closely as possible the sequence in my narrative account, *The Catholic Peace Tradition,* and of the subject divisions in the *Annotated Bibliography.* This is so that the user can have an easy frame of reference to this narrative history, and that the reader of the narrative and annotated bibliography can easily sample the most important of the primary sources available for the history of Catholic peacemaking in any given period.

For ease of reference, texts are numbered consecutively throughout both parts of this collection. Each text or group of texts is preceded by my introductory comments, with full bibliographical references to the texts cited. One major concern of this collection is that the documents be presented in sufficient length to speak for themselves, both in their overall context and full meaning. Peacemaking and peace texts are often ambiguous records of human history, fraught with the ambiguities between action and force, passivity and contemplation inherent in all human activity. Therefore, to be as faithful to the meanings of the texts as possible, I have tried to present them fully, not simply highlighting selected "famous" or "quotable" passages out of context.

Many of the texts are translated here into English for the first time. I have tried to remain as close to the original as possible, while providing readable modern versions. In some cases my own version reflects the difficulty inherent in the ideas or style of the original, or the sometimes preliminary quality of the modern edition. Biblical citations are taken directly from the *New Jerusalem Bible* (Garden City, NY: Doubleday, 1985), except where time-honored usage, or the Latin Vulgate version used by the medieval author, dictated otherwise.

At the same time I have attempted to provide introductions that will fill two purposes. The first of these is to give historical and biographical information on the text and its writer. The second is to offer both an introduction and a meditation on the text, a series of reflections and questions for the reader. For not only does a text offer itself to be read, it also engages the reader in a dialogue, and it offers a series of questions. While each reader will inevitably come away from each document, or approach that text, with his or her own questions, I hope that the questions and problems that I have raised will aid in reading and thinking about the particular selection and about broader questions in

xliv

the history and living tradition of peacemaking.

Finally, I should note several areas covered in this collection of sources that were only partially treated or not dealt with at all in *The Catholic Peace Tradition* but that were included in the *Annotated Bibliography*. Among these are the vision and mystical literature of the Middle Ages; the revolutionary situation in Central America, including Nicaragua; the martyrdom of the American churchwomen in El Salvador; and the United Farm Workers, the Sanctuary Movement in the United States; and Catholic opposition to the Persian Gulf War of 1991. Since the narrative history could not possibly encompass every group or individual in the history of Catholic peacemaking, it had to select cases that spoke for a region or a period as a whole. In this documentary history I have tried to amplify this treatment.

I hope that I have not, but suspect I still have, omitted many peacemakers that I invite readers to bring to my attention through criticism and suggestions for revisions. Again, my purpose here is not to retreat within the walls of narrow Roman Catholic interest but to break down those walls by showing that the Catholic tradition has much to share with all people of good will.

* *
*

CHAPTER 6
The Third World:
Catholic Peacemaking and Liberation

INTRODUCTION

The term "Third World" is of very little use to us today, for it classifies as inferior to the cultures and powers of the U.S., Europe, and the former Soviet Union, cultures and nations as ancient as India or Korea and as economically powerful as Brazil or Indonesia, grouping them as one with nations like Haiti and El Salvador, which now suffer the results of five centuries of oppression, poverty, and violence.

Popes John XXIII and Paul VI and Vatican Council II brought world attention to the role of the Catholic church in the Third World. It came as a shock at that time, and still comes as a surprise to many in Europe and North America, that the majority of all Catholics today live in the "Third World": in Central and South America primarily, but also in Africa and on the rims of Asia: in India, Korea, and the Philippines.

Catholicism in the Third World began as the product of European expansion and colonialism and brought with it the marriage of European culture with Christian religion that had been epitomized in the notion of medieval and early-modern Christendom. Yet over the centuries both the former colonies of Europe and their religious life have slowly undergone their own development, and in the late twentieth century these separate traditions impressed the church with the need to define new forms of Catholic life. This transformation coincided with the era of Vatican II, when the church began to end what many critics have termed its "Constantinian" era. The development of new forms of Catholicism in the Third World also coincided with the devastating effects of three decades of Western-style "development." This process drastically redirected national economies into rapid industrialization, exploitation of natural resources, and unbridled participation in the world economic system of free trade and international finance.

More often than not this development left Third World countries better off only on paper: yearly increases in GNP, per capita GNP, industrial production, miles of paved roads, capacities of modern ports and airports, and the prevalence of Western consumer products and market economies. Yet, despite improved official statistics, the living conditions of the vast majority of the peoples of the Third World have continued to deteriorate.

The disparities between the fortunes of the educated, Westernized, and affluent international elites and the rest of the peoples have grown more and more glaring by the year as greater proportions of national wealth continue to flow into fewer hands. We need not cite many of the same development statistics to illustrate our point. If the 1992 per-capita GDP of the average American was $24,205 and of the average West German $17,400, that of the average Filipino was $860, Brazilian $2,350, and Haitian $340. Meanwhile 50% of the people in Latin America earned only 14% of the region's total income, while over 200 million people in its most populated countries earned less than $100 a year in 1990.

In 1979 fourteen families in El Salvador controlled 90% of the wealth, 2% owned 58% of the arable land, 90% of the peasants had no land at all, and the average monthly income of 50% of the population was $12. These figures do not reveal how the rich in Latin America live far better than their counterparts in the United States, with an almost feudal grip on the lives and "services" of the vast majority of the people.

While the extremes of poverty and wealth continued to fly apart, most of the nations of the Third World had fallen under the iron glove of the "National Security State" [see 333]. Closely connected with development, this system protects the process of forced economic modernization through a highly centralized and authoritarian military state calculated to destroy all dissent in the name of anti-communism. As poverty increased, arms budgets to support ever-larger armies, security forces, and police grew out of all proportion to human needs: health care, literacy and education, proper housing, land reform, employment and fair wages, well-functioning systems of justice, and popular rule.

Thus by 1960 and Vatican II several trends had come together in a uniquely new situation for Catholic peacemakers. These combined a new spirit of renewal and reform within the Catholic church, while the impact of Marxism made itself felt profoundly throughout Latin America as a result of the successful Cuban revolution, and all over the post-colonial Third World as a new generation sought modes of existence that steered a careful course between what many perceived as the extremes of both Western and Soviet camps in the Cold War.

Oppression, poverty, and injustice cried out as never before for new solutions: yet the last three decades have not been easy ones to have foreseen: violent revolution often gave rise to even more violent repression, while first isolated individuals and then – with the help of a reform-minded church hierarchy – entire social movements and then nations began to experiment with and finally to learn the lessons of true nonviolent struggle. This culminated in successes for peacemaking that rivaled, and often exceeded anything we have seen in Europe.

We cannot hope to survey the entire range of thought and action of peacemaking in the Third World; yet we shall attempt to present some representative selections from Africa, from Asia and the Asian rim, and then most especially from Latin America. Here we shall first focus on the decisive church councils of the region: Medellín in 1968 and Puebla in 1979, then survey the thought of leading liberation theologians on the relationship between the Gospels, society, and change, including the options for violent and nonviolent change. We shall then profile some of the leading individuals and movements around Latin America, before focusing on texts from Nicaragua, El Salvador, and Haiti.

AFRICAN THEOLOGY: JEAN-MARC ÉLA

Issues of cultural identity, the dignity of the vast majority of the people, and the role of violence and nonviolence in the struggle for liberation are perhaps nowhere stronger than in Africa, where a legacy of colonialism and deep racism have left their marks on all forms of life and thought. Growing from this is a theology that owes much to both the liberation theology of Latin America and to the civil-rights movement of the United States. In African theology this has sought to find meaning in the biblical book of Exodus: the liberation of the people of Israel from their bondage under the Pharaohs. Liberation takes on not only theological and ecclesiological meaning in the freeing of the African from Eurocentric forms of liturgy and theology; but also in the political realm.

The following text offers a good example of a meditation on Exodus by one of Africa's leading Catholic theologians. Jean-Marc Éla was born in Ebolowa in Cameroon in 1936. He studied at the universities of Paris and of Strasbourg and completed a doctorate in theology in 1969 and a doctorate in sociology in 1978.

On returning to Cameroon he took up pastoral work among the impoverished Kirdis of the northern Sahel region, where the forest gives way to the ever-advancing Sahara and its millions of refugees displaced by both nature and human warfare. The following is excerpted from Jean-Marc Éla, *African Cry*, Robert R. Barr, trans., Maryknoll, NY: Orbis Books, 1986, pp. 28-38.

320. Jean-Marc Éla, An African Reading of Exodus

What is the message of the Book of Exodus today for so many millions of Africans in their religious, cultural, political and socioeconomic situations? What can men and women in black Africa who seek deliverance from political and economic oppression look for in a reading of Exodus? This is a towering question facing us. I shall examine it here....

And so the questions arise: In the colonial or neocolonial situation that has marked Christianity in Africa, is Exodus not a book terribly absent to us? And is the reason for this absence not that the message it delivers calls into question not only a certain theology but also an ecclesiastical praxis, a worship, and a spirituality?

The God of missionary preaching was a God so distant, so foreign to the history of the colonized peoples. Exploited and oppressed, they find it difficult to identify this God with the God of Exodus, who becomes aware of the situation of oppression and servitude in which the people find themselves. The primary role of the Bible, and of the Old Testament in a special way, in African religious movements is to express the reaction and revolt of African Christians within the institutional churches in which the despised, humiliated human being lives a relationship to God under the rubric of absence....

If the exodus has any meaning for us, it will be first and foremost in its capacity to illuminate the living relationship between revelation and history. The central event through which God is revealed by intervening in people's history is the exodus. God utters the divine being definitively in the action by which God snatches the people from the servitude of Egypt, and leads them, with mighty hand and outstretched arm, to the very land of Canaan, the land of the promise Abraham had received: "When Israel was a child I loved him, and out of Egypt I called my son" [Hos. 11:1]. Deuteronomy capsulizes Israel's religion thus: "We were once slaves of Pharaoh in Egypt, but the Lord brought us out of Egypt with his strong hand" [Deut. 6:21]....

In a perspective in which the history of human beings is of value for God, who gets involved in that history and fulfills the divine promise there, we cannot posit the happiness of human beings, justice and freedom, reconciliation and peace, in a beyond having no connection with the realities and situations of the present world....

For millions of Africans, the signs of a world in quest of freedom and justice are too evident not to attract the attention of churches that boast the Judaeo-Christian revelation or claim that the message of the exodus occupies a central place. How many illiterate people are paralyzed today by their ancestral [and modern] fears in societies in which the accumulation of new knowledge operates according to the model of an elitist culture? Ignorance is not limited here to an inability to read and write. It extends to the functioning of political institutions, to the mechanisms of economics, to the laws of society. In the face of the manifold harassments and blind bullying of which they are the victims, the illiterate African rural masses are ignorant of the very law designed to protect them. Their very fear of defending themselves, even when they know they are in the right, itself constitutes a stumbling block, one from which many human groups need to be liberated.

In any breach with situations of servitude, a first step will be to promote a mentality of active solidarity. Of course no such mentality can exist without an inventory of the factors or mechanisms of oppression. No change is possible without an awareness of injustices such as will render them intolerable in the mind of the people. Ultimately, in raising up leaders for a determinate community who will perform the function of prophets in that community, the group will receive a "word" from which it can draw the strength to forge ahead. There must be individuals to take up the questions and traumas of a group and awaken the group to injustices from within and injustices from without. Certain individuals must decide to speak, in the conviction that many in the group are aware of their suffering.

In any community, village or city neighborhood, the prime interest in reading the Book of Exodus is to rescue the majority of African Christians from ignorance of the history of liberation. After all, this text is about nothing else. Moses is not sent to Egypt to preach a spiritual conversion, but to lead Israel "out of the house of slavery." In this escape God is revealed as the unique, matchless God. In today's world changes do result from liberation movements, and Africans must not be kept from knowing that, in our age, living communities are struggling for respect for their rights.

A knowledge of the history of today's liberation movements will spur on communities held down by fatalism and resignation. It will be crucial to remember that through this history God's spirit is at work, toiling internally for the transformation of the world, in view of the fact that injustice and domination, with contempt for men and women and the violence all these things engender, constitute a key aspect of the sin of the world....

Beyond the shadow of a doubt, a reading of the Exodus is a must in the Christian communities of Africa today. As the oppressed of all times have turned to this primordial event, thence to draw hope, we shall never come to any self-understanding without ourselves taking up that same history and discovering there that God intervenes in the human adventure of servitude and death to free the human being. The exodus event is the grid permitting the deciphering of human history and the discovery of its deeper sense – that of an intervention of God revealing the divine power and love.

SOUTH AFRICA

The election of April 1994 that made Nelson Mandela the first president of post-apartheid South Africa was the culmination of a generation of struggle – both violent and nonviolent. Yet ultimately it was the nonviolence of South Africa's majority that convinced that nation's Europeans and the rest of the world of the injustice of apartheid and that gave South Africa as a whole the maturity and trust to enter a new era. While religious nonviolence was one of the main forms of this struggle, most have come to see it symbolized by Anglican Archbishop Desmond Tutu. The Catholic role in the revolution, as in South Africa as a whole, was largely overlooked.

Chapter 6: The Third World and Liberation

Between the years 1911 and 1960 the Catholic church in South Africa grew from an insignificant minority of 50,000 to a major force numbering nearly two million members out of a total current population of about 30 million. More significant is the fact that three-quarters of South Africa's Catholics are black. This has been due largely to the Catholic missions' linguistic and anthropological approach and to the church's decision to create an indigenous black leadership. In this approach to evangelization it has been far more serious than many other religious groups in the country.

At the same time, however, the Catholic Church remained a minority church in South Africa. Its early immigrant base was content to leave politics to the Protestant majority, especially the Dutch Reformed Church, which saw biblical roots for the white minority's racism and played a large role in developing South Africa's apartheid system. By the end of World War II the Catholic church thus found itself both highly committed to the religious life of its black majority and an outsider to the structures of white power. In 1948 it was therefore among the first churches in South Africa to denounce the system of apartheid. In 1952 and again in 1957 its bishops' pastorals repeated the church's denunciation of oppressive racial policies. In 1960 the bishops reiterated this opposition by calling on Catholics to obey God's law over man's.

By the 1970s the influence of Vatican II, of Paul VI's *Populorum Progressio*, and of the developing theology of liberation had moved the church to a new level of struggle. In 1972 the Catholic Bishops Conference unanimously adopted its *Call to Conscience* condemning detention without trial, banning, and the exploitation of black labor. In 1976 the bishops announced their intention of breaking South African law by integrating two Catholic schools.

Through its membership in the Christian Institute the church put itself firmly behind the black theology and liberation theology movements, South African Catholics actively began to pursue a theology of nonviolence, while government repression by naked force became the chief means of defending apartheid against an increasingly active black majority. The Sharpeville massacre of 1960 and the brutal repression of the Soweto demonstrations in June 1976, in which South African police and army killed over 175 and injured over 1,000, has come to symbolize this oppression. The role of the military and the police have therefore become crucial to any attempt to establish a just society. The

Catholic church therefore joined the South African Council of Churches in strongly advocating the right of conscientious objection. Through its Justice and Reconciliation Commission the Bishops' Conference also attempted to raise the consciousness of youth, worker, and student groups to the need for liberation and justice.

ARCHBISHOP DENIS HURLEY OF DURBAN

One should not exaggerate the activism or commitment of most South African Catholics to the end of apartheid, especially among the church's hierarchy. Among the more outspoken critics of the system, however, was the young archbishop of Durban. Denis Hurley was born on Nov. 9, 1915 in Cape Town, educated at St. Charles College, St. Thomas University, and the Gregoriana in Rome. He was ordained in 1939 and from 1940 to 1943 served as a curate at Emmanuel Cathedral in Durban. From 1944 to 1946 Hurley was superior of St. Joseph's Scholasticate in Prestburg (now Cedera), and in 1947 was appointed Apostolic Vicar for the Natal. He moved quickly through the hierarchy and in 1951 became archbishop of Durban. As the youngest president of the South African Catholic Bishops Conference from 1952 to 1960, he moved his colleagues to outspoken opposition to apartheid. After attending Vatican II from 1962 to 1965 Hurley returned home to found and serve as president of the South African Institute of Race Relations, moving on to found *Diakonia*, an interracial, interfaith communications center in 1975. With his increasingly outspoken stance and high profile, in 1984 he was accused of making false charges when he accused South Africa's paramilitary police of committing atrocities. The charges were finally dropped in 1985. Hurley's efforts to bring about racial and economic justice in South Africa have received worldwide attention. He is the recipient of many honorary degrees and other awards.

The following selection is taken from Marjorie Hope and James Young, *The South African Churches in a Revolutionary Situation*, Maryknoll, NY: Orbis Books, 1983, pp. 155-57.

321. *Denis Hurley, Interview with Hope and Young*

...We were fortunate enough to meet Archbishop Hurley on both our trips to South Africa. When we told him that we found his record to be an impressive one, he shook his head. "Speaking is easy – action is difficult."

Chapter 6: The Third World and Liberation

We asked him to tell us about his own life. He spoke slowly. "It was an intellectual journey before an emotional one. I was born in Cape Town, subject to South African cultural values. Whites here have been brought up with the paternalist attitude that only the White man can run African activities. My intellectual interest grew out of studies at the Gregorian University in Rome, where I finished in 1940. Much was said there about the social teachings of the church, and especially Leo XIII's letter on the condition of workers and the evils of capitalism. Later, in South Africa, I began to talk on the 'native' problem. But my attitude was still basically academic.

"I was still isolated – nervous about getting involved in 'radical' activities. It wasn't till the late '50s that I saw one couldn't be authentic without knowing the *people* in the situation, and without taking sides. I was elected chairman of the Durban branch chapter of the South African Institute of Race Relations, and our big task was to save the land at Cato Manor for the Africans. We went on deputation to the city council – and lost. But I was becoming an activist, in a minor way. In the late '50s too – I forget the date – I attended a conference on racial affairs called by Anglican Bishop Ambrose Reeves. Many radicals were present. When a Black reporter commented, 'It is surprising for Catholic clergy to be "involved,"' it made me think.

"Then the Sharpeville massacre in 1960 stimulated me to do more with the Durban branch of Race Relations. But I was still mostly making speeches. It was through women – members of the Black Sash – that I learned about demonstrating. When an Indian was detained in Durban and committed 'suicide' from a prison window, we had a big demonstration here. I felt nervous the first day. Later I became intrigued by demonstrating – by the way people stared at me, taking a sneaky look, then ducking away."

In the late 1960s, Hurley went on, he was invited by Cosmas Desmond, a young Catholic priest, to see Limehill, a resettlement village of "discarded people." Black families were simply dumped in the bare veld, where there was nothing but a pile of folded tents and a water tank some distance away. "They even took a picture of me driving in a tent peg. More important, I was getting to know the people. They were dying, like flies, of an epidemic – especially the children. One afternoon, we counted ninety little graves. We sent their names to the Bantu Administration – which never answered the letter. I was realizing these people as beings who were suffering enormously. Also there was a certain excitement in taking action....

"One night in Milan, going over a speech I was to give in Germany, I suddenly realized that I *myself* was part of an oppressive people. They were oppressors, and I was one of them. It was a terrible feeling. It may seem strange that it took so long to realize, *to feel this*. But that is South Africa.

"That experience fired me with the desire to do something – to try changing attitudes. Though I often felt powerless, especially when the guerrilla movements began spreading through Mozambique and Angola, and then Soweto broke out. It looked as if violence would be the only outcome."

Diakonia and the Human Awareness Program emerged from Hurley's belief that social attitudes are the crux of the problem, and that carefully planned small group experience can change them. "It's true," Hurley conceded, "that the social attitudes that do most harm are those of the establishment. But I still feel that attitudes must change before political structures. It does take a war effort to change attitudes. Too often I feel utterly helpless to avoid a holocaust.

"But Christians must never yield to pessimism, no matter how 'correctly' the judgment is calculated. And the essential task of the church remains that of giving practical expression to Christian faith. The real test of hope is when the situation is hopeless."

THE KAIROS COVENANT

In July 1985 an ecumenical group of Christian theologians met in Soweto to attempt to come to grips with their churches' response to apartheid and the government's increasingly desperate suppression of protest. By September 1985 they had formed a working committee to gather statements and suggestions from all over the country and had published the first edition of what has come to be called the "Kairos Document." The Document rejects pious calls that condemn revolutionary violence while remaining silent and acquiescent in the face of the state violence of oppression, poverty, and military and police force. In section 3.3 on "Non-Violence, " it thus challenges many received notions of peacemaking, including many already documented here, with the theory of the "just-revolution," based on both the European just-war and crusade traditions.

Chapter 6: The Third World and Liberation

Central to understanding the Document and its sense of urgent anger is the classic contrast between traditional interpretations of Roman 13 (obedience to the state as the instrument of God) and Apocalypse 13 (martyrdom under the state as the servant of Satan). This dichotomy reflects both the crisis of the 1986 State of Emergency and a growing frustration, even among churchpeople, with nonviolence. Its central call: that only repentance can produce forgiveness, and only a fundamental change in South Africa can demonstrate repentance is a radical restatement of the Gospel call to love enemies and a contemporary interpretation of satyagraha.

The following selections are taken from *The Kairos Covenant: Standing with South African Christians,* Willis H. Logan, ed., New York: Friendship Press and Meyer-Stone Books, 1988, pp. 1-43.

322. The Kairos Document

Chapter One: The Moment of Truth

The time has come. The moment of truth has arrived. South Africa has been plunged into a crisis that is shaking the foundations; and there is every indication that the crisis has only just begun and that it will deepen and become even more threatening in the months to come. It is the *kairos,* or moment of truth, not only for apartheid but also for the church and all other faiths and religions.

We as a group of theologians have been trying to understand the theological significance of this moment in our history. It is serious, very serious. For very many Christians in South Africa this is the *kairos,* the moment of grace and opportunity, the favorable time in which God issues a challenge to decisive action. It is a dangerous time because, if this opportunity is missed and allowed to pass by, the loss for the church, for the gospel, and for all the people of South Africa will be immeasurable. Jesus wept over Jerusalem. He wept over the tragedy of the destruction of the city and the massacre of the people that was imminent, "and all because you did not recognize your opportunity *(kairos)* when God offered it" [Luke 19:44].

A crisis is a judgment that brings out the best in some people and the worst in others. A crisis is a moment of truth that shows us up for what we really are. There will be no place to hide and no way of pretending to be what we are not in fact. At this moment in South Africa the church is about to be shown up for what it really is and no cover-up will be possible.

What the present crisis shows up, although many of us have known it all along, is that *the church is divided.* More and more people are now saying that there are in fact two churches in South Africa: a white church and a black church. Even within the same denomination there are in fact two churches. In the life and death conflict between different social forces that has come to a head in South Africa today, there are Christians (or at least people who profess to be Christians) on both sides of the conflict and some who are trying to sit on the fence!...

The church is divided against itself and its day of judgment has come....

Chapter Two: Critique of State Theology

The South African apartheid State has a theology of its own, and we have chosen to call it "State Theology." State Theology is simply the theological justification of the status quo with its racism, capitalism, and totalitarianism. It blesses injustice, canonizes the will of the powerful, and reduces the poor to passivity, obedience, and apathy.

How does State Theology do this? It does it by misusing theological concepts and biblical texts for its own political purposes. In this document we would like to draw your attention to four key examples of how this is done in South Africa. The first would be the use of Romans 13:1-7 to give an absolute and "divine" authority to the State. The second would be the use of the idea of "Law and Order" to determine and control what the people may be permitted to regard as just and unjust. The third would be the use of the word "communist" to brand anyone who rejects State Theology. And finally there is the use that is made of the name of God.

2.1 [Quotes Romans 13:1-7 in full. See **39**]

...Paul is simply not addressing the issue of a just or unjust State or the need to change one government for another. He is simply establishing the fact that there will be some kind of secular authority and that Christians as such are not exonerated from subjection to secular laws and authorities. *"The State is there to serve God for your benefit,"* says Paul. That is the kind of State he is speaking of. That is the kind of State that must be obeyed. In this text Paul does not tell us what we should do when a State does *not* serve God and does *not* work for the benefit of all but has become unjust and oppressive. That is another question.

Chapter 6: The Third World and Liberation

If we wish to search the Bible for guidance in a situation where the State that is supposed to be "the servant to God" betrays that calling and begins to serve Satan instead, then we can study chapter 13 of the Book of Revelation. Here the Roman State becomes the servant of the dragon (the devil) and takes on the appearance of a horrible beast. Its days are numbered because God will not permit his unfaithful servant to reign forever.

Consequently those who try to find answers to the very different questions and problems of our time in the text of Romans 13:1-7 are doing a great disservice to Paul. The use that State Theology makes of this text tells us more about the political options of those who construct this theology than it does about the meaning of God's Word in this text. As one biblical scholar puts it: "The primary concern is to justify the interests of the State and the text is pressed into its service without respect for the context and the intention of Paul."

2.2 Law and Order

The State makes use of the concept of law and order to maintain the status quo which it depicts as "normal." But this *law* is the unjust and discriminatory laws of apartheid, and this *order* is the organized and institutionalized disorder of oppression. Anyone who wishes to change this law and this order is made to feel that they are lawless and disorderly. In other words they are made to feel guilty of sin.

It is indeed the duty of the State to maintain law and order, but it has no divine mandate to maintain any kind of law and order. Something does not become moral and just simply because the State has declared it to be a law, and the organization of a society is not a just and right order simply because it has been instituted by the State. We cannot accept any kind of law and any kind of order. The concern of Christians is that we should have in our country a just law and a right order.

In the present crisis and especially during the State of Emergency [declared on June 12, 1986], State Theology has tried to re-establish the status quo of orderly discrimination, exploitation, and oppression by appealing to the consciences of its citizens in the name of law and order. It tries to make those who reject this law and this order feel that they are ungodly. The State here is not only usurping the right of the church to make judgments about what would be right and just in our circumstances; it is going even further than that and demanding of us, in the name of law and order, an obedience that must be reserved for God alone. The South African State recognizes no authority beyond itself and therefore it will not allow anyone to question what it has chosen to define as "law and order." However, there are millions of Christians in South Africa today who are saying with Peter: "We must obey God rather than man [human beings]" [Acts 5:29, see **44**].

State Theology further believes that the government has the God-given right to use *violence* to enforce its system of "law and order." It bases this on Romans 13:4: "The authorities are there to serve God: they carry out God's revenge by punishing wrongdoers." In this way *state security* becomes a more important concern than *justice*, and those who in the name of God work to change the unjust structures of society are branded as ungodly agitators and rebels. The State often admonishes church leaders to "preach the pure gospel" and not to "meddle in politics," while at the same time it indulges in its own political theology which claims God's approval for its use of violence in maintaining an unjust system of "law and order."

The State appeals to the consciences of Christians in the name of "law and order" to accept this use of violence as a God-given duty, in order to re-establish the status quo of oppression. In this way people are sacrificed for the sake of laws, rather than laws for the sake of people, as in the life of Jesus: "The sabbath was made for man [the human person]; not man [the human person] for the sabbath" [Mark 2:27]. The State's efforts to preserve law and order, which should imply the protection of human life, means the very opposite for the majority of the people, namely the suppression and destruction of life.

2.3 The Threat of Communism

...State Theology like every other theology needs to have its own concrete symbol of evil. It must be able to symbolize what it regards as godless behavior and what ideas must be regarded as atheistic. It must have its own version of hell. And so it has invented, or rather taken over, the myth of communism....

...From a theological point of view the opposite of the God of the Bible is the devil, Satan. The god of the South African State is not merely an idol or false god; it is the devil disguised as Almighty God, the antichrist.

Chapter 6: The Third World and Liberation

The oppressive South African regime will always be particularly abhorrent to Christians precisely because it makes use of Christianity to justify its evil ways. As Christians we simply cannot tolerate this blasphemous use of God's name and God's Word. State Theology is not only heretical, it is blasphemous....

South African State Theology can be compared with the Court Theology of Israel's Kings, and our false prophets can be compared with the Court Prophets of Israel, of whom it is said:

> They have misled my people by saying: Peace! when there is no peace. Instead of my people rebuilding the wall, these men come and slap on plaster. I mean to shatter the wall you slapped with plaster, to throw it down and lay its foundations bare. It will fall and you will perish under it; and so you will learn that I am Yahweh. [Ezek. 13:10,14, Jer. 6:10-15, see 22]....

Chapter Three: Critique of Church Theology

3.1 Reconciliation

There can be no doubt that our Christian faith commits us to work for *true* reconciliation and *genuine* peace. But as so many people, including Christians, have pointed out there can be no true reconciliation and no genuine peace *without justice*. Any form of peace or reconciliation that allows the sin of injustice and oppression to continue is a *false* peace and *counterfeit* reconciliation. This kind of "reconciliation" has nothing whatsoever to do with the Christian faith....

In our situation in South Africa today it would be totally un-Christian to plead for reconciliation and peace before the present injustices have been removed. Any such plea plays into the hands of the oppressor by trying to persuade those of us who are oppressed to accept our oppression and to become reconciled to the intolerable crimes that are committed against us. That is not Christian reconciliation, it is sin. It is asking us to become accomplices in our own oppression, to become servants of the devil. No reconciliation is possible in South Africa *without justice*, without the total dismantling of apartheid.

What this means in practice is that no reconciliation, no forgiveness, and no negotiations are possible *without repentance*. The biblical teaching on reconciliation and forgiveness makes it quite clear that nobody can be forgiven and reconciled with God unless he or she repents of their

537

sins. Nor are *we* expected to forgive the unrepentant sinner. When he or she repents we must be willing to forgive seventy times seven times, but before that we are expected to preach repentance to those who sin against us or against anyone. Reconciliation, forgiveness, and negotiations will become our Christian duty in South Africa only when the apartheid regime shows signs of genuine repentance. The State of Emergency, the continued military repression of the people in the townships, and the jailing of all its opponents is clear proof of the total lack of repentance on the part of the present regime.

There is nothing that we want more than true reconciliation and genuine peace – the peace that God wants and not the peace the world wants [John 14:27, see **38**]. The peace that God wants is based upon truth, repentance, justice, and love. The peace that the world offers us is a unity that compromises the truth, covers over injustice and oppression, and is totally motivated by selfishness. At this stage, like Jesus, we must expose this false peace, confront our oppressors, and be prepared for the dissension that will follow. As Christians we must say with Jesus: "Do you suppose that I am here to bring peace on earth. No, I tell you, but rather dissension" [Luke 12:51]. There can be no real peace without justice and repentance.

It would be quite wrong to try to preserve "peace" and "unity" at all costs, even at the cost of truth and justice and, worse still, at the cost of thousands of young lives. As disciples of Jesus we should rather promote truth and justice and life at all costs, even at the cost of creating conflict, disunity, and dissension along the way. To be truly biblical our church leaders must adopt a theology that millions of Christians have already adopted: a biblical theology of direct confrontation with the forces of evil rather than a theology of reconciliation with sin and the devil.

3.2 Justice

...There have been reforms and, no doubt, there will be further reforms in the near future. And it may well be that the church's appeal to the consciences of whites has contributed marginally to the introduction of some of these reforms. But can such reforms ever be regarded as real change, as the introduction of a true and lasting justice? Reforms that come from the top are never satisfactory. They seldom do more than make the oppression more effective and more acceptable. If the oppressor does ever introduce reforms that might lead to real change this will come about because of strong pressure from those who are oppressed. True justice, God's justice, demands a radical change of structures. This can only come from below, from the oppressed themselves. God will bring about change through the oppressed as he did through the oppressed Hebrew slaves in Egypt. God does not bring his justice through reforms introduced by the Pharaohs of this world.

Why then does Church Theology appeal to the top rather than to the people who are suffering? Why does this theology not demand that the oppressed stand up for their rights and wage a struggle against their oppressors? Why does it not tell them that it is *their* duty to work for justice and to change the unjust structures? Perhaps the answer to these questions is that appeals from the "top" in the church tend very easily to be appeals to the "top" in society. An appeal to the conscience of those who perpetuate the system of injustice must be made. But real change and true justice can only come from below, from the people – most of whom are Christians.

3.3 Non-violence

The stance of Church Theology on non-violence, expressed as a blanket condemnation of all that is *called* violence, has not only been unable to curb the violence of our situation; it has actually, although unwittingly, been a major contributing factor in the recent escalation of State violence. Here again non-violence has been made into an absolute principle that applies to anything anyone *calls* violence without regard for who is using it, which side they are on, or what purpose they may have in mind. In our situation, this is simply counter-productive.

The problem for the church here is the way the word "violence" is being used in the propaganda of the State. The State and the media have chosen to call violence what some people do in the townships as they struggle for their liberation, i.e., throwing stones, burning cars and buildings, and sometimes killing collaborators. But this *excludes* the structural, institutional, and unrepentant violence of the State and especially the oppressive and naked violence of the police and the army. These things are not counted as violence. And even when they are acknowledged to be "excessive," they are called "misconduct" or even "atrocities" but never violence. Thus the phrase "violence in the townships" comes to mean what the young people are doing and not what the police are doing or what apartheid in general is doing to people. If one calls for non-violence in such circumstances one appears to be criticizing the resistance of the people while justifying or at least overlooking the violence of the police and the State. That is how it is understood not only by the State and its supporters but also by the people who are struggling for their freedom. Violence, especially in our circumstances, is a loaded word.

It is true that church statements and pronouncements do also condemn the violence of the police. They do say that they condemn *all violence*. But is it legitimate, especially in our circumstances, to use the same word "violence" in a blanket condemnation to cover the ruthless and repressive activities of the State and the desperate attempts of the people to defend themselves? Do such abstractions and generalizations not confuse the issue? How can acts of oppression, injustice, and domination be equated with acts of resistance and self-defense? Would it be legitimate to describe both the physical force used by a rapist and the physical force used by a woman trying to resist the rapist as violence?

Moreover, there is nothing in the Bible or in our Christian tradition that would permit us to make such generalizations. Throughout the Bible the word "violence" is used to describe everything that is done by a wicked oppressor [for example Ps. 72:12, 14; Is. 59:1, 8; Jer. 22:13-17; Amos 3:9-10, 6:3; Mi. 2:2, 3:1, 6:12]. It is never used to describe the activities of Israel's armies in attempting to liberate themselves or to resist aggression. When Jesus says that we should turn the other cheek [Mt. 5:38-48, see **34**], he is telling us that we must not take revenge; he is not saying that we should never defend ourselves or others. There is a long and consistent Christian tradition about the use of physical force to defend oneself against aggressors and tyrants. In other words there are circumstances when physical force may be used. They are very restrictive circumstances, only as the very last resort and only as the lesser of two evils, or, as Bonhoeffer put it, "the lesser of two guilts." But it is simply not true to say that every possible use of physical force is violence and that no matter what the circumstances may be it is never permissible.

This is not to say that any use of force at any time by people who are oppressed is permissible simply because they are struggling for their liberation. There have been cases of killing and maiming that no Christian would want to approve of. But then our disapproval is based upon a concern for genuine liberation and a conviction that such acts are unnecessary, counter-productive, and unjustifiable, and not because they fall under a blanket condemnation of any use of physical force in any circumstances.

And finally what makes the professed non-violence of Church Theology extremely suspect in the eyes of very many people, including ourselves, is the tacit support that many church leaders give to the growing *militarization* of the South African State. How can one condemn all violence and then appoint chaplains to a very violent and oppressive army? How can one condemn all violence and then allow young white males to accept their conscription into the armed forces? Is it because the activities of the armed forces and the police are counted as defensive? That raises very serious questions about whose side such church leaders might be on. Why are the activities of young blacks in the townships not regarded as defensive?

The problem of the church here is that it starts from the premise that the apartheid regime in South Africa is a *legitimate authority*. It ignores the fact that it is a white minority regime which has imposed itself upon the majority of the people, that is, blacks, in this country and that it maintains itself by brutality and violent force and the fact that a majority of South Africans regard this regime as illegitimate.

In practice what one calls "violence" and what one calls "self-defense" seems to depend upon which side one is on. To call all physical force "violence" is to try to be neutral and to refuse to make a judgment about who is right and who is wrong. The attempt to remain neutral in this kind of conflict is futile. Neutrality enables the status quo of oppression (and therefore violence) to continue. It is a way of giving tacit support to the oppressor, a support for brutal violence....

Chapter Four: Toward a Prophetic Theology

4.5 Liberation and Hope in the Bible

The Bible, of course, does not only *describe* oppression, tyranny, and suffering. The message of the Bible is that oppression is sinful and wicked, an offense against God. The oppressors are godless sinners and the oppressed are suffering because of the sins of their oppressors. But there is *hope* because Yahweh, the God of the Bible, will *liberate* the oppressed from their suffering and misery. "He will redeem their lives from exploitation and outrage" [Ps. 74:14]. "I have seen the miserable state of my

541

people in Egypt. I have heard their appeal to be free of their slave-drivers. I mean to deliver them out of the hands of the Egyptians" [Exod. 3:7].

Throughout the Bible God appears as the liberator of the oppressed: "For the plundered poor, for the needy who groan, now I will act, says Yahweh" [Ps. 12:5]. God is not neutral. He does not attempt to reconcile Moses and Pharaoh, to reconcile the Hebrew slaves with their Egyptian oppressors, or to reconcile the Jewish people with any of their later oppressors. "You have upheld the justice of my cause...judging in favor of the orphans and exploited so that earth-born man [human beings] may strike fear no more. My enemies are in retreat, stumbling, perishing as you confront them. Trouble is coming to the rebellious, the defiled, the tyrannical city" [Ps. 9:4; 10:18; 9:3; Zeph. 3:1]. Oppression is a crime and it cannot be compromised with, it must be done away with. "They [the rulers of Israel] will cry out to God. But he will not answer them. He will hide his face at that time because of all the crimes they have committed" [Mi. 3:4]. "God, who does what is right, is always on the side of the oppressed" [Ps. 103:6]....

Not that Jesus is unconcerned about the rich and the oppressor. These he calls to repentance. At the very heart of the gospel of Jesus Christ and at the very center of all true prophecy is a message of hope. Jesus has taught us to speak of this hope as the coming of God's Kingdom. We believe that God is at work in our world turning hopeless and evil situations to good so that God's Kingdom may come and God's Will may be done on earth as it is in heaven. We believe that goodness and justice and love will triumph in the end and that tyranny and oppression cannot last forever. One day "all tears will be wiped away" [Apoc. 7:17; 12:4] and "the lamb will lie down with the lion" [Is. 11:6]. True peace and true reconciliation are not only desirable, they are assured and guaranteed. This is our faith and our hope. We believe in and hope for the resurrection....

Chapter Five: Challenge to Action

5.5 Civil Disobedience

Once it is established that the present regime has no moral legitimacy and is in fact a tyrannical regime, certain things follow for the church and its activities. In the first place *the church cannot collaborate with tyranny*. It cannot or should not do anything that appears to give legitimacy to a morally illegitimate regime. Secondly, the church should not only pray for a change of government; it should also mobilize its members in every parish to begin to think and work and plan for a change of government in South Africa. We must begin to look ahead and begin working now with firm hope and faith for a better future. And finally the moral illegitimacy of the apartheid regime means that the church will have to be involved at times in *civil disobedience*. A church that takes its responsibilities seriously in these circumstances will sometimes have to confront and to disobey the State in order to obey God....

ASIA

Since World War II Asian Catholicism has emerged as one of the most vital test cases of the post-Constantinian church. The arrival of the church on the continent and in its eastern island rim accompanied European expansion and colonialism. It remained attached to the cities and the Westernized elites and therefore grew and stagnated along with the authoritarian, dependent cultures that the Europeans imposed. By the twentieth century therefore Catholicism encountered the growing hostility of Asian societies in the midst of liberation, often in the form of Marxist revolutions against Western, capitalist, and imperialist pasts. As Marxism spread the Westernized nations of the region responded by embracing the "National Security" doctrine. Most often the Christian churches found themselves aligned through their cultural affinities to the national-security regimes and their ruling elites. Furthermore, in Asia Christians represent only five percent of the population and only ten percent of the world-wide Christian total. Asian Christianity was and remains, therefore, a truly marginal religion.

By the 1960s, however, all the factors of the Asian Catholic scene – marginality, the increasing poverty of the continent, the pressing need for social change caught between Marxist revolution and national-security reaction, and the church's tradition of criticism – combined to make necessary a new pastoral mission. The church, already on the fringes in most of Asia, began to adopt the message of Vatican II and to accept its proper place with the poor and oppressed – the truly marginal in Asian society. By the late 1960s and early 1970s two organizations, PISA (Priests' Institute for Social Action) and FABC (Federation of Asian Bishops' Conferences), began directing the Asian church toward the pressing issues of justice and nonviolent change.

In a series of meetings, at Manila in 1970 and 1977 and Taipei in 1974, the FABC reaffirmed the Catholic church's "preference for the poor," the young, and the oppressed. In so doing it combined the historical experiences of the Asian church with the lessons of Vatican II and the liberation theology of Latin America. Most noteworthy in this new alignment was the attempt within the Asian hierarchy to forge a new synthesis between the Gospel message and the methods of Marxist social and economic analysis. To this synthesis have also been added the examples of Gandhi, Martin Luther King, the Buddha, and, for many, Mao.

THE INDIAN SUBCONTINENT: ALOYSIUS PIERIS

According to pious legend, which may have some basis in fact, Christianity first arrived in India along with Thomas the Apostle. Certainly the subcontinent had had many ties with the Mediterranean world for centuries before Christ, and upon their arrival in Goa in 1510, Portuguese explorers encountered Nestorian Christians who had perhaps established communities there by the early seventh century. Nevertheless, Christianity remained the religion of a small, foreign elite until the post-Gandhian era. Yet with the withdrawal of the British, these very characteristics gave Indian Christianity a new dimension; for it then became the religion of the poor.

As the following text explains, however, the Christian teaching of poverty and nonviolence that we have already seen at work in the peace movements of the Middle Ages [146-157] found a deep resonance among the ascetic and mendicant practices of Indian Buddhism. The Christian God, as the God of the poor and of the monk, thus takes on new social meaning in a struggle for liberation that we have seen at work in the first era of Christian monasticism in Europe [87-95].

Aloysius Pieris, SJ was born in Ampitiya in Sri Lanka on April 9, 1934. He entered the Jesuits in December 1953 and was ordained a priest in 1965. He earned a Licentiate in Philosophy from Sacred Heart College in Shembaganur, India in 1959, a BA in Pali and Sanskrit from London University in 1961, a diploma in early music from the academy of San Giorgio in Venice in 1963, and a Licentiate in Theology from the Pontifical Faculty of Theology in Naples, Italy in 1966. In 1972 Pieris earned the first doctorate in Buddhist studies ever awarded to a non-Buddhist at the University of Sri Lanka. He has taught at Cambridge University, Graduate Theological Union in Berkeley, the Gregorian University in Rome, Washington Theological Union and at Union Theological Seminary in New York. In 1974 Pieris founded the Tulana Research Centre in Kelaniya, Sri Lanka and has remained its director ever since. Since 1974 he has been professor of Asian Religions and Philosophies at the East Asian Pastoral Institute in Manila and the editor of the journal *Dialogue,* and of *Concilium* since 1986. Since 1979 he has been a member of the Ecumenical Association of Third World Theologians.

This passage is excerpted from Aloysius Pieris, SJ, *An Asian Theology of Liberation,* Maryknoll, NY: Orbis Books, 1988, pp. 120-24.

323. *Aloysius Pieris, SJ, The Biblical Perspective: The Messianic Role of the Masses*

No liberation theology can claim to be rooted in the word of God if it does not hold together the two biblical axioms mentioned above: (1) the irreconcilable antagonism between *God and Mammon,* and (2) the irreconcilable covenant between *God and the poor* (i.e., a defense pact against their common enemy: mammon).

As already observed, the first axiom is a universal spiritual dogma that defines the very core of practically all religions of Asia and manifests itself symbolically in the figure of the *monk/nun* or any of its many equivalents. This universal symbol of *opted poverty* can never be dispensed with in any liberational action or speculation in our continent, because it is the symbol by which our cultures have, for centuries, affirmed (1) not only that the Absolute alone is the ultimate source and the intimate moment of liberation, but (2) also that the cult of mammon or the enthronement of capital (profit-accumulation) is not merely *not* the guarantee of human liberation but is certainly the very negation of that liberation. Thus the negation of this negation – that is to say, the open repudiation (not necessarily the overthrow) – of any order of society based on a cult of mammon is an essential ingredient of Asian religiousness as symbolized in the monastic ideal of *voluntary poverty.*

In fact, Buddhism stands out in bold relief among the gnostic religions in making this important deduction from the first axiom. Concealed beneath the mythical language of the *Agganna Sutta, Cakkavatti-Sihnada-Suttanta,* and the *Kutanada Suttanta,* taken together, is the

Buddha's explosive social message: that it is *tanha* – the acquisitive tendency, the accumulative instinct in the human heart – that generates all social evil; that it lays the foundation for the vicious idea of private property in place of the saner practice of common ownership. It thus brings about class divisions and absolute poverty, which lead to all types of human misery and have repercussions on the cosmos itself, affecting the quality of life and reducing the life span of humankind. Amid such a society, the monastic community ideally composed of greedless men and women presents itself as an eschatological community that symbolizes and even anticipates what *could* be everybody's future.

This explains the effectiveness of the already mushrooming *basic human communities* with Christian and non-Christian membership, which give testimony to this universal dogma of spirituality: the God-mammon antinomy. Christian members would describe such communities as "sacraments" of the kingdom or social embodiments of the Beatitudes. Many such ashrams and their equivalents by their practice of voluntary poverty (rejection of mammon) remain the only dream of a new social order....

...It is not enough to consider the poor passively as the sacramental recipients of our ministry, as if their function in life were merely to help us, the rich, to save our souls by our retaining them as perpetual objects of our compassion. That would be to take Matthew 25:31ff. out of the general context of the gospel teaching on the role of the poor in the coming of the kingdom, a teaching in continuation, albeit in a more subdued tone, with the more forceful doctrine contained in the Jewish scriptures. The poor must be seen as *those through whom God shapes our salvation history....*

In the light of this observation, we can now review the various perceptions of liberation – namely, (1) that of pagan Rome, (2) of Christian Rome, (3) of non-Christian Asia, and (4) of Marxism, and thus discover what is specific to the biblical faith.

The stoic perception, which is the ideological substratum of Roman theology, sees liberation primarily as spiritual/ personal/interior. It does, however, tolerate an individual's search for freedom from external social structures that are oppressive – as exemplified in the case of slavery. But it does not envisage any radical change of social structures.

The Roman theology that christianized stoic ethics goes further. It clearly mitigates, with Christian love, social antagonisms between the various divisions of society. Moreover, it also earnestly pleads for change of evil social structures. But it clearly upholds that such structural change is secondary to and a consequence of interior spiritual liberation achieved through love. In this matter, "Buddhism of the texts," as shown above, takes a similar stand.

The minimal view commonly attributed to Marxists restricts liberation to a class struggle of the poor (= proletariat) aimed at socio-economic justice (beginning with common ownership of the means of production and ending up, it is hoped, in a classless and stateless society).

In contrast to these three positions, biblical revelation seems to advocate a unitary perception of all these aspects of liberation so that it admits a mutuality in dyads – personal/ social, spiritual/material, internal/structural – whenever these are predicated of "sin" and "liberation from sin."

Secondly, liberation in the Bible is a *religious experience of the poor,* for what liberates is the redeeming love of God, and the final fruit of liberation is the saving knowledge of God! Biblical liberation is *more* than class struggle. It is the God-encounter of the poor, the poor by choice (the renouncers) and the poor by circumstances (the *anawim* of Yahweh).

Thirdly, the liberation that the Bible speaks of is a *joint venture of God and the people (poor) covenanted into one indivisible Saving Reality.* Human efforts and divine initiatives merge into one liberating enterprise. Yet even the highest human achievement either in the personal perfection of the individual (as in traditional spiritualities) or in the collective perfection of a social group (as in a liberation spirituality) does not even approach the final glory, which remains a grace, a gratuitous gift of God, immeasurable by any human criterion.

Fourthly, it is not merely individuals, but also racial groupings, cultures, peoples, and *nations* that are called to be perfect as the heavenly Father is perfect. But the crucial fact is that nations are judged by their *victims,* Christ himself being the "victim-judge" of nations [Mt. 25:31ff.]. Hence, the missionary mandate to make "disciples of all nations" is an invitation to all minority churches of Asia to join in the process of educating the nations to fear the judgments of the victims they themselves create!

Such a project is possible in Asia only if we Christians judiciously appropriate the *religiousness of the poor* as our own spirituality, for it is the locus for a theology of liberation in Asia....

KOREA: KIM CHI HA

While most North Americans will associate Korea with the devastating war between communist North and pro-Western South in the early 1950s, since the 1970s South Korea has become one of the most rapidly industrializing and wealthy nations in the world, by the 1980s challenging Japan itself as a powerhouse of heavy industry and export consumer goods. Yet this rapid industrialization came at a very high cost for most Koreans who produced the goods and yet who did not share in the enormous wealth generated.

The last three decades have seen all the key elements of the "National Security State" at work in South Korea: an obvious threat of Communist aggression combined with new "development" models that vastly transformed a traditional agricultural society into a modern industrial one and an authoritarian government that allowed no dissent to the rule of an enriched oligarchy. Yet dissent was inevitable and came from many sectors of Korean society: the left, especially the students and intellectuals, a blend of Confucian pragmatism and peasant resistance that had seen many popular uprisings throughout the century, and the role of the Christian minority in Korea as an agent of protest. The development of *minjung* (people's) theology also went hand in hand with the growing conscientization of Korea's industrial workers – especially women – into movements of protest.

A good example of these trends is the life and thought of poet and activist Kim Chi Ha. Born on February 4, 1941, he matriculated at the National University in Seoul in 1959. After wandering around the countryside for two years, in 1964 he joined the student protest movement against the Park government's policies. After graduating in 1966 he worked as a screenwriter and in 1970 published his poem *Five Bandits,* a satire of government corruption. Arrested for that poem in 1971, he was imprisoned for his *The World of Chang Il Tam,* about a converted thief who goes on to preach liberation to his fellow prisoners.

Kim' own conversion to Catholicism dates from 1971; and from that time his poetry takes on a thorough integration of biblical themes with those of liberation in both a spiritual and political sense. Poverty, oppression, the destruction of indigenous culture, and an economy and political oligarchy kept in place by violent repression, are among the themes of his work that made him an internationally known poet and political prisoner in the 1970s.

Kim wrote the following text while in Seoul's West Gate prison in May 1975. He entrusted it to a prisoner who was about to be released, and it eventually passed through several hands before reaching Maryknoll. Among its key themes is that of the proper Christian response to violence, nonviolence, and passive acquiescence to injustice. Like the Kairos Document its acceptance of certain forms of violence as Christian responses to tyranny derive from the just-war tradition. The "violence of love" will emerge as a theme again in the writings of Ernesto Cardenal [343].

This passage is excerpted from Kim Chi Ha, *The Gold-Crowned Jesus & Other Writings,* Chong Sun Kim and Shelly Killen, eds., Maryknoll, NY: Orbis Books, 1978, pp. 13-23.

324. Kim Chi Ha, A Declaration of Conscience

Democracy, Revolution, Violence

I want to identify with the oppressed, the exploited, the troubled, and the despised. I want my love to be dedicated, passionate, and manifested in practical ways. This is the totality of my self-imposed task for humanity, the alpha and the omega of my intellectual search. I hope that my odyssey will be understood as a love for humankind.

My desire to love all people as my brothers and sisters makes me hate the oppression and exploitation that dehumanizes life. Those who exploit others dehumanize themselves. Thus I fight against oppression and exploitation; the struggle is my existence.

I became a Catholic because Catholicism conveys a universal message. Not only the spiritual and material burdens could be lifted from people but also oppression itself could be ended by the salvation of *both* the oppressor and the oppressed. Catholicism is capable of assimilating and synthesizing these contradictory and conflicting ideologies, theories, and value standards into a universal truth.

My beliefs spring from a confident love for the common people. I have opposed the Park regime and ridiculed the "Five Bandits" because they are the criminal gangsters looting this country. I have grown up as one of the oppressed masses. That perspective enabled me to see that a pernicious, elitist bias permeates our society. The oppressors say the masses are base, ugly, morally depraved, innately lazy, untrustworthy, ignorant, and a spiritless inferior race....

I have total confidence in the people. Given the opportunity, they will find correct solutions to their problems. And their time is coming. The people cannot be denied their rights and justice much longer. My confidence in the people has led me to trust their ability to determine their own fate. Those who fear the people, who find the masses despicable, are not democrats. When the going gets rough, they will stand at the side of tyranny.

What is democracy? It is an ideology opposed to silence, a system that respects a free logos and freedom of speech. It encourages the cacophony of dissent. A political system where everything is not revealed to the public is not a democracy. I believe that the truth, only the truth, will liberate people. A public consciousness dulled by soporific incantations and smothered in darkness can only be liberated by the truth. Only when the people struggle out of the darkness, driven along by the very chaos of their opposition to tyranny, will they reach the sun-drenched fields. Then they can head toward Canaan, the land of justice and freedom promised by the Creator. This is my dream, my faith.

I cannot describe this Promised Land in detail. No one person can do that. I think it will be created by the collective effort of all the people. My task is to fight on until the people hold in their own hands the power to shape their destiny. I want a victory for real democracy, complete freedom of speech. Nothing more, nothing less. In this sense, I am a radical democrat and libertarian. I am also a Catholic, one of the oppressed citizens of the Republic of Korea, and a young man who loathes privilege, corruption, and dictatorial power. This defines my political beliefs. I have nothing more to add....

Catholic political thought since Thomas Aquinas has explicitly recognized the people's right and duty, based on natural law, to overthrow a tyrant who threatens their existence and common good. Resistance abruptly changes the course of human affairs. The people themselves recover their humanity. The masses undergo a sudden and profound awakening; history makes up for lost time by encouraging the people to miraculous feats.

Sooner or later resistance and revolution lead to the phenomenon of violence. When the violence of authority sustains oppression, the people's will is crushed, their best leaders are killed, and the rest are cowed into

submission. The "silence of law and order" settles grimly across the land. Then an antithetical situation exists where violence must shatter this macabre order. To a degree, I approve of this kind of violence. I must approve of it. I reject the violence of oppression and accept the violence of resistance. I reject dehumanizing violence and accept the violence that restores human dignity. It could justly be called a "violence of love."
Jesus used his whip on the merchants defiling the temple. That was the "violence of love." It was force suffused with love. Jesus wanted the afflicted *and* their oppressive rulers to be reborn again as true children of God.

Violence and destructiveness obviously bring suffering and hardship. But we must sometimes cause and endure suffering. Never is this more true than when the people are dozing in silent submission, when they cannot be awakened from their torpor. To preach "nonviolence" at such a time leaves them defenseless before their enemies. When the people must be awakened and sent resolutely off to battle, violence is unavoidable. Gandhi and Frantz Fanon agonized over this dilemma. Father Camilo Torres took a rifle and joined the people. He died with them, the weapon never fired. The fallen priest with his rifle epitomized godliness. I do not know if his beliefs and methods were correct or not, but the purity of his love always moves me to tears. He staggered along his road to Golgotha with uncertain tread. He was prepared to commit a sin out of a love for others. He was not afraid to burn in the depths of eternal hell.

True nonviolence requires total noncompliance and noncooperation. It concedes nothing to the oppressors. The superficial kind of nonviolence, which makes limited gestures of opposition, is just another form of craven cooperation with the oppressors. Cowardly nonviolence is morally equivalent to cruel violence because with both the people get crushed. On the other hand, the "violence of love" is essentially the same as a "courageous nonviolence" in that it arms the people against their foes. I approve of the "violence of love" but I am also a proponent of true nonviolence.

The revolution I support will be a synthesis of true nonviolence and an agonized violence of love. (I am now working on a long ballad, *Chang Il Tam*, set against this background.)

To reach that golden mean – a nonviolence that does not drift to cowardly compromise and a violence that does not break the bonds of love and lapse into carnage – humankind must undergo an unceasing spiritual revival and the masses must experience a universal self-awakening.

While I grant that the violence of Blanquism [socialist revolution of the workers themselves] can light the psychological fuse to revolution, I do not anticipate or support a "lucky revolution" achieved by a small number of armed groups committing terrorist acts of violence. That is why I have eschewed the formation of, or membership in, secret organizations and have participated in activities consistent with the democratic process: writing and petitions, rallies, and prayer meetings.

My vision of a revolution is the creation of a unified Korea based on freedom, democracy, self-reliance, and peace. More fundamentally, however, it must enable the Korean people to decide their own fate. I can confidently support such a revolution....

THE PHILIPPINES: PEOPLE POWER

The problems and possibilities of Catholic peacemaking in Asia are best illustrated in the Philippines. The country possesses the majority of Asia's Catholics, a cross-current of theological and ideological trends from Maoism to liberation theology, a highly literate and Christianized population, and a society brought to the brink of crisis by the increased poverty of "development," twelve years of martial law under Ferdinand Marcos' National Security state, and Maoist rebellion. Both because of its sheer size (83% of a 70 million population in 1995) and the rapid unfolding of its Christian witness the Filipino church has thus become the major influence in Asian Catholicism since the 1960s.

At the same time, development has widened the distance between the Westernized elite and the majority of the population, reducing them to even greater poverty as wealth shifted toward the top. Literally millions have been displaced from their homes and deprived of their livelihoods by large-scale capital development and infrastructure projects – dams, irrigation systems, new docks and airports, international class hotels – that benefit only a small sector of the population.

Meanwhile the Church's pastoral mission was heavily influenced by the teachings of Vatican II and such social encyclicals as Paul VI's *Populorum Progressio* [301]. The Filipino church took seriously its educational work of raising people's consciousness through basic Christian communities, Bible study and action groups within parishes, and through organizing farmers, workers, students, and young people to move toward a just society.

Chapter 6: The Third World and Liberation

By the 1970s the church had begun to emerge as the leading force for nonviolent change in the Philippines. From the early labor-union and cooperative organizing of the 1960s to its concerns with more general political and economic concerns in the 1970s, the church steadily pursued its goal of empowering the poor and the oppressed. President Marcos' declaration of martial law on September 21, 1972 caused the hierarchy to realize the true conditions of oppression.

By 1979 the church had finally found a voice and a unified position in Jaime Cardinal Sin, Archbishop of Manila and president of the Bishops' Conference. The archbishop was typical of a new breed of church prelates formed in the wake of Vatican II. At first Sin opted for a policy of "critical collaboration," attempting to remain personally friendly with Marcos while rebuking his "parishioner" for isolated human-rights abuses and refusing to support any mass protests against the regime. He soon began calling for an end of martial law, however, condemning the abuses of the military government, while he reminded the people that subversive violence only brings retaliation on the suffering poor it is intended to liberate. At the same time the Bishops' Conference issued a pastoral condemning violence on the right and the left and calling for nonviolent change.

The events of the 1980s showed the real impact of these choices. In February 1981 Pope John Paul II visited the country, publicly rebuked President Marcos for human-rights abuses, and stressed the laity's unique role in bringing about nonviolent change, reminding the clergy to restrict their leadership to magisterial functions.

The assassination of political opposition leader, Benigno Simeon Aquino, on August 21, 1983, as he stepped onto the tarmac of Manila airport on his return from exile in the United States, finally brought the Catholic struggle for nonviolent revolution in the Philippines to the attention of the world. The popular reaction to the assassination was overwhelming. In late August nonviolent demonstrations drew up to two million Filipinos, while Cardinal Sin became the most vocal leader of the Catholic opposition. Throughout the Fall the Filipino people kept up their nonviolent pressure to topple Marcos with demonstrations of up to 500,000, with strikes, protest jogs, motorcades of honking drivers, and with daily bell-ringings in all Catholic churches to protest the Aquino murder and demand justice. The business and middle-class communities soon joined in the demonstrations, despite Marcos' open threats of retaliation.

With the stunning electoral victories of the opposition in the May 1984 parliamentary elections, the nonviolent campaign of nine months had done more to cripple the Marcos dictatorship than twelve years of violent insurrection. The opposition had forced extensive modifications of the martial-law regulations on arrest, trial, and habeas corpus; had restored the vice-presidency and the beginnings of normal succession; had forced Ismelda Marcos out of the government and broken the family's dynastic dreams; had crippled the regime's image of stability that allowed foreign governments to continue to pour in economic and military aid in the name of development; and had even persuaded the U.S. Congress to halt military aid.

By August 1985 parliamentary investigations into Aquino's assassination and into widespread government corruption had put Marcos on the defensive; yet it came as a shock when he ordered new elections for February 7 1986. Despite the clear-cut election of Benigno Aquino's widow, Corazon, in a courageous and hard-fought campaign, Marcos and his cronies declared Marcos the winner. By February 13 the Catholic Bishops Conference condemned the election as fraudulent and called for nonviolent civil disobedience. On February 16 Corazon Aquino herself began the campaign.

When, on February 22, Defense Minister Juan Ponce Enrile and General Fidel Ramos withdrew their support from Marcos and called for his resignation, it appeared that the country was on the verge of a bloody civil war. But by February 25 Aquino had taken the oath of office as the duly elected president of the Philippines and Marcos and his followers had fled the country. The key events of the days in between were played out by hundreds of thousands of Filipinos, who formed nonviolent bulwarks between the two armed camps in the center of downtown Manila, at first preventing confrontation, and then actively making peace by bringing all the moral and political force of massive nonviolent action to bear. These days are the subject of the following eyewitness accounts of the "People Power" revolution.

The following texts are taken from *People Power: An Eyewitness History. The Philippine Revolution of 1986*, Monina Allarey Mercado, ed., New York: Writers & Readers Publishing, 1986, pp. 17, 54, 77-78, 105, 109-110, 122, 124-26.

Chapter 6: The Third World and Liberation

325. *Filipino Voices from the People Power Revolution of 1986*

Teodoro Benigno, bureau chief of Agence France Presse

…The death of Ninoy [Benigno Aquino] opened up a long gash of wound upon the Filipino nation. The unifying element was the Roman Catholic religion. It was a conscience brutalized and violated. All the things that made Jesus Christ a great leader of men and a great apostle at the same time – the values of human kindness, the values of Christian compassion – were brutalized with the death of Ninoy. All the people who had been going to church for years and years realized that their values as Christians would only be redeemed if they went out into the streets. So they went out.

In all my career as a journalist, I had not seen such crowds. The crowd of Mahatma Gandhi [at his funeral in 1948] was only one million. Ninoy's crowd was a very exceptional crowd, not only in size but also in reaction – a cry of lament, a cry of sadness. It was a cry of anger and it was a cry of outrage; it was a cry of being orphaned. It was a cry of distress. It was also a cry of courage. And Ninoy's death did the trick. They gained courage to face the future that they were not sure of. It was formless, in the very beginning – the Catholic population finally was able to get it into their system to say something, to do something, to react, to show their anger and their outrage against the government….

Corazon C. Aquino, From a Speech Delivered on 3 February 1986

I say to Mr. Marcos what Moses said to the cruel, enslaving Pharaoh – Let our people go! The nation has awakened. I, like millions of Filipinos, look on this awakening as the dawning of a new day.

Less than two months ago, I said yes to a million signatures that asked me to run; the people power phenomenon began and rallied around the widow of Ninoy.

The people are crying for change. Volunteers have bravely come forth in battalions. Even the poorest have offered gestures of support. And the women! They have cast caution to the winds to campaign and lead in the people's crusade. They are determined to prove that people power is mightier than all the men and money of the crumbling dictatorship.

I have crisscrossed the length and breadth of the nation. I have traveled by air, by plane and by helicopter; I have traveled by land.

I have seen the devastation wrought by a policy built on a mountain of lies.

I have seen the broken bodies of men, women and children buried under promises of peace and progress. I have heard the anguished voices of the victims of injustice answered only by hypocritical pledges of retribution.

I have been kissed by the poorest of the poor, and have felt the warmth of their tears on my cheeks. I have been emboldened by the eager embrace of throngs determined to put an end to this regime.

I have heard them shout that I must win. I have been electrified by their every cry for freedom, and inspired by their every clasp of hope.

I cannot shut my ears to them. I cannot turn my back on them.

The Catholic Bishops of the Philippines, Statement after the Election, 13 February 1986

The people have spoken. Or have tried to, despite the obstacles thrown in the way of their speaking freely, we, the bishops, believe that on the basis of our assessment, as pastors, of the recently concluded polls, what they attempted to say is clear enough.

In our considered judgment, the polls were unparalleled in the fraudulence of their conduct. And we condemn especially the following modes of fraudulence and irregularities:

§ The systematic disfranchisement of voters....

§ The widespread and massive vote-buying....

§ The deliberate tampering of the election returns....

§ Intimidation, harassment, terrorism, and murder. These made naked fear the decisive factor in people not participating in the polls or making their final choice. These and many other irregularities point to a criminal use of power to thwart the sovereign will of the people. Yet, despite these evil acts, we are morally certain the people's real will for change has been truly manifested.

According to moral principles, a government that assumes or retains power through fraudulent means has no moral basis. For such an access to power is tantamount to a forcible seizure and cannot command the allegiance of the citizenry. The most we can say then, about such a government, is that it is a government in possession of power. But admitting that, we hasten to add: Because of that very fact, that same government itself has the obligation to right the wrong it is founded on. It must

556

respect the mandate of the people. This is the precondition for any reconciliation.

If such a government does not of itself freely correct the evil it has inflicted on the people, then it is our serious moral obligation as a people to make it do so.

We are not going to effect the change we seek by doing nothing, by sheer apathy. If we did nothing, we would be party to our own destruction as a people. We would be jointly guilty with the perpetrators of the wrong we want righted.

Neither do we advocate a bloody, violent means of righting this wrong. If we did, we would be sanctioning the enormous sin of fratricidal strife. Killing to achieve justice is not within the purview of our Christian vision in our present context.

The way indicated to us now is the way of nonviolent struggle for justice.

This means active resistance of evil by peaceful means – in the manner of Christ. And its one end for now is that the will of the people be done through ways and means proper to the Gospel.

We therefore ask every loyal member of the Church, every community of the faithful, to form their judgment about the February 7 polls. And if in faith they see things as we the bishops do, we must come together and discern what appropriate actions to take that will be according to the mind of Christ. In a creative, imaginative way, under the guidance of Christ's Spirit, let us pray together, reason together, decide together, act together, always to the end that the truth prevail, that the will of the people be fully respected....

Now is the time to speak up. Now is the time to repair the wrong. The wrong was systematically organized. So must its correction be. But as in the election itself, that depends fully on the people; on what they are willing and ready to do. We, the bishops, stand in solidarity with them in the common discernment for the good of the nation. But we insist: Our acting must always be according to the Gospel of Christ, that is, peaceful, nonviolent way.

May He, the Lord of justice, the Lord of peace, be with us in our striving for that good. And may the Blessed Virgin Mary, the Queen of Peace, and patroness of our country, assist us in this time of need.

Jaime Cardinal Sin, Archbishop of Manila and Catholic Primate of the Philippines

On Saturday afternoon, as I was about to go to Ateneo [University] for the ordination of two Jesuits, Cristina Ponce Enrile called me, crying: "Cardinal, help us!"

Then Juan Ponce Enrile called: "Cardinal, I will be dead within one hour," he said. And he seemed to be trembling. "I don't want to die," he added. "But if it is possible, do something. I'd still like to live. I already heard the order to smash us." He was almost crying. Then Fidel Ramos, who is a Protestant, told me that he embraced the image of Our Lady of Fatima. "Dear Lady," he had said, "I know that you are miraculous." And he told me: "Cardinal, help us by calling the people to support us."

"All right, Fidel," I said, "Just wait. In fifteen minutes, your place will be filled with people." I immediately called the contemplative sisters. There are three communities – the Carmelites in Gilmore, the Pink Sisters in Hemady, and the Poor Clares. I called them one by one: "Prioress, right now get out from your cells and go to the chapel and pray with outstretched arms before the Blessed Sacrament. And fast until I tell you to stop. We are in battle and, like Moses, you have to stretch out your arms." I said I will tell them why later.

I called Radio Veritas [the Catholic station] immediately. This was my statement: "I want you to pray because it is only through prayer that we can resolve this problem. I am deeply concerned about the situation of General Ramos and Minister Enrile. I am calling on our people to support our two good friends at the camp. Go to Camp Aguinaldo [the military HQ of the anti-Marcos forces] and show your solidarity with them in this crucial period. Our two good friends have shown their idealism. I would be very happy if you would help them. I wish that bloodshed will be avoided. Pray to Our Lady that we will be able to solve our problems peacefully. I am sorry to disturb you at this late hour, but it is precisely at a time like this that we most need your support for our two good friends."…

Teresa C. Pardo, Wife and Mother

"Please stay at home because it's dangerous. You have to think of the children," my husband said.

I got angry. Precisely it was for the children that I was going to risk life and limb – so that they could hope for a better future. I had to be where the action was. My younger children were safe with a trusted nursemaid. I had encouraged the older kids to go and join the crowd. It was Cardinal Sin, no less, who had exhorted people to come out to defend the military and to pray. How could I now not practice what I preach?

For a second I sat down on the sofa; I was immobile and close to tears. I heard on the radio that people were being urged to man the barricades and that they were arriving even from the provinces. Here I was in White Plains [just outside Manila], just a stone's throw from the barricades, and I was I kept in the house.

The decision did not take long to make: going out there to do my share. This was the relevance I had been searching for: to express my faith in God, who is sometimes so near and yet often so far away. He was here, right now, asking me to prove myself by going out to be counted.

I couldn't stay put in my comfortable house while thousands from the depressed areas were doing their share to fight for me.

With towels and lemon juice to lessen sting of tear gas, I walked out into the early morning alone, out of the house into the street. I walked out of grace – from my marriage, so I thought at the time – into independence and into freedom.

Amado L. Lacuesta, Jr., Screenwriter

We park along White Plains Road, about two blocks away from EDSA [the main circuit road in Manila]. Dozens of vehicles already line both sides of the road and the island. We begin to sense some of the excitement as we walk towards EDSA. A group of religious and lay people mill under a loose makeshift awning just outside a secondary gate into Aguinaldo. A large banner identifies their cause. Another restless group is organizing itself across the road in front of a gate into Corinthian Gardens....

All around us, people are coming and going in every direction. Everyone seems to know why he is there and where he is going. A cheer gathers momentum. People applaud a truck loaded with empty sacks – presumably to be used for sandbags – as it passes on its way to Ortigas.

More people, vehicles, laughter, cheers. I shake my head. This isn't revolution. It's fiesta, only more fun. Towards the main gates of Aguinaldo and Crame, the festive crowds thicken. Vehicles are parked everywhere.

The island and sidewalks are littered with mats, cardboard sheets, even makeshift cooking stands where people must have kept vigil last night....

I run into friends and acquaintances I haven't seen in months, even years. One, an executive of a telephone company, is with his wife and son. Another, the president of his own bank, is with his son and two daughters. A third, a senior executive of the investment bank I used to work with, has an expensive camera. I remember deciding not to bring my own camera. I would be concerned more with taking photographs and protecting my equipment than participating in...in whatever. Thus, I have brought only Lolly's Instamatic.

Even then, we decline to take each other's picture. It seems petty, even sacrilegious, to be concerned with souvenir I-was-there snapshots at a time like this....

Vic Helly, S.J.

A platform had been erected in the middle of EDSA and comedians were entertaining the crowds. The entertainment was suddenly broken off for an announcement: "Government tanks are on their way to attack the camps. It is necessary for a large crowd to meet the tanks and to immobilize them." A large segment of the crowd nearest Ortigas turned and went off to stop the tanks. When we arrived at what we were made to understand was to be the first line of defense against the tanks, we stopped.

A low wall of sandbags stretched across EDSA. (Not really a wall; only one bag high.) A man was giving instructions over the PA system mounted on top of a station wagon: "Listen carefully. Pray to God that you will not have to follow these instructions, but just in case, they are important. When the tanks come, if they start firing into the crowds – I hope it will not happen – but if it does, then...." I felt a little queasy at the moment. I looked at the people standing on the sandbags. They were young people in their late teens, early twenties, with their entire lives stretched out before them. Young men and women stolidly looking down EDSA, a view which in ten minutes might become the barrel of a machine gun mounted on a tank. Behind them, backing them up, were all sorts of people, a young mother with a baby in her arms and another in her womb, families with toddlers, pre-teens, teenagers. Men and women of all ages. I saw one doctor there who was beyond seventy. They looked a little disturbed and uncomfortable with the instructions. I saw no one leave. I saw no one yield to fear. Instead many people prayed.

Lulu T. Castaneda, Wife and Mother

When we were alerted to meet the tanks, I was very self-conscious about two things: my hat and the person beside me.

I was wearing a Christian Dior hat because it was drizzling and I looked so bourgeoise. I wanted to take it off but my daughter Leia stopped me. She said: "Don't, Mommy. You'll get sick. You always catch a cold when you get wet in the rain." I told her: "What are you worried about? We are going to die. I have no time to catch a cold."

We were told to link arms. I looked at the faces of the people around me and especially at the man to my right who was holding on tightly to my arm. My big concern was: I am going to die with this man and I don't know his name. I wanted to ask his name, but then did not want him to think I was fresh. I did not ask his name. As utter strangers, we faced what seemed like imminent death together.

I did say the act of contrition – truly and heartily. And I said the Hail Mary, especially the part which goes: "pray for us now and at the hour of our death." That seemed the same at that moment: "now…the hour of our death." I really knew then what that means to ask the Blessed Mother to be with me – with all of us – at the hour of our death.

My deepest concern was for my daughter because she is so young, only 17. I looked at her with pain and said: She's only 17 and she is going to die. Then I also thought: But if she dies for the country, then it is a good way to die. I think a lot of people were there for the same reason.

Amado L. Lacuesta, Jr.

My curiosity leads me on. Soon I am on Ortigas, looking at my first APC [armored personnel carrier] although I initially think it is a tank. Its engine is off as it squats there, surrounded by the people. Even white-washed walls enclosing a vacant corner lot are lined with agitated people. The vacant lot is crowded with what must be tanks, although only their tops and red pennants are visible. It reminds me vaguely of a war movie. My heart starts to beat a little harder.

I squeeze through the crowd on the traffic island and suddenly I am standing on the edge of a sea of kneeling people. They are praying. A pious-faced matron in white is leading the Rosary, face lifted to heaven, praying in a loud, pleading tone. Around her, the crowd on its knees is mostly men and some young women. An Afro-haired mestizo is holding his rosary up before his chest, near a middle-aged man who looks like a long suffering government clerk. A young woman is weeping as she prays. Someone is holding up a small statue of the Blessed Virgin, similar to dozens I have seen today along EDSA.

My attention is drawn to a tight knot of civilians and camouflage-suited soldiers standing between the kneeling people and the APC, which looks even larger and more menacing. A man breaks away from the group and edges his way out. I recognize him – it is Teofisto Guingona, one of Cory's wise men.

Then someone, a civilian, is grudgingly given a hand by some grim-faced soldiers as he joins them atop the APC. He looks familiar – probably an ex-Atenean I saw during the Mass for Evelio Javier at the Ateneo campus. He looks very serious, very concerned. Someone calls for a megaphone.

Over the uneasy gathering, a military helicopter swoops low, one of several whose deep, dull throbbing as they hover overhead evokes *Apocalypse Now.*

The soldiers on the APC looks tough and deadly, ammunition strung around their bodies. People in the crowd talk to them with almost desperate kindness, toss packs of cigarettes to them. But they show no response. They survey the crowd with hard eyes from time to time, but avoid eye contact. They seem even more tense than the people before them. Their discipline is frightening.

Someone says these are Marines just in from Davao and somehow, I feel a disquieting sense of kinship. I want to say I, too, am from Davao, but I don't. The desperate Rosary pauses as the ex-Atenean starts to address us.

He and Guingona have been negotiating with General Tadiar of the Marines. While awaiting Guingona, who has gone to Ramos with a message from Tadiar, he informs us that Tadiar wants the crowd to let his armor through. The crowd turns ugly, boos, mutters angrily. He pleads for attention. Now, the General climbs up beside him, helped by his unsmiling Marines.

The General looks short, slightly stocky but, like his men, is brown and tough-looking, except that he is in combat fatigues. He takes the megaphone to address the crowd, fixing them with a hateful look when they hiss. I help quiet the crowd, afraid of trying this man's patience.

"I have my orders," he says. He explains (in the tone of one who is not used to having to explain what he wants) that he only wants to move his unit behind Aguinaldo, a simple request. He does not wish to harm anyone.

The ex-Atenean tells him, and us, that it is our decision. He reminds us that we are here because we want to prevent bloody confrontation. If the General's men and armor reach the back of Aguinaldo, they will come face to face with Enrile's and Ramos' men. Who knows what might ensue then?

The prospect wrenches angry, urgent "No's" from the crowd. Suddenly, I am no longer just curious. I, too, shout "No!"

From atop distant buses and the white-washed walls, the people begin to chant defiantly: "Coree!" Tadiar grimaces. The soldiers atop and before the APC hold their Armalites [automatic weapons] at the ready. I wonder if the safeties are off.

"I have my orders!" This time it's a threat. Darkness is less than an hour away, the general says. Who knows what might happen when darkness falls? Let us pass now in safety.

Butz Aquino [who was instrumental in organizing the nonviolent resistance to Marcos] arrives, clambers up unbidden, and takes the megaphone away. Tadiar looks piqued. Aquino plays to the crowd. He repeats what people power is all about – to prevent bloodshed. We are asked again whether we will let the Marines through. The response is unanimous, loud, defiant: "No!"

The General shrugs, says something to his soldiers. The soldiers prod Aquino, the ex-Atenean, and an intrepid Japanese journalist off the APC. Suddenly, the APC's engine coughs to life, spews black smoke.

Cries of surprise, of anguish. The Rosary starts again, more urgently this time. Panic sweeps over us all. Unthinking, I drop to my knees.

The APC's engine revs up again, spews black smoke again. In the back of my mind, I think of Lolly and our children – Sarge, Kite, Rock, and Andi. Tears rush to my eyes, unbidden; my chest heaves mightily, unbidden; a sob wrenches out of my throat, unbidden. Looking up, I see only the General and his Marines, disciplined, hard-eyed.

I am angry. I am hurt. I am desperate, not knowing exactly why. I only know those men in combat gear are Filipinos. I only know this should not be happening. But there is nothing else now, not here in the path of this huge mountain of ugly metal looming over us.

I shout and raise my hands, daring them: "Go on, kill us!" I am only dimly aware of angry booing and hissing, from the thousands on the streets, walls, and buses, of cameras clicking, motor-winders whirring furiously.

The metal mountain jerks forward. Defiant nervous shouts all around. The praying voices rise another key. I wonder what it is like to be crushed under tons of metal.

The metal mountain jerks forward again. But no one stirs except the excited journalists jockeying for better angles. Then the engine stops. There is an astounding split second of silence. The crowd erupts into wild cheers and applause.

General Tadiar looks at us, turns and shakes his head. He disappears somewhere to the rear. His soldiers look around uneasily, unwilling to concede eye contact.

For the first time, I notice the men around me. They are ordinary men. Some are in sneakers. Most are in t-shirts, some expensive, some cheap. The one next to me is in frayed jeans and rubber slippers, his bare feet unkempt and dirty. Not too many are visibly Cory-people. I feel conspicuous with my yellow plastic Cory-visor and blue headphone-radio around my neck.

For the first time also, I see that at the very front, within arms length of the APC, three nuns are kneeling, praying. They are puny and incongruous, in front of the APC and the soldiers. They look serene....

LATIN AMERICA:
OFFICIAL CHURCH TEACHING

If the history of Catholic peacemaking in Latin America began in the sixteenth century with Montesinos, Las Casas, and the other missionary prophets of nonviolence [224-228, 239-246], the rebirth of their tradition of liberation has come only in the era after Vatican II. Like the rest of the Third World, Latin America passed through its stages of colonialism only to enter a new age of dependency on Western, especially U.S., economic interests and "development" plans.

During the late 1960s and the 1970s both the massive scale of many development projects and the desire to protect the wealth of the oligarchs against the needs of an increasingly impoverished majority led to the creation of the "National-Security State" in one Latin American republic after another. Authoritarian regimes kept power by military force and the widespread suspension of human rights, including imprisonment without trial, torture, disappearances, and murder. In country after country, from Brazil in 1964 to Argentina in 1983, the military juntas or lifetime dictators excused their actions against scores of Catholic laypeople, priests, monks, nuns, and bishops in remarkably similar words: as the defense of "Western Christian Civilization."

Meanwhile, however, the church in Latin America had undergone fundamental changes. By the late nineteenth century the colonial alliance of church and state had changed radically. Liberal governments and popular and official anticlericalism stripped the churches of their privileged positions of power and expropriated most of their monastic and episcopal lands. The Latin American church, impoverished and deprived of official political power, also felt itself ignored by Europe and became increasingly understaffed and incapable of maintaining its pastoral and evangelizing missions to large segments of the Latin American population. In addition, indigenous forms of belief and practice commingled and survived along with the official cult and teaching of the Catholic church. Thus by the twentieth century a form of Catholicism particular to Latin America had developed.

The Catholic church that faced the era of development was thus truly marginal – deprived of real wealth, political power, and connection to the European center – even though on its upper, official levels it may have retained the illusion of being at the center of Latin American developments. The growth and appeal of Marxism in Latin America to wide segments of the population, especially following the success of the Cuban Revolution in 1959 and the reaction of the National Security State, found the church beset by new realities on both sides that threatened both its official authority and its power among the people.

Despite these realities, many in the church, especially among the hierarchy, maintained their Constantinian alliance with the state. The state, for its part, tolerated the notion of Christendom as long as the alliance aided its authoritarian purposes and maintained harmony among the ruling elite. At the same time, however, Marxist criticism of development and of increasing poverty combined with the prophetic tradition of protest in Latin American Catholicism to produce a new commitment among large segments of the church, which suddenly emerged as the only voice of dissent to national-security repression left. The changes affected first the lower clergy and the base Christian communities and slowly percolated up to the hierarchy, itself in the midst of interpreting and implementing the reform impulses of John XXIII's *Pacem in Terris* and *Mater et Magistra, Gaudium et Spes* of Vatican II, and Paul VI's *Populorum Progressio.*

THE MEDELLÍN CONFERENCE

The conference held in Medellín, Colombia from August 24 to September 6, 1968 was the second general meeting of CELAM, the Conference of Latin American Bishops. It brought together several of the developing strains of the last decade: the growing sense of unity among Latin America's Catholics, the impact of a developing liberation theology, and the influence of Vatican II and Paul VI's *Populorum Progressio.* Its major themes were the pressing issues of contemporary Latin America and the church's role in social change and its methods, political reform that would guarantee the participation of the people in decisions affecting the common good, and the process of conscientization.

The council documents touch on two essential areas: Justice and Peace. The document on Peace follows the same three-part form as that on Justice. Part I, Pertinent Facts, uses Paul VI's definition of peace in *Populorum Progressio* [development, a new name for peace: see 301] to raise the essential problem of peace and peacemaking in contemporary Latin America.

The church can no longer support conditions of oppression and poverty but must "call attention to those aspects which constitute a menace or negation of peace." These include the marginality of most of the people of Latin America, extreme social and economic inequalities, the growing frustration, disintegration, and proletarianization of the people, the oppression and insensitivity of the dominant groups, their unjust exercise of power, and the growing awareness among the oppressed of their state of oppression.

Part II, Doctrinal Reflection, provides some solutions by reviewing Christian views of peace, several of which we present here. The following selections are taken from Gremillion, pp. 445-76

Chapter 6: The Third World and Liberation

326. Medellín Documents on Justice and Peace, September 6, 1968

JUSTICE

I. Pertinent Facts

(1) There are in existence many studies of the Latin American people. The misery that besets large masses of human beings in all of our countries is described in all of these studies. That misery, as a collective fact, expresses itself as injustice which cries to the heavens [Paul VI, *Populorum Progressio,* §30].

But what perhaps has not been sufficiently said is that in general the efforts which have been made have not been capable of assuring that justice be honored and realized in every sector of the respective national communities. Often families do not find concrete possibilities for the education of their children. The young demand their right to enter universities or centers of higher learning for both intellectual and technical training; the women, their right to a legitimate equality with men; the peasants, better conditions of life; or if they are workers, better prices and security in buying and selling; the growing middle class feels frustrated by the lack of expectations. There has begun an exodus of professionals and technicians to more developed countries; the small businessmen and industrialists are pressed by greater interests and not a few large Latin American industrialists are gradually coming to be dependent on the international business enterprises. We cannot ignore the phenomenon of this almost universal frustration of legitimate aspirations which creates the climate of collective anguish in which we are already living.

(2) The lack of socio-cultural integration, in the majority of our countries, has given rise to the superimposition of cultures. In the economic sphere systems flourished which consider solely the potential of groups with great earning power. This lack of adaptation to the characteristics and to the potentials of all our people, in turn, gives rise to frequent political instability and the consolidation of purely formal institutions. To all of this must be added the lack of solidarity which, on the individual and social levels, leads to the committing of serious sins, evident in the unjust structures which characterize the Latin American situation.

II. Doctrinal Bases

(3) The Latin American Church has a message for all men on this

continent who "hunger and thirst after justice." The very God who creates men in his image and likeness, creates the "earth and all that is in it for the use of all men and all nations, in such a way that created goods can reach all in a more just manner" [Vatican II, *Gaudium et Spes*, §69], and gives them power to transform and perfect the world in solidarity [Ibid., §34]. It is the same God who, in the fullness of time, sends his Son in the flesh, so that He might come to liberate all men from the slavery to which sin has subjected them [John 8:32-35]: hunger, misery, oppression and ignorance, in a word, that injustice and hatred which have their origin in human selfishness.

Thus, for our authentic liberation, all of us need a profound conversion so that "the kingdom of justice, love and peace," might come to us. The origin of all disdain for mankind, of all injustice, should be sought in the internal imbalance of human liberty, which will always need to be rectified in history. The uniqueness of the Christian message does not so much consist in the affirmation of the necessity for structural change, as it does in the insistence on the conversion of men which will in turn bring about this change. We will not have a new continent without new and reformed structures, but, above all, there will be no new continent without new men, who know how to be truly free and responsible according to the light of the Gospel.

(4) Only by the light of Christ is the mystery of man made clear. In the economy of salvation the divine work is an action of integral human development and liberation, which has love for its sole motive. Man is "created in Christ Jesus" [Eph. 2:10], fashioned in Him as a "new creature" [2 Cor. 5:17]. By faith and baptism he is transformed, filled with the gift of the Spirit, with a new dynamism, not of selfishness, but of love which compels him to seek out a new, more profound relationship with God, his fellow man, and created things.

Love, "the fundamental law of human perfection, and therefore of the transformation of the world" [*Gaudium et Spes*, §38], is not only the greatest commandment of the Lord; it is also the dynamism which ought to motivate Christians to realize justice in the world, having truth as a foundation and liberty as their sign.

(5) This is how the Church desires to serve the world, radiating over it a light and life which heals and elevates the dignity of the human person [Ibid., §41], which consolidates the unity of society [Ibid., §42] and gives a more profound reason and meaning to all human activity.

Chapter 6: The Third World and Liberation

Doubtless, for the Church, the fullness and perfection of the human vocation will be accomplished with the definitive inclusion of each man in the Passover or Triumph of Christ, but the hope of such a definitive realization, rather than lull, ought to "vivify the concern to perfect this earth. For here grows the body of the new human family, a body which even now is able to give some kind of foreshadowing of the new age" [Ibid., §39]. We do not confuse temporal progress and the Kingdom of Christ; nevertheless, the former, "to the extent that it can contribute to the better ordering of human society, is of vital concern to the Kingdom of God" [Ibid.].

The Christian quest for justice is a demand arising from biblical teaching. All men are merely humble stewards of material goods. In the search for salvation we must avoid the dualism which separates temporal tasks from the work of sanctification. Although we are encompassed with imperfections, we are men of hope. We have faith that our love for Christ and our brethren will not only be the great force liberating us from injustice and oppression, but also the inspiration for social justice, understood as a whole of life and as an impulse toward the integral growth of our countries....

PEACE

I. The Latin American Situation and Peace

(1) If "development is the new name for peace" [*Populorum Progressio*, §87], Latin American under-development with its own characteristics in the different countries is an unjust situation which promotes tensions that conspire against peace.

We can divide these tensions into three major groups, selecting, in each of these, those variables which constitute a positive menace to the peace of our countries by manifesting an unjust situation.

When speaking of injustice, we refer to those realities that constitute a sinful situation; this does not mean however, that we are overlooking the fact that at times the misery in our countries can have natural causes which are difficult to overcome.

In making this analysis, we do not ignore or fail to give credit to the positive efforts made at every level to build a more just society. We do not include this here because our purpose is to call attention to those aspects which constitute a menace or negation of peace....

Tensions among the Countries of Latin America

(11) We here denounce the particular phenomenon of historico-political origin that continues to disturb cordial relations among some countries and impedes truly constructive collaboration. Nevertheless, the integration process, well understood, presents itself as a commanding necessity for Latin America. Without pretending to set norms of a truly complex, technical nature, governing integration, we deem it opportune to point out its multi-dimensional character. Integration, in effect, is not solely an economic process; it has a broader dimension reflected in the way in which it embraces man in his total situation: social, political, cultural, religious, racial.

Among the factors that increase the tensions among our countries we underline:

(12) An *exacerbated nationalism* in some countries: The Holy Father [*Progressio Populorum*, §62] has already denounced the unwholesomeness of this attitude, especially on a matter where the weakness of the national economies requires a union of efforts.

(13) *Armaments:* In certain countries an arms race is under way that surpasses the limits of reason. It frequently stems from a fictitious need to respond to diverse interests rather than to a true need of the national community. In that respect, a phrase of *Populorum Progressio* is particularly pertinent: "When so many communities are hungry, when so many homes suffer misery, when so many men live submerged in ignorance...any arms race becomes an intolerable scandal" [Ibid., §53].

II. Doctrinal Reflection: Christian View of Peace

(14) The above-mentioned Christian viewpoint on peace adds up to a negation of peace such as Christian tradition understands it.

Three factors characterize the Christian concept of peace:

a) Peace is, above all, a work of justice [*Gaudium et Spes*, §78]. It presupposes and requires the establishment of a just order [*Pacem in Terris*, §167, *Populorum Progressio*, §76] in which men can fulfill themselves as men, where their dignity is respected, their legitimate aspirations satisfied, their access to truth recognized, their personal freedom guaranteed; an order where man is not an object, but an agent of his own history. Therefore, there will be attempts against peace where unjust inequalities among men and nations prevail [Paul VI, *Message of 1 Jan. 1968*].

Chapter 6: The Third World and Liberation

Peace in Latin America, therefore, is not the simple absence of violence and bloodshed. Oppression by the power groups may give the impression of maintaining peace and order, but in truth it is nothing but the "continuous and inevitable seed of rebellion and war" [Ibid.].

"Peace can only be obtained by creating a new order which carries with it a more perfect justice among men" [*Populorum Progressio*, §76]. It is in this sense that the integral development of a man, the path to more human conditions, becomes the symbol of peace.

b) Secondly, peace is a permanent task [*Gaudium et Spes*, §78]. A community becomes a reality in time and is subject to a movement that implies constant change in structures, transformation of attitudes, and conversion of hearts.

The "tranquility of order," according to the Augustinian definition of peace, is neither passivity nor conformity. It is not something that is acquired once and for all. It is the result of continuous effort and adaptation to new circumstances, to new demands and challenges of a changing history. A static and apparent peace may be obtained with the use of force; an authentic peace implies struggle, creative abilities and permanent conquest [Paul VI, *Christmas Message*, 1967].

Peace is not found, it is built. The Christian man is the artisan of peace [Mt. 5:9, see **31**]. This task, given the above circumstances, has a special character in our continent; thus, the People of God in Latin America, following the example of Christ, must resist personal and collective injustice with unselfish courage and fearlessness.

c) Finally, peace is the fruit of love [*Gaudium et Spes*, §78]. It is the expression of true fraternity among men, a fraternity given by Christ, Prince of Peace, in reconciling all men with the Father. Human solidarity cannot truly take effect unless it is done in Christ, who gives Peace that the world cannot give [John 14:27, see **38**]. Love is the soul of justice. The Christian who works for social justice should always cultivate peace and love in his heart.

Peace with God is the basic foundation of internal and social peace. Therefore, where this social peace does not exist there will we find social, political, economic and cultural inequalities, there will we find the rejection of the peace of the Lord, and a rejection of the Lord Himself [cf. Mt. 25:31-46].

The Problem of Violence in Latin America

(15) Violence constitutes one of the gravest problems in Latin America. A decision on which the future of the countries of the continent will depend should not be left to the impulses of emotion and passion. We would be failing in our pastoral duty if we were not to remind the conscience, caught in this dramatic dilemma, of the criteria derived from the Christian doctrine of evangelical love.

No one should be surprised if we forcefully re-affirm our faith in the productiveness of peace. This is our Christian ideal. "Violence is neither Christian nor evangelical" [Paul VI, *Bogotá Homily,* 23 Aug. 1968]. The Christian man is peaceful and not ashamed of it. He is not simply a pacifist, for he can fight [Paul VI, *Message of 1 Jan. 1968*], but he prefers peace to war. He knows that "violent changes in structures would be fallacious, ineffectual in themselves and not conforming to the dignity of man, which demands that the necessary changes take place from within, that is to say, through a fitting awakening of conscience, adequate preparation and effective participation of all, which the ignorance and often inhuman conditions of life make it impossible to assure at this time" [Paul VI, *Bogotá Homily,* 23 Aug. 1968].

(16) As the Christian believes in the productiveness of peace in order to achieve justice, he also believes that justice is a prerequisite for peace. He recognizes that in many instances Latin America finds itself faced with a situation of injustice that can be called institutionalized violence, when, because of a structural deficiency of industry and agriculture, of national and international economy, of cultural and political life, "whole towns lack necessities, live in such dependence as hinders all initiative and responsibility as well as every possibility for cultural promotion and participation in social and political life" [*Populorum Progressio,* §30], thus violating fundamental rights. This situation demands all-embracing, courageous, urgent and profoundly renovating transformations. We should not be surprised therefore, that the "temptation to violence" is surfacing in Latin America. One should not abuse the patience of a people that for years has borne a situation that would not be acceptable to any one with any degree of awareness of human rights.

Facing a situation which works so seriously against the dignity of man and against peace, we address ourselves, as pastors, to all the members of the Christian community, asking them to assume their responsibility in the promotion of peace in Latin America.

(17) We would like to direct our call in the first place to those who have a greater share of wealth, culture and power. We know that there are leaders in Latin America who are sensitive to the needs of the people and try to remedy them. They recognize that the privileged many times join together, and with all the means at their disposal pressure those who govern, thus obstructing necessary changes. In some instances, this pressure takes on drastic proportions which result in the destruction of life and property.

Therefore, we urge them not to take advantage of the pacifist position of the Church in order to oppose, either actively or passively, the profound transformations that are so necessary. If they jealously retain their privileges and defend them through violence they are responsible to history for provoking "explosive revolutions of despair" [Paul VI, *Bogotá Homily,* 23 Aug. 1968]. The peaceful future of the countries of Latin America depends to a large extent on their attitude.

(18) Also responsible for injustice are those who remain passive for fear of the sacrifice and personal risk implied by any courageous and effective action. Justice, and therefore peace, conquer by means of a dynamic action of awakening *(concientizacion)* and organization of the popular sectors, which are capable of pressing public officials who are often impotent in their social projects without popular support.

(19) We address ourselves finally to those who, in the face of injustice and illegitimate resistance to change, put their hopes in violence. With Paul VI we realize that their attitude "frequently finds its ultimate motivation in noble impulses of justice and solidarity" [Ibid.]. Let us not speak here of empty words which do not imply personal responsibility and which isolate from the fruitful non-violent actions that are immediately possible.

If it is true that revolutionary insurrection can be legitimate in the case of evident and prolonged "tyranny that seriously works against the fundamental rights of man, and which damages the common good of the country" [*Populorum Progressio,* §31], whether it proceeds from one person or from clearly unjust structures, it is also certain that violence or "armed revolution" generally "generates new injustices, introduces new imbalances and causes new disasters; one cannot combat a real evil at the price of a greater evil" [Ibid.].

573

If we consider then, the totality of the circumstances of our countries, and if we take into account the Christian preference for peace, the enormous difficulty of a civil war, the logic of violence, the atrocities it engenders, the risk of provoking foreign intervention, illegitimate as it may be, the difficulty of building a regime of justice and freedom while participating in a process of violence, we earnestly desire that the dynamism of the awakened and organized community be put to the service of justice and peace.

Finally, we would like to make ours the words of our Holy Father to the newly ordained priests and deacons in Bogotá, when he referred to all the suffering and said to them: "We will be able to understand their afflictions and change them, not into hate and violence, but into the strong and peaceful energy of constructive works" [Paul VI, *Address to New Priests and Deacons*, Bogotá, 22 Aug. 1968]....

THE PUEBLA CONFERENCE

The second meeting of CELAM held at Bogotá Colombia, in December 1977, reaffirmed the thrust of Medellín, yet the third meeting of CELAM at Puebla, Mexico in 1979 put much of the progress of church reform in Latin America into serious doubt. Reaction had been growing ever since 1972 and the appointment of conservative Archbishop Alfonso Lopez Trujillo as secretary general of the bishops' conference. The anti-liberationist forces in Latin America and in Europe, funded by U.S. and West German conservatives, had been mounting a counterattack.

The conservatives' long preparations backfired, however, and the historical meeting at Puebla – at which Pope John Paul II played a public role – was a major media and international event and a landmark in church history. Its Final Document reconfirmed the positions of Medellín and deepened the church's commitment to the poor and the oppressed, especially after the past decade of repression and violence. It reconfirmed Vatican II's divorce of the church from the state and highlighted how far the Catholic church had come since the concordats of the 1930s. The Final Document rarely even uses the words "nation" or "state" that had so long dominated church thought on the problems of the world, replacing them, instead, with "the people" as the agency of change. It also sided decidedly with the prophetic tradition of Montesinos and Las Casas in Latin American history.

The council reaffirmed the message of Vatican II, of Medellín, and of Bogotá on Catholic peacemaking in Latin America. Peace is once again identified with justice. Yet justice itself cannot flourish under the present situation in Latin America, in which violence of all types prevails. This includes both the institutionalized violence of repression and the counter-violence of subversion. The council thus rejects the violence of the National Security State, "physical and psychological torture, kidnapping, the persecution of political dissidents and suspect persons, and the exclusion of people from public life because of their ideas," and condemns the excuses offered. It also condemns "terrorist and guerrilla violence" and rejects its role in the process of liberation.

The following selections are taken from John Eagleson and Philip Scharper, eds., John Drury, trans., *Puebla and Beyond*, Maryknoll, NY: Orbis Books, 1979, pp. 124-25, 190-98.

327. Puebla, The Final Document: Evangelization in Latin America's Present and Future, February 1979

PART I: PASTORAL OVERVIEW OF THE REALITY THAT IS LATIN AMERICA

Chapter 1, Historical Overview

...(4) Evangelization is the very mission of the Church. The history of the Church is fundamentally the history of the evangelization of a people that lives through an ongoing process of gestation, and that is born and integrated into the life of nations over the ages. In becoming incarnate, the Church makes a vital contribution to the birth of nationalities and deeply imprints a particular character on them. Evangelization lies at the origins of the New World that is Latin America. The Church makes its presence felt in the origins and in the present-day reality of the continent. And, within the framework of it own proper mission and its realization, the Church seeks to contribute its services to a better future for the peoples of Latin America, to their liberation and growth in all of life's dimensions. The Medellín Conference itself re-echoed the statement of Paul VI that the vocation of Latin America was to "fashion a new and genial synthesis of the ancient and the modern, the spiritual and the temporal, what others bequeathed to us and what is our own original creation" [Medellín, *Final Document*, §7].

(5) In the sometimes painful confluence of the most varied cultures and races, Latin America forged a new mixture of ethnic groups as well as modes of thinking and living that allowed for the gestation of a new race that overcame the hard and fast separations that had existed previously.

(6) The generation of peoples and cultures is always dramatic, enveloped in a mixture of light and shadow. As a human task, evangelization is subject to the vicissitudes of history; but it always tries to transfigure them with the fire of the Spirit on the pathway of Christ, the center and meaning of universal history and of each and every person. Spurred on by all the contradictions and lacerations of those founding epochs, and immersed in a gigantic process of domination and cultural growth that has not yet come to an end, the evangelization that went into the making of Latin America is one of the relevant chapters in the history of the Church. In the face of difficulties that were both enormous and unprecedented, the creative response was such that its vigor keeps alive the popular religiosity of the majority of our peoples.

(7) Our radical Catholic substrate, with its flourishing, vital forms of religiosity, was established and animated by a vast legion of missionaries: bishops, religious, and lay people. First and foremost, there is the labor of our saints: Toribio de Mogrovejo, Rosa de Lima, Martin de Porres, Pedro Claver, Luis Beltrán, and others.... They teach us that the weakness and cowardice of the people who surrounded and sometimes persecuted them were overcome; that the Gospel in all its plenitude of grace and love was lived, and can be lived, in Latin America as a sign of spiritual grandeur and divine truth.

(8) And then there were the intrepid champions of justice and proponents of the gospel message of peace [see **224-229, 239-246**]: e.g., Antonio de Montesinos, Bartolomé de las Casas, Juan de Zumárraga, Vasco de Quiroga, Juan del Valle, Julian Gracés, Jose de Ancheita, Manuel Nóbrega, and all the others who defended the Indians against *conquistadors* and *encomenderos* – even unto death, as in the case of Bishop Antonio Valdivieso. They prove, with all the force of actual fact, in what way the Church promotes the dignity and freedom of the Latin American person. And that is a reality thankfully acknowledged by John Paul II when he first stepped on the soil of the New World: "...those religious who came to announce Christ the Savior, to defend the dignity of the native inhabitants, to proclaim their inviolable rights, to foster their inte-

gral betterment, to teach brotherhood as human beings and as children of the same Lord and Father God."...

PART II: GOD'S SAVING PLAN FOR LATIN AMERICA

5.4 Reflections on Political Violence

(531) Faced with the deplorable reality of violence in Latin America, we wish to express our view clearly. Condemnation is always the proper judgment on physical and psychological torture, kidnapping, the persecution of political dissidents or suspect persons, and the exclusion of people from public life because of their ideas. If these crimes are committed by the authorities entrusted with the task of safeguarding the common good, then they defile those who practice them, notwithstanding any reasons offered.

(532) The Church is just as decisive in rejecting terrorist and guerrilla violence, which becomes cruel and uncontrollable when it is unleashed. Criminal acts can in no way be justified as the way to liberation. Violence inexorably engenders new forms of oppression and bondage, which usually prove to be more serious than the ones people are allegedly being liberated from. But most importantly violence is an attack on life, which depends on the Creator alone. And we must also stress that when an ideology appeals to violence, it thereby admits its own weakness and inadequacy.

(533) Our responsibility as Christians is to use all possible means to promote the implementation of nonviolent tactics in the effort to reestablish justice in economic and sociopolitical relations. This is in accordance with the teaching of Vatican II, which applies to both national and international life: "We cannot fail to praise those who renounce the use of violence in the vindication of their rights and who resort to methods of defense which are otherwise available to weaker parties too, provided that this can be done without injury to the rights and duties of others or of the community" [*Gaudium et Spes*, §78].

(534) "We are obliged to state and reaffirm that violence is neither Christian nor evangelical, and that brusque, violent structural changes will be false, ineffective in themselves, and certainly inconsistent with the dignity of the people" [Paul VI, *Address in Bogotá*, 23 Aug. 1968]. The fact is that "the Church realizes that even the best structures and the most idealized systems quickly become inhuman if human inclinations are

not improved, if there is no conversion of heart and mind on the part of those who are living in those structures or controlling them" [*Evangelii Nuntiandi*, §36]....

REFLECTION ON PRAXIS: LIBERATION THEOLOGY

We have elsewhere and at some length examined the theology of liberation (see *Liberation Theologies: A Research Guide*, New York: Garland Publishers, 1991). Here, therefore, we will give only a brief introduction to the topic and to the texts that follow. By the mid-1960s theological and practical elements had combined to produce a new theology of liberation in Latin America and a new definition of peacemaking for the majority of the world's Catholics. Essentially liberation theologians and educators reject the European dualism between an inner pietistic spirituality and a neutral or hostile attitude toward the world. Instead, following the new directions of papal and conciliar thought, they embrace the complete integration of the individual and of the world. Individual salvation and the salvation of the world are thus seen as one.

Liberation theologians put less emphasis on traditional doctrine, conventional spirituality, and liturgical devotion – *orthodoxy* – than on the visible imitation of Christ in the world and the life of committed love and justice – *orthopraxis*. Like the medieval mendicants [146-160] and the Renaissance Humanists [212-223], they emphasize less the intellectual and individualist aspects of piety and salvation, than the ethical demands of Christianity: the duty of each Christian to live the Beatitudes and to contribute to making the kingdom of god a reality not only in a spiritual afterlife but in concrete terms in the world, through social justice and peace. The world and its history are thus one, and the church is neither above nor outside this profane history. The church is, instead, the sacrament of the world, that is, the visible manifestation of God's kingdom and his plan for the salvation of all creation. As such it cannot act as an institution, protecting a specific and privileged position within the world, but must act as the chief agency of this salvation, not only for its immediate members but for all of God's creation.

This mission cooperates with and contributes to God's original creation by restoring and renewing the earth by liberating humans from sin. In keeping with its integral approach, however, liberation theology defines sin as the modern popes and councils have: as social and economic injustice, as oppression and the will to dominate, as the violence that maintains injustice. The church's role is both prophetic and teaching: it exposes sin wherever it finds it and condemns it for what it is; it also educates those enslaved and blinded by sin – those oppressed by unjust economic and social systems and those who maintain and extend this oppression – to their own human dignity, freedom, and solidarity with all other men and women. Liberation theologians call this process "conscientization." The church thus seeks not to replace one oppressor with another but to liberate both the oppressed and the oppressors at the same time and to reunite them in the kingdom of god.

In true adherence to the Christian message, however, liberation theology takes its inspiration from the Bible: from the archetypal story of liberation from oppressive bondage, the story of Exodus, which we have already seen as key in African theology [320] and from Christ's own definition of his mission. Luke's Gospel [4:1-19, see 30] is cited frequently for this model As Jesus returns from his fasting and temptation in the desert he enters the synagogue at Nazareth and begins preaching:

> The Spirit of the Lord is upon me
> for he has anointed me
> to bring good news to the afflicted.
> He has sent me to proclaim liberty to captives,
> sight to the blind,
> and to let the oppressed go free,
> to proclaim a year of favor from the Lord.

The two passages, the temptations and the announcement of the mission, form an essential unit: having rejected the materialism, power, and despair of the world, the church and its members must now embrace hope and preach the good news to the poor, the oppressed, the jailed, and the blind – in short they must bring the Gospels not to the rich, the powerful, and the comfortable but to the marginal, the outcasts, and those who neither can nor will see the truth. Liberation theology therefore takes up the call of Vatican II and the modern popes in its "option for the poor." Liberation itself, however, must be won by the oppressed themselves once they have become assured of their own dignity and freedom.

The revolution of liberation theology is based on nonviolence, but it realizes that the struggle for peace and justice necessitates conflict. This has led some liberation theologians to seek new formulations for Catholic peacemaking in the context of Latin America's revolutionary situation, to speak of "prophetic subversive violence," rather than "nonviolence," as the Christian alternative to the "institutionalized" and "oppressive" violence of the ruling elites and to the "subversive armed violence" of the terrorist or the guerrilla.

Theology thus remains true to its call to define doctrine in relationship to the developing practice of Catholics and their gradual process of revelation through history. Practice in turn is defined and modified by theology in an unfolding dialogue.

We can only illustrate by examples; we cannot examine the entire scope of peacemaking in Latin America today. Our selections therefore range from general theological principles to discussion of the church in the world, to "liberation ethics," to the issues of suffering, violence, persecution, martyrdom, and revolution; and hence back to the root issues of praxis in the world that give rise to the theology of liberation.

GUSTAVO GUTIÉRREZ

Liberation theology has often been brushed aside, disparaged as a naive formulation of political goals and methodologies: a Marxist Trojan Horse posing as discourse: yet one need only look at the work of Peruvian theologian Gustavo Gutiérrez' to see the fallacy of such a caricature.

Gutiérrez was born in Lima, Peru on June 8, 1928 and studied at the Universidad Nacional Mayor de San Marcos in Lima. He holds a doctorate in theology from the Catholic University of Louvain, Belgium. Ordained in 1959, in 1960 he became an advisor for the National Union of Catholic Students and a professor at the Catholic University at Lima. From 1967 to 1968 he also served on the Pastoral Advisory Team of CELAM. In 1974 he and several colleagues founded the Bartolomé de Las Casas Center in the Lima slum of Rimac where he lives. Since 1980 he has been its associate vicar.

Gutiérrez is the author of several of the most important theological works of this century, including the landmark *A Theology of Liberation* (1971), *The Power of the Poor in History* (1979), *We Drink from Our Own Wells: The Spiritual Journey of a People* (1983), and *On Job: God-Talk and the Suffering of the Innocent* (1985). In the 1980s liberation theology came under careful scrutiny and outright attack from many circles in North and South America, Europe and the Vatican itself. In September 1984, therefore, Gutiérrez was called to Rome by Joseph Cardinal Ratzinger, head of the Sacred Congregation of the Doctrine of the Faith (the former Inquisition) to defend his views on several subjects, including authority, violence, and the influence of Marxism on his thought. Ironically, the encounter brought worldwide attention to Gutiérrez and to liberation theology.

Even a casual reading of *A Theology of Liberation* will reveal the author's large number of sources: primarily the Bible, such progressive theologians as Henri de Lubac, Karl Rahner, Karl Barth, Johann Baptist Metz, Ives Congar, Edward Schillebeeckx, Harvey Cox, Jürgen Moltmann, political theorists Marx, Althusser, and Gramsci, Peruvian novelist José María Arguedas, Dom Helder Camara, the documents of Medellín, of Vatican II, especially *Gaudium et Spes*, John XXIII, Paul VI, all in a synthesis archetypal of liberation theology.

The following excerpts are taken from Gustavo Gutiérrez, *A Theology of Liberation*, Caridad Inda and John Eagleson, trans. and ed., 15th Anniversary Ed., Maryknoll, NY: Orbis Books, 1988, pp. 3-12.

328. Gustavo Gutiérrez, A Theology of Liberation

Chapter One. Theology: A Critical Reflection

Theological reflection – that is, the understanding of the faith – arises spontaneously and inevitably in the believer, in all those who have accepted the gift of the Word of God. Theology is intrinsic to a life of faith seeking to be authentic and complete and is, therefore, essential to the common consideration of this faith in the ecclesial community. There is present in *all believers* – and more so in every Christian community – a rough outline of a theology. There is present an effort to understand the faith, something like a pre-understanding of that faith which is manifested in life, action, and concrete attitude. It is on this foundation, and only because of it, that the edifice of theology – in the precise and technical sense of the term – can be erected. This foundation is not merely a jumping-off point, but the soil into which theological reflection stubbornly and permanently sinks its roots and from which it derives its strength.

But the focus of theological work, in the strict sense of the term, has undergone many transformations throughout the history of the Church. "Bound to the role of the Church, theology is dependent upon its historical development," writes Christian Duquoc. Moreover, as Congar observed recently, this evolution has accelerated to a certain extent in recent years: "The theological work has changed in the past twenty-five years."...

Theology as Critical Reflection on Praxis

The function of theology as critical reflection on praxis has gradually become more clearly defined in recent years, but it has its roots in the first centuries of the Church's life. The Augustinian theology of history which we find in *The City of God* [**86**], for example, is based on a true analysis of the signs of the times and the demands with which they challenge the Christian community.

Historical Praxis

For various reasons the existential and active aspects of the Christian life have recently been stressed in a different way than in the immediate past.

In the first place, *charity* has been fruitfully rediscovered as the center of the Christian life. This has led to a more Biblical view of the faith as an act of trust, a going out of one's self, a commitment to God and neighbor, a relationship with others. It is in this sense that St. Paul tells us that faith works through charity: love is the nourishment and the fullness of faith, the gift of one's self to the Other, and invariably to others. This is the foundation of the *praxis* of Christians, of their active presence in history. According to the Bible, faith is the total human response to God, who saves through love. In this light, the understanding of the faith appears as the understanding not of the simple affirmation – almost memorization – of truths, but of a commitment, an overall attitude, a particular posture toward life.

In a parallel development, Christian *spirituality* has seen a significant evolution. In the early centuries of the Church there emerged the primacy, almost exclusiveness, of a certain kind of contemplative life, hermetical, monastic, characterized by withdrawal from the world, and presented as the model way to sanctity. About the twelfth century the

Chapter 6: The Third World and Liberation

possibility of sharing contemplation by means of preaching and other forms of apostolic activity began to be considered. This point of view was exemplified in the mixed life (contemplative and active) of the mendicant orders and was expressed in the formula: *contemplata aliis tradere* ("to transmit to others the fruits of contemplation"). Viewed historically this stage can be considered as a transition to Ignatian spirituality, which sought a difficult but fruitful synthesis between contemplation and action: *in actione contemplativus* ("contemplative in action"). This process, strengthened in recent years by the search for a spirituality of the laity, culminates today in the studies on the religious value of the profane and in the spirituality of the activity of the Christian in the world.

Moreover, today there is a greater sensitivity to the *anthropological aspects* of revelation. The Word about God is at the same time a promise to the world. In revealing God to us, the Gospel message reveals us to ourselves in our situation before the Lord and with other humans. The God of Christian revelation is a God incarnate, hence the famous comment of Karl Barth regarding Christian anthropocentrism, "Man is the measure of all things, since God became man." All this has caused the revaluation of human presence and activity in the world, especially in relation to other human beings. On this subject Congar writes: "Seen as a whole, the direction of theological thinking has been characterized by a transference away from attention to the being *per se* of supernatural realities, and toward attention to their relationship with man, with the world, and with the problems and the affirmations of all those who for us represent the *Others*."There is no *horizontalism* in this approach. It is simply a question of the rediscovery of the indissoluble unity of humankind and God.

On the other hand, *the very life of the Church* appears ever more clearly as a *locus theologicus*. Regarding the participation of Christians in the important social movements of their time, Chenu wrote insightfully more than thirty years ago: "They are active *loci theologici* for the doctrines of grace, the Incarnation, and the redemption, as expressly promulgated and described in detail by the papal encyclicals. They are poor theologians who, wrapped up in their manuscripts and scholastic disputations, are not open to these amazing events, not only in the pious fervor of their hearts but formally in their science; there is a theological datum and an extremely fruitful one, in the *presence* of the Spirit." The so-called new theology attempted to adopt this posture some decades ago. The fact that the life of the Church is a source for all theological analysis has been recalled to mind often since then. The Word of God gathers and is incarnated in the community of faith, which gives itself to the service of all.

Vatican Council II has strongly reaffirmed the idea of a Church of service and not of power. This is a Church which is not centered upon itself and which does not "find itself" except when it "loses itself," when it lives "the joys and the hopes, the griefs and the anxieties of persons of this age" *(Gaudium et Spes,* §1). All of these trends provide a new focus for seeing the presence and activity of the Church in the world as a starting point for theological reflection.

What since John XXIII and Vatican Council II began to be called a theology of the *signs of the times* can be characterized along the same lines, although this takes a step beyond narrow ecclesial limits. It must not be forgotten that the signs of the times are not only a call to intellectual analysis. They are above all a call to pastoral activity, to commitment, and to service. Studying the signs of the times includes both dimensions. Therefore, *Gaudium et Spes,* §44, points out that discerning the signs of the times is the responsibility of every Christian, especially pastors and theologians, to hear, distinguish, and interpret the many voices of our age, and to judge them in the light of the divine Word. In this way, revealed truths can always be more deeply penetrated, better understood, and set forth to greater advantage. Attributing this role to every member of the People of God and singling out the pastors – charged with guiding the activity of the Church – highlights the call to commitment which the signs of the times imply. Necessarily connected with this consideration, the function of theologians will be to afford greater clarity regarding this commitment by means of intellectual analysis. (It is interesting to note that the inclusion of theologians in the above-mentioned text met opposition during the conciliar debates.)

Another factor, this time of a *philosophical* nature, reinforces the importance of human action as the point of departure for all reflection. The philosophical issues of our times are characterized by new relationships of humankind with nature, born of advances in science and technology. These new bonds affect the awareness that persons have of themselves and of their active relationships with others....

To these factors can be added the influence of *Marxist thought,* focusing on praxis and geared to the transformation of the world. The Marxist influence began to be felt in the middle of the nineteenth century, but in recent times its cultural impact has become greater. Many agree with

Sartre that "Marxism, as the formal framework of all contemporary philosophical thought, cannot be superseded." Be that as it may, contemporary theology does in fact find itself in direct and fruitful confrontation with Marxism, and it is to a large extent due to Marxism's influence that theological thought, searching for its own sources, has begun to reflect on the meaning of the transformation of this world and human action in history. Further, this confrontation helps theology to perceive what its efforts at understanding the faith receive from the historical praxis of humankind in history as well as what its own reflection might mean for the transformation of the world.

Finally, the rediscovery of the *eschatological dimension* in theology has also led us to consider the central role of historical praxis. Indeed, if human history is above all else an opening to the future, then it is a task, a political occupation, through which we orient and open ourselves to the gift which gives history its transcendent meaning: the full and definitive encounter with the Lord and with other humans. "To do the truth," as the Gospel says, thus acquires a precise and concrete meaning in terms of the importance of action in Christian life. Faith in a God who loves us and calls us to the gift of full communion with God and fellowship with others not only is not foreign to the transformation of the world; it leads necessarily to the building up of that fellowship and communion in history. Moreover, only by doing this truth will our faith be "verified," in the etymological sense of the word. From this notion has recently been derived the term *orthopraxis*, which still disturbs the sensitivities of some. The intention, however, is not to deny the meaning of *orthodoxy*, understood as a proclamation of and reflection on statements considered to be true. Rather, the goal is to balance and even to reject the primacy and almost exclusiveness which doctrine has enjoyed in Christian life and above all to modify the emphasis, often obsessive, upon the attainment of an orthodoxy which is often nothing more than fidelity to an obsolete tradition or a debatable interpretation. In a more positive vein, the intention is to recognize the work and importance of concrete behavior, of deeds, of action, of praxis in the Christian life....

Critical Reflection

All the factors we have considered have been responsible for a more accurate understanding that communion with the Lord inescapably means a Christian life centered around a concrete and creative commitment of service to others. They have likewise led to the rediscovery or explicit formulation of the function of theology as critical reflection. It would be well at this point to define further our terms.

Theology must be critical reflection on humankind, on basic human principles. Only with this approach will theology be a serious discourse, aware of itself, in full possession of its conceptual elements. But we are not referring exclusively to this epistemological aspect when we talk about theology as critical reflection. We also refer to a clear and critical attitude regarding economic and socio-cultural issues in the life and reflection of the Christian community. To disregard these is to deceive both oneself and others. But above all, we intend this term to express the theory of a definite practice. Theological reflection would then necessarily be a criticism of society and the Church insofar as they are called and addressed by the Word of God; it would be a critical theory, worked out in the light of the Word accepted in faith and inspired by a practical purpose – and therefore indissolubly linked to historical praxis.

By preaching the Gospel message, by its sacraments, and by the charity of its members, the Church proclaims and shelters the gift of the Kingdom of God in the heart of human history. The Christian community professes a "faith which works through charity." It is – at least ought to be – real charity, action, and commitment to the service of others. Theology is reflection, a critical attitude. Theology follows; it is the second step. What Hegel used to say about philosophy can likewise be applied to theology: it rises only at sundown. The pastoral activity of the Church does not flow as a conclusion from theological premises. Theology does not produce pastoral activity; rather it reflects upon it. Theology must be able to find in pastoral activity the presence of the Spirit inspiring the action of the Christian community.

A privileged *locus theologicus* for understanding the faith will be the life, preaching, and historical commitment of the Church.

To reflect upon the presence and action of the Christian in the world means, moreover, to go beyond the visible boundaries of the Church. This is of prime importance. It implies openness to the world, gathering the questions it poses, being attentive to its historical transformations....

This critical task is indispensable. Reflection in the light of faith must constantly accompany the pastoral action of the Church. By keeping historical events in their proper perspective, theology helps safeguard society and the Church from regarding as permanent what is only temporary. Critical reflection thus always plays the inverse role of an ideology which rationalizes and justifies a given social and ecclesial order. On the other hand, theology, by pointing to the sources of revelation, helps to orient pastoral activity; it puts it in a wider context and so helps it to avoid activism and immediatism. Theology as critical reflection thus fulfills a liberating function for humankind and the Christian community, preserving them from fetishism and idolatry, as well as from a pernicious and belittling narcissism. Understood in this way, theology has a necessary and permanent role in liberation from every form of religious alienation – which is often fostered by the ecclesiastical institution itself when it impedes an authentic approach to the Word of the Lord....

Finally, theology thus understood, that is to say as linked to praxis, fulfills a prophetic function insofar as it interprets historical events with the intention of revealing and proclaiming their profound meaning.... Theologians will be personally and vitally engaged in historical realities with specific times and places. They will be engaged where nations, social classes, and peoples struggle to free themselves from domination and oppression by other nations, classes, and peoples. In the last analysis, the true interpretation of the meaning revealed by theology is achieved only in historical praxis.

Conclusion

...This kind of theology, arising from concern with a particular set of issues, will perhaps give us the solid and permanent, albeit modest, foundation for the *theology in a Latin American perspective* which is both desired and needed. This Latin American focus would not be due to a frivolous desire for originality, but rather to a fundamental sense of historical efficacy and also – why hide it? – to the desire to contribute to the life and reflection of the universal Christian community. But in order to make our contribution, this desire for universality – as well as input from the Christian community as a whole – must be present from the beginning. To concretize this desire would be to overcome particularistic tendencies – provincial and chauvinistic – and produce something *unique*, both particular and universal, and therefore fruitful....

It is for all these reasons that the theology of liberation offers us not so much a new theme for reflection as a *new way* to do theology. Theology as critical reflection on historical praxis is a liberating theology, a theology of the liberating transformation of the history of humankind and also therefore that part of humankind – gathered into *ecclesia* – which openly confesses Christ. This is a theology which does not stop with reflecting on the world, but rather tries to be part of the process through which the world is transformed. It is a theology which is open – in the protest against trampled human dignity, in the struggle against the plunder of the vast majority of humankind, in liberating love, and in the building of a new, just, and comradely society – to the gift of the Kingdom of God.

LEONARDO AND CLODOVIS BOFF

When Cardinal Ratzinger called Gustavo Gutiérrez to Rome in the Fall of 1984, he also, and perhaps more to the agenda, summoned Leonardo Boff, OFM. The result of that inquisition begun in May 1984 and completed at a meeting in Rome on September 7, 1984 was the silencing of the Franciscan liberation theologian in March 1985, forbidding him to teach or publish for an indefinite period, and firing him from his editorship of the *Revista Eclesiastica Brasiliera*. The silencing became a cause célèbre and was widely interpreted as one of the key elements of a "Restoration" of papal autocracy under John Paul II and Ratzinger, in open reaction to many of the liberalizing tendencies of Vatican II.

Of the two brothers, Leonardo is the better known outside Latin America and the more widely published. He was born in Concordea in southeastern Brazil on December 14, 1938 and went on to earn a doctorate in theology at the University of Munich. He entered the Franciscans and went on to study philosophy and theology at Curitiba in the state of Paraña, and at the Petrópolis Institute of Philosophy and Theology just outside Rio de Janeiro. Boff was ordained a priest in 1964. He then went on to study theology at Würzburg and at Louvain and from 1965 to 1970 was a student of Karl Rahner at the University of Munich. He earned a Ph.D. in theology from Munuch in 1972. Returning to Brazil, Boff worked throughout the country helping found and guide the new base Christian communities, a process that took him into the 1980s.

Meanwhile he taught as a professor of systematic theology at the seminary at Petrópolis. He also served as an advisor to the Brazilian Conference of Bishops and the Latin American Confederation of Religious. He is the author of many of the most important works of liberation theology, including *Jesus Christ Liberator* (1972), *Liberating Grace* (1976), *Passion of Christ, Passion of the World* (1977), *Ecclesiogenesis: The Base Communities Reinvent the Church* (1977), *God's Witness in the Heart of the World* (1977), *Way of the Cross, Way of Justice* (1978), *Church, Charism and Power: Liberation Theology and the Institutional Church* (1985), and *Trinity and Society* (1986). Popular and clerical outrage over the "penitential silencing" was so great that the ban was lifted ahead of schedule in April 1986.

Clodovis Boff was born in 1944 in Concordia, Brazil and is a member of the Servite Order. He is a professor at the Catholic University of São Paulo and remains active in work among the base Christian communities. He is the author of numerous works, including *Theology and Praxis: Epistemological Foundations* (1978), *Feet-on-the-Ground Theology: A Brazilian Journey* (1984), and, with his brother Leonardo, of *Salvation and Liberation: In Search of a Balance between Faith and Politics* (1979), and *Introducing Liberation Theology* (1986).

The following is taken from Leonardo and Clodovis Boff, *Introducing Liberation Theology*, Paul Burns, trans., Maryknoll, NY: Orbis Books, 1988, pp. 1-9.

329. Leonardo and Clodovis Boff, How to Be Christians in a World of Destitution

Chapter 1: The Basic Question

A woman of forty, but who looked as old as seventy, went up to the priest after Mass and said sorrowfully: "Father, I went to communion without going to confession first." "How come, my daughter?" asked the priest. "Father," she replied, "I arrived rather late, after you had begun the offertory. For three days I have had only water and nothing to eat; I'm dying of hunger. When I saw you handing out the hosts, those little pieces of white bread, I went to communion just out of hunger for that little bit of bread." The priest's eyes filled with tears. He recalled the words of Jesus: "My flesh [bread] is real food...whoever feeds on me will draw life from me" [John 6:55, 57].

One day, in the arid region of northeastern Brazil, one of the most famine-stricken parts of the world, I (Clodovis) met a bishop going into his house; he was shaking. "Bishop, what's the matter?" I asked. He replied that he had just seen a terrible sight: in front of the cathedral was a woman with three small children and a baby clinging to her neck. He saw that they were fainting from hunger. The baby seemed to be dead. He said: "Give the baby some milk, woman!" "I can't, my lord," she answered. The bishop went on insisting that she should, and she that she could not. Finally, because of his insistence, she opened her blouse. Her breast was bleeding; the baby sucked violently at it. And sucked blood. The mother who had given it life was feeding it, like the pelican, with her own blood, her own life. The bishop knelt down in front of the woman, placed his hand on the baby's head, and there and then vowed that as long as such hunger existed, he would feed at least one hungry child each day.

One Saturday night I (Clodovis) went to see Manuel, a catechist of a base community. "Father," he said to me, "this community and others in the district are coming to an end. The people are dying of hunger. They are not coming: they haven't the strength to walk this far. They have to stay in their houses to save their energy...."

Com-passion, "Suffering with"

What lies behind liberation theology? Its starting point is the perception of scandals such as those described above, which exist not only in Latin America but throughout the Third World. According to "conservative" estimates, there are in those countries held in underdevelopment:

§ five-hundred million persons starving;

§ one billion, six-hundred million persons whose life expectancy is less than sixty years (when a person in one of the developed countries reaches the age of forty-five, he or she is reaching middle age; in most of Africa or Latin America, a person has little hope of living to that age);

• one billion persons living in absolute poverty;

• one billion, five-hundred million persons with no access to the most basic medical care;

• five-hundred million with no work or only occasional work and a per capita income of less than $150 a year;

• eight-hundred-fourteen million who are illiterate;

• two billion with no regular, dependable water supply.

Who cannot be filled with righteous anger at such a human and social hell? Liberation theology presupposes an energetic protest at such a situation, for that situation means:

- on the social level: collective oppression, exclusion, and marginalization;
- on the individual level: injustice and denial of human rights;
- on the religious level: social sinfulness, "contrary to the plan of the Creator and to the honor that is due to him" [Puebla, *Final Document*, §28].

Without a minimum of "suffering with" this suffering that affects the great majority of the human race, liberation theology can neither exist nor be understood. Underlying liberation theology is a prophetic and comradely commitment to the life, cause, and struggle of these millions of debased and marginalized human beings, a commitment to ending this historical-social iniquity. The Vatican Instruction, *Some Aspects of Liberation Theology* (August 6, 1984), put it well: "It is not possible for a single instant to forget the situations of dramatic poverty from which the challenge set to theologians springs – the challenge to work out a genuine theology of liberation."…

Meeting the Poor Christ in the Poor

…From all this, it follows that if we are to understand the theology of liberation, we must first understand and take an active part in the real and historical process of liberating the oppressed. In this field, more than in others, it is vital to move beyond a merely intellectual approach that is content with comprehending a theology through its purely theoretical aspects, by reading articles, attending conferences, and skimming through books. We have to work our way into a more biblical framework of reference, where "knowing" implies loving, letting oneself become involved body and soul, communing wholly – being committed, in a word – as the prophet Jeremiah says: "He used to examine the cases of poor and needy, then all went well. Is not that what it means to know me? – it is Yahweh who speaks" [Jer. 22:16]. So the criticisms made of liberation theology by those who judge it on a purely conceptual level, devoid of any real commitment to the oppressed, must be seen as radically irrelevant. Liberation theology responds to such criticism with just one question: What part have you played in the effective and integral liberation of the oppressed?

Inevitably the thrust of most liberation theology is upon the nature of God, God's manifestation in human society, its image of the heavenly city, and humans' ability to mold earthly society in this image. Change, resistance of change, oppression and violence, inevitably raise questions of violence and peace. Here Leonardo Boff meditates upon the traditional Franciscan union between poverty and peacemaking and spells out a compelling theology of nonviolence.

The following selections are taken from Philip McManus and Gerald Schlabach, *Relentless Persistence: Nonviolent Action in Latin America*, Philadelphia and Santa Cruz: New Society Publishers, 1991, pp. vii-xi.

330. Leonardo Boff, Active Nonviolence: The Political and Moral Power of the Poor

Besides everyday violence, three great forms of violence confront us today: originating violence, consequential violence, and revolutionary violence.

Originating violence has its roots in the elite institutions of power, in a social structure that protects the interests of the dominant groups, and in the extreme right, which will not tolerate any social change out of fear of losing its privileged status. As a result, many countries of the Third World are in the grips of state terrorism. Those who oppose the interests of capital or of the totalitarian state find themselves monitored, imprisoned, tortured, "disappeared" or assassinated.

Out of this first violence comes a second: consequential violence. To counter the first violence, or to show that they can and will fight back, resistance groups or terrorists use violent means. Undeniably, consequential violence has a component of legitimate indignation at injustice. At the same time it reflects a less admirable sentiment: revenge. Revenge is an attempt to pay back in kind. But returning violence to the violent does not change the social structure that produces the violence. To the contrary, as the Brazilian religious leader Dom Helder Camara [**338**] says , it creates an endless spiral of violence.

Finally, there is revolutionary violence. Behind revolutionary movements there is an immense thirst for justice in the face of a fundamentally unjust social system. A revolutionary desires an alternative society that offers a greater possibility of life, the full participation of all citizens, and greater equity among them. Revolution is complex, perhaps the most complex process of history. After all, it involves nothing less than remaking an entire social edifice and cultivating new values and new ways of relating. A revolution has many fronts: the popular, the legal, the diplomatic, the political, the pedagogical, the religious, the class, and, historically, also the military front. It is with the military front that the question of violence as a means to overthrow the old, oppressive regime surfaces most obviously. For revolutionary violence may have a different purpose than originating violence, but it also produces victims.

History is full of examples of these three responses to a situation of social inequity. Can we break this vicious cycle of violence? Is it at least possible to limit violence in such a way that we neither become accomplices of injustice nor lose our human dignity?

Throughout the world an alternative movement called *active nonviolence* answers with an emphatic "Yes!" This answer is inspired in part by the extraordinary example of persons who have successfully demonstrated another way of confronting highly conflictive situations. Some of the best known are Mahatma Gandhi, Martin Luther King, Jr., Dom Helder Camara, and Adolfo Perez Esquivel [**339**]....

...Behind every concerted nonviolent struggle there is a powerful *mística:* the conviction that truth, justice, and love are ontological. That is to say, these are objective forces tied to the very structure of reality, of human society, of being human. No matter how much they are violated, they always persist, and they find an echo in both the consciousness of people and in historical processes. These are the banners that never fall. Under them people accept death with honor.

The *mística* of active nonviolence implies changing ourselves as well as working to change the world. We must live the truth. We must be just, our integrity transparent. We must be peacemakers. It is not enough simply to confront external violence. We must also dig out the roots of violence in our own hearts, in our personal agendas, and in our life projects. In both a personal and a political sense we must seek to live today in miniature what we are seeking for tomorrow. Otherwise the glorious tomorrow of the revolution will never come....

Human history is not ruled by our desires, nor by the high-mindedness of our ethical and political ideals. It is dramatic and at times tragic. For Christians, the brokenness of our world reflects the presence of sin and evil. And that brokenness results in violence, whether through weakness, malice, or the selfish interests of individuals or groups. In this world the

593

struggle is for life, for justice, and for solidarity in social relations. It is not against the bosses or the powerful. Struggle *with* passion but never *for* passion. And always struggle with compassion. With good reason Gandhi used to say, "Nonviolence has as an essential condition the ability to both move others and to be moved to compassion by others."

The theology of liberation is not an alternative to active nonviolence, nor vice versa. On the contrary, they are born of the same inspiration, which is the commitment to transform a violent social reality to one based on justice and fraternity through peaceful means. Theologians of liberation always speak with confidence of the historic power of the poor. The process of liberation comes from the oppressed themselves.

It begins with a pedagogy of liberation. Paulo Freire, the great pedagogue of the poor of the Third World, has outlined this. The first task of the process consists of ejecting the oppressor who lives within the oppressed. The goal is not to become another oppressor, but to be free and to establish ties of solidarity, which are the building blocks of collective freedom. When popular movements turn to action, their vision may be initially more tactical than strategic. They may struggle to fill a very particular need or to claim a specific right. But their small victories serve both to redeem hope and gradually to destabilize the oppressive system.

In this struggle, theologians of liberation give clear preference to peaceful means because these are the means that generate life. We find in the gospel the renunciation of all vengeance, of all domination of one over another. We learn solidarity and love of enemy. But traditionally this gospel has only been preached at the personal level. We must reclaim it for our politics as well.

Like liberation theology, active nonviolence – also called *firmeza permanente* or relentless persistence – is centered on the conviction that liberation is only possible when the oppressed are the subjects of their own history. Active nonviolence has contributed to the theology of liberation through its pedagogy, through its gospel-based *mística* of peace based on justice, and through its creative means of confronting conflict by applying gospel teachings in political action.

Thus active nonviolence and liberation theology are two facets of a single reality. The two facets are not opposed. On the contrary, they inform and complete each other. As the Chilean Bishop Jorge Hourton observed at an international meeting on active nonviolence in 1977, nonviolence is "a vibrant, rich, and valid vein of liberation theology."

To a great degree the future of active nonviolence depends on nurturing a culture of solidarity, dialogue, and participation. It is in the absence of these practices that a society turns violent. When such values are real social practices, they constitute the necessary preconditions for a network of cooperative relationships and for controlling the violence that continues to plague humanity.

Finally, we must not limit the renunciation of violence to human relations. It must also include relations with nature. The stones, the plants, the animals, the air, and the water are our sisters and brothers. We need to cultivate tenderness for all beings. Democracy should be not only political, but cosmic. When there are open relationships based on solidarity with all of creation and especially between people, then we can hope that the era of violence will belong to the dark past of humanity and that a new era of universal love will be inaugurated.

JUAN LUIS SEGUNDO, SJ

Born in Montevideo, Uruguay on October 31, 1925, Segundo entered the Jesuits and was ordained a priest in 1955. He earned a Licentiate in Philosophy from the Faculty of Philosophy at San Miguel, Argentina in 1948, a Licentiate in Theology from the University of Louvain in 1956, and a Doctorate of Letters from the Sorbonne in Paris in 1963. In the 1970s he taught at Harvard Divinity School and at the universities of Chicago, of Montreal, of Birmingham, England, and of São Paulo. Segundo serves as a chaplain to various Christian groups in Uruguay. He is the author of the five-volume *A Theology of Artisans of a New Humanity* (1973-74), *The Liberation of Theology* (1976), the five-volume *Jesus of Nazareth Yesterday and Today* (1982), and *Theology and the Church: A Response to Cardinal Ratzinger and a Warning to the Whole Church* (1985).

The following selection focuses on some of the immediate connections between theology and political action and is taken from Juan Luis Segundo, SJ, *The Liberation of Theology*, John Drury, trans., Maryknoll, NY: Orbis Books, 1976, pp. 3-6, 71-72.

331. Juan Luis Segundo, The Liberation of Theology

Theological Reservations about the Political Realm

Let us start with several highly significant facts. And here we can assume that Gustavo Gutiérrez has paved the way for our discussion by his remarks in his important book *(A Theology of Liberation)*. He notes: "Theology is reflection, a critical attitude. Theology *follows*, is the second step. What Hegel used to say about philosophy can likewise be applied to theology; it rises only at sundown." As we go on it will become clear that here we have a basic principle for dealing with the whole question of the relationship between theology and politics....

Whatever one may think about the political stance or the political neutrality of Jesus himself, it seems evident that his commandment of love and his countless examples and admonitions concerning it in the Gospels must be translated to an era in which real-life love has taken on political forms. To say that machines have nothing to do with the gospel message because it says nothing about machines is to fail to understand that message. To suggest that almsgiving should continue to be the Christian response to the whole problem of wealth and its relationship to love is also to seriously distort the gospel message (see Vatican II, *Gaudium et Spes*, §30, see **299**). And the same thing applies to any attempt to inculcate an apolitical love today – presuming that love can be apolitical at all in a world where politics is the fundamental human dimension. And once we discover that liberation theology can and must engage in ideological analysis, and that it cannot look to sociology for fully scientific proof or support, then some relationship between theology and politics becomes necessary and in fact decisive.

Taking due account of all that, we should not be surprised to find that the more recent documents emanating from the Vatican on social matters are in fact *political*. From *Mater et Magistra* [see **297**] to *Octogesima adveniens* all the encyclicals purportedly dealing with what used to be called the "social doctrine" of the Church have concentrated on what is really the "political doctrine" of the Church. Only the general appellation has remained the same, for whatever reasons. The fact is that those recent documents have not focused as much on such issues as social classes, wages, and work conditions as they have on national and international political structures. Yet curiously enough, except for a few strong reactions against *Populorum Progressio* [**301**] (in one instance [by the *Wall Street Journal*] labeled "warmed-over Marxism"), the popes have not been accused of mixing religion and politics....

Chapter 6: The Third World and Liberation

PABLO RICHARD

Richard was born in Chile and earned degrees in both sociology and biblical studies. He was exiled from Chile in 1973 and is now a professor of theology at the National University of Costa Rica.

Many key ideas of liberation theology's political analysis find their clear expression here: that of "Christendoms" as opposed to Christianity, of systems of domination, and like the thought of the Eastern European dissidents [311-319] a deep concern to form a "civil society" that will reestablish right relations among people in the image of the Heavenly Jerusalem: the clearest image of peace. The themes of idolatry, domination, and the church's alliance with the powers of this world are central to all his writings. These include *The Idols of Death and the God of Life: A Theology* (1983), *The Battle of the Gods* (1984), and *Death of Christendoms, Birth of the Church* (1987).

The text that follows is taken from Pablo Richard, *Death of Christendoms, Birth of the Church: Historical Analysis and Theological Interpretation of the Church in Latin America*, Philip Berryman, trans., Maryknoll, NY: Orbis Books, 1987, pp. 1-16.

332. Pablo Richard, The Death of Christendoms

3. Basic Working Hypothesis

My general hypothesis deals with the crisis of Christendoms in Latin America, and in particular, the crisis of the New Christendom, which began during the 1960s. My definition of Christendom comes from the relationship encompassing the terms "church," "state," and "civil society." Within Christendom the relationship of church and civil society is mediated by the church-state relationship. A study of the crisis of Christendom in Latin America basically involves analyzing the crisis of the church/state/ civil society relationship. It is my hypothesis that, beginning in the 1960s, this relationship has moved into an irreversible structural crisis in Latin America. My hypothesis is not directly centered on the crisis of the *church* but on the crisis of *Christendom*, which indirectly means a crisis for that form or type of church that has been linked to the workings (project) of Christendom. By the same token, my hypothesis is not directly concerned with the crisis of the state in Latin America, but with the crisis of the church-state relationship, as a mediation of the larger church-civil society relationship.

597

Consonant with the methodology adopted, one that is determined by the object under study, I have sought to provide an interpretation for the crisis of Latin American Christendom, starting from Latin American social formation. In analyzing this crisis I have centered on the processes that have a direct bearing on the church/state/civil society relationship. With regard to the crisis of New Christendom that began around 1960, I put forward the hypothesis that there are three basic processes at work in this crisis: the crisis of the state and of the dominant social bloc, the rise of the mass movement, and the appearance of a new model of domination. *Initially,* these three processes provoked a crisis in the church-state relationship, and hence a crisis in New Christendom, with the result that the church linked to New Christendom has been unable to retain its hegemony in civil society; *subsequently,* there has occurred a direct contradiction between New Christendom and a new kind of church that seeks to be set up outside any existing or possible kind of New Christendom and even in opposition to that kind of project. This direct contradiction between church and Christendom has had the effect of accelerating and deepening the process of crisis and dissolution affecting New Christendom.

It is my hypothesis that this process of crisis is of such a nature and is so great that the crisis of New Christendom is *structural* and *irreversible*. This means that there are two possibilities for the New Christendom that has prevailed in Latin America since the 1960s: one possibility is that there could begin a process of restructuring out of which would emerge a *new* model of New Christendom; the other possibility is that a decisive majority in the church could begin a process of once and for all ending New Christendom and going beyond it. For the first possibility to be realized, two things would have to take place. First, there would have to be set up a new relationship between the church and the new model of domination (more precisely, between the church and the new model of the state implied in this new model of domination), a relationship that constitutes the foundation for a new project of New Christendom. Secondly, it would be necessary to cut down, dominate, or suppress the form of church that stands in direct contradiction to any real or possible project of Christendom. On the basis of my analysis of the crisis of New Christendom during the 1960s and 1970s, and on the basis of my assessment that this church standing in opposition to Christendom has in fact come into existence, I propose the general hypothesis that the crisis of New Christendom in Latin America is *final* and *definitive*. The obverse side of that hypothesis is that a significant majority within the hierarchical church in Latin America has begun an irreversible process of dismantling New Christendom and moving decisively beyond it, and that that majority will continue to reject any model or possible project of New Christendom....

JOSÉ COMBLIN

Comblin was born in Brussels, Belgium on March 22, 1923. He was ordained a priest in 1947. He received a doctorate in theology from the University of Louvain in 1950, specializing in New Testament studies. In 1958 Comblin traveled to Brazil. He taught at the Catholic University of Campinas, Brazil from 1958 to 1961, at the University of Santiago, Chile from 1962 to 1964, and at the Theological Institute of the Northeast at Recife, Brazil from 1965 until he was expelled by the military government in 1972. He then served on the faculty at Talca, Chile from 1972 to 1979, and at the Latin American Pastoral Institute in Quito, Ecuador from 1968 to 1973. In the late 1970s Comblin also taught at Harvard Divinity School and at the Catholic University of Louvain. In the late 1980s he returned to Latin America to continue his pastoral work in northeastern Brazil. He is the author of over forty books, including *The Church and the National Security State* (1979), *Cry of the Oppressed, Cry of Jesus: Meditations on Scripture and Contemporary Struggles* (1986), *The Holy Spirit and Liberation* (1987).

While the explicit identification of a "National Security" ideology among the Third World's military dictatorships seems to be the work of Brazil's Bishop Cândido Padín in 1968, and Hugo Assmann had examined the expropriation of Christian symbolism to justify their rule in 1971, Comblin articulated the elements of this ideology – and theology – throughout the 1970s, making the concept of the "National Security state" widely known.

These excerpts are taken from José Comblin, *The Church and the National Security State*, Maryknoll, NY: Orbis Books, 1979, pp. 64-78.

333. José Comblin, The National Security System in Latin America

The Creation of the National Security System

No theology and no institutional church can be examined in a vacuum;

they must be considered in the context of the political and social reality in which they exist and act. In Latin America today political and social reality means being part of the postwar American Empire and living under its farthest-reaching export – the national security state.

In 1947, the United States created two new political institutions which established a new pattern for the state and, in the long run, a new pattern for society. The National Security Council (NSC) and the Central Intelligence Agency (CIA), both established by the National Security Act, were organs invented to fulfill and further the new imperial role the United States had undertaken.

The NSC caused a radical change in the state's balance of power. More and more the Executive Branch, through this new agency, reserved for itself the initiative, direction, supervision, and responsibility for defense and foreign policy. The Congress – and even other departments of the Executive Branch – witnessed or rubber-stamped accomplished facts. Meanwhile, the CIA became a secret service that assumed (often illegally) the right to supervise the lives of citizens and officials and the right of intervention in foreign countries according to the secret interests of the United States – or more precisely, those of the National Security Council....

And as these [Latin American Security] councils, which are basically military dictatorships, came to power, they organized duplicates of the CIA – the SNI (National Information Service) in Brazil, the DINA (National Intelligence Division) in Chile, and so on.

These new organizations had a more immediate and profound effect on the social lives of Latin America because these nations are quite different from the United States. Neither the national security councils nor the secret services in Latin America have to cope with the limits of constitutions or the reaction of a congress. There is no longer either a constitution or a functioning congress in most Latin American countries [as of 1979]. Sometimes appearances are maintained, but they are only appearances....

Any institutions that have so changed society need an ideology, and the new institutions of the state have one. Although their ideology looks relatively modest in comparison with traditional philosophical systems (indeed, it is almost worthless from the philosophical point of view), its persuasive power is great, and we may not ignore it.

This ideology has no official name, but I call it the national security ideology because it is the ideology of the national security system, the new political system of today. This ideology has not yet been philosophically elaborated by its disciples, but since it covers virtually all individual and social activities of the nation and gives a new meaning to all human existence, it is universal and totalitarian enough to exclude any interference by another philosophy....

Necessity of War

The other reason used by the national security ideology to justify military takeover of the entire control of the state is the seriousness of the present war. At this point geopolitics, total strategy, and military government meet. The present condition, according to the national security ideology, makes evident what geopolitics and strategy have been studying and perceiving all over the world: military government is necessary because the nation is involved in a total war....

The war against Marxism is an all-out war within the present definition of total war. The communist world is making (total) war against the West. The survival of the West compels the Latin American peoples to make war using all their resources. Their own survival can be achieved only by the total integration into the war against communism as led by the United States. (It is assumed that the United States, by its very ideology, is the leader of the West's total war, just as the Soviet Union is seen to be leading the war of the communist world.)

Only a military government is able to lead such a war. Experience shows that civilian governments are dangerous because they open the nation to its worst enemies: Marxist management. To protect democracy and achieve a Christian society, the most far-reaching dictatorship is established, a dictatorship that may be called the image of Hobbes's Leviathan, a dictatorship that has nothing to do with democracy or Christianity. A basic postulate of the ideology is that war and dictatorship are the means with which to establish democracy and Christianity. In actual practice, war and dictatorship never end; the promised utopia never does reach the level of concrete beings. The Declaration of Principles and all similar statements will remain "future utopia" forever. The armed forces will never want to relinquish the power that they have monopolized. They will never believe that the country is now sufficiently protected against its enemies, sufficiently regenerated, sufficiently free from corruption. Their ideology of national security contains nothing that is able to justify the end of the war; it does not even encompass a need to clear the way for a peaceful government.

The ideology of national security is generally called nationalism by its authors. But it is a radical, absolute nationalism. As General Golbery [do Couto e Silva] described it in his master book [*Geopolitica do Brasil,* Rio de Janeiro: Olympio, 1967, pp. 101 ff.]:

> To be nationalist is to be always ready to give up any doctrine, any theory, any ideology, feelings, passions, ideals, and values, as soon as they appear as incompatible with the supreme loyalty which is due to the Nation above everything else. Nationalism is, must be, and cannot possibly be other than an Absolute One in itself, and its purpose is as well an Absolute End – at least as long as the Nation continues as such. There is no place, nor should there be, nor could there be place for nationalism as a simple instrument to another purpose that transcends it.

Consequently, the nation takes the place of God. What happens then to the God whom the military elite claim they want to worship by establishing a "Christian society"? This Christian God is only a cultural symbol. In actual practice the action is commanded by no god other than the nation and national security, the unconditional goals of all citizens....

ENRIQUE DUSSEL

Dussel was born in Mendoza, Argentina on December 24, 1934. He earned a Licentiate in Philosophy from the University of Mendoza, a Doctorate in Philosophy from the University of Madrid, a Ph.D. in history from the Sorbonne in Paris, a Licentiate in Theology from the Catholic Institute of Paris, and studied at both Munster and Mainz in Germany and in Israel. He taught at the National University of Cuyo in Mendoza, Argentina until he was exiled by the military dictatorship in 1976. He then lived and taught at the University of Mexico City. He is a member of the advisory committee for the theological journal, *Concilium,* and has served as president of the Commission on the Study of the History of the Church in Latin America. He is the author of the classic, *A History of the Church in Latin America: Colonialism to Liberation* (1964 & subsequent editions), *History and Theology of Libera-*

Chapter 6: The Third World and Liberation

tion (1976), *Ethics and the Theology of Liberation* (1978), *Philosophy of Liberation* (1985), and *Ethics and Community* (1986), among others.

Like Comblin's, Dussel's work deals with the structures of domination and their theological manifestations as sin. The following selections focus on some of the more apparent forms of analysis: the business and economics of war and violence, their meaning for the everyday suffering of the impoverished peoples of the world, the manifestation of the apocalyptic beast in this system with an analysis of Apocalypse 13 similar to that of the Kairos Document [322]. Also like the Kairos Document, Dussel outlines some of the alternatives open to the oppressed: including an option for self-defense, the "just revolution" that draws on the theory of the just war. Dussel's examples, drawn from the 1960s, are still valid categories for most of the developing world today.

The following selections are taken from Enrique Dussel, *Ethics and Community,* Robert R. Barr, trans., Maryknoll, NY: Orbis Books, 1986, pp. 158-80.

334. Enrique Dussel, On Violence, Oppression and Liberation

Chapter 15: International Loans and Weaponry

15.1 State of the Question

Let us consider another aspect of the transnationalized structure of sin/domination. Our new considerations will bear not only on the productive level of this sinful domination, but on its financial or monetary level as well.

We read in magazines, and in all our dailies, of huge international loans that have been made to poor nations. How did this come about? In 1967, world capitalism entered a state of crisis. The demand for goods and services in the central capitalist countries had suddenly dropped, resulting in restricted production. But this caused unemployment, so that now still less money was available to consumers for goods and services. And the vicious spiral proceeded apace.

Now financiers needed a new way to use the money left over from production. One of the ways they found was to lend it irresponsibly to needy countries. Another way consisted in increasing arms production. And so we have two types of investment that reproduce not life, but death....

15.7 War As Business

For the pre-Socratic Greek philosopher Heraclitus it was "war," strife, contention that generated all things and systems. "War is the origin of all," said this philosopher of domination. In the same fashion, capital thinks: competition, this death struggle waged by all against all, is the source of life and wealth. Indeed, in the United States today, for example, war is a *business*.... Military expenditures have multiplied twenty-five times since the turn of the century....

The destructive capacity of today's nuclear weaponry outstrips that of conventional armaments thousands of times over. For the first time in history, and the first time in the life of our planet, we face the possibility of the *total extinction* not only of the human race, but of all life on earth. The human species is at the mercy of a force too great for it. Should that force be activated in error, or by a fanatic or terrorist, or by way of a "preemptive strike," it would drag us all down to death. Christian ethics faces the possibility of our suicide as a species, and the North American bishops addressed this threat in their pastoral letter of 1983, *The Challenge of Peace*.

15.8 Sinfulness of the Arms Race

The "arms-race complex" represents sin, and this in various aspects of its structure. In the first place the industrial production of arms is an activity performed by capital in order to make profit. This profit, as we have seen (12.5-6), is extracted from arms-industry workers and scientists as "surplus life." "The population lives on weaponry."

In the second place, in the United States for instance, the arms race syndrome takes on a particular physiognomy. The fulcrum of all the other relationships is the unit formed by the Pentagon with the weapons industry. The Pentagon assigns 80 per cent of its contracts directly to industrial corporations without public bidding. A good part of the citizen's budget, then, is spent on instruments of destruction without any competition. It is all done behind the public's back. This is another aspect of the sin in question.

The Strategic Defense Initiative, or "Star Wars," which the Reagan administration has proposed to Congress and the countries of Western Europe, would compound the sin. It would call for unheard-of expenditures incurred for the sake of enormous new profits on the part of the weapons industry. In 1968 President Reagan's home state of California hosted 17 percent of the war industry, followed by Texas (where so many chicanos are pressured to work in war factories) with only 9 percent. The North American episcopate went so far as to say that "those who in conscience decide not to participate in defense activities will find support in the Catholic community" *(The Challenge of Peace,* IV, C: "To the Men and Women of the Defense Industries").

Worst of all, poor countries fall into the same vices. There are countries with workers who earn less than $200 per year, and nevertheless the government invests less in agriculture than in military activities.

15.9 Unproductive Investment: Instruments of Death

The implicit contradiction of weapons production carries the seeds of its own rejection. Let us consider a few figures:

	Military Spending: Percentage of National Budget 1966	Percentage of Rate of Increase of Production, 1950-65
United States	8.5	2.4
West Germany	4.1	5.3
Japan	1.0	7.7

(Source: Melgan, *The Capitalism of the Pentagon,* p. 296*)*

The difference between the figures for the United States and Japan is arresting. The United States *wastes* on weaponry what Japan spends *usefully* on increased production. Evidently there is a direct correlation between military spending and negative economic effects.

After all, weapons (instead of Isaiah's plowshares) are tools and means precisely for the elimination of life. A plow is a tool for working the land – for acquiring the "bread of life" that produces life as it is consumed. Jet fighters, bullets, nuclear warheads detonated or stockpiled, reproduce no life, serve no useful purpose. They all represent a recessionary, inflationary investment, producing crises in production and consumption, and wiping out wealth acquired by the blood of the worker and bought with the work of the people

Military production in the United States grew by 2.3 percent in the first half of 1983, and industrial production fell by 1.6 percent. There is evidence that military expenditures currently exert a harmful effect on the productivity of labor. Such expenditures compete for scarce resources with capital employed in civilian industries just when they are being so mightily pressured to increase their level of production in view of the threat posed by international competition, especially by Japan and Europe.

Hunters used their weapons to hunt animals. They needed to eat. But soon they were using them to wage war – to hunt their human enemies. And "the military" was born. Jesus "died *under* Pontius Pilate" – a military man – as have nearly all the martyrs ever since.

15.10 Armed Might of the Beast

In the Book of Revelation the Beast is invested with power; and all of its might is in weaponry:

> The dragon conferred upon it its power.... Who shall be able *to fight against* it? It has been permitted to *wage war* against the anointed and vanquish them, and has been given authority over every race, people, tongue and nation [Apoc. 13:2, 7].

When all is said and done, the strength of the Prince of "this world" (2.10) – the way in which Satan in fact exercises power – is through coercion by the instruments of death, coercion through weaponry. The martyr's "cross" (3.10) is the actual use of the weapon that kills the innocent, the people (an innocent civilian population fanatically defined in advance as "the enemy").

There would be no *real* sin if it were not effectuated by the use of arms. It was Pilate's soldiers, once more, who crucified Christ.

The sin of the violent murder of one's neighbor by the use of weapons of war is intimately bound up with economic and social injustice. The mighty, the dominators, must control the oppressed, must keep them subdued, keep them "pacified," by means of weaponry. "Bread," that biblical symbol of all productivity, has become the "bread of death."

The circle of death is complete. Sin is domination, and as domination of the life of the other (2.2) it is the extraction of surplus life (12.6). But now this structure of sin (2.6) must be guaranteed. It must be endowed with permanency. Weaponry and military power constitute the highest court of the effectiveness of sin. Arms and armed might are the ultimate demonstration of the power of the reign of the Prince of "this world." The torture of heroes and martyrs, then (9.3), and their actual death on their "cross," is the consummation of sin upon earth. And yet this torture and death are also the means by which the glory of the Infinite is made manifest. Crucified by the military power of his age (the Romans), Jesus manifests the absolute contradiction of history....

Chapter 16: Class Struggle, Violence, and Revolution

16.1 State of the Question

We frequently hear in the church, both in the documents of the social teaching of the church and in the mouths of individual Christians, that neither the class struggle nor violence may be approved or practiced by Christians. Like so many other questions, however, this one too is fraught with confusion, both terminological and conceptual, especially at the theological level.

The daily newspapers carry news stories of strikes, worker demonstrations, and police repression of these expressions of a struggle on behalf of workers' interests. We likewise read of wars, guerrilla actions, air highjackings, and attempts on the lives of industrialists or politicians. All around us we see violence, and sudden social change.

We read in holy scripture:

> I saw no temple in the city. The Lord, God the Almighty, is its temple.... Nothing deserving a curse shall be found there. The throne of God and of the Lamb shall be there, and his servants shall serve him faithfully. They shall see him face to face and bear his name on their foreheads. The night shall be no more. They will need no light from lamps or the sun, for the Lord God shall give them light, and they shall reign forever [Apoc. 21:22, 22:3-5, see **46**].

For the Christian, the reign of God is to be the perfect community (1.5). In the reign, injustice, social classes, inequalities, sin, violence, will be no more – only a continuous movement from the new to the newer, from discovery to exciting discovery. Revolution will no longer need to be fostered; it will be ongoing and permanent. After all, in perfect love, newness prevails; no structure is ever needed but the ongoing creativity of new structures. And this is to be "forever," as our text from Revelation tells.

16.8 Violence

As Paul VI declared in Bogotá, Colombia, on August 23, 1968, "violence is neither evangelical nor Christian." Of course, the pope was referring to the violence of force, in Latin *vis*, the coercion of the will of others against their rights, against their justice. He spoke of the violence of sin. "It is clear," said Medellín, "that in many parts of Latin America we find a situation of injustice that can be called *institutionalized violence*"[*Medellín Document on Peace*, §16, see **326**). This is the more visible violence, the violence of every day, the violence of sin (2.2), institutional violence (2.5), the violence that produces weapons (15.10) or obliges the poor to sell their work (12.3).

This violence, that of the Prince of "this world," is frequently practiced with the consent of the oppressed. There is an ideological hegemony and domination in which the poor *accept* the system of domination, as something natural, as an obvious, eternal phenomenon (3.9). But the moment the oppressed (oppressed classes, oppressed nations, the poor) get on their feet, the moment they rebel, and oppose the domination under which they sweat and strain – this is the moment when *hegemonic* violence becomes *coercive*. Oppression becomes repression. All repression is perverse. There can never be a "legitimate" repression, as a certain conservative, right-wing group of bishops and others in the Latin American church say there can be.

Confronted with the active repression or violence of sin, many adopt the *tactics* or stance of "non-violence," as Mahatma Gandhi in India, Martin Luther King, Jr., in the United States, or Miguel D'Escoto in Nicaragua. This courageous position cannot, however, be elevated to the status of an absolute theoretical principle, an exclusive strategy for any and all situations. To the violence of sin the martyr opposes the valor of the suffering servant, who builds the church with his blood (9.2-3). But this martyr, this prophet, is not the political hero.

16.9 Just Defense and a People's Right to Life

The exact contrary of the repulsive, unjust violence of the oppressor is the active *defense of the "innocent,"* of the oppressed poor, the repressed people. Saint Augustine teaches us that it is a requirement of charity or Christian love to *re-act* to unjust violence: "matters would be still worse, after all, were malefactors to lord it over the just" *(The City of God, IV,* 15). Saint Thomas likewise teaches that struggle is not sin *(Summa Theologiae,* II-II, q. 40, a. 1) if its cause is just. Further, he adds, "force is repelled with force" in the case of defending *life* (ibid., q. 64, a. 7).

Chapter 6: The Third World and Liberation

The church has always held the "just-war theory" where the authority of governments is involved, even in the Second Vatican Council *(Gaudium et Spes,* §79). But it happens that an innocent person or a people can be oppressed, repressed, colonized by a government. In that case the war is not a war of one state with another, but a liberation struggle between oppression and the defense of the innocent. Joan of Arc against the English, Washington against the established order, the *Resistance française* against Nazism, Bolivar or San Martin against Spain, Sandino against the North American occupation – none of these heroes (9.3) represented the established *governments* of a state (9.8). They have their legitimacy in virtue of their *just cause* and their *right intention,* in virtue of their right to employ *adequate* means (even arms, as a "last resort") for the defense of the people – keeping in mind the principle of due proportion, of course, and not using more force than necessary to attain the realistic ends at stake. These are precisely the requisites that church tradition, including Saint Thomas, has always demanded for the use of force in defense of the innocent, the poor, the oppressed, in order that the use of force be just and legitimate. The Sandinista National Liberation Front, for example, complied with these requirements in its struggle with Somoza. And yet its members were labeled "subversives," "violent," and so on. In his Peace Day Message of 1982, Pope John Paul II asserted: "In the name of an elementary requisite of justice, peoples have the right and even *the duty* to protect their existence with *adequate means"* (no. 12). Peoples, then, and not merely governments, have this right and duty, and the means they are allowed to employ are "adequate means," in other words, even force of arms when necessary as a last resort to "repel force," as Saint Thomas put it, the force of sin and oppression....

JON SOBRINO

Sobrino was born in Barcelona into a Basque family in the midst of the Spanish Civil War. He earned a master's degree in mechanical engineering from St. Louis University in Missouri in 1965 and a doctorate in theology from the Hochschule Sankt Georgen in Frankfurt in 1975. He is a Jesuit priest and has been a professor of philosophy and theology at the Universidad José Simeón Cañas in El Salvador, a position that has placed his life in jeopardy more than once. On November 16, 1989, while Sobrino was away on business, six of his Jesuit community, their cook and her teenage daughter were murdered at their residence at the university by the Salvadoran military.

Sobrino is the author of many books and articles, including *Christology at the Crossroads* (1978), *The True Church and the Poor* (1981), *Jesus in Latin America* (a collection of articles, 1978-82), *Spirituality of Liberation* (articles from 1980-84), and, with Juan Hernández Pico, *Theology of Christian Solidarity* (1983). He recently edited the writings of the Jesuit martyrs of El Salvador in *Companions of Jesus* (1990).

The following selections analyze the spirituality of martyrdom and its meaning in a world of injustice and violence in terms that recall the witness of the early church [see 63-75]. They are taken from Jon Sobrino, *The True Church and the Poor,* Matthew J. O'Connell, trans., Maryknoll, NY: Orbis Books, 1984, pp. 160-80.

335. Jon Sobrino, *Witness of the Church in Latin America: Between Life and Death*

The Subjective Testimony of the Church in Persecution and Martyrdom

I turn now to the subjective aspect of the testimony the Church gives through the objective promotion of a just life. This subjective testimony is another name for the holiness of the Church. But what repays analysis here is not holiness in the abstract, as though we already knew that holiness was independent of objective testimony. I am interested rather in the kind of Christian holiness, attitudes, and virtues that are generated in the process described in the first part of this chapter. More concretely, I want to show that when the Church gives the objective witness described, there is generated at the historical level what the New Testament regards as holiness in its supreme form: the giving of one's life for the community as the greatest possible proof of love.

I need not dwell on the fact that the Church, which has given its testimony on behalf of life, has been persecuted and has produced martyrs. Thousands of peasants, workers, catechists, students, and intellectuals have suffered persecution and death. There is something new and eye-catching: hundreds of priests, religious women and men, and bishops have been attacked, slandered, threatened, expelled, tortured, and murdered. I want to undertake a theological analysis of persecution and martyrdom and to show that these two are the most typical and most complete form of holiness for the Church, precisely because the Church therein gives testimony in behalf of the just life.

Chapter 6: The Third World and Liberation

Theological Reflection on Persecution and Martyrdom

The Second Vatican Council acknowledged the importance of witness as a form of life that opposes faith and spiritual values to the reigning materialism. It also emphasized – and this was something new – that the laity have the duty of giving this kind of witness to the world. The Council did not, however, analyze theologically the importance of persecution and martyrdom....

Theology of Persecution

The inchoative theology of persecution sketched at Puebla [327] represents a recovery of a fundamental dimension of New Testament ecclesiology, although this in turn needs a fuller theological development and translation into historical terms. It is clear from the New Testament that persecution came upon the Church at a very early date [see 65-75] and that being persecuted was soon declared to be a de jure characteristic of the true Church. In other words, the new Church at an early date experienced persecution from the Jewish and Roman authorities. Soon there was a declaration of principle regarding the Christian necessity of such persecution. In the earliest New Testament document Paul says: "You yourselves know that this is to be our lot. For when we were with you, we told you beforehand that we were to suffer affliction" [1 Thes. 3:3-4]. The communities see this necessity as having its theological ground in the lot of Jesus [John. 15:18, 20; Mt. 10:24-25] and the prophets [Mt. 5:11-12].

The persecution of Jesus, which from a theological standpoint has to be understood in terms of the Father's will, has a clear historical cause: his activity in opposing, denouncing, cursing, and unmasking the powerful and the rich, the Pharisees, scribes, and rulers. Jesus fought against every kind of oppressive and unjust power, in order to promote and defend a life of justice for the poor. The struggle was not simply a personal conflict between Jesus and other individuals, that is, a conflict between "mediators." It was a struggle between different "mediations." On the one hand, the defense of a just life for the poor; on the other, the defense of a life of injustice exercised by the powerful. This emerges clearly in the death of Jesus. The *pax romana* and the Jewish society symbolized by the Temple are unjust sociopolitical formations that oppressed the poor masses. Because Jesus attacked both in the name of the reign of God, he was persecuted and put to death.

The gospel narratives supply abundant evidence of the persecution against Jesus, and they present this persecution as religious. Beneath the religious level lies the properly human level. If the apparent issue in the persecution of Jesus is his religious orthodoxy, the real issue is the *doxa* or glory of God, which is manifested in a life of justice for the poor....

Martyrdom

The persecution here described can generate and in fact does generate a series of Christian attitudes and virtues that are difficult to come by apart from persecution. The most noteworthy of these are impoverishment, solidarity with the poor, courage in suffering, and hope against hope. All these form an important part of the subjective witness of the Church and reach their climax in what has traditionally been regarded as the supreme testimony: martyrdom.

I maintain that martyrdom is the most complete form of holiness, not only for general theological reasons but also for contemporary historical reasons, which make martyrdom a real and not a remote possibility and show clearly that it is the greatest proof of love. Although martyrdom will obviously not be the lot of all Christians, it is theologically and historically the *analogatum princeps* (primary analog) on the basis of which, and in relation to which, the holiness of the Church and what I have been calling the Church's subjective witness are to be understood.

In theory this has always been the case in the Church. The important thing is to specify in a historically concrete way what martyrdom is and how it should be understood at the present time. The usual definition of martyrdom is "the free and patient acceptance of death for the sake of the faith (including its teaching on morality) either as a whole or in regard to a particular doctrine (which in turn is always seen in relation to the faith as a whole)." This definition captures the basic idea of martyrdom as a bearing witness to Christ (this element of martyrdom is clear in the New Testament) and as a bearing witness with one's own life (martyrdom has been thus understood since the middle of the second century). It implicitly includes another New Testament tradition according to which the giving of one's life for another is the greatest act of love [cf. John. 15:13; 1 John. 3:16], that is, the supreme form of holiness.

If we are to understand the death of so many present-day Latin American Christians as martyrdom, we must give historical concreteness to some of the ideas contained in the definition just given. Three points need to be stressed.

(1) The "confession of faith," which is an inherent element in martyrdom, must be historically specified in the way indicated earlier as a confession of the just life. According to the usual definition, martyrdom is a bearing witness with one's life to a basic moral teaching, namely, the call for a just life, with this teaching seen as related to faith in the God of life.

(2) At the present time, it is necessary to give a different historical content to the notion of "patient" (the "patient" acceptance of death) [see vol. 1:86-89]. It usually means "not provoked by acts of physical or moral violence," as the working document for Puebla puts it. As I said earlier in speaking of persecution, death normally comes through the struggle in behalf of justice. Objectively, every struggle generates some kind of violence. Martyrdom in our day cannot be understood without this element of violence, just as Christian life in general cannot be understood without it, although it is of course necessary to determine what kind of violence is just. Martyrdom cannot be understood without bringing in this element of violence, just as the death of Jesus cannot be understood without it, since, at least objectively, Jesus made use of moral violence. It would be ironic if we found ourselves unable for purely terminological reasons to speak of "martyrdom" in contemporary Latin America when in fact so many Christians suffer the same fate as Jesus and when many of them use the same kind of violence that he did.

(3) Finally and most importantly we must see death suffered out of love for one's neighbor as taking the historical form of death out of love for an entire people and for the sake of the liberation of this people. As Saint Thomas shows, love is the formal element that gives martyrdom its excellence. This love need not be a love directed exclusively to one or another individual; it may be a love for an entire people.

The reality of martyrdom is today abundantly present in Latin America, where it takes various forms. I shall analyze two of these. There is first the kind of martyrdom that most clearly reproduces the characteristics of the martyrdom of Jesus. There are many Christians – simple faithful, community leaders, priests, religious women and men, and bishops – who have denounced the sin of the world, struggled to promote justice, come in conflict with the powerful, done violence to the mighty in the name of God, and been murdered for their deeds. These Christians have been murdered because of their love for their people and their desire that the poor might have a just life. This is the kind of martyrdom suffered by the priests Hector Gallegos, Rutilio Grande, Hermogenes Lopez. In the light of what I have said there is no doubt that these men were martyrs; the people celebrate them as such, and some of the hierarchy acknowledge them, though others are skeptical.

There is another way of giving one's life. It has some of the same traits as the first kind of martyrdom but it also has characteristics proper to itself. I am referring to the martyrdom of a people as a people. Given the situation in so many Latin American countries, the sufferings and struggles of the people of Nicaragua, and the state of affairs in El Salvador and Guatemala, it would be scandalous to pass over these deaths and the kinds of holiness they reflect, whether or not we call the deaths martyrdom....

LATIN AMERICA: INDIVIDUAL WITNESS

BRAZIL

Brazil offers the most frightening, and in many ways one of the most hopeful, situations in Latin America. The largest and richest country on the continent, with a 1995 population of 158.7 million, and one of the major economies of the world, with a 1992 GDP of $369 billion, in the 1970s and 1980s Brazil was also a disastrous example of the doctrine of development, with a foreign debt of $93 billion in 1984, then the Third World's highest, and vast differences of wealth between a small ruling elite and an impoverished majority.

Between 1960 and 1970 the top one percent of the population increased their share of the national wealth from 11.7% to 17%, while the income of the bottom 50% of the population dropped from 17% to 13.7% of the total. The wealth accumulated in 1970 by one percent of the population was greater than that of 50% of the people. Meanwhile in the northeast, one of the poorest, but still "developed," parts of the country, per-capita income reached $200 a year in 1970, and over 52% of the people earned less than $20 a month. Unemployment in Recife ran an average of 40%.

By the late 1960s "development" had dislocated thousands of small farmers, turned an indifferent ear to the conscious extermination of entire Indian tribes in the Amazon valley, and left the country in debt to foreign, mostly North American, banks and governments. Meanwhile, Brazil's oligarchs had created the largest military establishment in Latin America and made the country the largest arms exporter in the Third World and the fifth-largest in the world.

The pressures and dislocations of development brought continual political unrest in the early 1960s and threatened the position of the oligarchy. In 1964 the military under Gen. Castello Branco staged a coup and brought the country under a harsh military dictatorship that ended only with direct presidential elections in 1985. With the help of the U.S.A. the generals created a national security state. In defense of "Western Christian Civilization" the military suspended all constitutional and human rights, and jailed and executed thousands of political opponents, including many Catholic lay and church people.

In keeping with its traditional alliance with the state and with the interests of the ruling elite, at first many in the Catholic church supported the military regime. Yet gradually and in small but significant ways, the work first of base Christian communities and then of more and more members of the regular clergy and hierarchy began addressing such issues as poverty, dislocation of small farmers by huge development projects and private interests, the increasing use of violence to squelch union and reform movements, and the lack of human rights on any level in Brazilian society.

The following selection describes the persecution of leaders of the basic Christian communities and is taken from Martin Lange and Reinhold Iblacker, *Witness of Hope: The Persecution of Christians in Latin America,* William E. Jerman, trans., Maryknoll, NY: Orbis Books, 1981, pp. 37-46.

336. Bishop Tomas Balduino of Goiás, The Amazon and the Landworkers, Pastoral Letter, February 1, 1976

On January 23 our community was stunned by the arrest of six landworkers *(camponeses)* and fathers of families, members of our evangelization groups. The arrest of our brothers was "justified" by apparent discrepancies as to where they lived, as given in diverse personal papers. But another thought comes to mind; another question comes to the surface.

All those arrested are members of evangelization groups. They are mature persons who know what they are doing, who freely made a serious decision to take on a Christian commitment in the new directions being explored by our Catholic church.

Is it the case that we have some persons here who call themselves

Catholic and yet want to suppress others who are struggling on the side of the gospel? Will there be organized religious persecution in Itaguaru, aimed at the weakest and poorest, at those for whom Jesus Christ has become the fount of life and liberation? Is it possible that hypocritical brothers live among us and, under the veil of a Christian life, worship and defend the golden calf of money and might?

It is my duty as a bishop to make two points perfectly clear:

(1) If someone is of the opinion that these Christians have chosen a mistaken path and are going to harm society, and hence they should be punished, then that someone should not blame those persons but the bishop, because he is the one in charge of this church and he approves of and supports the evangelization groups.

(2) If someone is going to punish the members of this church, then let it be done openly, without evasion, without hiding the hand that throws the stone. The laws on making accusations are better observed by opening a lawsuit, as also the laws regarding the defense of an accused person. It is cowardly to resort to defamation of character, and thence to "justify" the use of physical force and intimidation.

DOM PEDRO CASALDÁLIGA

Casaldáliga was born in Balsareny in Catalonia, Spain in 1928. His youth was spent amid the horrors of the Spanish Civil War (1936-39), and Casaldáliga soon entered the diocesan seminary at Vic. He joined the Claretian Order and was ordained a priest in 1952. From that time until 1958 he taught at Claretian schools in Sabadell, and then moved to Barcelona where he worked in various pastoral posts. In 1965 he became prefect of the Claretian seminary at Barbastro and then editor of *Iris de Paz* in Madrid. In 1967 he was named representative to the Claretian Chapter General in Rome. In 1968 Casaldáliga was sent on missionary work to the Mato Grosso in Brazil's Amazon interior and was named bishop of São Félix do Araguaia by Pope Paul VI in 1971. His diocese stretches over a thinly populated area of nearly 58,000 square miles that is home to several Indian communities and a few larger towns. The region offers vast wealth to developers and foreign investors who are displacing the local peoples with huge cattle ranches – largely to feed a North American hamburger culture. But because of its remoteness the government has exempted the Mato Grosso from reform laws meant to slow unbridled development. In its place has come money muscle: when small landowners, and those granted holdings under agrarian-reform laws resist buyouts, displacement, threats, torture, and murder follow. Those who have attempted to organize resistance, to begin agricultural and marketing communes, have been assassinated almost with impunity. Yet the work of Bishop Casaldáliga and the cooperation of many of Brazil's highest-ranking church officials and lay activists have had some hand in checking the violence and establishing some beginnings of nonviolent change and civil society in the region.

He is a proponent of nonviolent action and of resistance to capitalist development not only in Brazil but also in such "front-line" nations as Nicaragua, which he visited in 1985 at the invitation of Miguel D'Escoto [345] to show solidarity with the Sandinista revolution. During the same tour Casaldáliga also visited El Salvador and Cuba. In 1987 he repeated his visit to Central America, including Mexico and Panama. His activities on behalf of the popular church soon aroused the opposition of many conservative circles in Latin America; and in June 1988 he was summoned to Rome for an inquisition similar to that already undergone by Gutiérrez [328] and Boff [329-330]. Only the outspoken support of his fellow Latin American bishops prevented a Vatican rebuke. Casaldáliga has continued his journeys to Central America. There, as in Brazil, he makes the connection between the just life and the poverty that it must embrace if talk of "solidarity" with the people is to be more than a tired cliché. He thus hearkens back to the connection between justice, nonviolence, and voluntary poverty first forged by the medieval mendicant movements [146-168]. In 1989 Casaldáliga was nominated for the Nobel Peace Prize and in 1990 the government of his native Catalonia awarded him the St. George Cross.

These excerpts are taken from Lange and Iblacker, pp. 46-53.

337. Dom Pedro Casaldáliga, On Authentic Voluntary Poverty

We have all been taught, to a greater or lesser degree, the meaning or meanings that poverty has in the Bible. And we know that, in the final analysis and to the extent that we approach the fullness of time – when the Son of God will come as judge – the poor in the Bible are the downtrodden, the oppressed. They live on the other side of the divide from the rich, the mighty, and the exploiters.

617

The poor, as poor, open themselves to God. The rich, as rich, close themselves off from God. God, for his part, can communicate himself only to the poor, those who are ready for him.

Mary, mother of Jesus, expressed it in her Magnificat [quotes Luke 1:46-55]

She thereby framed the best theology of poverty, uniting the legacy of the Old Testament with the new theology of poverty that Jesus would live – in his words, his deeds, his family and work conditions, his messianic struggles with the established powers, his final, magnanimous surrender in his death on the cross.

In practice all of us "educated" Christians talk about poverty of spirit. And we are, to a greater or lesser degree, romantically enthusiastic about it. Bethlehem, Nazareth, Francis of Assisi, Charles Foucauld – they all figure easily in our spiritual conversations, in our dreams.

But can poverty be only a dream? How great an abyss is there between our spiritual poverty and the objective poverty of "the others"? How could the religious orders and congregations, looking back over the centuries, and without pangs of conscience, reconcile the individual poverty(!) of their members with the collective wealth that cries to heaven? How can we, well fed and well established, keep our peace of conscience vis-a-vis the two-thirds of humankind that are not well off and suffer hunger?

In view of the poverty of the majority of humankind, the children of God, our brothers and sisters, is spiritual poverty anything else but social sarcasm? Is it anything other than anti-evangelical blasphemy?

All must answer for themselves, before God and in the light of the objective circumstances of their life. I cannot in this context give any universally valid advice. But I believe that, in any event, we can discourse on poverty only if we also discourse on justice and liberation, if we discourse on all aspects of life.

It has been said that "love that is not political is not love." Obviously, this is also applicable to Christian love. The poverty of the gospel is necessarily political. Because it shows how the two-edged sword of the Word of God penetrates to the core of the structures of exploitation, dominance, avarice, luxury, and consumerism that dehumanize the lives of millions of human beings, the life of entire peoples and continents: those who terrorize as oppressors, living in superfluity, and those who are enslaved as the oppressed, living in hunger.

Voluntary poverty, therefore, necessarily includes a political option, a decision, a true class-option. My putting it this way must not be more scandalous than the tragic reality that we have around us, that of a people in fact divided into classes.

The gospel is, to be sure, for all classes. But differently. For the oppressor and rich classes it is a condemnation and an insistent cry for a radical change of life. For the oppressed poor class it is a liberation to encouragement and hope.

The Spirit of Jesus, of course, goes behind and beyond all theologies. And the poverty of the gospel is something more than political and social protest and solidarity.

Certainly it is in no way conformism.

It can no longer be a "good excuse" for those who retreat before the conflict, thereby leaving their brothers and sisters alone in the conflict.

Nor can voluntary poverty – the poverty of the gospel – be reduced to the performance of acts of self-denial.

Nor does it consist in simply giving away what is superfluous, being generous in a "charitable" way....

It is more, much more. As with Jesus, who, "was rich, yet for your sake became poor, so that through his poverty you might become rich" [2 Cor. 8:9] with the life of God, so true evangelical poverty must be a true incarnation in the life and struggle of the poor.

It means to lose oneself, to lose one's class, to lose respect and security; with one's own life as the scandal of the cross, to give an answer to idolatrous and enslaving greed and the consumer mentality, to exploitive and colonialistic economy and politics. It means to accept the risk that corresponds to the daily risk of the life of the poor. It means to strip one's own family or one's own institution of privileges – especially when it is a matter of something that boastfully calls itself religious and evangelical.

It means simply to live from the work and with the insufficient wherewithal that the poor must be content with. To eat, dress, travel as the poor eat, dress, travel. To struggle with them in society and in the church (it too is divided into classes) in their political and trade-union struggles and for the other needs of the poor as a class.

It is not a question of letting misery alone, much less of harmonizing it for the others.

What it is a question of is to search for an ever-growing equality of opportunity, in fellowship, always with the participation of the poor and together with them.

If it is not so, then our poverty has nothing to do with the gospel of the poor of our Lord Jesus Christ, the Son of God, who became a poor and marginalized human being, before the Sanhedrin and the Pretorium, but who is the only true liberator of humankind....

Dom Helder Camara

Perhaps the most significant figure in the process of nonviolent change in Latin America has been the Archbishop of Recife, "the voice of the Third World," and Nobel Peace Prize nominee, Dom Helder Camara. He was born in 1909 in Fortaleza, Brazil, the son of a middle-class family and brought up with a devout but conventional spirituality that led to the priesthood. In 1931 his Catholic fear of communism prompted him to join the fascist Integralist movement, which he soon repudiated. In 1936 Camara became an advisor of the Brazilian Secretariat of Education and rose quickly through the bureaucracy in an age when educated churchmen mingled easily in the Brazilian government. Consecrated a bishop in 1952 and auxiliary bishop of Rio de Janeiro in 1955, by 1951 he had already founded the Brazilian National Conference of Bishops with the help of Cardinal Giovanni Battista Montini, his close friend and later, as Paul VI, his loyal protector. During his fourteen years as head of the conference he was instrumental in founding the Latin American Bishops' Council, CELAM.

During the late 1950s and early 1960s Dom Helder was closely involved with Brazil's development schemes and was at various times invited to run for the mayoralty of Rio de Janeiro and the vice-presidency of the country. By 1960, however, he had begun to pay close attention to the reform ideas of Pope John XXIII and to have serious doubts about the wisdom of capitalist development. The works of the Brazilian educator Paolo Freire on conscientization and the church's real role in educating the people added to these doubts; and in 1960 Camara negotiated with the government on behalf of the bishops to establish the Movement for Basic Education (MEB), the origin of the basic Christian communities, organized along Freire's theories and consciously modeled on the achievements of Danilo Dolci in Sicily [304-305].

By 1963 Dom Helder had come to repudiate the U.S. Alliance for Progress with its emphasis on grand development projects imposed from above. Shortly after he criticized the program to the U.S. ambassador to Brazil, he fell from the ruling elite's favor. Newspapers began to vilify him, and in April 1964, immediately after the coup, he was transferred from Rio to the oblivion of Recife in Northeast Brazil. He continued to call on the military government to make necessary reforms and had become such a problem for the generals that in 1967 the neofascist "Tradition, Family, Property" (TFP) movement began to call for his purging from the church.

Despite the TFP denunciations of all reform attempts as communist subversion, Dom Helder vigorously pursued the new directions laid out by Vatican II, John XXIII and Paul VI, condemning both extremes of capitalism and communism and denouncing the U.S. and the U.S.S.R. for their selfishness in the face of world poverty.

In October 1968 Camara united 43 of Brazil's 253 bishops and thousands of Catholic laypeople to launch his "Action, Justice, and Peace" movement, an attempt at nonviolent "revolution through peace." His methods included the witness of religious processions, of human chains to prevent violence between police and protesters, as in Rio in 1968, and his own decision to embrace voluntary poverty. He abandoned his bishop's palace, which he used only as an office.

Most important to this revolution, however, was Camara's foundation of Operation Hope, a grass-roots organization, coordinating the basic Christian communities. Serving somewhat the same function as the medieval Third Orders [see 157-160], these are essentially small groups within a parish devoted to Bible study and its application to the problems of society, a most fundamental form of conscientization. This effort starts with the premise that change cannot be forced from above or led by an elite but must come from the people themselves. These basic Christian communities therefore aim first to overcome the alienation and fragmentation of urban life for the poor, to provide basic vocational training, health care and literacy education, and then to raise people's consciousness so that they can begin deciding the directions of their own lives and planning their own communities. The efforts of Camara and other bishops have been a huge success. By 1979 there were 80,000 basic Christian communities throughout Brazil.

The process of nonviolent revolution has been a dangerous one as well. The basic Christian communities faced continuous harassment and physical violence from the military government. Its members have been arrested, tortured, and killed. Foreign missionaries, priests, nuns, and bishops helping their work have been vilified, arrested, tortured, and expelled. Camara himself was declared a "nonperson" in Brazil, the press and the electronic media were forbidden to mention his name or report on his activities. He was denied all media access, except for a five-minute homily broadcast every morning. His bishop's palace was attacked by the police with machine guns, and on May 27, 1969 his personal assistant, Fr. Henrique Neto, was brutally assassinated and his body dismembered as a clear warning.

In 1973, the year the Nobel Peace Prize was awarded to Henry Kissinger and North Vietnam's Le Duc Tho, Camara was awarded the Alternate Peace Prize by European peacemakers. After his retirement he continued to travel, lecture and to keep the unsolved problems of the oppressed in the consciousness of the world.

The venue of the following talk – Paris in April 1968 – is as emblematic of a revolutionary situation as can be imagined. In the United States protest against the Vietnam War was rapidly reaching its peak, while the ferment of the counter culture combined with the civil rights movement, the assassinations of Robert Kennedy and Martin Luther King, the uprisings of the poor in New York, Detroit, and Chicago, the take-over of Columbia and other universities by students to bring government and society to a crisis point. Throughout Europe the spring of 1968 saw revolutionary movements from East to West: Prague, Warsaw and Gdansk, Rome, and especially Paris as the De Gaulle government collapsed. For a while it looked as if the nation itself might face civil war between entrenched bourgeois and an alliance of students (also bourgeois and Camara's audience here) and workers. In Latin America the Marxist revolution symbolized by Castro and Che Guevara had yet to crest, and two decades of fierce military repression in reaction were yet to come.

Yet here in Paris, in the spring of 1968, many idealistic – and some truly revolutionary – students came to hear the famed bishop from Brazil talk to them as a fellow radical. The impact of the Latin American reality on these "First World" children of privilege is as fresh and important today as it was a generation ago.

The following selection is taken from Dom Helder Camara, *The Church and Colonialism: The Betrayal of the Third World*, William McSweeney, trans., Denville, NJ: Dimension Books, 1969, pp. 101-11.

Chapter 6: The Third World and Liberation

338. Dom Helder Camara, Violence the Only Way? A Lecture Given in Paris on 25 April 1968.

The subject is certainly topical. It is true that violence belongs to all ages, but today it is perhaps more topical than ever; it is omnipresent, in every conceivable form: brutal, overt, subtle, insidious, underhand, blind, rational, scientific, solidly entrenched, anonymous, abstract, irresponsible.

It isn't difficult to speak of violence if it is either to condemn it out of hand, from afar, without bothering to examine its various aspects or seek its brutal, and regrettable, causes; or if it is to fan the flames from a safe distance, in the manner of an "armchair Che Guevara."

What is difficult is to speak of violence from the thick of the battle, when one realizes that often some of the most generous and the most able of one's friends are tempted by violence, or have already succumbed to it. I ask you to hear me as one who lives in a continent whose climate is pre-revolutionary, but who, while he has no right to betray the Latin American masses, has not the right either to sin against the light or against love.

Here is a first basic remark, necessary to the understanding of the problematic of violence: the whole world is in need of a structural revolution. With regard to the underdeveloped countries, this fact is self-evident. From whatever standpoint one approaches the question – economic, scientific, political, social, religious – it soon becomes obvious that a summary, superficial reform is absolutely insufficient. What is needed is a reform in depth, a profound and rapid change; what we must achieve – let's not be afraid of the word – is a structural revolution.

As Paul VI has recently said:

> One thing is certain, the present situation must be faced courageously, and the injustice it comprises must be fought and overcome. Audacious transformations and a profound renewal are the price of development. Reforms must be urgently undertaken, without delay. Everyone must generously play his part.

Economically speaking, it is common knowledge that the underdeveloped countries suffer from internal colonialism. A small group of rich and powerful people in each country maintains its power and wealth at the expense of the misery of millions of the population. This regime is still semi-feudal, with a semblance of a "patriarchal" system, but in reality a total absence of personal rights; the situation is sub-hu-

623

man, the conditions those of slavery. The rural workers, who are nothing more than pariahs, are denied access to the greater part of the land, which lies idle in the hands of rich landowners who are waiting for its value to rise.

With such a situation in a continent like Latin America, which is wholly Christian – at least in name and tradition – one realizes the great responsibility borne by Christianity in such countries. Without forgetting the fine examples of devotion, of sacrifice, of heroism even, we must admit that in the past – and the danger still persists – we Christians in Latin America have been, and are, seriously responsible for the situation of injustice which exists in this continent. We have condoned the slavery of Indians and Africans; and now are we taking a sufficiently strong stand against the landowners, the rich and the powerful in our own countries? Or do we close our eyes and help to pacify their consciences, once they have camouflaged their terrible injustice by giving alms in order to build churches (very often scandalously vast and rich, in shocking contrast with the surrounding poverty), or by contributing to our social projects? In practice, don't we seem to have vindicated Marx, by offering to pariahs a passive Christianity, alienated and alienating, justly called an opium for the masses?

And yet Christianity exists, with its demands of justice and fraternity; Christianity exists, with its message of eternal redemption. Indeed, our love for mankind is inspired from within by a love which is greater than the dimensions of the world and which provides it with a radically new element. In this way Christianity too is a motive force working for an integral development – including economic development – for scripture teaches that God gave man his image and likeness and wished him to subdue nature and bring creation to perfection.

If we Latin-American Christians assume our responsibility in face of the underdevelopment of the continent we can and must work to promote radical changes in all sectors of social life, particularly in politics and education. Politics must not remain the preserve of a privileged few, who stand in the way of basic reforms by betraying them or agreeing to them on paper only. Education is so far below the needs of technology – itself in constant evolution – that the unrest of our students is easy to understand. They have no time for the superficial, timid, and empty university reforms that are imposed upon them.

My remarks about Latin America can, more or less, be transposed to the whole of the underdeveloped world, which is in crying need of a structural revolution.

It is harder to understand that the developed countries are also in need of a structural revolution. Isn't their advanced state of development a proof that they have achieved success? Why should they need a revolution? Let us glance for a moment at the two most successful forms of development, under the capitalist and socialist regimes, as exemplified by the United States and the Soviet Union.

The United States is a living demonstration of the internal contradiction of the capitalist system: it has succeeded in creating underdeveloped strata within the richest country in the world – 30 million Americans live in a situation below the dignity of the human condition: it has succeeded in provoking a fratricidal war between whites and blacks; under the guise of anti-communism, but in fact driven by a lust for prestige and the expansion of its sphere of influence, it is waging the most shameful war the world has ever known [in Vietnam]. The dominant system in the United States is so irrational in its rationalization, as they call it, that it has succeeded in creating a one-dimensional, "robot" existence, to such an extent that young Americans of different cultural traditions feel called to build a more just and more human society by transforming the social context and humanizing technology.

The Soviet Union considers itself motivated solely by scientific humanism, since it takes its inspiration from Marxism. In practice, however, under the pretext of defending itself from the contamination of capitalism it perpetuates the iron curtain and the wall of shame; it refuses all pluralism within the socialist camp – the Soviet Union and red China face each other like two capitalist powers; and it considers Marxism to be an untouchable dogma.

Marx failed to distinguish between the essence of Christianity and the weakness of Christians who, in practice, often reduced it to an opium for the people. But today there is a change of attitude among Christians. Now, even in practice, there is an effort to preach and live a Christianity that is by no means an alienated or alienating force, but that is incarnated among men, following the example of Christ. This change has not yet been understood by the Soviet Union....

Who can now fail to understand the need for a structural revolution in the developed world?

Before asking whether the structural revolution needed by the world necessarily supposes violence, it must be underlined that violence already exists and that it is wielded, sometimes unconsciously, by the very people who denounce it as a scourge of society.

It exists in the underdeveloped countries: the masses in a sub-human situation are exploited violently by privileged and powerful groups. It is well known that if the masses attempt to unite by means of education at grass roots level based on the popular culture, if they form trade unions or cooperatives, their leaders are accused of treason or communism. This has aptly been described as follows: "they rebel against the established disorder, so they are classed as outlaws.... They must disappear so that order may reign." An orderly disorder!

As for "law," it is all too often an instrument of violence against the weak, or else it is relegated to the fine phrases of documents and declarations, such as the Declaration of the Rights of Man, whose second decade the world is commemorating this year. A good way of celebrating this anniversary would be for the United Nations Organization to verify if one or two of these rights are in fact respected in two-thirds of the world.

Violence also exists in the developed world, whether capitalist or socialist. In this respect, there are certain disquieting signs which speak for themselves. Negroes pass from non-violence to violence [in the urban uprisings of the late 1960s]. The black apostle of non-violence [Martin Luther King, Jr.] is felled to the consternation and shame of all men of goodwill. We are filled with horror when we see, on the one hand, young Americans forced to raze whole regions [of Vietnam] by means of "overkill," supposedly in order to protect the free world (we know the real reason); and on the other hand young men, children almost, obliged to kill in order to defend their lives, or rather sub-human existence. The youth of Western Germany, of Italy, of Spain, of Poland rise simultaneously in revolt [in 1968]. There is also the unique protest movement of the hippies. The arms race continues, and risks contaminating the space race. How splendid would be this glorious achievement of our age if the cosmonauts were not instruments of belligerence, of political and military prestige. Faced with the new Czechoslovakia, the Soviet Union's uneasiness is evident and, under the pretext of safeguarding the unity of the socialist camp, it rekindles the ideological battle against the capitalist world....

Faced with this triple violence – that which exists in the Third World, or in the developed world, or that done to the former by the latter – it isn't hard to understand the possibility of thinking, speaking and acting in terms of a liberating violence, of a redemptive violence.

If the elites of the Third World haven't the courage to rid themselves of their privileges and to bring justice to the millions living in sub-human conditions; if the governments concerned content themselves with reforms on paper, how can one restrain the youth who are tempted by radical solutions and violence? In the developed countries on both sides, how long will it be possible to restrain the ardor of youth, the spearhead of tomorrow's unrest, if the signs of disquiet and violence continue to multiply? How long will nuclear bombs be more powerful than the poverty bomb which is forming in the Third World?

Allow me the humble courage to take up a position on this issue. I respect those who feel obliged in conscience to opt for violence – not the all-too-easy violence of armchair guerilleros – but those who have proved their sincerity by the sacrifice of their life. In my opinion, the memory of Camilo Torres and of Che Guevara merits as much respect as that of Martin Luther King. I accuse the real authors of violence: all those who, whether on the right or the left, weaken justice and prevent peace. My personal vocation is that of a pilgrim of peace, following the example of Paul VI; personally, I would prefer a thousand times to be killed than to kill.

This personal position is based on the gospel. A whole life spent trying to understand and live the gospel has produced in me the profound conviction that if the gospel can, and should, be called revolutionary it is in the sense that it demands the conversion of each of us. We haven't the right to enclose ourselves within our egoism; we must open ourselves to the love of God and the love of men. But is it enough to turn to the beatitudes – the quintessence of the gospel message – to discover that the choice for Christians seems clear: we Christians are on the side of non-violence, which is by no means a choice of weakness or passivity. Non-violence means believing more passionately in the force of truth, justice and love than in the force of wars, murder and hatred.

If this appears to be mere moralizing, be patient a moment. If the option for non-violence has its roots in the gospel, it is also based on reality. You ask me to be realistic? Here is my answer: If an explosion of violence should occur anywhere in the world, and especially in Latin America, you may be sure that the great powers would be immediately on the spot – even without a declaration of war – the super-powers would arrive and we would have another Vietnam. You ask for more realism?

627

Precisely because we have to achieve a structural revolution it is essential to plan in advance a 'cultural revolution' – but in a new sense [from that of China from 1965 to 1968]. For if mentalities do not undergo a radical change then structural reforms, reforms from the base, will remain at the theoretical stage, ineffective.

I should like now to address a few remarks especially to the young. To the youth of the underdeveloped countries I put this question: what is the point of acceding to power if you lack models adapted to your situation, to your countries? Up till now you have been offered solutions which are viable only for developed countries. While we Christians try to exert a moral pressure, ever more courageously, on those who are responsible for the situation in our countries, you should try to prepare yourselves for the responsibilities that await you tomorrow; try above all to help the masses to become a people. You know only too well that material and physical underdevelopment leads to intellectual, moral and spiritual underdevelopment.

To the youth of developed countries, both capitalist and socialist, I would say: Instead of planning to go to the Third World to try and arouse violence there, stay at home in order to help your rich countries to discover that they too are in need of a cultural revolution which will produce a new hierarchy of values, a new world vision, a global strategy of development, the revolution of mankind.

Allow me to make one final remark. I have just come from Berlin, where I was invited to the World Congress of International Catholic Youth Movements. In that divided city I wondered how Europe could accept the dismembering of Berlin – symbol of so many divisions in the whole world. Why does mankind allow itself to be divided and torn asunder, from east to west, and even more profoundly from north to south?

It is only those who achieve an inner unity within themselves and possess a worldwide vision and universal spirit who will be fit instruments to perform the miracle of combining the violence of the prophets, the truth of Christ, the revolutionary spirit of the gospel – but without destroying love.

ARGENTINA: ADOLFO PÉREZ ESQUIVEL

Pérez Esquivel was born in Buenos Aires in November 1931. Though poor as a youth, he received a good, Catholic education and

took up a successful career as a painter and sculptor. On an early trip to Ecuador he was moved by a conversion to take up the cause of the poor and oppressed. Pérez Esquivel claims to have been most influenced by several peacemakers: John the Baptist, Francis of Assisi [147-157], Gandhi, Lanzo del Vasto [303], Dom Helder Camara [338] Ernesto Cardenal [343], Charles de Foucauld, the Goss-Meyrs, Teilhard de Chardin, and Thomas Merton [366-370]. The council of Medellín [326] gave his work even greater meaning and urgency.

Pérez Esquivel has pursued peacemaking as an organizer and a coordinator, bringing together Latin America's various peace movements, lending them advice and logistical help, cross-fertilizing the efforts under regimes that use every method to prevent the dissemination of information, curtail travel, and prohibit open meetings and free expression. In the 1970s Pérez Esquivel began his work as an organizer, traveling around Latin America, participating in nonviolent actions and learning the varieties of peacemaking. In 1971 in Costa Rica he helped plan for nonviolent liberation, founding the Servicio de Paz y Justicia (SERPAJ, see 340), and participated in similar efforts in Colombia in 1974. Later that year he was named general coordinator of Paz y Justicia and continued to work throughout Latin America through the 1970s. He also helped lay the groundwork for the *Latin American Charter of Nonviolence* issued by the bishops gathered at Bogotá in the fall of 1977.

By 1976 he had begun leading the human rights movement in Argentina, denouncing the government, and helping bring together the women who would found the Mothers of the Plaza de Mayo [341]. Later that year the junta ordered the destruction of his Paz y Justicia headquarters and his arrest. He was imprisoned, without charges, for fourteen months in a cramped cell, repeatedly tortured, denied the Bible or any other religious reading. An international campaign led by Mairead Corrigan and Betty Williams of the Peace People [306], Amnesty International, and the U.S. Carter administration finally secured his freedom. On his release he was held under house arrest for another nine months. In 1980, Pérez Esquivel received the Nobel Prize for peace. He has continued his work throughout the 1980s and lives in a now democratic Argentina. He is the author of *Christ in a Poncho* (Maryknoll, NY: Orbis Books, 1983).

The following selection is taken from an interview between Philip

McManus and Adolfo Pérez Esquivel published in McManus and Schlabach, pp. 238-51.

339. Adolfo Pérez Esquivel, To Discover Our Humanity

McManus: Can you tell us something about your personal history and how you became interested and involved in active nonviolence?

Pérez Esquivel: My concern for nonviolence began when I was young, for several reasons. First, I rediscovered the power of the gospel. My upbringing had been religious, but it was very systematized, very formal – more of a religious culture than a religious formation. With time I began to understand more deeply the gospel's power, and I also discovered the struggles of a man called Mahatma Gandhi. I was always impressed by Gandhi's saying he had found the strength of nonviolence in the ancient sacred books of India and in the Sermon on the Mount. One of the fundamental books that Gandhi always had with him was the Bible, along with the sacred books of his country, the Upanishads, and others.

Many Christians who were friends of Gandhi asked him why he wasn't a Christian. He replied that he would be a Christian the day that he saw Christians living the teachings of their teacher. He asked very clearly for one thing: consistency between what we say and what we do. Of course in a violent society like ours you have to reflect on what nonviolence means; it is not simply being opposed to physical violence. There is a violence that is structural. And there is also personal, psychological, and spiritual violence. One must begin the task of discovering the "why" of the violence. The fact is that the societies in which we live are violent in their roots, in their education, in their culture.

When studying history one sees that what is taught is always the history of violence. We were never taught history from the point of view of the people. Instead we learned about heroes of war. But I believe that the world exists not because of violence but rather because human beings have the capacity to survive....

McManus: One can see that in Latin America people generally seek to avoid violence in their efforts to make change. Quite apart from this, one also encounters an appreciation of what we call active nonviolence as a positive force for change. What are the historical and cultural roots of this understanding in Latin America?

Pérez Esquivel: In Latin America, long before Gandhi, there were nonviolent struggles. The indigenous people are actively nonviolent. And their social structure is nonviolent too, even with their ups and downs and the problems of being marginalized and exploited communities. Think about the fact that after five hundred years the communities still exist, still survive. Some survive in bad conditions, some in better conditions, but they show the capacity to resist through nonviolent means. We see this continually. Traveling through Latin America one begins to discover the wisdom in the people. We think we have just recently discovered that wisdom; but we must take care. They have long known the methods of nonviolent struggle. It is just that they have used it as a way to survive, not to try to overturn a whole system.

But Latin American nonviolence has other origins as well, especially among intellectuals. It has roots in the experience in Europe and also in the influence of Mahatma Gandhi, Martin Luther King, Jr., and others such as Jean and Hildegard Goss-Mayr. In recent times the Goss-Mayrs were among the first to promote nonviolence in Latin America through networking among many groups. They were the first who began the work that eventually resulted in what is now the Service for Peace and Justice in Latin America, or SERPAJ. They began from a gospel perspective even as they delved into the methodology of the Gandhian struggle. They began to help Dom Helder Camara and Mario Carvalho de Jesus in Brazil....

I first had contact with Jean and Hildegard many years ago. I read a report of theirs and then we had a long correspondence and later a long friendship. They began to visit Argentina and got to know us and our work. Another person who was a friend of mine was Lanzo del Vasto of the Community of the Ark in France [see **303**], who also visited here.

McManus: When was this?

Pérez Esquivel: Oh, about twenty-five years ago, about the same time that Jean and Hildegard came. He was a disciple of Gandhi, and worked a lot with Vinoba Bhave in the movement to secure land donations [in India]. Here in Argentina many groups of the Ark formed – nonviolent but with a communal life, working the earth, making handicrafts. For many years we ourselves belonged to the Community of the Ark [**303**].

McManus: To return to the present, do you see differences between how Latin Americans understand nonviolence and how North Americans or Europeans understand it?

Pérez Esquivel: There are differences and I believe they are root differences, not just differences of form. With regard to principles, such as the ethical principle of giving respect to one's neighbor, we are all in agreement. I believe that the differences that exist are historical and conceptual. For example, for Gandhi nonviolence was not only getting the English out of India. That's why his conception is so close to that of Latin America. He said that getting the English out of India was only the first step; the liberation of India would not be achieved until the last of the Untouchables had the same rights as the Brahmins. So he was speaking of a much deeper liberation.

In the United States and Europe there are important, serious nonviolent movements, but many of them aim more at modifying an unjust situation or conflict than at changing a structure. For example, the Martin Luther King, Jr. movement, with all of its importance for his black brothers and sisters, aimed at securing recognition of civil rights. King didn't really challenge the system.

McManus: Not at first…

Pérez Esquivel: Yes.… There was injustice, a conflict, but within the framework of the U.S. system. In Latin America we find ourselves in a process of liberation. We do call into question the system and the structures, the life to which we are subjected because we are dependent countries, exploited countries, shaped by the major international interests.

McManus: Then what does liberation mean?

Pérez Esquivel: We think of liberation holistically. It isn't only the resolution of a conflict; it is also a liberation of the social, the economic, and the political. And of the spiritual. One must understand that Latin America is a continent where religiosity is part of life itself. It is not incidental. The Latin American being is a deeply religious being. Maybe that's why I feel so close to the spirituality of Gandhi, who achieved a balance between the spiritual and the social, political, and economic.

This explains some of the difference in social movements. Many movements think economic life is the central issue, that overcoming the economic problems will solve the social problems. This is a utopia – more of a utopia than nonviolence. We aim for a change in the social structures, but also for the liberation of the person. I have said many times that the first step in the whole process of liberation is for men and women to realize that they are people. If they never discover themselves as people they will never know what liberation is. From that point we can open the doors to liberation, because then a person will recognize others as equals. And, logically, as people of faith we will recognize our neighbors as our brothers and sisters and as children of God....

McManus: You spoke before of religious faith as a key support in the struggle for liberation. One hears much about the theology of liberation. To what degree – in theory and in practice – has the theology of liberation had an impact as a support for armed struggle, and to what degree has it had an impact in promoting nonviolent struggle in Latin America?

Pérez Esquivel: A theologian friend of mine told me that theologians can't write or make theology if there is no one to "do" the theology. Theology is not theoretical reflection. A theology arises from a praxis [an ongoing dynamic process of action and reflection]. This is fundamental. If not, it isn't theology; it's a theory.

After the Second Vatican Council [1962-65, see **299-300**] and after the [Latin American bishops'] meeting in Medellín in 1968 [**326**], there was a revisioning of the attitude of how to assume a commitment to the process of liberation of the people. This happened principally in the Catholic Church but also in the evangelical churches.

Religion had been used to dominate, not liberate. But the gospel is liberating. In it one finds the greatest song of liberation – in the mouth of a woman, Mary of Nazareth. It's not in the mouth of a man. It is not in the mouth of a brave and powerful warrior. I find this important. God puts the greatest song of liberation, the Magnificat, into the mouth of a humble woman who suffered persecution, exile, fears [Luke 1:46-55].

So one begins to see the real meaning of liberation from the perspective of the gospel. Through a commitment of faith and what I was saying about recognizing one's brother as an equal, as a child of God, many Christians have begun to assume the commitment of freeing themselves from the structures, to build the kingdom of God and God's justice, to seek liberation. It is as much spiritual liberation as social, political, and economic liberation. And it is always *within* a historical situation. Not outside, not disconnected.

In this situation, the people don't choose violence. They have been submerged in violence. People who have come to the point of desperation resort to meeting that oppressive violence in any way possible. That's how armed struggles arise in many Latin American countries – some with success, many failures. We see the armed struggle in the Cuban revolution, in the present Nicaraguan revolution. We see that the people resort to armed struggle, but that is not what they seek.

At the same time, parallel to this in Latin America, there are also many nonviolent struggles – a great chain of them across the whole Latin American continent. However, because of the cultural mentality of violence, very little is said of those nonviolent struggles. We could go on talking for hours and hours about all the struggles in Latin America, but I can point out some to you....

McManus: In all of this, what attraction does nonviolence have for the marginalized?

Pérez Esquivel: Dom Helder Camara used to say that nonviolence is the weapon of the poor. What is attractive is that it enables organization, joining together in action, and reducing risks through collective actions. (This doesn't mean that the poor aren't going to be repressed, only that the risks are less.) Nonviolence makes it possible to respond to aggression and to repression in a way that is original – with an alternative totally distinct from the game of the aggressor. One of the positive things to understand, and which the people are understanding more and more, is that you don't have to confront the aggressor on his own turf. The people, the poor, must select the field of struggle and act from a position of strength.

McManus: What is the strength of the people?

Pérez Esquivel: Their numbers, their organization, their collective actions, their solidarity and mutual support, the development of what we might call a chain of solidarity and resistance. There are many elements.

But I think we still have not advanced in the political dimension of nonviolent struggle. All nonviolent movements must seriously consider this. Up to now we have not gone beyond acts of recovery. Isn't that so? There is a conflict and there is the nonviolent action to overcome that conflict. There is aggression against Nicaragua so people react with campaigns, international mobilizations, marches, the sending of aid. It's a form of pressure. But we must seek a political dimension of nonviolence that we have not explored deeply enough.

Most of the time when people talk of nonviolence, they talk about street action, about confrontation with the police. But the issue goes beyond the police to the system. Nonviolence means work in education, in health, in the environment, in economics – a nonviolent economics, because the economy we now have is very violent. We lack alternatives that expand the social, political, economic, and technological horizons of nonviolence to their fullest extent. It is necessary to begin to have a much more holistic vision of how nonviolence can liberate.

McManus: In other words you mean we should not just propose a new society but also start to construct it not wait until political power is achieved but begin the task now.

Pérez Esquivel: That is the difference. We have to begin it from the micro and move to the macro. There are stages. We can't expect that we are going to change everything from the top down; change will never come that way. No, we must work in health care, in education with children, in energy alternatives, in the means of production, in the training of professionals and technicians.

McManus: But at the same time you propose to work in national politics?

Pérez Esquivel: Of course, because it's the only way to make a real change in the structures. If you don't have the political and transforming dimension, things end up in the same place. They move a little but then they settle back again.

That's why what Gandhi says is so important when he speaks of the Untouchables. He speaks to the root of the problem. Here we say, "Yes, we're going to get rid of the dictatorship in Argentina." We did manage to get rid of the dictatorship. But now we see that in some respects things are getting back as they were. They move a little but they come back to the same place.

To synthesize, I believe we need to understand the structural origins of violence, the response nonviolence can offer, and the alternatives that can make a new, liberated society a reality....

And we must analyze history. I believe that nonviolence has much to do and much to offer, just as it has much left to discover. We still don't know the full potential of nonviolent struggle. We have found that nonviolent struggle is effective to the extent that the people understand it and join together to take it up. It is effective when their collective actions develop the capacity of resistance, of solidarity, of pressure, of protest, but also of proposals, of alternatives.

Once in a while individual initiatives may be effective, if they aim at moving the people as a whole. I support some isolated, testimonial acts of nonviolence. But these are not going to change the system. Real change will happen only when the people have their objectives clear and have a critical consciousness of their responsibility to create liberating change. I believe that nonviolent struggle is what enables people to be fully aware as they participate. A good example is the process of reflection and action

635

within the base communities in Latin America. For me the base communities are the seed of a wholly new social vision. And it is a nonviolent vision.

When we talk about nonviolence, we have to also speak about the relationship to power. Nonviolent struggle seeks to reinstate more horizontal social relations. People in power should place themselves on the same level as others, because it is not necessary that one be more than another. I think that the nonviolent movement must deepen its reflection on the meaning of power as a means of service. The one who has a higher position should be the servant of the most lowly. And this is the teaching of Gandhi. Gandhi made himself an Untouchable.

McManus: Now we are talking not just about a new society but also of building a new culture.

Pérez Esquivel: Right, a new culture. We must begin to see this — what sort of relations power implies, how nonviolent struggle may achieve power. The aim of a socio-political process is to achieve power, to gain the capacity to make decisions. But so often what happens is that small groups take power and the rest stay at the bottom. The people are always made to believe that they don't have any capacity to exercise power. But a people in power. And a people that begins to discover its power can begin to control its own life....

Servizio Paz y Justicia (SERPAJ)

Founded as a result of the work of the Latin American Bishops Conference (CELAM) in the 1970s, SERPAJ has deepened its original inspiration in the words of John XXIII, *Pacem in Terris,* Vatican II's *Gaudium et Spes,* and Paul VI's *Populorum Progressio* [see **297-301**] to spell out the methods of nonviolent struggle and its practical organizing and spiritual underpinnings.

Long discontented with notions of peace as "passive" resistance or quietude, Latin Americans have had to face the fact of the violence of oppression and the choices of violent insurgency, passivity, or nonviolent action. Their theory and practice have therefore evolved the notion of *firmeza permanente,* which is explained below.

This selection is taken from McManus and Schlabach, pp. 282-91.

340. Servizio Paz y Justicia (SERPAJ), Preparing for Nonviolence

Convictions and Consequences of Active Nonviolence

Active nonviolence offers to both the oppressed and the oppressor the possibility of safeguarding their honor and their person. In the unjust, it attempts to nurture understanding, transformation, and even collaboration toward the good of all. It does not seek the humiliation of the enemy, nor his or her destruction, and it is careful not to be unnecessarily provocative.

This struggle enriches the adversaries – both aggressor and victim. Even if in the first stage of the struggle the victims are not able to achieve their objectives or to emerge victorious, they should not allow apparent failure to discourage them or diminish their struggle. Even without immediate positive or visible results, our conviction – and the guarantee of nonviolent action – is that truthful and loving action has within it an all-encompassing, redeeming, and life-giving value: "To wish to save all humankind, including the oppressor."

This "universality" of the act of liberating nonviolence has infinite repercussions in the lives of men and women. Active nonviolence seeks to be the expression of authentic love at the core of political combat.

Some Principles of Nonviolence

(1) In order to attain a just society, we need means that are better than intrigue, plotting, coups d'état, torture, murder, and terrorism. To achieve justice and peace it is necessary to find just and peaceful means. Since such means are consistent with the ends we desire in the long run, they will be simpler and more effective.

(2) *Firmeza permanente* [or relentless persistence, a term sometimes used in place of active nonviolence] is in no way cowardly submission to the oppressors. To the contrary, it opposes the tyrants and the violent ones with all its strength. The *queixada* continually attempts to overcome bad with good, lies with truth, hatred with love.

(3) The struggle of *firmeza permanente* draws all of its strength from truth. To withdraw from truth is to withdraw from the source of our strength. Therefore the struggle cannot be clandestine. If you act in secret, you end up lying in order to disguise your efforts.

(4) Violence may be impressive at first sight if it is part of a courageous search for justice. With time however, we find that the way of violence does not deliver the hoped for result.

(5) Courage in isolation is not enough. The struggle must be collec-

tive and organized. The struggle brings persecutions, but persecution and the action of the group nurture a class consciousness.

(6) If the people do not want to use the very weapons that dehumanize the oppressor, the only solution is to accept, without retreating, the blows and the brutality of the adversary. There is no such thing as a human being who wishes to be inhuman until the end. Such is our hope.

(7) Those who use violence attempt to provoke the *queixadas* in order to get them to abandon their principal weapon: the use of *firmeza permanente*.

(8) In a situation of weakness, *firmeza permanente* is more effective than violence.

(9) By overcoming the oppressor through violence, one achieves only a partial victory. The roots of injustice remain within the oppressor who was defeated and within the victor who is liberated from the oppressor, since both used violence and so kept within themselves the evil that they fought.

(10) We cannot offer any guarantees to anybody that they will not be imprisoned. We can only guarantee that we will go together and nobody will skip out on the others.

(11) Since its first commitment is to truth and justice, *firmeza permanente* is not limited to strictly legal actions.

(12) Violence comes from aggressive impulses that are not channeled constructively. Since it is irrational it leads to hatred. The *queixada*, fed by the conviction that we are all brothers and sisters, aspires to act for justice through the control of reason over instinct.

(13) Violence is often impatient. *Firmeza permanente* endeavors to wait and to respect the necessary stages, recognizing that the conservatives know how to compromise or to change when they need to.

(14) In the face of the *queixada*, the anger and the might of the oppressor are useless. He loses his sense of self-assurance because of the attitude of the victim and the appeals to reason that the victim makes. The transformation and the defeat that he suffers then are moral. Instead of humiliating him, they enrich him.

(15) The important thing is not to be brave once in a while, but rather persistent all of the time. "We may die, but we are not going to run," pledged the workers of PERUS in the strike of 1967.

(16) If you cannot commit yourself to be nonviolent, be violent. What you cannot be is submissive.

(17) When somebody attacks another in an act of physical violence

and the victim replies in kind or flees, the response of the victim gives the aggressor a great security and moral support, since it shows that the moral values of the victim are the same as those of the attacker. Any attitude of fight or flight on the part of the victim reinforces the morale of the aggressor. But if the attitude of the victim is calm and firm, the fruit of self-discipline and self-control, the aggressor is disarmed by the show of love and the respect for him or her as a person. This only happens because the victim does not respond to the violence of the aggressor either with cowardice or with counter-violence. Instead the victim attacks the aggressor at the level of thought, of intelligence, of reason, using the weapons of truth, justice, and love.

Training For Nonviolent Action

Firmeza permanente is not improvised. We must take *training* for nonviolent action seriously. *Firmeza permanente* requires training that is as much spiritual as practical, as much in the inspiration as in the tactics of nonviolence....

Spiritual Training

Finally, we cannot forget this fundamental aspect of training. The apostle Paul reminds us that even in the most dramatic situations, "the fruit of the Spirit is love, joy, peace, patience, kindness, goodness, trustfulness, gentleness, and self-control" [Gal. 5:22].

Fasting and prayer are powerful weapons of nonviolence. Before any action that is likely to awaken the strongest passions, everyone should do such things as increase their vigils of prayer, ask the pardon of their brothers and sisters, purify themselves of evil, do justice in their own life, and fast.

Why all of this? Because we believe in the power of truth. It is truth that is going to triumph in the social, political, and other realms of human endeavor. Gandhi wrote: "By its very nature, truth gives evidence of itself. From the moment we leave behind all the stubborn webs of ignorance, the truth shines in splendor.... The way of truth is full of unimaginable obstacles. But in the faithful lover of truth there is neither deception nor defeat. For the truth is all-powerful, and the disciple of truth can never be overcome."

THE MOTHERS OF THE PLAZA DE MAYO

Following Gen. Videla's coup in Argentina in March 1976, as fathers and mothers, brothers and sisters, sons and daughters were taken away from homes and work – 1,400, fifteen a day, by the end of the year – never to be seen again, a group of women came to Pérez Esquivel's Peace and Justice Service's center in Buenos Aires to ask for advice and help. At first the center simply provided a outlet for their sorrow and despair. One day, however, the team suggested that they unite to bring their grievances before the government by a silent protest in the Plaza de Mayo, Buenos Aires' main square, in the heart of the government district. One April 30, 1977, the first fourteen mothers went into the Plaza. Their weekly protests were at first ignored and ridiculed, later harassed and sometimes driven off violently by police. The Mothers persisted, taking out paid ads in *La Prensa*, and circulating petitions. By 1980 the Mothers had grown to 3,000 regular members and had become known worldwide as the major symbol of Argentina's opposition to the generals, an opposition that stood, peacefully, protesting and giving witness to the truth that the generals would prefer to bury.

In July 1980 Pérez Esquivel and the Mothers issued a statement that summarized their philosophy. The Gospel had become a guide to their lives. They condemned violence as an attack on the family, on society, and on the body politic, especially the institutional violence of injustice, and offered instead nonviolence as a means of liberating the poor and the oppressed. Despite dangers, they were willing to become martyrs for a more just society, to answer evil and injustice with truth, and hate with love.

The Plaza de Mayo Mothers immediately began to encourage other Argentines to open their mouths in protest and by the early 1980s found themselves a focus of much of the nation's opposition forces that finally toppled the generals in massive nonviolent protests following the Malvinas-Falklands War in December 1982, leading to the democratic restoration of 1983. Since then they have continued to press for the location of all the missing and dead, the punishment of the military criminals, and the work of peace and justice.

In the late 1980s Marjorie Agosin, a widely published poet and activist, conducted a series of interviews with the Mothers, focusing on their founder, Renée Epelbaum. Born in Paraña, Argentina and the winner of the Henrietta Szold Peace Award, Epelbaum was an educator and a businesswomen when, in 1976 her son Luis disappeared, followed by the abduction of her younger children, Claudia and Lilafour, months later by an Argentine commado unit. She soon began demonstrating in the Plaza de Mayo, holding placards with the dates of her children's "disappearance." The following text is taken from Marjorie Agosin, *The Mothers of the Plaza de Mayo: the Story of Renée Epelbaum,* Janice Molloy, trans., Trenton, NJ: Red Sea Press, 1990, pp. 34-37, 71-73.

341. Mothers of the Plaza de Mayo, Interviews with Marjorie Agosin

Renée speaking: In the beginning, when we would first meet in the Plaza, we were a powerless group. People laughed at us. When it rained, we looked like a bunch of heads smothered by enormous, white kerchiefs. In the beginning of 1983, with a democratic Argentine government facing a discredited military regime, we became stars because we had legitimacy in the eyes of the new government. Remember this word well, legitimacy. Our battle was legitimate; that of the military was something hidden, monstrous, and illegal.

You must also remember that, during the Falklands War [April-June 1982], we were viciously attacked. In the newspapers there were caricatures of us as horrible old women with huge knives in our backs, showing that we were traitors against the great Argentine nation.

We were the only group to oppose that war publicly, and we published numerous articles against the Falklands War. We began with the following statement: "The Mothers of the Plaza de Mayo know pain. We ask the two governments of Argentina and Great Britain to renew talks."

Too much has been said about the politicization of the Mothers of the Plaza de Mayo. Politics has always interested me, but I would prefer it to be less tortuous.

I repeat that we began and continue as a movement because we are mothers; we became involved because our children disappeared. I remember that Maria Adela [one of the founders of the Mothers of the Plaza de Mayo] went to the Plaza on April 30, 1977. She and her three sisters were there alone, completely alone. You can't imagine how afraid they were; it is almost impossible to explain because this doesn't happen in other countries. In this way, mothers began to meet in the Plaza. At first, there weren't fourteen; there were three or four. We formed strategies such as petitioning for writs of habeas corpus, because we wanted to recover the bodies or for the military to at least tell us where they were.

We were desperate, but we were also rationally searching for an immediate solution. We always thought that our children would reappear, and so we went from court to court, from police station to police station.

At three-thirty p.m. on the dot we continued to meet to share our news. I remember a particularly interesting episode. One of the first mothers of the Plaza de Mayo, Azuzena de Vicente, who later disappeared, had an audience with one of the Pope's representatives in 1976. He told us that he couldn't do much, that he had spoken with [General] Videla and there were gray zones, as if there were some hope, gray zones...

I often thought: I don't want to be the mother of Christ. I want to be a mother who does things, who helps people, who occasionally bakes cakes, but I don't want to be the mother of Christ. For this reason, I demand that you return my son to me alive.

Ester speaking: I accompanied the Mothers when no one else would go near the Plaza. No one was with them. In those moments, I felt so helpless. Being there, not being able to do anything and knowing what had happened to the children. To think about torture, to think that all these women didn't know anything about their children and that their children had died, not through sickness or accident. They simply disappeared.

I went to the Plaza and felt that I could see their pain.

Renée speaking: One Thursday at about four-thirty in the afternoon, on my way home from the Plaza a car stopped and its occupants tried to grab me. In the car was a woman who tried to pass herself off as a French tourist, but who spoke perfect Spanish. She said, "This woman is being disorderly on a public street."

After a long struggle, I threw myself to the ground so they couldn't drag me into the car. I thought they wouldn't torture me because I was sprawled on the ground, and that's how I saved myself.

The next Thursday I returned to the Plaza, but I wore a different coat.

Ester speaking: The men were impotent when faced with the reality. The few that remained didn't want to appear in public, like at the Plaza. In addition, being the father of a disappeared person was a great stigma. Also, many of the mothers were widows like the señora, and for that reason they went alone.

Chapter 6: The Third World and Liberation

Marjorie Agosin speaking: Many people greet her, I don't know how it is other Thursdays, but at least this Thursday. Distant, she smiles, telling them, I am marching, circling the Plaza for Luis, Claudio, and Lila, and also for you. A very small child watches Renée and smiles with her.

At the Plaza she wore a Cossack hat. She had watery eyes and delicate skin. She told me she was from Odessa, and that she was searching for her daughter, Graciela. Then she took off her Cossack hat to reveal a wrinkled kerchief covering her head. She said, "I am another in this Plaza," and she looked more and more like the photograph of Graciela that she carried, her eyes crazy with pain, holding her Cossack hat.

When we join arms, we form a single alliance, a single embrace, and we cross the Plaza like sleepwalkers, asking: "Where are the missing? How can we talk with them?" And a great procession of white kerchiefs blesses our innocent steps.

The crazy women of the Plaza de Mayo surround the cold obelisk. They look for their children but they know they are dead. They walk but they know there are no corpses. They walk and choose to put on masks: they stop being Renée and Adela. It is easier to be the Mothers of the Plaza de Mayo, or the crazy old women. It is easier to imagine that perhaps they will be joined with their children again, as before birth.

The crazy women of the Plaza de Mayo spin and, dizzy, we watch them ascend through the demonic air of an indifferent Buenos Aires.

The end of winter. The sun shelters us like a generous embrace. I accompany her to the Plaza. Slowly, I follow her steps and she rises as if she were an immense white kerchief watching over the ceremonies. She seems to be someone else, or am I someone else as I watch her? I see her growing and growing, and with each lap around the obelisk her steps begin to resemble the rhythms of life and death.

In the Plaza de Mayo, we are all someone else, but when the shadows fuse everything together we return to her home, and she falls silent. She is no longer a Mother of the Plaza de Mayo. She is a woman, so alone, a mother with three missing children, dead or alive.

El Porteño, January 1984. The Mother's Column: Why We Continue to Go to the Plaza

We, the Mothers, share the happiness of the vast majority of Argentines at the restoration of democracy. We participated in the general rejoicing on December 10 in celebration of the inauguration of the constitutional president, Dr. Raul Alfonsin, although this event was inevitably tainted with mixed feelings of grief and hope.

As citizens and as mothers of the "missing and disappeared," we have participated and continue to participate in this new democracy in which the Argentine people have invested so many expectations and dreams.

This active participation implies an unconditional support of the constitutional government. All Argentines must work to prevent future coups. But this active participation also means that we must voice, publicly if necessary, our disagreement with policies or decisions that we judge to be of dubious effectiveness or to be mistaken. It is our obligation to do so, since this is the duty of all good citizens within the framework of a pluralistic and free democracy in which dissent should be expressed in a civilized manner.

To confuse critical support and the honest questioning of the methods that a constitutional government may adopt with a questioning of the legitimacy of that same government is out of the question. Firm adherence to the republican and democratic principles that mark our Constitution does not require unanimity of opinion or the concealment of dissent, since those are the characteristics of dictatorship.

It is healthy and necessary to exercise this critical support and to point out both errors and good judgment.

For this reason, we, the Mothers, will keep up our activities, without becoming involved in subordinate interests or games.

And for this reason, we continue to come to the Plaza de Mayo every Thursday. Our cry still has not been answered. The "detained and disappeared" who are alive must be released, and the government owes us the most detailed information concerning the fate of each and every one of them.

Finally, those guilty of the kidnappings, tortures, and assassinations must be tried and sentenced according to the magnitude of their crimes, the greater the responsibility, the greater the punishment. This judgment must be exemplary and known by the entire nation so it will be certain that this horror will never be repeated, that NEVER AGAIN will truly mean never again.

For this reason, we question why the accused military officers are being tried in a military court and not by an ordinary penal court like any other citizens. For this reason, we insist on the formation of a bicameral investigatory commission, since Congress, as a reflection of the general public, is the proper forum for the consideration of a problem that affects all citizens, just as the Plaza de Mayo, scene of our resistance against the dictatorship for seven long years, is the natural arena for the Mothers to continue to protest.

Only through Truth and Justice will Argentines be able to regain an ethical sense of life. Without ethics, nothing lasting, nothing that is worthwhile can be constructed.

CHILE: WOMEN ARTISTS AND CRAFTSPEOPLE AS PEACEMAKERS

When the military under General Augusto Pinochet Ugarte deposed President Salvador Allende in a violent military coup on September 11, 1973, they ended 150 years of uninterrupted democratic rule and set of a reign of terror unmatched on the continent: of a total population of 13 million 500,000 were arrested and imprisoned in concentration camps (the equivalent of 9.6 million Americans). This included kidnapping, disappearances, torture and rape, executions of an estimated 5,000 Chileans in a right-wing campaign to "exterminate Marxism" and to defend "Western Christian Civilization." Despite protests from around the world, the junta appeared to have U.S. backing – if not outright participation. They soon followed political repression with a development scheme actively implemented by a team of University of Chicago economists guided by Milton Friedman: radical free enterprise, privatization and "trickle down" that made the 20% in the elite even richer and left millions jobless, destitute, and homeless – a decade before the Third-World experiment was brought home to the U.S.A. under the Reagan administration.

Whenever the poor attempted to organize: for a local cooperative, a trade union, to inquire into the fate of the disappeared or the imprisoned, the result was the same: massive sweeps of barrios by tanks, helicopters, heavily armed soldiers, roundups, summary imprisonment, torture, and exile, a pattern that would take on greater brutality only under the South African apartheid regime.

Yet in 1977 SERPAJ began to organize a nonviolent resistance in Chile, weaving together the strands of dissent into at first localized, and then nationally organized demonstrations, work and craft centers, soup kitchens, gardening clubs, food banks, bakeries, larger economic cooperatives, study, and nonviolence training groups. By the late 1980s nonviolent demonstrations were growing larger and larger and pushing for the overthrow of the generals. In a plebiscite forced on Pinochet by growing nonviolent revolt, voters rejected the junta, and a democratic government was restored in elections held in December 1989.

One of the more interesting examples of this type of work – and of the vivid link between the arts and the building of a nonviolent life and society – is the following account of the work of the *arpilleras,* weavers of traditional (and not-so-traditional) patchwork quilts that not only gave work to dispirited and dislocated women of the barrios, but also gave a voice to their despair and to their cry for justice, at the same time creating a product that would appeal to international tourist and eco-industry dollars. It tells the story of a young woman artist who in finding work for the poor and marginalized also found meaning for her own life and helped end a brutal dictatorship.

The following text is taken from Marjorie Agosin, *Scraps of Life: Chilean Arpilleras, Chilean Women and the Pinochet Dictatorship,* Cola Franzen, trans., Toronto: Williams-Wallace, 1987, pp. 93-99.

342. A Woman Artist, On the Role of the Arpilleras

...I was born in Chile, a country of mountains, three hundred years of struggle did not save us from the conquest and independence from Spain did not save us from madness.

My interest in art arose naturally from my contact with other students, in the face of family opposition I entered the school of Fine Arts in the University and there became involved in movements interested in working with community groups, in literacy work in marginal sectors of the city, finding for the first time the gratifying sensation of giving something and not only that but contributing something of great value to others, such as the ability to read and write.

This short period of work in the poor neighborhoods was a great help for me in defining many things in my life, the coming in direct contact with different social classes and opportunities, such different rights, such a different sense of justice from one side to the other, and yet so equal in the right to life and to love.

Slowly I entered a period of personal confrontation with myself, of questioning. Trying to be aware above all of the fact of being a woman, I began to work with women.

Together we began the search for our own cultural roots, those that were most pure, the least contaminated ones, the women learned to value and to feel pride in their past and in their origins by showing their work, in that way recuperating their lost self-esteem. We were happy they and I.

But we are not only our origins, we are our origins plus everything that happens in our history, we are the result of three hundred years of struggle, we are the result of the cultural influence and the slow impoverishment of our land, of the importation of luxurious goods that we don't need, of the propaganda that transforms us into a society that consumes products that we don't make, of seeing every day on television a luxurious and exotic life that we try to imitate and in that way we again repeat the cycles of our earlier history when we embraced foreign cultures and values instead of treasuring our own.

As an artist I am the mixed result of my history, my actions, my process and my commitment. Based on my commitment I have carried out a long and varied career trying to open other areas that are less individualistic, to find other possibilities of expression. Especially since as artists we have always provided the testimony of our epoch.

And here I wish to speak about a part of my work, the *arpilleras*. Their beginning, their expression, their possibilities and their future.

After the military coup [of Pinochet and the military junta on Sept. 11, 1973] I was out of a job like so many others, in a short time the Pro-Paz committee [of the Chilean church's Peace an Justice service] asked me to develop some craft-work projects with women. The first group assigned to me were women of families of the detained-disappeared: mothers, wives, sisters. At the end of my first interview with them, it was clear to me that in their state of anxiety they would not be able to concentrate on anything except their own pain. I went back to my house, their anxiety embedded in me, I could hardly believe what I had heard, sons, husbands, brothers snatched with blows and threats to their families, pregnant women carried off, couples including their small children, all disappeared for weeks and even months, with nobody knowing anything about them, not even about the newborns or the older children and even less about the adults.

Everything I had been thinking of doing with these women was useless, since the future work we would undertake together ought to serve as a catharsis, every woman began to translate her story into images and the images into embroidery, but the embroidery was very slow and their nerves weren't up to that, without knowing how to continue I walked, looked and thought and finally my attention was attracted by a Panamanian *mola,* a type of indigenous tapestry, I remembered also a foreign fashion very much in vogue at that time: "patchwork" [quilts]. Very happy with my solution the very next day we began collecting pieces of fabric, new and used, thread and yarn, and with all the material together we very quickly assembled our themes and the tapestries, the histories remained like a true testimony in one or various pieces of fabric, it was dramatic to see how the women wept as they sewed their stories, but it was also very enriching to see how in some way the work also afforded happiness, provided relief, happiness to see that they were capable of creating their own testimony, relief simply from the fact of being together with others, talking together, sewing, being able to show that by means of this visual record others would know their story.

This *collage* of fabric, mixture of *mola* and patchwork, was not, as a technique, new, but we all liked it and were satisfied with it. Some visitors and foreign journalists saw the result and took them away, other people, all motivated by our problems, acquired them and they began to be in demand inside the country as well as abroad, the demand for the *arpilleras* had begun.

Two months after beginning this work, seeing the results, Pro-Paz assigned me to other groups, the [trickle-down] economic model [of Milton Friedman] imported from [the University of] Chicago by the military regime began to cause havoc, this time among industrial workers. Unemployment was going up, imported goods arrived by the tons, propaganda helped turn us into a grossly overblown importer-country. And with this primitive streak that still remains in us to be dazzled by glass beads of beautiful colors, we bought and bought without realizing that by doing so we were closing down our own industry, and as our factories closed there were hundreds and thousands of unemployed workers and the workers had wives and children and all of them needed to eat.

The Church assumed a historic role, opening its doors and taking on as its own the problems of the most needy. In a desperate attempt to stave off malnutrition the first child-feeding programs were begun in various churches. The mothers in the communities organized, going out every morning to collect left-over foodstuffs, from stores, private houses, restaurants, in produce markets, even going out into the countryside and there gathering produce of poor quality that could not be sold in the markets, it was painful to see how few resources they had to work with. Many times, the good half of a half-rotten tomato was used, and the same thing went for potatoes and other vegetables and fruits. It was an impressive effort to cook something with the poor and miserable things they were able to collect.

Then we saw heartbreaking situations when women recently confronted by the drama of hunger would arrive at the church dining rooms for the first time with their children, only to find all the places taken, but it never failed that some woman would give up her place to the newcomer, saying "My child ate yesterday and the day before, let your child eat now."

That was the atmosphere I found when I arrived, and these things I am telling I learned from the women there, I began to take real account of the unemployment and the effect produced by the continuing closing and more closing of factories.

Also there were anguished women, another kind of anguish, first of all, hunger, and another equally painful, to see a child slowly becoming thinner and thinner, slowly being consumed, not having means to go to a hospital, nothing with which to buy medicine, is always painful. And with these groups the story of the *arpilleras* continued.

The women didn't know how to begin, one of my volunteer companions, Gloria Torres, a lawyer, suggested to the children that they draw the dining rooms. New collages of fabrics appeared with enormous pots, enormous tables filled with children and long lines awaiting their turn. These were the things they began to tell in different *arpilleras*, then they began to make their own drawings, mamas collecting foodstuffs, cooking, serving steaming hot plates, mamas waiting. We should add here that the only income some of these women received at all was from the sale of *arpilleras*....

One of the groups of women had formed a little laundry service when their husbands lost their jobs,... I was called in to see what I could do with this group, and other *arpilleras* appeared telling other stories. These women were very imaginative and began the evolution of the *arpilleras*, incorporating volume and other materials to the work, it was very heart-warming to see reflected in the new *arpilleras* the very busy little chapel, and so much laundry hanging on the line. In addition to picturing the stories of the women washing clothes they told how their husbands had lost their jobs when the factories and plants had closed, of the interminable treks that the men made in search of work, of how they slowly used up their few possessions, of the solidarity that developed around the common soup pots. Other artists began to be inspired by this experience and that's how the theatrical work called "Tres Marias y una Rosa" (Three Marias and a Rose) came about.

Many other groups were formed from the arpillera groups, carrying out different activities, within the limits of my possibilities....

CENTRAL AMERICA: NICARAGUA

For North Americans Nicaragua needs little introduction: the scene of one of the most savage of "low intensity conflicts" launched by the United States against a nation of 4.1 million people (roughly the population of Brooklyn, NY), Nicaragua, its dictatorship under U.S.-backed Anastasio Somoza Debayle, the Sandinista Liberation Front that took power in a violent revolution in July 1979, and the subsequent guerrilla war waged by the Contras – Ronald Reagan's "freedom fighters" – from the day Somoza fled Managua to the electoral defeat of Sandinista president Daniel Ortega on February 25, 1990.

That purely political story also reveals one of the most intriguing events in the entire history of the Catholic peace tradition, for many of the members of the original Sandinista front, and subsequently of the highest levels of their government, were not only fervent Catholics, but also priests, poets and educators. The presence of Ernesto and Fernando Cardenal and of Miguel D'Escoto, as well as dozens of other priests and religious in the Sandinista government – and the role of base Christian communities in supplying some of the critical material and spiritual supports for the incipient revolt – have been the subject of intense media and scholarly scrutiny, in addition to conservative political attacks in both South and North America for over a decade. The testimony of what constitutes Christian love, Christian witness, and the manifestations of this love in just revolution must give pause to any easy definition of Catholic peacemaking.

ERNESTO CARDENAL

Poet and intellectual, monastic founder and educator, friend of

Chapter 6: The Third World and Liberation

Lawrence Ferlinghetti, Daniel Berrigan and Thomas Merton, Ernesto Cardenal led a life in many ways reminiscent of many a medieval peacemaker. He was born in Granada, Nicaragua on January 20, 1925. After attending Jesuit primary and secondary schools, he studied at the National Autonomous University in Mexico City from 1942 and in 1947 received an MA in literature. Already a published poet, he studied American literature at Columbia University from 1948 to 1949. After travel in Europe, he returned to Nicaragua in 1950 and began work as a translator and writer. Always a strong, perhaps romantic revolutionary, in 1954 he took part in an unsuccessful uprising against Somoza.

In 1956 Cardenal experienced a religious conversion and in 1957 entered the Trappist monastery of Gethsemani, Kentucky under the spiritual guidance of Thomas Merton [366-369]. For health reasons Cardenal left the strict Trappists in 1959 and entered a Benedictine monastery in Cuernava, Mexico, continuing to write and publish poetry there. He then went on to study for the priesthood in Colombia from 1961 to 1965. With the blessing of his old friend Merton, Cardenal returned to Nicaragua in 1966 to found the quasi-monastic community of Solentiname, on Lake Nicaragua.

By the 1970s the ferment of Latin American revolution had combined with Cardenal's own intellectual and political commitments. In 1970 he visited Cuba to experience the revolution first-hand, and by 1976 had joined the FSLN (Sandinista Liberation Front), providing the Front with a base at Solentiname that helped launch the opening of the guerrilla war in 1977. With the overthrow of Somoza, Cardenal was named minister of culture, a post he still held during the famous visit of Pope John Paul II to Nicaragua in March 1983 and the pontiff's rebuff to Cardenal's show of obedience with a harsh warning to the priest to choose between his government and his church post.

Ernesto Cardenal is the author of many books of poetry and of popular religious works. Perhaps his best known in North America are *The Psalms of Struggle and Liberation* (New York: Herder & Herder, 1971) and the four volumes of *The Gospel in Solentiname* (Maryknoll, NY: Orbis Books, 1982).

The following excerpts are taken from an interview with Ernesto Cardenal in Teofilo Cabestrero, *Ministers of God, Ministers of the People:*

Testimonies of Faith from Nicaragua, Robert R. Barr, trans., Maryknoll, NY: Orbis Books, 1983, pp. 24-30.

343. Ernesto Cardenal, From Monk to Minister

...First, I had a religious conversion, in which I discovered God as love. It was an experience of a loving faith, a falling in love. It made me want to live in the most isolated, lonely place I could find, to be alone with God. And I felt that the ideal place would be a Trappist monastery. So I entered the Trappists. There I renounced everything, even my interest in poetry and my interest in politics. And my novice master, Thomas Merton, showed me that it shouldn't be this way. He showed me that just because I surrendered myself to God, that didn't mean I was supposed to change my personality. I should keep being the same as before, just as interested in what I was interested in before, interested in the fate of Nicaragua, in Somoza's dictatorship, and in everything that had been important to me before.

Merton didn't just say this to me conceptually, he taught it to me especially by the way he acted. He was already starting to get acquainted with Zen, and it seemed to me that he used a Zen method with me. He would get together with me for a spiritual conference – then, instead of talking to me about "spiritual things," he'd start asking me about Somoza, or about the dictator of Venezuela, Perez Jimenez, or the one in Colombia, and so on, or about the poets of Nicaragua. Then he would start telling me about his poet friends. And so our precious "spiritual direction" time all went by, "wasted." I'm sure he did this deliberately.

Merton was very interested in politics, and in all sorts of social problems. About this same time, too, he had discovered Gandhi and had become a great Gandhian. He was making Gandhians of us novices. It was also about this time that he started being a great proponent of nonviolence in the United States. He was also very interested in dialogue with Marxists and was sympathetic with them. This was before Vatican II, before anybody talked about that.

I had to leave the Trappists, for health reasons, but Merton saw this as providential: he was already thinking of founding a community different from the Trappists in Latin America, and he wanted to found it with me. As we said good-bye he told me that if he couldn't leave the Trappists I would found this community myself, and so I ought to study for the priesthood. He told me that there was still a great deal of clericalism in the church, and so, to direct a little foundation, a small community, it was very important to be a priest, to have more influence.

So I started studying for the priesthood. I still hoped he'd get permission to leave the Trappists to found this community, but I finished my studies and was ordained a priest and he still didn't have permission. So, right after my priestly ordination, I founded the little Solentiname community. The bishop of that region had agreed that I was being ordained a priest to found his community, and not for other pastoral work somewhere else....

Merton had told me many times that the contemplative life would have to "go political." That's why he was afraid of starting an official Trappist community in Latin America. He said that those North American monks, with their conservative ideas, and their admiration for Franco, would go along with a dictatorship in Latin America, and maybe the community would be founded in a country with a dictatorship: most had dictatorships anyway. So our Solentiname community, inspired by this spirit of Merton's, was a "politicized" community right from the start, involved with the Nicaraguan people, and with its liberation. Eventually this brought me into contact with the Sandinista Front.

First, there was a letter from Tómas Borge, which he sent me from where he was hiding. Tómas said this was the first contact the Sandinista Front had had with priests, and he invited me to come to see him. So I had my first talk with him. And afterward there were other talks, with him and Carlos Fonseca. Later I went to Cuba, and there I saw that the Cuban revolution was love for neighbor – the gospel in action, "efficacious charity."

We were also evolving with respect to our position of nonviolence. We saw that in Nicaragua an armed struggle was becoming more and more necessary. We recalled that Gandhi had said that in certain circumstances his doctrine of nonviolence couldn't be put into practice – in Hitler's Germany it could not have been put into practice [see **278-291**], and it was the same in Somoza's Nicaragua. Merton had already died, but I'm sure he would have thought the same as we.

About this same time, the current of liberation theology began to well up in Latin America, and it was gradually identifying us with our people's revolution, with the Sandinista National Liberation Front....

The young men in my Solentiname community had been wanting to leave for some time now, to go and fight with the guerrillas in the mountains. I had to hold them back, because if they left, our community would be destroyed. So I had to make them see that the community represented something good for the nation. They were not very convinced, but we received a message from Eduardo Contreras saying that our community should be kept going because it had political and military importance, and tactical and strategic importance, for the Sandinista Front. We quickly understood what he meant by military importance when we learned that there was going to be a Sandinista offensive in which that whole region of the country would be involved. The offensive would need the participation of the young Solentiname members as guerrillas. They accepted the invitation with enthusiasm. They trained, preparing for the offensive.

Earlier, I had met with Carlos Fonseca and Tómas Borge. They had told me they wanted me to be one of the three members of a government junta; they were sure that the guerrilla war was about to be won. I was told that I would soon get word to head for the mountains. But a few months later, Eduardo Contreras and Carlos Fonseca died, one day apart. Later the order came from the Sandinista Front for the attack in which the Solentiname members were to take part, in the city of San Carlos. Boys took part in this attack and so did girls.

A few days before, I'd been called out of the country by the Front. The first task I was given was to handle the formal introductions of the new government that would be set up. There was already a government ready and waiting, made up of the Group of Twelve. So I was the one who formally presented this new government to Carlos Andrés Pérez, who was president of Venezuela, and from then on it was one trip after another taking me to so many countries.

I was also appointed spokesperson for the Sandinista Front because the others, in their clandestine operations, could not make public statements to the press or on radio or television. I kept at this work until the revolution was victorious.

When the new government was being set up, in Costa Rica, I received a phone call asking me if I would be minister of culture. I said I didn't want to, but that if they thought it was necessary I would agree. They asked me again – did I accept or not – I repeated that I didn't want to accept, but that if they ordered me to do it, I would. And again they asked me if I was saying yes or no. After the third request I answered, 'Then, yes, I accept' – thinking it would be for three months or so.

A little later it occurred to me that three months wouldn't be long enough, and that maybe it would have to be six months. And the time has been drawn out like that, as circumstances in the country kept requiring me to continue in this duty. I didn't ask for it, in fact I had never even thought of it: there was no ministry of culture before, and Sandinista Front plans never mentioned creation of a ministry of culture. This was a last-minute decision, it would seem. I had thought that I'd just go back to Solentiname, back to my former life....

FERNANDO CARDENAL

Fernando Cardenal was born on January 26, 1934, also in Granada, Nicaragua, and like his brother Ernesto attended Jesuit schools through college, when he entered the Jesuit novitiate at Santa Tecla in El Salvador. From 1954 to 1961 he attended the Catholic University of Quito, Ecuador, taking degrees in philosophy and humanities. He earned a degree in theology in Mexico and was ordained a Jesuit priest in 1967.

After serving his tertianship in a slum of Medellín, Colombia, he experienced a conversion to the new liberation theology. On his return to Nicaragua, he was appointed vice-rector of the Central American University in Managua, but that December was expelled from the university for supporting a student strike. Cardenal went on to work among the base Christian communities, in 1973 founding the revolutionary Christian Movement, out of which emerged many leaders of the Sandinista Front. He was placed under internal house arrest in 1976 following his testimony to the U.S. Congress of Somoza's repression and North American support for it. His response was to found the Nicaraguan Commission for Human Rights.

In August 1979, following the revolution, Cardenal was named national coordinator of the Crusade for Literacy, a campaign that earned world-wide acclaim for its reduction of illiteracy in Nicaragua from 51 to 12 percent.

The following excerpts are taken from Cabestrero, *Ministers*, pp. 70-71, 78-79, 84-85, 88-89.

344. Fernando Cardenal, Ministry of Charity and Love

...I can state publicly that, on numerous occasions, I have communicated directly with the leaders of the revolution, to ask them questions or to transmit my reservations or my suggestions, and that I continue to do so. Any sort of "blind obedience," in the pejorative sense, is foreign to everything I stand for. I have never practiced it, not even in the religious life – and nobody normal practices it, because it's beneath human dignity. Still less would it be an act of religion or a Christian practice. Those who know us know that we've always been very independent persons; we say what we think.

But there is something more complex and deeper here. I feel very deeply the religious call to obedience to God. Never in my life have I made greater sacrifices out of obedience to God than in the revolution. And never, in my thirty years of religious life, have I understood more profoundly the importance of "obedience in faith," which is obedience to the will of God. I hear this call of obedience to God in the voices and cries of our people suffering in poverty. I seek to obey God more than anything else on the face of this earth, and I feel that no one, nothing, can separate me from the path of obedience. And I can say without exaggeration (and without vanity – we've had enough training in risking our lives) that I'm not afraid even of death. I'm not afraid. I'm ready to do anything to be obedient to my conscience. And my conscience tells me to obey God by being unconditionally faithful, always, every moment, to my people – to a people still suffering in a country where three years is too short a time for the miracle of a passage from misery to development, where there are so many needs, where there is such a heritage of pillage and destruction, where there's been a blockade, where we're under attack....

I'd like to make it very clear that, by my faith in our Lord and my obedience in faith to our Lord to whom I've consecrated myself in the religious life and the priesthood, my conscience obliges me, after considering everything involved, to make this irreducible, irrevocable, irreversible commitment to the people. And for me it's clear that this is what God asks of me, that this is what God wishes. And I'm ready to obey his will even if it leads to my death. And there's nothing, there's no one, that can make me abandon it. For me, anything else, anything against a commitment to the people, goes clearly against the will of God and would be a sin.

I've had very striking personal experiences in which I've seen that I'd be betraying God, and failing in the accomplishment of his will, if, in the name of some "law" or other, I were to abandon my people – the poor in Medellín, or the students who went on a hunger strike for their comrades who were being abused by Somoza's National Guard. And I feel the same thing now. Only, I feel it much more profoundly, because that was just the beginning....

We've already defined ourselves. We've been defining ourselves for years. We've always spoken and acted as Christians, priests, and persons of faith, committed to our people's struggle, by the power of the gospel and for the sake of the gospel.

Our service of God in the priesthood has led us to the ministry of charity and love, which in Nicaragua has been translated into a ministry in support of the forward march of the people, the ministry of accompanying our people from within, by participating in a transformation of structures, so that the poor may have justice. Our first definition, then, our essential definition, must include, because of the concrete historical exigencies of the ministry of charity, the element of support for the Sandinista popular revolution....

If we study the defense of the cause of the poor with the eyes of faith, we find God deep within it. In defending the cause of the poor we're defending God's cause. God's cause is transcendent, this is true. But it includes all the positive causes of history, and preferentially the cause of the poor, for God has caught them up in history in a preferential option. We believe we can reach God in Nicaragua only through the mediation of the struggle for and with the poor....

...In Nicaragua there has been a positive integration of Christians in the popular revolution. This is precious for the church. It's the first revolution in the history of the human race that Christians have been this deeply and this positively involved in. If any of us left the revolution, I would consider it a loss for the church, because the church would lose its presence in the revolution. If the church doesn't want the revolution to be atheistic, and atheizing, then the first thing it should do is to be present in it as God's witness. If the church pulls Christians out of the revolution, it will be cooperating in the "atheization" of the revolution: the revolution will become atheistic and it will make atheists of others.

I doubt if there has ever been another revolutionary party or revolution anywhere in the world that's entrusted the formation of its youth – its future as a revolution – to a Catholic priest. But Nicaragua did it. The church has always been most zealous for the education of youth, has it not? So, then, ought it not to see my presence in the Sandinista Youth Movement as a guarantee of, and an advantage for, its educational mission?

I don't understand how the same ones who complain that Christians aren't allowed to join the Communist Party of Cuba then turn around and complain that the Sandinista Party in Nicaragua not only allows Christians to join it but appoints them members of the Sandinista Assembly and entrusts the political directioning of its youth movement to a priest! This ought to be seen as something positive. It ought to be recognized that if this were to be lost, the church would suffer a loss. I could be replaced, of course, but my replacement might be someone who, by training and experience, would have no appreciation of the Christian faith or the church....

At the same time, I have to restate all I've said concerning my commitment – to the death, if need be – to this revolution. I hope that no one will put asunder what God has joined together here in Nicaragua. In my case God has united my priesthood to the Sandinista popular revolution, which I love so much, and to which I feel committed with all the strength of my heart, with all my enthusiasm – and for this revolution I'm ready to shed the last drop of my blood....

MIGUEL D'ESCOTO

As much a product of North American progressivism as Latin American revolutionism, D'Escoto was born in Hollywood, CA on February 5, 1933, the son of well-off Nicaraguans. The family returned to Nicaragua shortly after, and Miguel was educated at the La Salle institutes in Diriamba and Managua. He returned to the U.S. for college at St. Mary's in Moraga, CA and at Manhattan College in New York City. After studying Greek at Scranton, he received a licentiate in philosophy and entered the Maryknoll novitiate in 1956. By 1961 he had received degrees in theology from Maryknoll and in education from the State University of New York.

D'Escoto then worked as a journalist and political economist at Columbia University, and following his ordination in 1962 at Maryknoll's Department of Social Communications. He was appointed its director from 1970 to 1979 and helped found Maryknoll's Orbis Books. From 1963 to 1969 he worked in the barrios of Santiago, Chile. Back in Nicaragua, he launched the Foundation for Integral Community Development in Léon in 1979. With the Sandinista revolution, he was named foreign minister of Nicaragua in July 1979 and joined the Sandinista Assembly in September 1980.

The following selection is taken from Cabestrero, *Ministers,* pp. 96-97, 100-101, 109-13, 117, 126.

345. Miguel d'Escoto, Power as Cross

...I'd been born in the United States. My father had quite a life story. When his father died, he was taken on as a page in the household of Archbishop Pereira y Castellon, in Managua. My father was a seminarian then. But he left the seminary, at the age of seventeen, and went to study in the U.S.A. He even acted in the movies. Then he met my mother. They got married, I came along, and they took me to Nicaragua. I was just over a year old. We got there just days after Sandino was killed, in 1934. My father entered the diplomatic corps under Somoza.

But anyway, back in the United States, I began to live a lonely life, far from home. I was at Saint Mary's in Berkeley, which was a Christian Brothers school. I was an angry young man. I was angry at my country's predicament. I remember one time I was talking with Brother Edward, who was the dorm prefect. I was telling him about the situation in my country. And I told him, "I hate the rich."

And Brother Edward said, "I'm sure you don't hate them. You couldn't hate anybody."

"What are you saying that for? "I replied. "I do too hate them!"

And he asked me, "Do you want something bad to happen to them? Do you wish evil on them?"

"I wish they wouldn't be the way they are."

"Ah, then you're using the wrong word. You don't hate them."

This made me realize that what I really wanted was for the rich to change, not that something bad would happen to them. I just wanted those in misery to stop suffering, and I thought this would happen if the rich changed. I couldn't ever wish any evil on anybody....

Here I should say that the person who had the most impact on my life at that time, by his way of living his Christianity, was Martin Luther King, Jr. I carried a little picture of him with me. There were photos of him on the walls of my room. I looked at Martin Luther King as a very special human being – someone very consistent. I'd taken steps to get him to visit Chile before I came back to the United States, and he'd accepted, but he didn't make it. He was killed. I always thought of Martin Luther King as a kind of reproach to myself, because I was so afraid to follow in his footsteps. I looked on him as a guide, as a standard. And yet at the same time I tried to excuse my mediocrity by saying that he was one of those special persons, persons whom God had made different – not me, I was afraid. Then one day I came to the conviction that this wasn't really the way it was. No, we were all equal – and by the grace of God we could overcome any situation, any fear.

Reflections such as these had led me to the prayer: "Lord, help me understand the mystery of your cross. Help me love your cross. Give me the strength I need to accept and embrace it always." This was the beginning of the stage in my spiritual life in which the cross, and reflection on the cross, became the main thing for me. Before, the cross was something I felt sad about. And logically, if you think about it enough, what you're going to do is cry. But all of a sudden it changed into something different. The cross transformed itself into a cradle. One symbol of the cross is the lily – the Easter flower. I entered into a dialectical process in which cross and resurrection are altogether inseparable. Cross *is* resurrection....

When you identify with those who suffer, you take the risk of reprisals. *This* is the cross....

What was asked of me in this struggle was something altogether compatible and consistent with my vocation. I was to make known what Nicaraguans were going through, why they were struggling, and why they had considered themselves obliged to take up armed struggle – because there was no other way out of the armed violence of the repressive Somoza dictatorship.

My initial mission was twofold. My comrades told me, "Miguel, we're getting ready for an insurrection, and then the revolution. We want to create a new, democratic society of brothers and sisters." You could have knocked me over with a feather! My fellow freedom fighters had exactly the same concept of what Nicaragua was crying for as I did. They knew the work I was already doing. And now they were asking me to work in their international mission and to help form a new government. All this seemed to me to be a service that was completely consistent with the duties of anyone who, besides being a Nicaraguan, pursued a mission that included being a builder of peace – which requires that one also build justice, because there's no peace without justice – and building justice included defusing the time bomb of a situation of chronic, deep injustice afflicting our people and capable of exploding at any moment....

You see – how shall I put it...? For me the whole war was a great Eucharist, because, in all my comrades there was this disposition to give all, to give their lives. It wasn't just one person ready to give up his or her life for all the others. Every one of us had to be ready for death. Every one of us knew that death could come at any moment....

...Never before had I seen a situation where a whole country so clearly needed the church to try to influence the hearts of its members and incline them toward the gospel, so that the people would be equal to the demands of this unique stage in its history. What Nicaraguans are trying to do, of course, is create a genuine society of sisters and brothers. And I kept thinking: the atmosphere is right, the soil is right, we've got this determination to make our revolution succeed – but we always have to fight selfishness, and this is the essential moral ministry of the church, its basic ethical task....

As a human being, as a Nicaraguan, as a Christian, and as a priest, I have to react in view of the de facto situations in which my life places me. In my opinion, there is no real contradiction between my priestly ministry and my complementary ministries in service to the people – though in the mind of someone else, who might happen to be my superior at the moment, such a contradiction might seem to exist. But I'm always going to be obedient.

On the other hand, I'll never betray my conscience out of false obedience. And I have a clear awareness that loyalty to the people, especially to the most oppressed and marginalized and historically exploited of my people, has to be the concrete form my fidelity to Christ will take.

I don't think there's any doubt, then, what my response would be in case I were called on to do something that I'd consider a betrayal of the people. My response will be (and God grant that it may be this): to be able to embrace the cross in whatever form I'm asked to accept it....

CENTRAL AMERICA: EL SALVADOR

Like Nicaragua's, the recent history of El Salvador has been very much part of the conscious political life of the United States in the 1980s and 1990s. With a population of 5.7 million, and a per-capita GDP of $1060 in 1992, one might be led to expect a better life in that country than in many parts of Latin America. Yet such "development" statistics are very much part of the problem of perceiving life in Central America. In

1979 fourteen families in El Salvador controlled 90% of this wealth, 2% owned 58% of the arable land, 90% of the peasants had no land at all, and the average monthly income of 50% of the population was $12.

Little has changed since. In 1992 literacy was 75% after twenty year of "reform"; yet infant mortality remained at 41/1000 as opposed to 7/1000 in France or 9/1000 for the United States; life expectancy was 64 years and 75.5 in the USA; and there was 1 physician per 1,322 persons, as opposed to 1 to 381 in the USA.

As the tide of revolution and liberation began to sweep over Central America in the 1970s, and the teachings of Medellín and the efforts of CELAM began to have an effect on the organization of small farmers and city dwellers into base Christian communities, in union organizing and in human-rights campaigns, the ruling elite stepped up its campaign of oppression. They used as their model the ideology of the National Security State and of clandestine repression. El Salvador made the words "death squad" a daily occurrence around the world as extreme right-wing groups, with the covert support of the government and through them of the United States government, applied terror tactics against churchpeople, union members, and suspected leftists. By the end of the decade resistance had become organized and violent, as El Salvador became an ideological and physical battleground between the United States and its opponents in Latin America. Yet those who suffered and died were almost solely the poor of El Salvador. By the time the civil war had ended in January 1992, at least 75,000 people had died, 600,000 were exiles, and 500,000 were refugees within the country; while the U.S. government had spent $1.5 million a day to fund the killing.

OSCAR ROMERO

Oscar Romero was born in the mountain village of Ciudad Barrios in the southern region of San Miguel in 1917, the son of a local postmaster and a family of small coffee planters. He was brought up in a conventional Catholic piety and apprenticed to a carpenter when young. In 1937 he entered the seminary and was sent to Rome for theological studies. Ordained there in 1942, he returned to El Salvador in 1943. As a priest he fostered a simple, fervent spirituality centered around the imitation of Christ. In the 1960s he rose gradually through the hierarchy and in 1970 was ordained a bishop. At first he was attracted to the message of Vatican II and Medellín, but by the 1970s, as editor of *Orientación*, Romero had turned fully against the new liberation theology and activist priests of Central America, attacking the Jesuits for their Medellín ideas and shifting away from the social implications of the Gospel. He generally supported the status quo and the conservatives in the church and in the country's ruling elite.

As late as 1976 he continued to attack Peace and Justice activities, conscientization programs, and "Marxist" priests, even while admitting that the military used repressive means and maintained a cruel social system. In February 1977, however, the elderly Archbishop Chavez y Gonzalez of San Salvador stepped down from his post. In the past few years he had energetically mobilized the clergy of the archdiocese, the center of the country's population, around the commitments of Vatican II and Medellín, encouraging the basic Christian communities, worker priests, and the progress of peace and justice. Oscar Romero's choice as his successor initially came as a great disappointment to his clergy and concerned laity. Events, however, would soon bring drastic changes throughout El Salvador and to Archbishop Romero. In February 1977 General Carlos Humberto Romero was also elected El Salvador's president in a fraudulent campaign. The election spurred mass protests that ended in the government's "Monday Massacre" of over one hundred protesters in San Salvador's main plaza. Even before his installation Romero found himself consulting with his activist clergy and finally coming out with pointed denunciations of government repression and violations of human rights. By the time of his first formal meeting with his diocesan clergy, Archbishop Romero had turned against El Salvador's ruling class with disgust.

He and the church could not do so with impunity, however. Several days later, Romero's dear friend and mentor, Rutilio Grande S.J., a worker priest and organizer in the countryside around Aguilares, was murdered by a death squad. By March 1977 Romero had begun speaking out against the violence and oppression of the government. He refused to participate in government events and declared that the church was being persecuted for its adherence to Vatican II and Medellín. Despite the opposition of the papal nuncio, a close ally of the ruling families, and of conservative colleagues in the El Salvador's Bishops' Conference, Romero forged a solid alliance with progressive clergy and with the hundreds of thousands of Salvadoran campesinos who attended protest masses, listened to his sermons on YSAX, the diocesan radio, and continued to work in basic Christian communities. He repeatedly wrote and traveled to Rome and received continued support from popes Paul VI and John Paul II.

In response to church criticisms the government used a variety of tactics reminiscent of the Nazis in the 1930s: attacks on the orthodoxy of the schools, accusations of Marxist infiltration and the teaching of hate there, attacks on individual priests, campesinos, and basic Christian communities, assassinations by death squads, expulsion of foreign missionaries, and the organization of pseudo-Catholic groups like the "Association of Catholic Women" and the "Followers of Christ," that were, in reality, thinly disguised fronts for government death squads. Threats to kill all the Jesuits in the country or the distribution of handbills urging Salvadorans to "Be a Patriot: Kill a Priest" were typical.

Romero kept up his criticisms of the government through a series of nationally broadcast pastoral addresses and through his weekly Sunday homilies, some of which are excerpted below. The government's response to the church's increased campaign for nonviolent change was stupefying. The incident of Aquilares is typical of what was then happening all over Central and Latin America. On May 17, 1977, the same day that the bishops had joined Romero in condemning the violence and exploitation of the country, 2,000 soldiers backed by planes, helicopters, and tanks surrounded the small town just north of the capital in what the government obscenely dubbed "Operation Rutilio" after the slain Jesuit. In a sudden raid troops armed with machine guns slaughtered between 350 and 400 unarmed farm workers and arrested hundreds more over the next eight days. Three foreign Jesuits were arrested, tortured, and expelled from the country for the crime of union organizing. When the archbishop arrived the next day to remove the sacrament, the soldiers were using the church as a barracks and refused him entry. Calling on the president, Romero condemned "these unspeakable outrages on the part of a security force in a country that we call civilized and Christian." From that point on the archbishop broke openly with the government and ruling class of El Salvador.

By the end of 1977 Romero had boycotted the inauguration of Gen. Romero, had publicly called for disobedience to the Law of Public Order, the basic martial-law statute, and had condemned the country's Supreme Court and judiciary for corruption and cowardice. By 1978 he had brought worldwide attention to El Salvador's torment and had gained international support. He had journeyed to Puebla and there met with bishops Proaño, Mendez-Arceo, Lorsheider, Camara and other proponents of nonviolent change. In November 1978 he was nominated for the Nobel Peace Prize.

By May 23, 1979 and the declaration of a state of siege followed by a massacre of protesters outside the cathedral, the archbishop condemned both the government and acts of terrorism. He was subjected now both to physical searches by the government as a publicly-accused subversive and to condemnations of accommodation by the underground. The last few months of the archbishop's life saw the bloody repression of a January march by 100,000 in commemoration of the 1932 peasants' uprising, increased assassinations on both sides, and the intensification of the guerrilla campaign. Despite repeated death threats now leveled against him, attacks on friends, and the bombing of his radio YSAX, Romero continued his call for peace and justice.

Finally on March 23, 1980 the archbishop shocked the nation with an impassioned plea for the end of violence. The former pillar of the established order climaxed his sermon by calling on El Salvador's army to lay down its arms and stop the repression of the Salvadoran people.

The next day, the archbishop was saying mass in the chapel of the Carmelite hospital. As he raised the chalice for the consecration, an unknown assassin shot him from behind. In a few minutes Oscar Romero was dead. The next week millions around the world watched on television as government-incited violence rocked the archbishop's funeral. U.S. government sources and the Salvadoran judge named to investigate the assassination, who has since fled to Costa Rica for his life, put the blame squarely with Operation Piña, planned and authorized by Gen. José Alberto Medrano and Major Roberto D'Aubuisson, then head of El Salvador's ARENA Party.

These texts are taken from James R. Brockman, SJ, *The Word Remains: A Life of Oscar Romero*, Maryknoll, NY: Orbis Books, 1982, pp. 201-23.

346. Oscar Romero, Final Sermons and Homilies

Sunday, January 27, 1980

As pastor and as a Salvadoran citizen, I am deeply grieved that the organized sector of our people continues to be massacred merely for taking to the street in orderly fashion to petition for justice and liberty [the San Salvador massacre of January 22, 1980 in front of the cathedral]. I am sure that so much blood and so much pain caused to the families of so many victims will not be in vain. It is blood and pain that will water and make fertile new and continually more numerous seeds – Salvadorans who will awaken to the responsibility they have to build a more just and human society – and that will bear fruit in the accomplishment of the daring, urgent, and radical structural reforms that our nation needs. The cry for liberation of this people is a shout that rises up to God and that nothing and no one can now stop.

When some fall in the struggle, provided it be with sincere love for the people and in search of a true liberation, we should consider them always present among us – not only because they stay in the memory of those who continue their struggles, but also because the transcendence of our faith teaches us that the destruction of the body does not end human life. Rather, we hope that by the mercy of God it is after death that we humans will achieve the full and absolute liberation. Temporal liberations will always have to be imperfect and transitory. They are valid and are worth struggling for only insofar as they reflect on this earth the justice of the kingdom of God....

In response to the violence of the armed forces, I must recall their duty to be at the service of the people and not of the privileges of a few.... In response to this intransigent violence of the right, I repeat once more the severe admonition of the church, when it declares them guilty of the anger and despair of the people. They are the real germ and the real peril of the Communism that they hypocritically denounce....

To the government junta, I must say with my people that it is urgent to show by ending the repression that it is able to control the security forces, which at present seem to be a parallel government that is doing great harm to the junta. Each day that passes, marked by the security forces' repression, is a further weakening of the government and a new frustration for the people....

[The Church] expects of you, the organized, to be reasonable political forces for the common good of the people. Making the revolution is not killing other persons, because only God is the master of life. Making the revolution is not painting slogans on walls or shouting in the streets without thinking. Making the revolution is thinking out political designs that better build a people of justice and brotherhood....

Chapter 6: The Third World and Liberation

Sunday, February 24, 1980

...If they [El Salvador's ruling elite] don't want to listen to me, let them at least listen to the voice of Pope John Paul II, who this very week, at the beginning of Lent, exhorted the Catholics of the world to give up superfluous wealth in order to help the needy as a sign of Lenten penance.... The pope said that the church's concern is not only that there be a fairer sharing of wealth, but that this sharing be because people have an attitude of wanting to share not only possessions but life itself with those who are disadvantaged in our society. This is beautiful. Social justice is not just a law that orders to share. Seen in a Christian manner, it is an internal attitude like that of Christ, who, being rich, became poor so as to be able to share his love with the poor. I hope that this call of the church will not further harden the hearts of the oligarchs but will move them to conversion. Let them share what they are and have. Let them not keep silencing with violence the voice of those of us who offer this invitation. Let them not keep killing those of us who are trying to achieve a more just sharing of the power and wealth of our country. I speak in the first person, because this week I received notice that I am on the list of those who are to be eliminated next week. But let it be known that no one can any longer kill the voice of justice....

Sunday, March 16, 1980

...How much we need here in El Salvador to meditate a little on this parable of the prodigal son.... The denouncements of the left against the right and the hatred of the right for the left appear irreconcilable, and those in the middle say, wherever the violence comes from, be tough on them both. And thus we live in groups, polarized, and perhaps even those of the same group don't love each other, because there can be no love at all where people take sides to the point of hating others. We need to burst these dikes, we need to feel that there is a Father who loves us all and awaits us all. We need to learn to pray the Our Father and tell him: "forgive us as we forgive."

You [the elite] are the principal protagonists in this hour of change. On you depends in great part the end of the violence.... If you realize that you are possessing the land that belongs to all Salvadorans, be reconciled with God and with fellow humans, yielding with pleasure what will be for the peace of the people and the peace of your own consciences....

[To the government]: I see two sectors: those who have goodwill but cannot do what they want, and those stubborn and powerful ones who are responsible for the repression. To the first I say: make your power felt or confess that you cannot command and unmask those who are doing great harm to the country. And to those who are in power and do not want to cooperate with the reform and instead are hindering it by the repression that they foment, I say: do not be an obstacle – at so historic a moment for the nation you are performing a sad role of betrayal....

[To the Coordinating Commission]: You are a hope if you continue to mature in your opening and in your dialog.

[To the guerrilla groups]: Someone criticized me as if I wanted to lump together in one sector the popular forces and the guerrilla groups. My mind is always clear about the difference. To them, and to those who advocate violent solutions, I want to call to understanding. Nothing violent can be lasting. There are still human perspectives of reasonable solutions. And above all there is the Word of God, which has cried to us today: reconciliation! God wills it – let us be reconciled, and we shall make of El Salvador a land of brothers and sisters, all children of one Father who awaits us all with outstretched arms....

Sunday, March 23, 1980

...I know that many are scandalized at this word [of the Gospels] and want to accuse it of forsaking the preaching of the gospel to meddle in politics. I do not accept that accusation. I make an effort for us not merely to have on paper all that Vatican Council II and the meetings at Medellín and Puebla have tried to further, but to translate it, preaching the gospel as it should be preached for our people in this conflict-ridden reality. I ask the Lord during the week, while I receive the cries of the people and the sorrow of so much crime, the disgrace of so much violence, to give me the fitting word to console, to denounce, to call to repentance. And though I continue to be a voice that cries in the desert, I know that the church is making the effort to fulfill its mission....

We run the risk of wanting to get out of pressing situations with quick solutions and we forget that the quick solutions can be patches but not true solutions. The true solution must fit into God's definitive plan. Every solution that we want to give to a better distribution of land, to a better administration of money in El Salvador, to a political organization

668

fitted to the common good of Salvadorans, will have to be sought always in the totality of the definitive liberation....

There can be quick liberations, but only those of faith can bring about definitive, solid liberations.... If I had the time at this point, I might make an analysis of these months of a new government that meant to get us out of this horrible environment. If it intends to behead the people's organization and block the political development that the people want, no other program can succeed. Without roots in the people, no government can avail, much less so when it wants to impose its program through bloodshed and sorrow.

I would like to make an appeal in a special way to the men of the army, and in particular to the ranks of the Guardia Nacional, of the police, to those in the barracks. Brothers, you are part of our own people. You kill your own campesino brothers and sisters. And before an order to kill that a man may give, the law of God must prevail that says: "Thou shalt not kill!" No soldier is obliged to obey an order against the law of God. No one has to fulfill an immoral law. It is time to recover your consciences and to obey your consciences rather than the orders of sin. The church, defender of the rights of God, of the law of God, of human dignity, the dignity of the person, cannot remain silent before such abomination. We want the government to take seriously that reforms are worth nothing when they come about stained with so much blood. In the name of God, and in the name of this suffering people whose laments rise to heaven each day more tumultuous, I beg you, I ask you, I order you in the name of God: Stop the repression!... Thou shalt not kill!... Stop the repression!...

The church preaches its liberation just as we have studied it today in the Holy Bible – a liberation that has above all, respect for the dignity of the person, the saving of the common good of the people, and a transcendence that looks before all to God, and from God derives its hope and its force.

From an interview with José Calderón Salazar, Guatemalan correspondent of the Mexican newspaper *Excelsior,* March 1980

I have often been threatened with death. Nevertheless, as a Christian, I do not believe in death without resurrection. If they kill me, I shall arise in the Salvadoran people. I say so without meaning to boast, with the greatest humility.

As pastor, I am obliged by divine mandate to give my life for those I love – for all Salvadorans, even for those who may be going to kill me. If the threats come to be fulfilled, from this moment I offer my blood to God for the redemption and for the resurrection of El Salvador.

Martyrdom is a grace of God that I do not believe I deserve. But if God accepts the sacrifice of my life, let my blood be a seed of freedom and the sign that hope will soon be reality. Let my death, if it is accepted by God, be for the liberation of my people and as a witness of hope in the future.

You may say, if they succeed in killing me, that I pardon and bless those who do it. Would that thus they might be convinced that they will waste their time. A bishop will die, but the church of God, which is the people will never perish....

THE WOMEN MARTYRS OF EL SALVADOR

On December 4, 1980, U.S. Ambassador to El Salvador Robert E. White was informed that the bodies of what were believed to be four American women had been found buried near a small village in the countryside. Two days before they had been forced out of their van by Salvadoran soldiers acting under direct order, stripped and raped, shot in the head and then thrown into a ditch. The ambassador could hardly believe his eyes as he witnessed the gruesome exhumation, for the four women had just days before been dinner guests of his and his wife's at the U.S. chancellery in San Salvador.

Ita Ford (April 23, 1940-Dec. 2, 1980) and Maura Clarke (Jan. 13, 1931-Dec. 2, 1980) both Maryknoll Sisters, Dorothy Kazel (June 30, 1939-Dec. 2, 1980), an Ursuline, and Jean Donovan (April 10, 1953-Dec. 2, 1980), a lay volunteer, were four American churchwomen who had been doing missionary work in El Salvador in the late 1970s. Yet their life became increasingly difficult and dangerous in the midst of El Salvador's repression and the guerrilla war that was fast approaching; for the women missionaries worked in areas that protected the guerrillas, they did things that the campesinos dared not: bury the victims of death squads, visit the homes of grieving relatives, aid in the work of organizing unions, agricultural cooperatives, and base Christian communities, seeking and obtaining the release of suspects detained by the police and military. As they saw their neighbors, and then their friends slain one after another, they carried on their work convinced that the church was the one agent for nonviolent change left in a country quickly being swallowed by the devil.

Jean Donovan's life illustrates the passage from North American affluence to martyrdom in Central America. She was born in Westport, CT in 1953, into comfortable Irish-Catholic family. Her father was an executive for United Technologies, and part of the team that built the Huey helicopter, the archetypal symbol of the Vietnam War for a generation of Americans. After taking a bachelor's degree from Mary Washington College in Fredricksburg, VA – a college chosen largely based on her love of horseback riding – Jean Donovan went on to take a masters degree in economics from Case Western Reserve University.

In an era when many of her contemporaries were "dropping out" or organizing protest against the Vietnam War, Donovan went on to take a high-paying job for the Cleveland office of Arthur Anderson, the large accounting firm. Yet already as a college student she had been disconcerted by an encounter with the Third World, ironically during a stay in Ireland. There her suburban attitudes and tastes clashed repeatedly with the simple and frugal ways of her neighbors; and there she was to meet the missionary priest Michael Crowley, who had recently concluded ten years of work in Trujillo, Peru. She also befriended Maura Corkery, a member of the Cork Legion of Mary, which was active in social programs for the poor and elderly. The experience challenged the North American student both materially and spiritually.

By the end of 1977 Donovan had experienced some sort of conversion – whether aided by an unhappy romance, or by a realization that her professional life left something to be desired – and after visiting Crowley in Ireland, eventually decided to go to El Salvador as a lay missionary. The Cleveland archdiocese agreed to her request on the condition that she take training at Maryknoll, New York. By the spring of 1979 she had left her former life and had joined the work in El Salvador.

The following selections are taken from Ana Carrigan, *Salvador Witness: The Life and Calling of Jean Donovan,* New York: Ballantine Books, 1984, pp. 161-87.

347. Jean Donovan, Diary

April 26, 1980: Eleven-fifteen PM. Barrio La Cruz. Army trucks and civilians decapitated catechist Elizio Diaz, twenty-four years, Miguel

Hernandez, thirty years old. Teresita Mejia, fifteen years old. Cut off the feet of Antonio Hernandez, nineteen years old, Teodorio Hernandez, twenty-six years old, and killed beyond identification two others.

April 28: In the early morning in San Martin, armed civilians with military equipment destroyed the altar, violated the tabernacle, and destroyed the house of the pastor.

May 1: One AM in the morning. Rosario de Mora Church and Convent both destroyed.

May 17: Eleven Thirty, San José Villa Nueva. The Guardia Nacional captured and held Sister Teresa Barrios until six PM when [Monsignor, vicar-general of the archdiocese] Uriosti obtained her release. Stole money from Church building.

May 20: Nine fifty-five PM. San Salvador. Attempt to blow up Radio YPAX (Archdiocescan radio station]
Ilopango, Parroquia San Lucia. Attack on the Church.
Citala, Chalatenango. Community of nuns was threatened to leave.

May 22: Three people killed in Santa Cruz – Pastors and Julio – two of the *juvenes* that helped me in the celebrations.

June 7: Four men entered the church of San Pedro Nonualco, Diocese of San Vincente, and assassinated Padre Cosme Spezzatto, a Franciscan [from Italy], while he was praying.

June 12: In the evening, soldiers raid the Sisters of the Sagrado Corazón School – destroying the door and rip up pictures of Monsignor [Oscar] Romero.

June 13: In the evening soldiers break into the Instituto Secula de Lacamel – a community of religious lay people.

June 20: In the evening, at the High School Sagrada Familia, more than 100 soldiers circled the school. Said they were looking for arms, medical clinics, and fugitives. Ripped up pictures of Monsignor Romero. Took copies of *Orientación* [the archdiocescan newspaper] because they were dangerous. Captured one religious sister and 5 employees.

June 21: The Guardia and one ex-member of the FPL [a guerrilla group] accused the Church of helping import arms – Jesuits especially –

and said P. de Sebastian, de Monchi, Hernandez, are part of Fuerzas Populares de Liberación.

June 22: Two men killed bus driver in Tamonique. Dorothy [Kazel], Paul [Schindler, OMM] and I go to bless bodies. Pass by armed drunk camp of ORDEN [Salvadoran security forces]. Other organizer killed. Two shots fired in cemetery. Leave quickly.

July 6: Three men, one with a pistol, shot the sacristan and another young man – Armando Avelae [Jean's best friend] and Carlos Hernandez [Paul Schindler's adopted son] – both in the head at 10:30 PM in the evening in front of the Parochial School [and Jean Donovan's home] in Puerto de la Libertad.

From a Letter to Fr. Michael Crowley, Summer 1980

Chalatenango is absolutely civil war at the moment. They've got bodies lying all over – no one can bury them because they get shot at if they try. Some nuns were up there. ORDEN just really turned on the nuns. They got a message to leave in six days or you're going to be killed, and they burned their jeep to prove it. So they believed it, and left. People don't have liberty to do anything. They have to take a side. And it's very hard not to take a particular side. It's so much harder to fight for your liberty in a nonviolent way than it is with a gun. It's funny – people very close to me have been killed now, and yet I still think that. So I'm starting to think maybe I really do believe it. At the moment, the only nonviolent voice in the whole country is the Church, and I think they have to remain in a neutral position....

The Jesuit Martyrs of El Salvador

On November 16, 1989, Salvadoran troops entered the University of Central America in San Salvador, burst into the Jesuit residence and massacred six priests, their housekeeper and her daughter. The murders of Joaquin López y López (1918-1989), Ignacio Ellacuría (1930-1989), Juan Ramón Moreno (1933-1989), Segundo Montes (1933-1989), Amando López (1936-1989), Ignacio Martín-Baró (1942-1989), Elba Ramos (1947-1989), and Celina Ramos (1973-1989) revealed the lengths to which the Salvadoran oligarchy was prepared to go – with the support of the Reagan administration – to suppress any form of dissent in El Salvador, and how the church in that country had ultimately come to fully endorse the call of liberation theology to end the oppression of the poor and the marginalized.

IGNACIO ELLACURÍA

Ignacio Ellacuría was probably the best known of the slain Jesuits. He was born in Spain, entered the Jesuits in 1947, was ordained a priest in 1961, and earned a Ph.D. in philosophy in 1967 from the University of Madrid. During his Jesuit training he first traveled to El Salvador in 1955 where he lectured, taught, and wrote for *Estudios Cetroamericanos* until 1958, when he went to Innsbruck for further study in theology.

Soon after his return from Europe in 1967 Ellacuría had become Central America's leading liberation theologian. His works focus not only on traditional theological topics, such as Christology, but in *Estudios Centroamericanos* he also addressed issues of war and peace, poverty and wealth within El Salvador, making him one of the oligarchy's most hated enemies. As rector of the National University, he made the school a leading agent for change in the country, not only attacking the excesses of the elite but also distancing himself and his school from the Marxism of the violent revolutionaries. By the late 1980s Ellacuría had taken a leading role in attempting to bring the warring sides together for peace talks and other exchanges. As his influence grew, so did the strength of his enemies. With the election of ARENA party leader Alfredo Cristiani as president in 1989, the guerrillas launched a new offensive that November that brought harsh government reaction, including the massacre of Ellacuría and his companions on November 16.

In the following passage Ellacuría raises a central point for all Christians: if we do not reject all violence, or at least any notion of just war, then how can we counter these very cogent arguments for just revolution. If violence waged in the name of revolution disturbs us, why then does not violence carried out in the name of the nation-state or of economic and political interests not cause us the same revulsion?

These excerpts are selected from Ignacio Ellacuría, *Freedom Made Flesh: The Mission of Christ and His Church,* John Drury, trans., Maryknoll, NY: Orbis Books, 1976, pp. 217-31.

Chapter 6: The Third World and Liberation

348. Ignacio Ellacuría, The Christian Redemption of Violence

Christian Approaches to the Redemption of Violence

Theological reflection should not offer a book of ready-made recipes or practical techniques. It is not for me to define here the concrete means that are to be used in combating and rooting out the sin of violence. But I do think it is proper to point out different Christian styles and approaches to the whole task of redeeming violence. Christianity is pluralistic, and it respects the differences that mark people's individual vocations. At this point, however, I think it would be useful to consider three different styles and approaches that have been used by Christians in trying to solve the conflict raised by violence. All three have been more practical than theoretical in nature.

Charles de Foucauld

The first approach rejects not only all violence, understood in the context of injustice, but also all use of physical force to achieve the gospel's objectives of peace and love among human beings. This approach is exemplified by Charles de Foucauld and the Little Brothers of the Gospel, the group which he established. They go out to live with the victims of violence, but not to fight on their behalf. Their aim is to bear witness to peace and universal love, to serve as the leaven in the dough and the condensation of those values that should be present in any Christian commitment.

According to René Voillaume, three great realities underlie the attitude of the Little Brothers: (1) the immortality of man, who is a spiritual being waiting for the definitive establishment of a new order in and through Christ's resurrection; (2) the violent and sorrow-filled nature of man's brief existence; (3) the reality of universal love. This outlook should not be viewed as a dreamy disembodied idealism. It should be seen as the pursuit of an ideal of love which looks beyond this world towards the living, resurrected Christ, but which does not cease to be faithful to the human condition and its limitations.

Holding this outlook, what is one to do in the face of violence? The temptation is to repel force with force, but Charles de Foucauld chose another approach instead of active forceful resistance to violating force. He chose the silent witness of kindness, humility, and peace; one does not defend himself but rather hands himself over to death meekly for the

675

sake of those whom he loves. Violence will not disappear from the world until its roots are eliminated, and the witness of Christ is directed against the roots of violence. In the face of the desire to possess wealth, he preaches poverty. Against the concupiscence of power, he preaches humility. In the face of hatred, he preaches kindness. Over against the strict rigor of an all too human justice, he proposes mercy and respect for the most lowly....

Martin Luther King, Jr.

There is a second Christian approach to the whole problem of violence. It is alluded to in *Gaudium et Spes:* "Motivated by this same spirit, we cannot fail to praise those who renounce the use of violence in the vindication of their rights and who resort to methods of defense which are otherwise available to weaker parties too, provided that this can be done without injury to the rights and duties of others or of the community itself" (§78). The martyred Martin Luther King, Jr., stands as an admirable example of what this approach can achieve in theory and in practice. Here it will suffice to summarize the Christian interpretation that he himself put on his overall attitude towards violence.

He tells us that we must move from passive conformity to direct action, but without falling into the snares of hatred and vengefulness. Effective action of nonviolent character lies between two extremes. One extreme is exemplified by those who are content with "tokenism," who for the most part let things go on as usual. The other extreme is represented by those who launch into action of a violent and uncontrolled nature.

Nonviolent action is born of two very powerful forces: the absolute and total rejection of injustice committed against human beings, and a love that impels one towards the construction of a new society. It transforms hatred into a constructive force. The process of Christian interpretation helps us to see that the real enemy is not another human being but the system that has made individuals evil. These individuals are the oppressors, who must be liberated from their active oppression. By dramatizing the injustice in a social context, one obliges consciences to face up to the injustice that is there. The oppressor is forced to recognize his injustice in an explicit and public way. The repression he uses to stifle nonviolent action makes clear his usual pattern of conduct, and nonviolent resistance reveals his own moral inferiority....

Chapter 6: The Third World and Liberation

Camilo Torres

A third approach has arisen from the Christian's painful experience of violence. Its most startling representative may well be Camilo Torres, the Colombian priest who died as a guerrilla fighter. Father Regamey has noted that the worst commitment that can be forced on the Christian is to see oneself forced to choose violence, and that was the case with Camilo Torres. A staunch proponent of nonviolence himself, Father Regamey does not rule out the possibility that such an approach may not only be heroic but also holy. But he goes on to say that there is a terrible temptation to establish this as the rule for our time.

Camilo Torres was motivated by two fundamental "passions": a passion for justice and a passion for charity. These two passions were fleshed out in the real-life situation of the people of Colombia. They did not allow him to stay on the sidelines, to evade any sort of activity that was necessary to change the structures that had led the people into such dire straits. To stay on the sidelines would be to betray Christianity and his own personal vocation. The guiding principle behind his outlook and activity was clear to him: When existing circumstances prevent people from giving themselves to Christ, it is part of the proper function of a priest to combat those circumstances. Torres had opted for Christianity because he saw it as the purest form of rendering service to others. His analysis of the situation of Colombian society forced him to conclude that a revolution was necessary, that the revolutionary struggle was a Christian and priestly struggle. Given the real circumstances, the love that people were supposed to show to their neighbors could only be fleshed out in and through the revolutionary struggle. So he felt compelled to commit himself to that struggle as a way of bringing men to love of God.

His ideas, his character, and the sociological conditions prevailing in his country drove him to specific means of political action, to the setting up of a political front and to dedicated efforts to make the masses more aware of their needs. He thus would help to create an authentic revolutionary spirit through his speeches, his writings, and his demonstrations. Eventually he joined the guerrillas and was slain in an encounter with the army. He did not see any way out of the problem by legal means. The only way left was recourse to arms....

Conclusion

Faced with the extensive and complex problem of violence, I have been forced to simplify and reduce its overall proportions. I have left many problems unconsidered, e. g., war, the existence of armies, the arms race, the use of propaganda at every level, and delinquency. Perhaps the basic perspective offered in these pages may help people to decide what the Christian should say about all these forms of violence which oppress human beings.

I have chosen a focus which may hopefully give us a clearer idea of what violence really is today. It is certainly not intended to provide a trigger for further violence; rather it is meant to be a summons to combat violence. I have discussed at length the reasons why the struggle against real violence should not itself be regarded as violence. No one can honestly say that I am preaching the use of violence to combat violence. And the social dimensions of the perspective presented here should help us to avoid those forms of struggle which are too strictly individualistic or too tainted with vengefulness. Violence is a sin which we all carry within ourselves, and we share responsibility for its objectified forms in societal life and structures. Advertence to these facts should dissuade us from entering the fray against violence for the sake of juvenile sport or mere political advantage.

Studying violence as a social phenomenon – be it revolutionary or counterrevolutionary violence – I began with its biological and psychic roots. Our analysis made it clear that aggressiveness is not only a dimension of nature but also a necessary one for the equilibrium and betterment of both the individual and the species. Hence there can and must be aggressive patterns of behavior. A pattern of conduct is not wrong or evil simply because it is aggressive.

But aggressiveness is also an ambiguous reality, a natural force which is dangerous by its very nature. It is a positive, natural force; but it also includes a truly daemonic element which appears on the scene with the advent of personal rationality. It is from the combination of natural aggressiveness and personal rationality that violence arises as a typically human phenomenon.

On the human level, violence shows up at once as a symptom. It is in and through its symptomatic character that we draw closer to the real meaning and import of violence. Violence is symptomatic of the fact that something is wrong. It is symptomatic in the sense that force is used to maintain the disordered setup, and in the sense that force is used to change and improve the situation. The two uses are clearly opposed to one another, but they both signify that a situation of injustice exists.

The twofold form of violence forces us to look for the element that differentiates violence and makes it what it is. That element is injustice. All injustice is violent, and it is injustice that points up the true gravity of violence. When such injustice is not present, we cannot speak about violence in any strict sense, although we may be able to speak about force, or coercive force, or painful force. Viewed in the context of injustice, violence must always be regarded as sin. It is the sin of violence, intimately bound up with the whole mystery of iniquity, which prevents the establishment of conditions that will allow Christian love and salvific justice to flower.

The Christian response to the sin of violence must take a specific form, i.e., the redemption of violence. This redemption must be understood in Christian terms, but it must also take on flesh and blood in the very realities and at the very levels where the sin of violence itself is present. The biblical message offers us many concepts that will help us to evade the danger of disembodied solutions on the one hand and of excessively politicized solutions on the other hand.

If there is to be a Christian redemption of violence, we must find Christian approaches to that task. In the immediately preceding pages I outlined three such approaches. It may well be that we will have to look for another solution rather than trying to synthesize those three. It is easy enough to orient ourselves in the right direction; it is not so easy to implement our ideas in the concrete. The realm of implementation is strictly political in any case. Operating from a Christian outlook we must denounce every sin of violence unceasingly; but from that outlook we cannot calculate and spell out the concrete means and techniques that are to be used. What ought to be done and the actual doing are two different things; confusing the two could be catastrophic. Keeping the two things clear and distinct must remain a permanent concern of all those who rightfully wish to see the Church taking action vis-a-vis the sin of violence.

The prevailing violence, however, is strictly unjust in character. The injustice of it calls for extreme remedies. Any moral evaluation of these remedies cannot start from the assumption that the situation is normal, that it is not violent. The use of force will always be dangerous. It should be reduced to the minimum so long as we are not faced with a grave injustice. Under normal circumstances, however grave they may be, we ought to avoid any force that coerces, compels, or wounds. But in cases of established violence, whatever form it may take, we may be not only permitted but even required to use the force that is necessary to redeem the established violence. The good being sought does not justify the evil entailed in the means to achieve it. But if evil is an achieved and concrete fact already, it must be reduced and eventually eliminated. The obligation to reduce and eliminate evil compels us to use all those means that will help to reduce evil in the world. But now I am getting into the whole ethics of violence, and my purpose here was simply to provide some basic theological orientation.

That does not mean I am trying to be evasive. The reflections contained in this volume were prompted by reflection on the concrete reality of the world around us, and that of the Third World in particular. They are intended to provide a theoretical framework for concrete Christian action designed to combat the violence of injustice and the sin of violence. This combative action must keep in mind two points of the utmost importance: (1) Not everything in the existing structures is evil, neither as structure nor as personal achievement; (2) the Christian message demands that we move out of the whole schema of violence versus resistance to violence by the use of force as quickly as possible. Why? Because in that struggle, even when viewed simply as a means, there is great danger that we shall lose sight of the very essence of Christianity. It is not just the sin of violence that is against the spirit of the gospel message. Resistance to violence is too, if it is adopted as a definitive attitude or if we allow ourselves to be taken over by its powerful dynamic. Christian redemption does not derive its power from hatred. It must derive its life from love, albeit a difficult love.

Theological reflection on violence tends, of its very nature, to be extremist. It must be complemented and completed by reflection on related themes. But though it may be partial and incomplete, it is still urgent and pressing. The eradication of violence in all its forms is an urgent task that cannot be postponed. But stress must be placed on that form of violence which is protected by legal forms, which entails the permanent establishment of an unjust dis-order, which precludes the conditions required for the human growth of the person, and which therefore gives rise to strong reactions. Our rejection of violence must be absolute. The paradox is that the absolute character of this rejection calls for attitudes and lines of action that cannot help but be extreme.

HAITI: JEAN-BERTRAND ARISTIDE

With a population of 6.5 million in 1995, Haiti had a per-capita GDP of $340, the lowest in the Western Hemisphere. Its average life expectancy is 43 years, its infant mortality 109/1000; it has 1 physician per 6,083 persons (1/20,000 by one estimate) and a literacy rate estimated at anywhere between 39% and 15%. Yet such statistics tell only part of the story; for of its 6.5 million people, 1.5 million live abroad for political and economic reasons. Most urban dwellers earn only $100 a year, and the vast majority of rural dwellers far less than that. AIDS, typhoid and TB are epidemic. Haiti's elite drive their Jaguars and BMWs to Tiffany's and Bonwit Teller in Manhattan, keep chalets in Switzerland, and entertain their friends in the First World's best restaurants and discotheques.

Discovered by Columbus in 1492, along with the Dominican Republic, the Hispaniola of the Spanish Main, it was ravaged and depopulated by the time Bartolomé de Las Casas began his mission there [225-226]. Granted to the French by the Treaty of Ryswick, which ended the War of the League of Augsburg in 1697, it finally revolted against Napoleon in 1804 under former slave Toussaint Louverture, thus becoming the first nation in the Americas after the United States to gain independence. Yet this independence was soon shackled by economic collapse and a virtual embargo by European powers. By the mid-nineteenth century its rulers were puppets of either France or the United States, which actually occupied the country from 1915 to 1934.

In 1957 François Duvalier was elected president, and in 1964 he took the office for life, backing his rule with a reign of terror that ensured the wealth and isolation of the elite and their foreign investors, while keeping the vast majority of the population in abject poverty. He and his son, Jean-Claude Duvalier, were kept in power not only by a military far out of proportion to the nation's size and economic strength, but by the private Duvalier army: the Tontons Macoutes. All opposition was destroyed, including that of the intellectuals, politicians, and union organizers. Fort Dimanche, the dreaded interrogation center in

681

downtown Port-au-Prince, saw thousands enter its gates, never to re-emerge. When death squads shocked the world in Central America, they were long the established practice in Haiti, every morning bringing to light new bodies, new disappearances.

After a series of natural disasters in the late 1970s and 1980s, the economy lay in ruins. When Pope John Paul II visited Haiti in 1983, he came away shocked by the disparity between the wealthy and the vast majority of Haitians. "Things must change" he declared publicly before his departure. His words startled the "Tontons" bishops – the conservative churchmen all appointed under Duvalier influence – and gave encouragement to *Ti Legliz*, the popular church, to stiffen its non-violent resistance to Duvalier. After weeks of unrest, in February 1986, Duvalier fled the country aboard a U.S. Air Force Jet. In 1987 Haitians approved a new constitution; yet 1988 elections were met with massacres at voting places by the Tontons Macoutes and boycotts by the opposition. Finally, in December 1990, Haitians elected as president Jean-Bertrand Aristide, a Salesian priest and worker among the base Christian communities, a vocal leader of the opposition. By September 1991, however, the military under General Raoul Cédras arrested Aristide, expelled him from the country and suppressed the democratically elected government. A reign of terror ensued that saw over 2,000 killed and 35,000 Haitian refugees reach U.S. waters between the Fall of 1991 and 1992, only to be turned back.

With Aristide in exile in the United States, pressure began mounting for a return to civilian government. With the election of the Clinton administration in 1992 and the imposition of a UN embargo the ground was set for an eventual multinational force, led by the U.S., to invade Haiti, restore civilian rule, and disband the Tontons and the army. By October 15, 1994 Aristide – now stripped of his priesthood by the Vatican – had been restored to the presidency. The hold of the new democracy in Haiti was reaffirmed by free elections held in June 1995 that gave a majority to Aristide's supporters.

The struggle of the Haitian people has become inextricably entwined with the life of its president, Jean-Bertrand Aristide. Most of the details of his life have become familiar to many Americans, largely through he publication of his *Autobiography* (with Christophe Wargny, Linda M. Maloney, trans., Maryknoll, NY: Orbis Books, 1993). Born into a family of small landowners in Port-Salut in southwestern Haiti on July 15, 1953, he emigrated to Port-au-Prince with his widow mother two years later. In 1958 he began grammar school with the Salesian Brothers and continued in their schools until his entry into the Salesian seminary at Cap Haïtien in 1966 and classes at the neighboring Notre Dame *lycée*. From an early age Aristide showed a great talent for writing and language, mastering French, Latin, Greek, English, Spanish and Italian, in addition to the native Haitian Creole. Aristide was also open to the flow of ideas springing from Latin America: the liberation theology of Boff, and magical realism of its novelists were among his major influences.

By 1974 he had completed the seminary and traveled to the Dominican Republic for the Salesian novitiate. In 1975 he entered the state university at Port-au-Prince, where he took a degree in psychology in 1979. By the 1970s Aristide was beginning to participate in the anti-Duvalier mood of the university, a spirit aided by the council of Puebla in 1979-80. He was soon sent by his Salesian superiors to Jerusalem for biblical studies. Aristide returned to Port-au-Prince in 1982, where he was ordained a priest. He was then reassigned to complete his psychology studies, this time at the University of Montreal, earning a master's in biblical theology and completing all course work for a doctorate in psychology before his return to Haiti in January 1985. After some negotiating Aristide was appointed master of studies at the National School of Arts and Crafts in Port-au-Prince and assigned to the parish of St. Jean Bosco there. He immediately threw himself into the effort to oust the Duvalier dictatorship.

Aristide's account of the attack on St. Jean Bosco church in September 1988 reads, all too appallingly, like that of Bartolomé de Las Casas' account of a similar massacre in Cuba [224] almost five hundred years before, or like that in the cathedral at Beziers during the Albigensian Crusades almost 800 years before [182]. But the heroic resistance that ensued reminds the reader of St. Ambrose's stand against imperial troops at his basilica in Milan 1600 years before [82]. The survival of the infant Esperancia recalls the passages in Apocalypse 12 describing the salvation of the woman attacked by the dragon.

The following excerpts are taken from Jean-Bertrand Aristide, *In the Parish of the Poor: Writings from Haiti*, Amy Wilentz, trans. and ed., Maryknoll, NY: Orbis Books, 1990, pp. 3-4, 15-17, 23, 35-37, 52-57, 62-69.

683

349. *Jean-Bertrand Aristide, A Letter to My Brothers and Sisters*

…Once, during a time of troubles when my country's government was particularly vicious – when base communities throughout the country were under physical attack and more than two hundred members of a large peasant movement in Jean-Rabel in our northwest province had been massacred – I spoke to the people of these groups, spoke to all my countrymen and countrywomen in the four dark corners of my nation. I spoke Jesus' words then, and now they, too, remind me of [Simon] Bolivar's blade [that liberated South America from the Spanish].

"And he that hath no sword," I quoted, "let him sell his garment, and buy one" [Luke 22:36]. With these words from the Gospels, I was urging my countrymen to defend themselves against the onslaught of the military and the paramilitary forces in Haiti; I was urging them to defend themselves against the diabolical, Machiavellian, satanic forces that were gathering against them, against the forces that were massing to extinguish what few little lights of solidarity we had managed to keep burning over the years.

The government – that is to say, the military and the paramilitary forces – did not take kindly to Jesus' words. The Minister of Information said that I was preaching armed struggle, and the campaign against me and against all those who worked with me, against the ecclesial base communities, against the peasant movements, against the vigilance brigades, and against so many comrades I did not know but who were on our side, grew more vicious, more violent.

More than two hundred had already died, and scores more would be martyred as the movement continued. Like all of you, brothers and sisters, I have lost friends in this long and bitter struggle. The blood of those beloved martyrs only makes the fight more valiant, and the distant goal sweeter. For their sakes, we must not lose sight of the path of liberation that we can cut through the jungle, with solidarity's sword.…

My story, and the story of my struggling Haitian brothers and sisters, is the story of your people, too, brothers and sisters. Listen, and then tell me you do not recognize yourselves, your brethren and – yes – your enemies, too, your evildoers, all of them characters in the story that is my life, that is your lives. All of them living in a land where there is darkness and shadow – but light also.…

The crime of which I stand accused is the crime of preaching food for all men and women. According to the authorities in my country and in Rome, this is tantamount to preaching revolution, war. But what war? I ask.

History has proven that some wars are just. This war I have been accused of advocating is an avoidable war, one that I and all men and women who care for peace and the well-being of our parishioners would wish to avoid. The men eating at the great table could avoid it if they wished to, and merely by the simple fraternal act of sharing: sharing wealth, sharing power, breaking bread with their brothers and sisters. But these men, among them bishops, do not wish for the well-being of their parishioners; they wish rather for their own well-being, and the well-being of those who sit at the great table. They remind me of the Pharisees who make clean the outside of the cup and the platter but their inward part is full of ravening and wickedness [Luke 11:39]. If they do not wish to share fraternally with those whom, before the world, they call brother and sister, then they must accept the fate that they have chosen. They must accept the simple fact that it is they, and not I and my colleagues, who are advocating war....

Let me begin with guns. In Haiti, guns are often at the vortex of current events. Does this sound like your countries, brothers? sisters? I know it does. This is the story of guns. (Notice, as you read, that it is always the wrong men who have the guns. This is one of the lessons that the men with guns taught me.)...

In the north of my country that summer, in July, at a place called Jean-Rabel, a massacre took place. Peasants marching to protest their condition and to demand an end to their exploitation by the ruling class of their region were cut down and slaughtered by the military and the agents of the large landholders there. Hundreds were killed; peasants' houses were looted and burned; the peasant movement was momentarily crushed.

Meanwhile, back in Port-au-Prince, my religious order had decided to move me out of the capital and into a parish filled with people who call themselves my enemies, former members of the Tontons Macoute, generals, the wealthy (the enemies of the Haitian people, in short). I obeyed. Not happily, for I had no wish to leave my people alone to face the repression that was coming. I obeyed because I had vowed to obey, and because to disobey might have brought down an even crueler fate upon my parishioners. So I moved to my new parish. (Such displacements and new assignments are not surprising to you, I am sure, brothers and sisters....)

The youth were worried. A massacre of a movement in the north, and now the displacement of one of their most visible colleagues. They sensed the wave of repression beginning to build against them, and took action to deflect it. Thus, they entered the great cathedral of Port-au-Prince, in all humility, and began a hunger strike before its altar. They called on my religious order and the Haitian bishops to rescind the directive moving me out of the capital, and they called on them to speak out against the massacre that had taken place in Jean-Rabel. After all, it was one of the bishops who, just before the massacre, had said that the peasants of the movement in Jean-Rabel were troublemakers. The Haitian proverb says: "He who says 'There is the serpent,' has killed the serpent."

After many days of starvation, the hunger strike was successful. It ended in a huge burst of joy within the cathedral as first the bishops and then I came to talk to the thousands who had gathered to support the strikers. I was returned to my parish, the bishops spoke out against what had happened at Jean-Rabel. But that was not the end of the story, my story. As I have said, there is always a first time, but never a last. While the hunger strike continued, it was always in the news. Perhaps there were men who were annoyed at hearing my name repeated. Perhaps there were men who did not like to see the youth take matters into their own hands, however peaceably....

The reading for the day [of Sept. 11, 1988, at the Church of St. Jean Bosco in Port-au-Prince] continues: "For whosoever will save his life shall lose it: and whosoever will lose his life for my sake shall find it." The words comforted me. They calmed me. They quieted my fears.

That Sunday, many people had decided to show their respect for the Constitution by wearing white (the color that was worn in March 1987, when the Constitution was approved by a popular vote), and some of my people were wearing white, it is true. But the rest of my people were dressed as they dressed every Sunday to come to my church: in the colors of love, in the colors of faith, in the rainbow colors of courage, in patriotic raiment. The fact that they were there at all, at St. Jean Bosco, on a day that everyone knew would be full of rage, was testimony to their patriotism and courage. They were not there naively, unknowing. They were there to show that they had taken up the cross of Jesus, and that they would carry that cross through a lifetime of menaces and threats.

Chapter 6: The Third World and Liberation

That Sunday, I told them that they did not really need to ask the Lord for his forgiveness for their sins, because the courage that had brought them to this particular church on this particular day had purified them utterly. My people were clothed in robes of crimson and of purple, waiting to be scourged and mocked, and crucified.

And so I said to the congregation: "Let us begin."

And we had just finished reading the Gospel – not more than five minutes had passed – offertory, consecration – when I heard the first cry go up from the street, the first smashing of rocks, a few first shots fired. A wind of panic rose up in the street and was blowing toward us in the church, blowing along the backs of the men who were shouting and throwing rocks, shooting guns. While I was trying to calm the congregation and stop them from hurting one another in the panic, bullets began crisscrossing the church in front of me. One round passed just in front of me and lodged itself in the tabernacle. They missed me and hit the tabernacle. With the microphone in my hand, I was thinking that a pastor must stay and die before, or in the place of, his sheep, and not run and leave them behind. I was wondering how to stop the panic from overwhelming the congregation. And I was wondering whether the power of our solidarity would make our force equal to theirs, whether we would be able to oppose them with a prophetic, evangelical resistance, and stop the panic that was about to disperse us, that was about to let them kill us more quickly, one by one. I shouted to my congregation: "Blessed be the Eternal! Blessed be the Eternal!" And the bullets kept smashing through the church.

People say that ten or twenty people died that day at St. Jean Bosco. The official version is ten to twenty. The exact number depends on your source. But it is the same as the massacre in front of Fort Dimanche: no one will ever be able to say with any certainty how many died that day at St. Jean Bosco. I myself could see them dragging bodies of parishioners out in front of the church in order to load them into cars, while the bullets were still flying through the chancel and the nave, and up and down the aisles, over the heads of my people, and piercing their flesh. The men with red armbands did not always drag the wounded and dead all the way out because there was so much confusion, and many of the injured and dead were left in the church, heaped in a pile, to die later by fire and be among the uncounted martyrs.

Everyone was running, trying to find a place to hide. One man was

shot in the outside courtyard, and collapsed and died in the inner courtyard, with his Bible in his hand. Bullets were zinging left and right. I saw
a pregnant woman screaming for help in the pews, and holding onto her
stomach. A man had just speared her there, and she was bathed in red
blood. Another priest was trying to organize people to give the woman
first aid. I saw an American journalist running up and down the aisle
with torn clothes; the men with red armbands had torn the clothing,
trying to hurt the journalist. A group of young women were in the front
courtyard and were attempting to resist the onslaught, attempting to
resist, with our own kind of arms, the heavy weapons that the men were
using against us from the street – this was a prophetic, historic resistance
that we will never forget.

Our weapon was our solidarity, as we stood together, unified, and
our weapons were rocks, that we used to stop the men from coming over
the top of the courtyard wall and getting into the church to murder us
all. If we had not resisted in this fashion, what happened to us at St. Jean
Bosco would have been a hundred times worse than the election day
massacre in November 1987. Hundreds and hundreds of us would have
died beneath the stick, or of punches and kicks, or speared at the end of
a steel pike, or shot through the head, or cut into pieces with machetes
and knives and daggers – the murderers were ready to do anything and
everything, and the Haitian Army had surrounded the murderers in silence, their guns at their sides, watching as the assassins went about their
business.

This was a great moment that showed pacifists against the bloody-
minded, the people of God against assassins. The criminals – Tonton-
Macoute Duvalierist thugs, paid with a few dollars and a bottle of rum,
and prepared for any act – were looking to spit death into the faces of
those who were fighting for life with no weapons of death in their hands.
During this whole time, as death rained down on us, across from the
church stood the Haitian Army, back behind the church stood Fort
Dimanche and, of course, neither one attempted to stop the killings.
They watched. God have mercy on those who watch evil and do nothing. They are as guilty as the murderer. Often, they are his accomplice.

Yes, this lasted three hours, and meanwhile, what did the Church do,
what help did it give us?

My Salesian superior heard about what was happening, he gathered
up his courage, he crossed through the battle zone and came to the court-

yard of St. Jean Bosco. A valiant man. He came into the midst of the battle and fought to save us, negotiated with the leaders of the criminals, allowed the assassins to humiliate him, offered them drinks, did everything to calm the situation, and bravely worked alongside us to end the killing.

At this same moment, where was the [papal] Nuncio? What was he doing? He was not there. He came late. When he finally descended from his house, he did not come all the way. He remained aloof. Across the street from the burning church, watching and waiting, I am not sure for what.

And then there was a Salesian sister, who is not afraid of anyone. And she came through the battlefield to help us, too. She braved all the dangers. But she was there only to save the Salesians, and was willing and ready to offer up to the wolves those of us who were not in the Salesian family, friends of mine, friends of other priests. She would save the Salesians and throw the rest to the devil. Ah, my sister! All persons are human beings, and to be cherished....

Meanwhile, fire had run its course through the church. The assassins had doused the building with gasoline and set it on fire. The roof of my beautiful, beloved church had fallen in, smoke was pouring out, and all Port-au-Prince could see that hell had burst up in our midsts, as though the end of the world had appeared in the fire's flames. It was odd for most people to watch St. Jean Bosco burn when on all sides, the church was surrounded by police headquarters. But the police crossed their arms, with their guns in hand, and protected the criminals who burned down the church, and who kept on killing and robbing with impunity. Fire in the church, fire in human minds....

This victory, our victory – for indeed, in the end, ours was the victory, the side of the martyrs triumphed – was achieved for and by the Haitian people in general, and in particular, it was achieved for and by the congregation of St. Jean Bosco, who were supposed to disappear in a hail of bullets and a ball of fire, and who, instead, reemerged from death carrying the embers of hope and life, and who stand today next to the bodies of their dead comrades, in the shadow of our burned-out church, and hold out hope and life to the rest of the Haitian people. We are more blessed when we preach to a hungry congregation from the top of a dusty pile of cinders than when we preach to the well-fed from a luxurious altar inside a magnificent cathedral....

Remember that young woman I saw that day, bleeding from her womb, clutching herself where they had speared her, sobbing that she would lose the baby that was growing inside her? Here again is a story of life coming where there should be death. This is the story – finally – of the child called Hope. The woman bled and bled as the assassins rampaged through my church; they had knifed her where they knew it would do the most damage. These are men who see a mother and want to damage what is within her. Insanity. Somehow, the woman, bleeding and sobbing, was brought to a hospital.

Everyone in Port-au-Prince had heard the story of the godless attack against the young mother and her unborn child. And the criminals, that night, after the massacre had ended, went to the university hospital, searching the maternity wards. They had heard that the woman had survived, and they wanted to kill her, to show the people that there was no hope in this world. They made the mothers in the maternity ward lift their white nightgowns to see if they were wounded in the stomach. Indecency. But they never found the woman. She had been taken to another hospital far away, and there – miracle, miracle – she was delivered, by cesarean, of a baby girl, a wounded baby girl, but fine, healthy, more or less undamaged. And that child she called Esperancia, or Hope. Because the baby's birth showed that the murderers, the assassins, the criminals, the police, the Army, the president and all the president's men could not put an end to Hope in Haiti, could not destroy us, could not wreck our infant aspirations with their knives and spears. Hope's birth showed that a new Haiti could emerge from the wounded body of the old, that in spite of the atrocities visited upon Haiti, she could give forth new life, if only her friends would help her, and shelter her, and protect her, and help her with the birth. Hope is the new generation of my country....

...Haiti is the parish of the poor. In Haiti, it is not enough to heal wounds, for every day another wound opens up. It is not enough to give the poor food one day, to buy them antibiotics one day, to teach them to read a few sentences or to write a few words. Hypocrisy. The next day they will be starving again, feverish again, and they will never be able to buy the books that hold the words that might deliver them. Beans and rice are hypocrisy when the pastor gives them only to a chosen few among his own flock, and thousands and thousands of others starve. Oh yes, perhaps that night, the pastor can sleep better, thinking, "Ti Claude's eyes looked brighter today; I do believe he is growing." Perhaps that will put the pastor's mind at rest. Hypocrisy. Because for every Ti Claude or Ti Bob or Ti Marie to whom the pastor gives his generous bowl of rice and beans, there are a hundred thousand more Ti Claudes, Bobs and Maries, sitting on bony haunches in the dust, chewing on the pit of a mango, finishing their meal for the day. I have seen them, I have seen the children the good pastor never feeds.

What good does it do the peasant when the pastor feeds his children? For a moment, the peasant's anguish is allayed. For one night, he can sleep easier, like the pastor himself. For one night, he is grateful to the pastor, because that night he does not have to hear the whimpers of his children, starving. But the same free foreign rice the pastor feeds to the peasant's children is being sold on the market for less than the farmer's own produce. The very food that the pastor feeds the peasant's children is keeping the peasant in poverty, unable himself to feed his children. And among those who sell the foreign rice are the big landholders who pay the peasant fifty cents a day to work on their fields; among those who profit from the food the pastor gives the peasant's children are the same men who are keeping the peasant in utter poverty, poverty without hope.

Would it not be better – and I ask the question in all humility, in its fullest simplicity – for the peasant to organize with others in his situation and force the large landholders to increase the peasants' pay? Would it not be wiser – more Christian – for the pastor, while he feeds those children, to help the peasant learn to organize? Isn't this a better way to stop the children's cries of hunger forever? As long as the pastor keeps feeding the peasant's children without helping deliver the peasant from poverty, the peasant will never escape the humiliating fate to which he has been assigned by the corrupt system. When the pastor only feeds the children, he is participating in that corrupt system, allowing it to endure. When the pastor feeds the children *and* helps organize the peasants, he is refusing the corrupt system, bringing about its end. Which behavior is more Christian, more evangelical?

I chose the second course, along with many of my colleagues here in the parish of the poor. You have chosen that course, too, brothers and sisters. I chose to help organize youth, I chose to preach deliverance from poverty, I chose to encourage my congregation into hope and belief in their own powers. For me it is quite simple: I chose life over death. I preached life to my congregation, not life as we live it in Haiti, a life of mud, dank cardboard walls, garbage, darkness, hunger, disease, unemployment, and oppression. But life as a decent poor man should live it, in

691

a dry house with a floor and a real roof, at a table with food, free from curable illness, working a meaningful job or tilling the fields to his or her profit, proud.

The only way to preach a decent poor man's life in Haiti is to preach self-defense, defense from the system of violence and corruption that ruins our own and our children's lives. I hope and trust that I have preached self-defense to my people. I would feel myself a hypocrite otherwise. And I would rather die than be a hypocrite, rather die than betray my people, rather die than leave them behind in the parish of the poor....

Let us leave our old homes of cardboard and mud floors. Let us make a plan to douse them with gasoline, and burn them to the ground. Let us turn our backs on that great fire and on that way of life, and hand in hand, calmly, intelligently, walk forward into the darkness toward the sunrise of Hope. Let us trust one another, keep faith with one another, and never falter.

Take my hand. If you see me stumble, hold me up. If I feel you weaken, I will support you. You, brother, hold up the lamp of solidarity before us. Sister, you carry the supplies. Yes, the road is long. I fear there are criminals on either side of us, waiting to attack. Do you hear them in the bushes, brothers and sisters? Hush! Yes, I can hear them loading their guns. Let us ignore their threats. Let us be fearless.

Let them come. They do not know it, but though they kill us, though they shoot and cut down every last one of us, there is another battalion about a mile back, coming and coming down this long path toward sunrise. And behind that battalion, another and another and another. God is for the big battalions, and the big battalions are the people. Let us keep the lamp of solidarity lit, and move forward. Amen.

The following selections are taken from Jean-Bertrand Aristide, *An Autobiography*, written with Christophe Wargny, Linda M. Maloney, trans., Maryknoll, NY: Orbis Books, 1993, pp. 52-53, 56, 164-65.

350. Jean-Bertrand Aristide, *No to Violence*

Seventh Commandment of Democracy: No to Violence, Yes to *Lavalas*.

A political revolution without armed force in 1991: is it possible? Yes. Incredible, but true. The pedagogy of *Lavalas* [i.e., a torrent], the tactical and strategic convergence of democratic forces, brandished the weapon of unity against that of violence. A stunning victory! An historic surprise!

Chapter 6: The Third World and Liberation

Schooled by the poor, the pedagogy of active nonviolence and unity triumphed over institutionalized violence. After 1804, the date of our first independence [from France], 1991 opened the era of our second independence.

Does there exist a democratic nation that is capable of remaining indifferent to that victory of nonviolence precisely in the place where the structures of economic violence still hold sway? Is it right to test the patience of the victims of economic violence? If there is no such thing as a politics unconnected with force, neither is there such a thing as an economy unconnected with interests.

The capital of nonviolence that the Haitians have already invested represents considerable economic interests, thanks to the restoration of peace. A simple social-psychological approach speaks volumes. In fact, the less the social self is under attack by the antiquated oligarchy, the more psychological, political and economic health it enjoys.

The pedagogy of nonviolence may support a collective raising of consciousness with regard to our country of nonviolence – a nonviolent country where, nevertheless, 85 percent of the population, crushed under the weight of economic violence, is still illiterate: illiterates who are not animals. Teaching these victims to read, today, is a challenge to the true friends of the Haitian people: I am not speaking of friends, but of true friends. You who are our true friends, do not be observers. Be actors, inasmuch as you are citizens of the world.

Together, let us participate in a campaign for literacy. Can we count on your cooperation? We hope so. All cooperation at this level testifies to a willingness to struggle against economic violence through active nonviolence.

Where the canons of violence are roaring, that is where the sun of nonviolence is shinning, *"lavalassement."*

* *
*

Dorothy Day in 1917. Protest against World War I. (Bettman Archive)

CHAPTER 7
Catholic Peacemaking in the USA

INTRODUCTION

There are several characteristics of American society that make American Catholic peacemaking unique. First among these has been the predominance of middle-class life in America. Its Catholic laity has been comparatively prosperous, literate, and well-educated, especially during the generation between World War II and the 1970s. Second, American Catholics, like the Romans of the first century A.D., have been at the focus of power in the world today: they have been – and more importantly have perceived themselves as – neither marginalized nor alienated in this respect, and their view of peace has therefore shared many of the qualities of the Pax romana. The maintenance of their own system of life and government, even brutally at times, continues to be an essential element of any American definition of peace. Third, American Catholics have had broad access to power, to communication, and to the protection of their opinions and dissent. Finally – and this is a point that is only beginning to be perceived – Catholics in the United States, unlike their contemporaries in Latin America or the Philippines, and unlike the Christians in the late Roman Empire or medieval Europe, are living in an essentially post-Christian society.

These conditions have combined to make peacemaking in America a special challenge. In a materialistic society that consumes over 60 percent the world's goods and resources for only six percent of its population, American Catholic peacemakers have come to realize the primary importance of conversion: lives of justice and solidarity with the poor and the oppressed will increasingly become not pious cliches but necessities of civilized life.

Yet Catholic peacemakers also live in a nation that has set about to defend its claim to the world's wealth with the capacity to destroy life on the planet itself. Its citizenship accepts the fact that violence must be used to protect this way of life and becomes increasingly insensitive to daily violence of every type. In a society that tolerates every form of expression and absorbs every shock to its sensitivities as quickly as it switches a television channel, Catholic peacemakers have therefore sought fresh and meaningful ways to dramatize and implement lives of peace. These methods may, however, have far greater difficulty converting individuals and society than the obvious and more painful witness of the martyrs and saints of the Catholic tradition.

HISTORICAL BACKGROUND

Catholics first arrived in North America as a persecuted minority. Through the colonial and early republican periods their growth was slow; and they were subject to suspicion and outright prejudice. The Catholic church's solution was to draw in on itself, to protect itself from hostility and to continue nurturing its own traditions and institutions in a society that it often viewed with suspicion and alienation. With the great waves of immigration of the late nineteenth and early twentieth centuries came millions of Catholics, predominantly from the impoverished classes of southern and eastern Europe and Ireland, who greatly increased Catholicism's presence in the United States but who also deepened its association with foreign cultures, alien political systems, and suspect allegiances.

Catholics of the immigrant generations remained urban, impoverished, and subject to the worst forms of prejudice and discrimination. They continued to view mainstream American culture from a safe distance, with equal suspicion, and with increasing defensiveness. Since the Council of Trent (1545-63) Catholicism had retained its Counter-Reformation suspicion of Protestantism and nonconformism and its hostility to much of the Protestant liberal economic, intellectual, and spiritual tradition that had built the United States.

Paradoxically, several of these traits were sources of strength for the Catholic peace movement. Many immigrants had come to America partially to flee conscription. Many retained emotional, familial, and certainly religious ties to the countries that they had just left. Peace in the Catholic tradition always retained a strongly "personalistic" strain that merged well with the immigrants' suspicion of institutions; Catholic moral teaching retained the medieval exaltation of conscience above human law that many Protestant mainline churches had abandoned in favor of the state's authority; Catholic social thought by the early twentieth century was beginning to be clearly critical of many aspects of capitalist industrial economy and society. The Catholic church's universality bound Catholics to their coreligionists all over the world; while the church's claims to being above society, and certainly to being distinct from the mainstream of American culture, provided it both institutionally and individually with a reservoir from which later dissent could flow.

WORLD WAR I

With the twentieth century and World War I, American Catholics began to emerge from their isolation. The immigrant church, in fact, began to go out of its way to assert its Americanness and ultra-loyalty. There was little Catholic protest against World War I. Of the 3,989 conscientious objectors to the conflict, only four were Catholic.

THE CATHOLIC BISHOPS

By the end of the war American bishops could write their pastoral letter, *The Lessons of War.* Good Catholics make good Americans, it asserts. Yet paragraph 72 offers implicit testimony of the great efforts needed to make this so. Despite the letter's Constantinian claims that God has especially favored America and its war aims, and its urging the U.S. to take its unique role to "restore peace and order" according to "the principles of reasonable liberty and of Christian civilization," the bishops can almost be accused of "protesting too much." The hierarchy seems to think it necessary to position itself between Catholics and American society as both mediator and bulwark, pledging Catholics loyalty to their nation not as individual citizens but as a special – and somewhat foreign – group.

Ultimately, however, the bishops reveal an uneasiness with America's display of power (§82-§83) and urge a return to the peaceful works of civilization (§85-§86). The triumphalism, the pride of good citizenship the somewhat naive hope that the war would bring good seems to have disappeared in the retrospection of this letter. Despite its patriotic prose, the letter betrays a deep and paradoxical disquiet with the role played by the church in supporting the war, whose prosecution it now

697

holds responsible for much of the moral and social upheaval that would soon characterize the 1920s.

The following selection is taken from Hugh J. Nolan, ed., *Pastoral Letters of the American Hierarchy, 1792-1970*, Huntington, IN: Our Sunday Visitor, 1971, pp. 230-33.

351. *National Catholic Welfare Council, The Pastoral Letter of 1919*

III. Catholic War Activities

(69) Once it had been decided that our country should enter the War, no words of exhortation were needed to arouse the Catholic spirit. This had been shown in every national crisis. It had stirred to eloquent expression the Fathers of the Third Plenary Council.

(70) "We consider the establishment of our country's independence, the shaping of its liberties and laws, as a work of special Providence, its framers 'building better, than they knew,' the Almighty's hand guiding them.... We believe that our country's heroes were the instruments of the God of nations in establishing this home of freedom; to both the Almighty and to His instruments in the work we look with grateful reverence; and to maintain the inheritance of freedom which they have left us, should it ever – which God forbid – be imperiled, our Catholic citizens will be found to stand forward as one man, ready to pledge anew 'their lives their fortunes and their sacred honor.'"

Catholic Patriotism

(71) Tho prediction has been fulfilled. The traditional patriotism of our Catholic people has been amply demonstrated in the day of their country's trial. And we look with pride upon the record which proves, as no mere protestation could prove, the devotion of American Catholics to the cause of American freedom.

(72) To safeguard the moral and physical welfare of our Catholic soldiers and sailors, organized action was needed. The excellent work already accomplished by the Knights of Columbus, pointed the way to further undertakings. The unselfish patriotism with which our various societies combined their forces in the Catholic Young Men's Association, the enthusiasm manifested by the organizations of Catholic women, and the eagerness of our clergy to support the cause of the nation, made it imperative to unify the energies of the whole Catholic body and direct

them toward the American purpose. With this end in view, the National Catholic War Council was formed by the Hierarchy. Through the Committee on Special War Activities and the Knights of Columbus Committee on War Activities, the efforts of our people in various lines were coordinated and rendered more effective, both in providing for the spiritual needs of all Catholics under arms and in winning our country's success. This unified action was worthy of the Catholic name. It was in keeping with the pledge which the hierarchy had given our Government: "Our people, now as ever, will rise as one man to serve the nation. Our priests and consecrated women will once again, as in every former trial of our country, win by their bravery, their heroism and their service new admiration and approval."

Tribute to Military Chaplains

(73) To our chaplains especially we give the credit that is their due for the faithful performance of their obligations. In the midst of danger and difficulty, under the new and trying circumstances which war inevitably brings, they acted as priests.

(74) The account of our men in the service adds a new page to the record of Catholic loyalty. It is what we expected and what they took for granted. But it has a significance that will be fairly appreciated when normal conditions return. To many assertions it answers with one plain fact....

V. Lessons of the War

(78) In order that our undertakings may be wisely selected and prudently carried on, we should consider seriously the lessons of the War, the nature of our present situation and the principles which must guide the adjustment of all our relations.

(79) Our estimate of the War begins, naturally, with the obvious facts: with the number of peoples involved, the vastness and effectiveness of their armaments, the outlay in treasure and toil, the destruction of life and the consequent desolation which still lies heavy on the nations of Europe. Besides these visible aspects, we know somewhat of the spiritual suffering – of the sorrow and hopelessness which have stricken the souls of men. And deeper than these, beyond our power of estimation, is the moral evil, the wrong whose magnitude only the Searcher of hearts can determine.

(80) For we may not forget that in all this strife of the peoples, in the loosening of passion and the seeking of hate, sin abounded. Not the rights of man alone but the law of God was openly disregarded. And if we come before Him now in thankfulness, we must come with contrite hearts, in all humility beseeching Him that He continue His mercies toward us, and enable us so to order our human relations that we may atone for our past transgressions and strengthen the bond of peace with a deeper charity for our fellowmen and purer devotion to His service.

(81) We owe it to His goodness that our country has been spared the suffering and desolation which war has spread so widely. Our homes, our natural resources, our means of intercourse and the institutions which uphold the life of our nation, have all been preserved. We are free, without let or hindrance, to go forward in the paths of industry, of culture, of social improvement and moral reform. The sense of opportunity has quickened us, and we turn with eagerness to a future that offers us boundless advantage.

(82) Let us not turn hastily. Our recent experience has taught us innumerable lessons, too full and profound to be mastered at once. Their ultimate meaning a later generation will ponder and comprehend. But even now we can recognize the import of this conspicuous fact: a great nation conscious of power yet wholly given to peace and unskilled in the making of war, gathered its might and put forth its strength in behalf of freedom and right as the inalienable endowment of all mankind. When its aims were accomplished, it laid down its arms, without gain or acquisition, save in the clearer understanding of its own ideals and the fuller appreciation of the blessings which freedom alone can bestow.

The Costliness of War

(83) The achievement was costly. It meant interruption of peaceful pursuits, hardship at home and danger abroad. Not one class or state or section, but the people as a whole had to take up the burden. This spirit of union and sacrifice for the common weal, found its highest expression in the men and women who went to do service in distant lands. To them, and especially to those who died that America might live, we are forever indebted. Their triumph over self is the real victory, their loyalty the real honor of our nation, their fidelity to duty the bulwark of our freedom.

(84) To such men and their memory, eulogy is at best a poor tribute. We shall not render them their due nor show ourselves worthy to name

them as our own, unless we inherit their spirit and make it the soul of our national life. The very monuments we raise in their honor will become a reproach to us, if we fail in those things of which they have left us such splendid example.

VI. The Present Situation

(85) We entered the War with the highest of objects, proclaiming at every step that we battled for the right and pointing to our country as a model for the world's imitation. We accepted therewith the responsibility of leadership in accomplishing the task that lies before mankind. The world awaits our fulfillment. Pope Benedict himself has declared that our people, "retaining a most firm hold on the principles of reasonable liberty and of Christian civilization, are destined to have the chief role in the restoration of peace and order on the basis of those same principles, when the violence of these tempestuous days shall have passed."

(86) This beyond doubt is a glorious destiny, far more in keeping with the aims of our people than the triumph of armies or the conquest of wider domain. Nor is it an impossible destiny, provided we exemplify in our own national life "the principles of reasonable liberty and of Christian civilization.". . .

BEN SALMON

The man often described as one of the most prominent resisters to World War I was virtually unknown until the 1980s when a young graduate student decided to investigate his life and thought. Benjamin J. Salmon was born in Denver in 1889 into an Irish-American working family. Keenly aware of the social injustices of the Gilded Age, he became an activist by the 1910s, and after the 1914 Ludlow Massacre of striking miners, their wives, and children by the Colorado National Guard, he joined the labor movement as an organizer of the Railway Clerk's Union.

Salmon campaigned for Woodrow Wilson in 1916, in the hope that the Democrat would keep the U.S. out of World War I. Meanwhile he was elected secretary of the People's Council of America for Democracy and Peace, a coalition of labor and peace activists, journalists, and intellectuals that opposed the new conscription law. Salmon registered for the draft in June 1917 but then refused to complete his

Army questionnaire, declaring himself a conscientious objector, a category forced upon the Wilson administration by the American Civil Liberties Union and other peace groups to make provision for the thouands of Quakers, Mennonites, and other members of traditional "peace churches." As a Catholic, however, Salmon's only choice was combat duty or death for treason.

In January 1918, therefore, he was arrested, tried and imprisoned at Fort Logan, Colorado under military jurisdiction. Here his noncooperation continued until he and three other COs were condemned to death after refusing noncombatant service on July 24, 1918, four months before the conclusion of the war. Their sentences were then reduced to 25 years at hard labor at Fort Leavenworth, Kansas. After organizing a strike by hundreds of prisoners there Salmon was eventually placed in solitary confinement and denied the most basic human rights, until his transfer to the Army War Prison at Fort Douglas, UT. Here in July 1920 he began his famous hunger strike that saw his transfer to Washington, DC and a ward for the criminally insane at St. Elizabeth's Catholic Hospital. By then the ACLU had taken up Salmon's case before the entire nation. Hundreds of letters of protest finally persuaded the War Department to release him, the last of the remaining 33 World War I COs, on November 26, 1920, with a dishonorable discharge from the U.S. Army. Hostility to Salmon's pacifism in Colorado forced the Salmons' to move to Chicago, where the rigors of his imprisonment, hunger strike, and the Great Depression led to his death in 1932.

According to Torin Finney, the author of his award-winning biography, Salmon was the first American Catholic to directly and explicitly challenge the "just-war" theory, and he was the only one of the four Catholic objectors to World War I to base his claim on Gospel teachings. He was reviled by Catholic laity and clergy during his lifetime and virtually ignored after his death, except for the *Catholic Worker's* description of him as "an unsung hero of the Great War."

Our selections are taken from Torin R.T. Finney, *Unsung Hero of the Great War: The Life and Witness of Ben Salmon*, New York: Paulist Press, 1989, pp. 118-20.

352. Ben Salmon, Conscientious Objection to World War I

Letter to Woodrow Wilson, President of the United States, Washington, DC, Denver, Colorado, June 5, 1917.

Chapter 7: Catholic Peacemaking in the USA

My Dear Mr. Wilson:

Complying with your edict, I registered today. Your mandate was autocratic, and contrary to the Constitution; nevertheless, acquiescence caused injustice against no one but myself; consequently, I submitted. But, I must now tell you that I refuse to submit to conscription.

Regardless of nationality, all men are my brothers. God is "our Father who art in heaven." The commandment "Thou shalt not kill" is unconditional and inexorable.

If the parent orders the child to do wrong, the child should disobey. If the State commands the subject to violate God's law, the subject should ignore the State. Man is anterior to the State, and God is supreme.

Both by precept and example, the lowly Nazarene taught us the doctrine of non-resistance, and so convinced was He of the soundness of that doctrine that he sealed His belief with death on the cross. The great mass of the people still adhere to Christ's teachings against war, regardless of the fact that cardinals, priests and ministers have repudiated the Christian ideal and bowed to the god of expediency.

There are many ways to avoid war. Now that you are in it, there are many ways to get out of it without sacrificing, or threatening to sacrifice, a single life. Solution of the problem, without breaking the commandments of God, is merely a question of desire and determination.

Aside from right or wrong, why concern ourselves about German injustice while unmindful of the disorder of our own house? In America, millions of impoverished citizens vainly send forth their mute appeal for justice. Their supplications are answered with greater tyranny, renewed iniquities, and a further disregard of their rights and their liberties. Show me any German cruelty that can outdo in horror the massacre of the women and children in the tent colony at Ludlow! And, the underlying cause of the Ludlow tragedy manifests itself daily throughout the length and breadth of this land of liberty, although it is only when given spontaneous expression that we even notice the misery and sorrow and seething despair that is slowly eating out the heart of our boasted civilization in America. Why not correct the wrongs at home? "…Hypocrite, cast first the beam out of thy own eye; and then shalt thou see clearly to take out the mote from thy brother's eye" [Luke 6:42].

I am not an alien sympathizer. I was born in Denver, of Canadian-American parents, and I love America. This letter is not written in a contumelious spirit. But, when human law conflicts with Divine law, my duty is clear [see Acts 5:29, **44**].

Conscience, my infallible guide, impels me to tell you that prison, death, or both, are infinitely preferable to joining any branch of the army, and contributing, either directly or indirectly, to the death of my fellow workingmen.

I voted for you and worked for your election in 1916, and I still have faith in you. Hopeful that you may see the right and have the courage to follow it, I am, sincerely yours,   – Ben J. Salmon.

Letter to Local [Draft] Board for Division Number 1, Denver, Colorado, December 26, 1917

Gentlemen:

The government's Questionnaire was received by me yesterday – Christmas day – the day we celebrated the birth of Him Who bade nations as well as individuals "Love one another."

"You have heard that it hath been said, Thou shalt love thy neighbor, and hate thy enemy. But I say to you, Love your enemies: do good to them that hate you; and pray for them that persecute and calumniate you" [Mt. 5:43-44, see **34**].

You may inform the proper officials that I refuse to answer the Questionnaire.

I am legitimately entitled to exemption: a wife and mother to support. However, I will not use my dependents to shield me from an institution against which my soul rebels.

War is incompatible with my conception of Christianity. I positively refuse to aid organized murder, either directly or indirectly. I must serve God first, and, in serving Him it [is] impossible to be other than loyal to my country – the world.

Ultimately, individuals and nations must awaken and rally to Christ's Standard or perish. Meantime, I must stand firm and trust in God.

Let those that believe in wholesale violation of the commandment "Thou shalt not kill" make a profession of their faith by joining the army of war. I am in the army of Peace, and in this army I intend to live and die.

Very truly yours,
Ben J. Salmon.

THE CATHOLIC WORKER

In May 1933 in New York City two legendary, some say saintly, American Catholics, Dorothy Day and Peter Maurin, founded a new Catholic peace group that would embody their ideals of pacifism, commitment to the poor and to fundamental change in American society. The stories of the Catholic Worker and Dorothy Day (1897-1980) are woven inextricably into the fabric of the American church.

Day was born in New York of Scot-Irish Calvinist parents. Her father was a journalist. She received a better than average education, joined the campus socialists at the University of Illinois, but by 1916 had returned to New York with her parents. Part of the Greenwich Village bohemian scene, she got jobs writing with the *Call,* the *Masses,* and the *Liberator.* She was involved with the Anti-Conscription League in World War I and the women's suffrage movement, for which she was arrested in Washington in 1917.

After 1918 and her return from jail, Day abandoned her political activism, worked as a nurse and in a variety of clerical jobs, married and divorced, traveled and began writing novels. In 1923 she married again and had a child. The marriage and its breakup brought her to a spiritual crisis, the rejection of her old friends, and conversion to Catholicism in December 1927. Between 1927 and 1933 Day traveled and took a variety and jobs, finally writing for both the Catholic lay paper *Commonweal* and the Jesuit magazine *America.* In December 1932 she met and gradually fell under the spell of Peter Maurin (1877-1949), with whom she would go on to found the Catholic Worker the following year.

Aristide Pierre Maurin was born in a family of farmers on May 9, 1877 in Oultet, a village in Languedoc, in southern France. After early study with the Christian Brothers, he was selected to attend a novitiate in Paris, taking his first vows in 1895. He was till in minor orders as a grammar-school teacher when he was called up for military service in 1899. With the secularization and closing of many Catholic schools under the Combe government in 1902, Maurin joined the liberal Catholic Sillon movement where he remained active until 1908.

Continued exposure to military service, his own sense of alienation from his farming background, and the lure of the New World, finally led to his emigration from France in 1909, and his attempt to set up a new life in Canada. Maurin came to the U.S. in 1911, and a long period of wandering eventually took him to New York by 1925. He brought with him his "gentle personalism": a Catholic radicalism based on the literal interpretation of the Beatitudes and of the Christian realities of sin, the fall, and the need of redemption, reconciliation, and community. Maurin had read widely in political theory, church history, economics, and law; and he rejected the liberal institutions of capitalism and the modern state and their faith in material progress and technology. He replaced them with a personal commitment to love and an eschatological vision of the Christian mission. He proposed a radical imitation of the Gospel life of voluntary poverty in solidarity with the weak, the poor, the sick, and the alienated.

Day and Maurin complemented one another well. To the pacifism and social commitments of the intellectual and bohemian Day, Maurin added the fundamental reality of human community, the radical social gospel, and the French farmer's disdain for institutions. Both drew strength and inspiration from the common source of the Sermon on the Mount; and they combined the commitment to nonviolence with the struggle for social justice that has always characterized true Catholic peacemaking. The result of this combination of talents and spirits was the Catholic Worker movement.

In New York City on May Day 1933, Day launched the *Catholic Worker* newspaper, the first fruit of her collaboration with Maurin. Between then and 1940 its distribution grew from the original 2,500 handed out at the Union Square rally to over 185,000 subscribers. A consistent intellectual position gradually emerged based on the radical interpretation of the Sermon on the Mount and papal social encyclicals. The *Catholic Worker* soon became a prophetic voice calling for nonviolent revolution against capitalism and began to attract a loose association reformers and radicals, Catholic intellectuals, scholars, and workers.

Essential to Maurin's Catholic vision was the Christian social ideal: the medieval hospice and the communal farm were models. Dorothy Day's apartment was his first attempt at communal life, and by 1933 the Catholic Worker had founded its first, St. Joseph's, House of Hospitality. The houses became hospices for Catholic Worker volunteers, soup kitchens and dining halls for thousands of unemployed and homeless. They housed meeting rooms, clothing centers, schools, and "revolutionary headquarters" for the movement. By 1941, thirty-two Worker houses were spread all across the United States, from Milwaukee to Chicago to Seattle, centers of radical hope amid the backdrop of America's depression. Despite this radicalism, the movement always retained its doctrinal and practical orthodoxy and accepted the loose supervision of the hierarchy.

Over the decades since its founding the visibility and impact of the Catholic Worker contracted and expanded along with the urgency of issues of peace and justice on the American psyche. Yet the Worker has maintained a consistent presence and message despite whims of fashion. As many of the selections that follow throughout this chapter testify, it has been both the nurturing garden and safe haven for countless Catholic peacemakers in the United States since its founding; and where it has not fostered the creation of this or that Catholic movement, its presence as both witness to enduring truth and counterweight to current fashion has made itself felt.

PETER MAURIN

The following is taken from Peter Maurin, *Easy Essays*, reprinted in *A Penny a Copy*, 2d. ed., Thomas C. Cornell, Robert Ellsberg, and Jim Forest, eds., Maryknoll, NY: Orbi Book, 1995, pp. 7-8.

353. Peter Maurin, Easy Essays

What The Catholic Worker Believes

The Catholic Worker believes
in the gentle personalism
of traditional Catholicism.
The Catholic Worker believes
in the personal obligation
of looking after
the needs of our brother.
The Catholic Worker believes
in the daily practice
of the Works of Mercy.
The Catholic Worker believes
in Houses of Hospitality
for the immediate relief
of those who are in need.

The Catholic Worker believes
in the establishment
of Farming Communes
where each one works
according to his ability
and gets
according to his need.
The Catholic Worker believes
in creating a new society
within the shell of the old
with the philosophy of the new,
which is not a new philosophy
but a very old philosophy,
a philosophy so old
that it looks like new.

No Party Line

The Catholic Worker
is a free-lance movement,
not a partisan movement.
Some of the Bishops
agree with our policies
and some don't. We are criticized
by many Catholics
for some of our policies
and especially
our Spanish policy [for not siding with Franco and his
Catholic-fascist alliance].
The Communist Party
has a party line.
The Catholic Worker
has no party line.
There is no party line
in the Catholic Church.

DOROTHY DAY

The following is taken from *The Catholic Worker* 6.4 (Sept. 1938): 1, 4, 7.

354. Dorothy Day, Editorial: Catholic Worker Stand on the Use of Force, September 1938

Dear Father:

You are one of many priests and laymen who have written to us of *The Catholic Worker* these past two years on the stand we have taken in the Spanish conflict. Many times we have been misquoted, or sentences from articles or public speeches have been taken from their context and distorted, and our friends have written us with pain that our attitude should seem to be at variance with that of Catholic leaders.

I am writing this letter to explain as best I can the points which we are trying to bring out in *The Catholic Worker*. I am writing it with prayer because it is so hard to write of things of the spirit – it is so hard to explain. If we had made ourselves clear before, we should not have to keep restating our position. But perhaps conflict is good in that it brings about clarification of thought.

We all know that there is a frightful persecution of religion in Spain. Churches have been destroyed and desecrated, priests and nuns have been tortured and murdered in great numbers.

In the light of this fact it is inconceivably difficult to write as we do. It is folly – it seems madness – to say as we do – "we are opposed to the use of force as a means of settling personal, national, or international disputes." As a newspaper trying to affect public opinion, we take this stand. We feel that if the press and the public throughout the world do not speak in terms of the counsels of perfection, who else will?

We pray those martyrs of Spain to help us, to pray for us, to guide us in the stand we take. We speak in their name. Their blood cries out against a spirit of hatred and savagery which aims toward a peace founded upon victory, at the price of resentment and hatred enduring for years to come. Do you suppose they died, saying grimly: "All right – we accept martyrdom – we will not lift the sword to defend ourselves but the lay troops will avenge us!" This would be martyrdom wasted. Blood spilled in vain. Or rather did they say with St. Stephen, "Father, forgive them," and pray with love for their conversion. And did they not rather pray, when the light of Christ burst upon them, that love would overcome hatred, that men *dying for* faith, rather than *killing for* their faith, would save the world?

Truly this is the folly of the cross! But when we say "Saviour of the

World, save Russia," we do not expect a glittering army to overcome the heresy.

As long as men trust to the use of force – only a superior, a more savage and brutal force will overcome the enemy. We use his own weapons, and we must make sure our own force is more savage, more bestial than his own. As long as we are trusting to force – we are praying for a victory by force.

We are neglecting the one means – prayer and the sacraments – by which whole armies can be overcome. "The King is not saved by a great army," David said. "Proceed as sheep and not wolves," St. John Chrysostom said.

St. Peter drew the sword and our Lord rebuked him [Mt. 26:52-53, see 37]. They asked our Lord to prove His Divinity and come down from the cross. But He suffered the "failure" of the cross. His apostles kept asking for a temporal Kingdom. Even with Christ Himself to guide and enlighten them they did not see the primacy of the spiritual. Only when the Holy Ghost descended on them did they see.

Today the whole world has turned to the use of force.

While we take this stand we are not condemning those who have seized arms and engaged in war.

Who of us as individuals if he were in Spain today, could tell what he would do? Or in China [during the Japanese invasion]? From the human natural standpoint men are doing good to defend their faith, their country. But from the standpoint of the Supernatural – there is the "better way" – the way of the Saints – the way of love....

We are afraid of the word love and yet love is stronger than death, stronger than hatred.

If we do not, as the press, emphasize the law of love, we betray our trust, our vocation. We must stand opposed to the use of force....

By the late 1930s it was plain that the United States was slowly abandoning neutrality and preparing for a war in Europe. The Catholic Worker therefore launched a multi-pronged attack on militarism, the sale of war bonds, and increased munitions production. It organized a "Non-Participation League" to press for neutrality, and opposed draft registration and conscription. Day, Joseph Zarella (of the pacifist group PAX), and Rev. Barry O'Toole testified before Congress on the traditional Catholic opposition to conscription on the basis of individual freedom of conscience and vocation. Day was personally chastised by the New York Chancery for her call for nonregistration.

Three decades before Vatican II, articles in the *Catholic Worker* by Paul Hanley Furfey called for abandoning the "Constantinian compromise" with the warmaking state; while Arthur Sheehan urged a return to Gospel pacifism and rejected the just war as an impossible position in the modern age of technological weapons and mass destruction. At the same time the *Catholic Worker* vigorously opposed the blend of isolationism and rabid anti-Semitism espoused by Fr. Charles Coughlin in his popular radio broadcasts.

By 1940, however, it was clear that the U.S. would soon be involved in war. The newspaper therefore adopted a new attitude toward the inevitable draft, pressing Selective Service to make provision for Catholic conscientious objection. In August 1940 Day published an open letter to all Catholic Workers insisting on the basic pacifist position of the movement in the coming war. The result was disastrous. Dissidents who believed in the primacy of the social mission of the movement or in the just-war tradition began abandoning the Worker. By 1945 twenty of the thirty-two Catholic Worker Houses had closed down and the *Catholic Worker* lost over 100,000 in circulation.

The disaster of World War II was to have profound effects on the Catholic Worker movement and great consequence for the history of peacemaking in the United States. In the first place it demonstrated the fragility of the Catholic peace movement on the brink of World War II and its inability to affect American policy. Through Day's insistence on pacifism, after 1940 the peace issue became the predominant characteristic of the movement and made the remnant of the Catholic Workers a committed seed for all further Catholic peacemaking after the war. By its shift in emphasis to the issue of conscientious objection in the 1940s the newspaper also helped lay the groundwork for a new form of Catholic resistance during the war.

The following is taken from *The Catholic Worker* 9.3 (Jan. 1942): 1, 4.

355. Dorothy Day, *Our Country Passes from Undeclared War to Declared War; We Continue Our Christian Pacifist Stand*

In Addition to the Weapon of Starvation of Its Enemy, Our Country Is Now Using the Weapons of Army, Navy and Air Force – In a Month of Great

Feasts, a Time of Joy in Christian Life, the World Plunges Itself Still Deeper into the Horror of War

...We are at war, a declared war, with Japan, Germany and Italy. But still we can repeat Christ's word, each day, holding them close in our hearts, each month printing them in the paper. In times past, Europe has been a battlefield. But let us remember St. Francis [**147-157**], who spoke of peace and we will remind our readers of him, too, so they will not forget.

In *The Catholic Worker* we will quote our Pope, our saints, our priests. We will go on printing the articles which remind us today that we are *all* "called to be saints," that we are other Christs, reminding us of the priest-hood of the laity.

We are still pacifists. Our manifesto is the Sermon on the Mount [**31**], which means that we will try to be peacemakers. Speaking for many of our conscientious objectors, we will not participate in armed warfare or in making munitions, or by buying government bonds to prosecute the war, or in urging others to these efforts.

But neither will we be carping in our criticism. We love our country and we love our President. We have been the only country in the world where men of all nations have taken refuge from oppression. We recognize that while in the order of intention we have tried to stand for peace, for love of our brother, in the order of execution we have failed as Americans in living up to our principles....

Our works of mercy may take us into the midst of war. As editor of *The Catholic Worker,* I would urge our friends and associates to care for the sick and the wounded, to the growing of food for the hungry, to the continuance of all our works of mercy in our houses and on our farms. We understand, of course, that there is and that there will be great differences of opinion even among our own groups as to how much collaboration we can have with the government in times like these. There are differences more profound and there will be many continuing to work with us from necessity, or from choice, who do not agree with us as to our position on war, conscientious objection, etc. But we beg that there will be mutual charity and forbearance among us all....

PAUL HANLEY FURFEY

Furfey was born in Cambridge, MA in 1896 and educated there in Catholic parochial schools and Boston College Prep. He earned a BA from Boston College in 1917, and after one year at Catholic University entered St. Mary's Seminary in Baltimore in 1918. After completing studies at Sulpician Seminary in Washington, DC he was ordained in Baltimore in 1922. Meanwhile he continued his studies and earned a Ph.D. in sociology from Catholic University in 1926, where he gradually rising from instructor to full professor, chairing the Sociology Department there from 1940 to 1963. He headed Washington's Bureau of Social Research from 1959 to 1971. Furfey gained a nation- and world-wide reputation as a sociologist, lectured at the universities of Berlin and Frankfurt, and served on many public committees, including a White House conference board. He wrote many articles and books, including *A History of Social Thought* (1942) and *The Morality Gap* (1968).

Furfey first read the *Catholic Worker* in 1934 while at Catholic University and became a fervent adherent to the movement, providing it with some of its most important intellectual foundations. His articles for the paper and his book, *Fire on the Earth* (1936), were infused with the Worker's social gospel and its nonviolence, a theme that Furfey would develop at great length. His thought rested firmly on the Sermon on the Mount, while he also used the strict application of just-war principles and 1930s economic critique of the arms industry and capitalism.

The following selection excerpts Furfey's dialogue between Christ and the modern Patriot, written six years before Pearl Harbor, ironically highlights the conflict between gospel nonviolence and the security of the nation state, a dilemma that has recently been addressed with fresh insights by Gene Sharp and his students. Furfey's dialogue recalls Erasmus' satires in *Charon* [219] and *Cyclops* [220].

It is taken from *The Catholic Worker* 2:10 (March 1935): 3.

356. Paul Hanly Furfey, Christ and the Patriot

The "Patriot": I love peace as well as any man, but I am a realist. A strong system of national defense is our best assurance of peace. National defense is the patriotic duty of every American citizen. The ROTC affords the Catholic college student a fine opportunity to fulfill this patriotic duty.

Christ: All that take the sword shall perish by the sword [Mt. 26:52-53, John 18:36].

The "Patriot": Yet we must be practical! There are, of course, some

713

nations whom we can trust. Canada is a good neighbor. We shall never have a war with her. But unfortunately not all nations are like that. Japan and Russia are casting jealous eyes at us. Our basic policies conflict. We must arm to defend ourselves against such nations.

Christ: You have heard that it hath been said, Thou shalt love thy neighbor and hate thy enemy. But I say to you, love your enemies, do good to them that hate you; and pray for them that persecute and calumniate you [Mt. 5:43-45, **34-35**].

The "Patriot": A noble doctrine! We must always keep before us the ideal of international good will. At the same time we must realize that it is merely common sense to be on our guard. We shall not start a war, but if some other nation starts one, then we must be in a position to defend our territory.

Christ: To him that striketh thee on the one cheek, offer also the other. Of him that taketh away thy goods, ask them not again [Mt. 5:40-42, **34-35**].

The "Patriot": But national defense is not merely a question of defending our material rights. It is a question of life and death. Only a strong system of national defense will guarantee our personal security.

Christ: Be not afraid of them who kill the body, and after that have no more that they can do.

The "Patriot": But there is such a thing as a just war. Under certain circumstances a nation has a right to declare war. In the Old Testament war is approved under certain circumstances.

Christ: You have heard that it hath been said, an eye for an eye, and a tooth for a tooth. But I say to you not to resist evil [Mt. 5:38-39, **34**].

Lord Jesus Christ, Lover of Peace, kindle in our poor hearts the flame of Thy heroic love, that we may see Thy beloved image in all men, our enemies as well as our friends, that we may rather suffer injury than protect our rights by violence, for Thy sweet sake Who died for all men. Amen.

WORLD WAR II

BISHOPS' STATEMENTS

In a poll published in the November 1939 issue of *America*, the Jesuit magazine, 54,000 Catholic college students of both sexes surveyed at 141 colleges and universities responded to the question whether they would become conscientious objectors in the event of war. Twenty percent said that they would volunteer, 44% that they would accept conscription, and a startling 36% said that they would claim conscientious objector status. By 1941, just before Pearl Harbor, 97% of all Catholics polled opposed U.S. entry into World War II, far greater than the percentage of any Protestant denomination. In theory and until the attack on Pearl Harbor, then, opposition to war, including pacifism, had a respectable and widespread appeal among American Catholics.

This opposition took several forms, including the internationalist approach of CAIP (Catholic Association for International Peace), which was rapidly moving toward the administration's collective-security approach, the Catholic Worker, and the Coughlinites. In general, however, mainstream Catholic opposition to the war and to conscription followed just-war criteria, resting on the belief that the United States would not be attacked and that to prepare for war would imply aggressive intent. The Catholic hierarchy was almost universally opposed to the Burke-Wadsworth conscription bill of 1940, both because of the priority of conscience in Catholic teaching and because of institutional concerns: fear that priests and religious would be subject to the draft.

With the Japanese attack on Pearl Harbor on December 7, 1941 Catholic opposition to the war and the draft collapsed. Catholics, like most Americans, became fervent supporters of the war, both out of patriotic duty and from a sense of the justness of the struggle. In their pastoral letter, *The Crisis of Christianity,* written three weeks before the Japanese attack, the Catholic bishops condemned the dangers of both Nazism and communism. The letter is a forceful counter to many pacifists' use of Acts 5:29 (obey God above man) and relies heavily on Leo XIII's appeal to the medieval theory of the "two swords" or realm of authority within Christendom [see 272]. The letter calls on the just-war theory [194-198], according to which, once an issue has been discussed and a consensus reached, the individual is bound to obey legal authority. Declaring that "we support wholeheartedly the adequate defense of our country," the bishops called on Catholics to "render to Caesar" [Mt. 22:21, Mk. 12:17] They reminded them that all authority comes from God, and that therefore, even in democratic countries, they must obey their rulers. Missing from their call, however, is any reminder of the prior authority of conscience, even within the just-war theory.

The following excerpts are taken from Flannery, pp. 329-35.

357. U.S. Catholic Conference, The Crisis of Christianity, November 14, 1941

...Defense of Our Country

We support wholeheartedly the adequate defense of our Country. Thoughtful statesmen are perplexed, patriotic citizens are divided in their opinions as to the procedure our Country should follow. In these crucial times, when the civil fabric of every country is threatened and when dictators would destroy all religion, we herewith restate the position of the Catholic Church in the language of the immortal Pope Leo XIII:

> The Almighty has appointed the charge of the human race between two powers, the ecclesiastical and the civil: the one being set over divine, and the other over human things. Each in its kind is supreme; each has fixed limits within which it is contained, limits which are defined by the nature and special object of the province of each, so that there is, We may say, an orbit within which the action of each is brought into play by its own native right.
>
> But inasmuch as each of these two powers has authority over the same subjects, and as one and the same thing, under different aspects but still remaining identically the same, might chance to fall under the jurisdiction and determination of both powers, God, who foresees all things and is Author alike of these two powers, has marked out the course of each in correlation to the other. "For the powers that are, are ordained of God" [Rom. 13:1]. Were this not so, deplorable contentions and conflicts would often arise, and not infrequently men, like travelers at the meeting of two roads, would hesitate in anxiety and doubt, not knowing what course to follow. Two powers would be commanding contrary things, and it would be a dereliction of duty to disobey either of the two.
>
> But to judge thus of the wisdom and goodness of God would be most repugnant.... One of the two has for its proximate and chief object the well-being of this mortal life; the other, the joys of heaven. Whatever, therefore, in things human is of a sacred character, whatever belongs, either of its own nature or by reason of the end to which it is referred, to the salvation of souls, or to

716

the worship of God is subject to the power and judgment of the Church. Whatever is to be under the civil and political order is rightly subject to the civil authority. Jesus Christ has Himself given command that what is Caesar's is to be rendered to Caesar, and that what belongs to God is to be rendered to God [Mt. 22:15-22].

Respect for Authority

Pondering this solemn teaching of Pope Leo XIII, we must recognize that all lawful authority is from God. "Let everyone be subject to the higher authorities, for there exists no authority except from God" [Rom. 13:1]. Disrespect for authority, both ecclesiastical and civil, must be condemned. In the confusion of the hour, we deplore the presumption of those who, lacking authority, strive to determine the course of action that the Church should take within her clearly defined field. Recognizing the liberty of discussion, and even of criticism, which our democratic form of government guarantees, we urge and commend respect and reverence for the authority of our civil officials which has its source in God.

At the present moment, in varying degrees, in every part of the world, the peaceful course of events is disturbed. People are called upon to make sacrifices and to suffer. Comparing our conditions in the United States with those of other lands, we must recognize that our country is singularly blessed. But we cannot avoid the repercussions of a world cataclysm. Our faith in a Divine Providence ruling the universe should inspire us to have confidence in the benevolent designs of a loving God who permits suffering to correct evil and to bring forth the fruits of justice and charity and peace.

In this solemn hour when fateful decisions are to be made, it is evident that a spirit of exemplary restraint should characterize our priests and people. In every national crisis and every danger, our priests have been an inspiration. We are confident that their good example of strong faith and courage, founded on the virtue of fortitude, will not be lacking now. As moral teachers, they show that freedom has its limitations. It is limited, first of all, by the rights of God, and next by the rights of others and by the interests of the common good....

CATHOLIC CONSCIENTIOUS OBJECTION

With the coming of war the 36% of Catholic students who favored conscientious objection evaporated. The hierarchy neither denied nor supported the Catholic right to pacifism and cut Catholic COs adrift. Out of a total of 21 million Catholics only 223 claimed IV-E CO status, conscientious objection to military service; 135 were eventually classified, a grand leap from the 4 Catholics out of the 3,989 COs to World War I [352], but a miniscule percentage of the total 11,887 conscientious objectors to World War II, still small enough for the hierarchy to safely ignore. Most Catholic objectors chose I-A-O status, noncombatant military service, generally as unarmed medics on the front lines. Unlike the exclusion of Catholics, Jews, and mainline Protestant churches from CO status in World War I, the Burke-Wadsworth Act did provide for Catholic objection, but the prejudice and scepticism of draft boards and of many potential Catholic supporters about the pacifist tradition in their own church made applications difficult. It is not surprising then that in addition to these 135 Catholic conscientious objectors, 61 Catholics refused induction and were imprisoned, again a small proportion of the 6,068 jailed during the war for noncooperation.

Even though the conscientious objector was ignored by the institutional church, by 1939 he had became central to the efforts of Dorothy Day and the Catholic Worker movement. In 1940 PAX, the pacifist offshoot of the Worker movement, had already transformed itself into the Association of Catholic Conscientious Objectors (ACCO) with the tacit consent of the hierarchy, and by April 1941 it had received 400 Catholic claims. Expecting a large groundswell of Catholic COs, ACCO had affiliated with the National Service Board for Religious Objectors (NSBRO), a consortium of the traditional Protestant peace churches – Brethren, Friends, and Mennonites. These groups formed the umbrella agencies that oversaw the camps as agents of the U.S. Selective Service System. While many pacifists objected to this obvious alliance with the state, the traditional peace churches, and the Catholic Worker, saw it as the only viable method of preserving the rights of individual conscience among those whom they served.

The 135 Catholics who had sought and obtained draft status IV-E were required to perform civilian alternative service, away from home, for a period roughly equivalent to that of draftees in military service.

718

With the coming of war this meant the duration of the conflict, plus six months, and for COs the prospect of unpaid service in a series of isolated work camps, doing forestry and other "labor in the national interest."

In August 1941 sixteen Catholics entered a Civilian Public Service (CPS) camp at Stoddard, New Hampshire where they and others remained until their transfer to a new camp at Warner, New Hampshire in November 1942. Collectively the two camps were dubbed "Camp Simon," after the biblical Simon also pressed into service to bear a cross. Here a maximum of 63 Catholics served until March 1943, when the Catholic COs were disbanded and sent to several other camps run by Protestant peace churches. About 100 Catholic COs eventually served at Swallow Falls Camp in Maryland or at Rosewood Training School where they cared for psychiatric patients.

Gordon Zahn was born on August 7, 1918 in Milwaukee. After high school he did office work until drafted in 1942 and sent to Camp Simon as a young CO. In February 1944 he published his first article for *The Catholic Worker*. Thereafter Zahn became a regular contributor to the paper. After the war he earned a Ph.D. from Catholic University and taught as a professor of sociology at Loyola University in Chicago from 1953 to 1967. During this period Zahn published two books of major importance to peace studies, his *German Catholics and Hitler's Wars* (1962, see 273) and his classic account on the life and death of Franz Jägerstätter [290-291], *In Solitary Witness* (1964). From 1968 to 1981 he served as professor of sociology at the University of Massachusetts, Boston, and has been Emeritus since 1981. His most recent book is *Vocation of Peace* (1993).

During the 1960s and the Vietnam War Zahn became an outspoken leader of the Catholic peace movement, emphasizing the historical roots of Catholic nonviolence and attempting to create the structures and organizations needed to support peacemaking. As early as 1957, on his return from a Pax Christi meeting in Europe, Zahn had attempted to found a U.S. branch, but the U.S. hierarchy preferred to retain CAIP and its just-war orientation. In 1964 he, Eileen Egan [379], his co-founder of PAX, and James Douglass [403] successfully lobbied for the inclusion of gospel nonviolence into Schema XIII and Vatican II [see 371]. In June 1972 Egan and Zahn finally achieved their goal and Pax Christi/USA [380] was born, with the pair as co-chairs.

Since the 1970s Zahn has been one of the mainstays of Pax Christi and its campaigns against the arms race and conscription. Zahn established the Center on Conscience and War in Cambridge, MA and through it and its counseling and publications programs Pax Christi maintained its opposition to the draft and conscription through the 1980s. In addition to many articles and the works already cited, Gordon Zahn is the author of *An Alternative to War* (1963), and *War, Conscience and Dissent* (1967), a collection of essays. He is the editor of Thomas Merton, *The Nonviolent Alternative* (1980, see 366-369).

In the selection below, Zahn describes the routine and the hardships, the sense of loneliness and futility experienced by most of the Catholic COs in the work camps during World War II. To the dissensions among differing groups of Catholic Worker pacifists, just-war Thomists, Coughlinites, intellectuals, anarchists, and plain misfits, was added their gradual realization that the administration of the program was arbitrary, suspended all civil and constitutional rights to the whim of Selective Service, and in the end performed little useful function. During the 1960s Selective Service Director Lewis B. Hershey revealed the government's true intent with the CO status: "The CO is best handled if no one ever hears of him." Inadequate housing, poor nutrition, and the unpaid and useless labor of the camps eventually brought many Catholics to organize hunger strikes and other acts of Gandhian civil disobedience to protest their conditions. In January 1946 the ACCO began withdrawing from NSBRO over what ACCO termed NSBRO complicity in the CPS system as a form of slavery, while the camp system was declared unconstitutional and closed down.

The following selection is taken from Gordon C. Zahn, *Another Part of the War: The Camp Simon Story,* Amherst: University of Massachusetts Press, 1979, pp. v-xiv.

358. Gordon Zahn: The Catholic Conscientious Objector in World War II

Introduction

There is little danger that the Second World War – the "big war," the "last good war" as some would have it – will pass unnoticed in the final recapitulation of human history....

This book addresses itself to another part of that war. For a period of slightly less than six years, approximately twelve thousand men were classified as conscientious objectors under the provisions of the Selective

Service and Training Act and assigned to duty in the one hundred and fifty or so camps and special units of Civilian Public Service. In obtaining their IV-E classification they had convinced either their local draft boards or other conscription authorities that they were opposed to all participation in war by reason of their religious training and belief.

The men assigned to alternative service were not the only conscientious objectors to World War II. A much larger number (Selective Service estimates suggest there were between twenty-five and fifty thousand) declared themselves willing to perform noncombatant service in the military forces and were classified I-A-O. Finally, another six thousand or so were sentenced to federal prison either because they failed to convince the designated authorities of the legitimacy or sincerity of their claim to the IV-E classification or because they refused to cooperate with the conscription program even to the point of registering and seeking such classification.

If one compares these modest totals with the millions of men who accepted the national call to military service, it is probably not surprising that so little is known about the conscientious objector and the alternative service program, or that what little is known is so often distorted and misinterpreted. It has been altogether too easy to take the CPS program at face value as clear evidence of democracy's tolerance and respect for the rights of individual conscience while, at the same time, dismissing those who took advantage of the alternative service option as an unpatriotic, self-centered, perhaps even cowardly dissident minority that was unwilling or unable to respond to the challenge presented by totalitarian tyranny in its drive for world domination. A quite contrary view was held by many, perhaps most, of the men who actually served in the program. In their eyes CPS was punitive in practice and intent, an experiment in the democratic *suppression* of a dissident religious minority in time of war....

This study proposes to tell only part of that story. Between late October 1942 and the middle of the following March, seventy-five conscientious objectors were assigned to a forestry camp located near Warner, New Hampshire....

...If a single camp is selected to serve as an illustration of the CPS program, its weaknesses, and its implications, it could be argued that one of the larger, more representative and more enduring camps operated by the major traditional peace churches would be better suited to that purpose.

Perhaps so. On the other hand, there are some perfectly good reasons behind my choice. The first is partly personal and partly professional. As one of the men assigned to perform alternative service there – my arrival actually coinciding with the official opening of the Warner camp – I can bring the benefit of personal interest and the methodological advantages to be gained from participant observation and insights. I cannot deny that this experiential dimension can be as much a liability as an asset, but in this particular instance the danger is outweighed by the deeper understanding of the events and personalities to be described, an understanding made possible by that more intimate association.

But there are other equally important considerations to be taken into account. Camp Simon was unique in several crucial respects....

...It was, in a very real sense, the first corporate witness against war and military service in the history of American Catholicism. Indeed, the claim might even be made that it was the first such witness in the entire history of the Church. Having said this, I must introduce some basic reservations and qualifications that would seem to negate both claims.

For one thing, to speak of Camp Simon as a corporate witness overstates the case if one takes that to mean that the men assigned there represented anything even approaching consensus in principle or application with respect to their opposition to the war. If anything, the reverse was true. As this record will show in occasionally shocking detail, the Warner campers as a group were extremely individualistic and ever on guard against anything that threatened to limit the intellectual and ideological independence that had brought them to camp in the first place. Partly as a result of this, the camp situation would be marked by dissension and disaffection throughout its brief history and, often enough, these conflicts were provoked by essentially trivial matters and incidents.

On a more positive note, however, there was a least common denominator in the obvious fact that all had rejected service and in the kind of unity that arose from the misery they were obliged to share under the compulsion of conscription. From these most of the men were able to fashion a sense of common identity and an awareness of mutual interest. One might even speak of an esprit de corps that, strangely enough, grew stronger once the Warner camp was closed and the men distributed among other CPS camps and units or returned to civilian life. I find it remarkable that today, more than thirty years later, the memory of that brief and generally unhappy association still serves as a continuing bond for a surprisingly large proportion of the Warner veterans. To this extent, certainly, the designation "corporate" is justified.

But how "Catholic" was that witness? The question raises a more complicated problem and one which accounts in great part for the severity of those shared deprivations. That single Catholic camp was in no sense officially Catholic, nor did its members receive encouragement from their spiritual leaders or fellow communicants. If it is too much to describe the Catholic conscientious objector as a religious outcast, this is only because the general Catholic population took no notice of him. Camp Simon was administered by the Association of Catholic Conscientious Objectors, an impressive sounding organization that was really nothing more than a "front" set up by the Catholic Worker movement. And as for the Worker itself, though it has achieved a considerable measure of respect and admiration today, in the 1930s and 1940s mainstream Catholics tended to view the movement and its radical teachings as being of doubtful orthodoxy if not actually heretical....

Even in the absence of more official support, however, the men of Camp Simon (or, at least, those who actively practiced their faith) had no doubts as to the Catholicity of their witness. This confidence extended further than the ability to defend the *legitimacy* of their refusal to serve with appropriate theological arguments. Most of them regarded their stand as the *correct* stand to be taken, a binding moral obligation for them and, presumably, for other Catholics as well. This is not to say, of course, that they regarded those who did not see things their way as guilty of sin; instead, they were more likely to make allowances for what they considered a tragic failure on the part of most to think the matter through. When they had the rare occasion to argue the case they would present conscientious objection as the logical and behavioral consequence of the faith they and their detractors alike professed....

There is another dimension to Camp Simon's uniqueness, however. Much of the turbulence that marked its brief history must be traced not only to the fact that they were out of place as far as their fellow Catholics were concerned but that they were also (and, moreover, considered themselves to be) out of place in CPS. This enhanced the sense of isolation and alienation that was theirs and served to intensify the hardships and burdens that formed the substance of most of the continuing complaints and protests directed against those held responsible for the defects and injustices of the alternative service program.

And they were outsiders in a number of ways. First, by taking a stand against a war supported by a nearly total national consensus, they justifiably felt alienated from family, friends, neighbors, and the whole of society around them. Even if they were not actually disowned or repudiated, as so many were, there was punishment enough in the sorrowful tolerance encountered in those closest to them and in the knowledge of having disappointed people who meant a lot to them. Add to this, then, the fact that they felt alienated as well from the Church, in a very real sense orphaned by that spiritual mother in whose name they had taken their unpopular stand. Now they found themselves in CPS, outsiders again in a program conceived by and clearly dominated by the traditional peace churches (Friends, Mennonites, Brethren) leaving them a small minority in an almost exclusively Protestant operation.

The time factor is relevant here, too. These were, one must remember, pre-ecumenical days, a matter of no small concern for Catholics whose orthodoxy was already suspect in the eyes of their religious community. It did not help when they found themselves patronized by some of their CPS counterparts who apparently shared the opinion that Catholic objectors were not really Catholic but had somehow freed themselves from the rigidity and narrowness usually ascribed by Protestants to the Catholic Church. In any event, this third level of alienation – from CPS itself – carried the heaviest load of resentment. Rightly or wrongly, many of the Catholic objectors believed they had been trapped into a situation not of their making, obliged to accept deprivations imposed by a set of concessions and compromises arranged without their approval or participation between the military officers who ran the show and the Protestant peace church leaders....

AFTER THE WAR

THE PAX AMERICANA

With the end of World War II the American Church entered into a wholehearted alliance with the U.S. government for the preservation of world order against international communism. America had achieved a power and control over world affairs not matched since the Roman Empire, and the American church fully accepted the chance to help define this new peace of imposed order. In their 1944 pastoral, *International Order*, the bishops declared, "we have met the challenge of war. Shall we meet the challenge of peace?" They called for a new international order based on moral law, the recognition of God, and the oneness of humanity and international community. Blaming "scholars" for unleashing the philosophy that "asserts the right of aggression," they also urged the people to press for a strong new international body that could apply force to punish international outlaws and preserve order.

At the same time, however, the bishops showed a recurrent distrust of U.S. policies and actions in the post-war world. In November 1945 they issued their letter, *Between War and Peace*, in which they warned the United States against the cynical temptation to make agreements with the Soviets based on simple power considerations, recalling the poverty and helplessness of the world's people as the greatest obstacle to true peace. The next year the bishops condemned the post-war order as no true peace that cynically imposed settlements on the war-torn and ignored the true calling of peacemakers: care for the imprisoned, the displaced, and all the victims of the conflict.

The following excerpts are taken from Flannery, pp. 346-50.

359. U.S. Catholic Conference, Between War and Peace, November 18, 1945

The war is over but there is no peace in the world. In the Atlantic Charter we were given the broad outline of the peace for which we fought and bled and, at an incalculable price, won a great martial victory. It was that ideal of peace which sustained us through the war, which inspired the heroic defense of liberty by millions driven underground in enslaved countries. It made small oppressed nations confide in us as the trustee of their freedoms. It was the broad outline of a good peace. Are we going to give up this ideal of peace? If, under the pretext of a false realism, we do so, then we shall stand face to face with the awful catastrophe of atomic war.

Since the Moscow Conference of 1943, the United States, Great Britain and Russia have undertaken to shape gradually the peace which they are imposing on the nations. From the conferences of these victorious powers there is emerging slowly their pattern for the peace. It is disappointing in the extreme. Assurances are given us in the announced peace principles of our country, but so far results do not square with these principles. We are in perhaps the greatest crisis of human history. Our country has the power, the right, and the responsibility to demand a genuine peace, based on justice, which will answer the cry in the hearts of men across the world.

We want to work in unity with other nations for the making of a good peace. During the war perhaps, it may have been necessary for strategic reasons to postpone final decisions on many questions mooted at the conferences of the three great powers.

Russia and Democracy

Now we must face the facts. There are profound differences of thought and policy between Russia and the western democracies. Russia has acted unilaterally on many important settlements. It has sought to establish its sphere of influence in eastern and southeastern Europe, not on the basis of sound regional agreements in which sovereignties and rights are respected, but by the imposition of its sovereignty and by ruthlessly setting up helpless puppet states. Its Asiatic policy, so important for the peace of the world, is an enigma.

The totalitarian dictators promised benefits to the masses through an omnipotent police-state which extends its authority to all human relations and recognizes no innate freedoms. Their theories, moreover, look to the realization of world well-being as ultimately to be secured by the inclusion of all countries in their system. Sometimes Russia uses our vocabulary and talks of democracy and rights, but it attaches distorted meanings to the words. We think in terms of our historic culture. We see God-given, inviolable human rights in every person, and we know democracy as the free collaboration under law of citizens in a free country.

There is a clash of ideologies. The frank recognition of these differences is preliminary to any sincere effort in realistic world cooperation for peace. The basis of this cooperation must be mutual adherence to justice. It would be unjust for us to be an accomplice in violating the rights of nations, groups and individuals anywhere in the world.

A first step towards effective negotiation for peace is to have a plan....

Our Program for Peace

Our peace program envisions a world organization of nations. The Charter which emerged from the San Francisco Conference [of the United Nations], while undoubtedly an improvement on the Dumbarton Oaks proposals, does not provide for a sound, institutional organization of the international society. The Security Council provisions make it no more than a virtual alliance of the great powers for the maintenance of peace. These nations are given a status above the law. Nevertheless, our country acted wisely in deciding to participate in this world organization. It is better than world chaos. From the provision in the Charter for calling a Constituent Assembly in the future, there comes the hope that in time the defects may be eliminated and we may have a sound, institutional organization of the international community which will develop, not through mere voluntary concessions of the nations, but from the recognition of the rights and duties of international society.…

The bishops continued this message throughout the 1950s, insisting on the importance of the individual and of personal conscience. Even at the height of Cold War tensions, during the Hungarian Revolt and the Soviet invasion, the bishops could declare: "'If you wish peace,' said the pagan axiom, 'prepare for war.' Christianity has revised that saying: 'If you wish peace, prepare for peace'."

The following excerpts are taken from Flannery, pp. 375-78.

360. U.S. Catholic Conference, The Hope of Mankind, November 18, 1956

Once again in our time the alarm bell is ringing in the night. The world, inured as it is to tragedy, is apprised of a tragedy still more profound [the Soviet invasion of Hungary and the brutal suppression of the Hungarian revolt against Soviet rule]. In the events of this hour at which the Bishops of the American hierarchy meet in annual session, they and all men concerned with human welfare under God read the threat of catastrophe so dire as to destroy the last bulwarks of civilization.

One voice, urgent and clear, has made itself heard above the tumult of the nations. The Common Father of Christendom, Pope Pius XII, has spoken out with unhesitating forthrightness [see 296]. To those peoples who have been made the victims of a brutality so gross as to defy historic comparison, he has addressed words of compassion which could only come from a father's heart. To those nations bent upon aggression and which have ignored the sacred rights of humanity and the instruments of justice upon which they rest, he has issued stern warning of their madness.

Primacy of Law and Order

To all, whether inspired by selfish interest or led astray by rash counsel, who would jeopardize the delicate balance of world peace he has recalled the primacy of law and order in the settlement of human disagreements.

In this crisis we can only add our voice to his. We echo his burning reproof of those who have dared to unleash the hounds of war in a world which has already suffered so long and so bitterly. With him we denounce with all our strength this fresh outbreak of aggression which sets at utter defiance the hard-won concert of the nations for the outlawing of international banditry. With him we plead for a renewal of that basic sanity among men and nations which will establish peace upon its only enduring foundations of justice and charity. With him we urge upon the world not the counsels of despair which would describe the situation as beyond salvation, but the promise of a better hope implicit in the dawning recognition of human solidarity under the universal fatherhood of God.

We share his anguish for those whose unmerited sufferings have again filled the cup of human misery to overflowing. Our eyes follow his as he surveys the ravaged cities, the desolated countrysides, the charred ruins of a thousand homes and shrines. We count with him the ghastly casualties of modern warfare, the broken bodies, the dead in their silent windows.

Foremost, inevitably, in our thinking are the heroic people of Hungary....

War Would Only Annihilate

It is not mere rhetoric to say that at this juncture the world is poised on the brink of disaster; it is grim realism. Yet war in modern terms would be a nightmare of unimaginable horrors. It can only annihilate; it has no power to solve our problems. If, in the ultimate resort, it is the duty of man to resist naked aggression, still it is obvious that every possible means consistent with divine law and human dignity must be employed and exhausted to avoid the final arbitrament of nuclear warfare. It has been the hope of humankind that a means adequate to the necessity might be found in the concert of the United Nations....

Threat of Disunity

Nothing could be conceived more disheartening for the cause of peace, nothing more discreditable to the honor of nations which have pledged themselves to peace, than the disunity which threatens to disrupt our immediate counsels and dissipates our strength. With the Sovereign Pontiff we recognize the urgency of prompt and effective intervention to silence the guns of war and to enforce the pacific arbitration of conflicting claims. With him, also, we emphasize the paramount need for a heightened concept of the universal validity of law among nations as among men. For unless God and His justice are acknowledged as basic to the very substance of law, there is no foundation upon which men may hope to build a lasting citadel of peace. There, for those who will read it, is the poignant warning of our present tragedy....

"If you wish peace," said the pagan axiom, "prepare for war." Christianity has revised that saying "If you wish peace, prepare for peace." Though the hour is late indeed, it is not yet too late. There is the Divinity which governs the destinies of this world, and the supreme folly is to leave God out of our reckoning. As the Bishops of the United States we solemnly call upon the faithful throughout the land to pledge themselves to a veritable crusade of prayer. Let it be for the specific ends that international sanity will triumph over war; that justice may be vindicated by the nations united under law; and that our own beloved country, under God, may lead the way to that better hope for all mankind. Nor let us forget those who have suffered and who suffer now; that out of the crucible of their sacrifice may come the minted gold of freedom. We stand with the Vicar of Christ, and our prayer is for peace for our country and all the world – a peace with justice and charity....

CATHOLIC PEACEMAKING IN THE ATOMIC AGE

With the end of World War II the American peace movement lay practically dead. The Hydrogen Bomb, the Korean War, and the Cold War stilled protest and silenced outrage. CAIP had fully adopted the role of the United States as the international policeman of world order, while the hierarchy seemed to move even closer to official U.S. policy. Among Catholics the *Catholic Worker* remained the sole voice for peace, yet even for it the post-war period was a low ebb of virtual inactivity.

Despite this, several voices continued the Catholic Worker struggle. Chief among these were Dortothy Day, Robert Ludlow, and Ammon Hennacy.

The following is from *The Catholic Worker* 12.7 (Sept. 1945): 1.

361. Dorothy Day, We Go on Record

Mr. Truman was jubilant. President Truman. True man; what a strange name, come to think of it. We refer to Jesus Christ as true God and true Man. Truman is a true man of his time in that he was jubilant. He was not a son of God, brother of Christ, brother of the Japanese, jubilating as he did. He went from table to table on the cruiser which was bringing him home from the Big Three conference, telling the great news; "jubilant" the newspapers said. *Jubilate Deo.* We have killed 318,000 Japanese.

That is, we hope we have killed them, the Associated Press, on page one, column one of the *Herald Tribune,* says. The effect is hoped for, not known. It is to be hoped they are vaporized, our Japanese brothers, scattered, men, women and babies, to the four winds, over the seven seas. Perhaps we will breathe their dust into our nostrils, feel them in the fog of New York on our faces, feel them in the rain on the hills of Easton.

Jubilate Deo. President Truman was jubilant. We have created. We have created destruction. We have created a new element, called Pluto. Nature had nothing to do with it.

"A cavern below Columbia was the bomb's cradle," born not that men might live, but that men might be killed. Brought into being in a cavern, and then tried in a desert place, in the midst of tempest and lightning, tried out, and then again on the eve of the Feast of the Transfiguration of our Lord Jesus Christ, on a far off island in the eastern hemisphere, tried out again, this "new weapon which conceivably might wipe out mankind, and perhaps the planet itself."

"Dropped on a town, one bomb would be equivalent to a severe earthquake and would utterly destroy the place. A scientific brain trust has solved the problem of how to confine and release almost unlimited energy. It is impossible yet to measure its effects."

"We have spent two billion on the greatest scientific gamble in history and won," said President Truman jubilantly....

Scientists, army officers, great universities (Notre Dame included), and captains of industry – all are given credit lines in the press for their work of preparing the bomb – and other bombs, the President assures us, are in production now.

Great Britain controls the supply of uranium ore, in Canada and Rhodesia. We are making the bombs. This new great force will be used for good, the scientists assured us. And then they wiped out a city of 318,000. This was good. The President was jubilant.

Today's paper with its columns of description of the new era, the atomic era, which this colossal slaughter of the innocents has ushered in, is filled with stories covering every conceivable phase of the new discovery. Pictures of the towns and the industrial plants where the parts are made are spread across the pages. In the forefront of the town of Oak Ridge, Tennessee, is a chapel, a large comfortable-looking chapel benignly settled beside the plant. And the scientists making the first tests in the desert prayed, one newspaper account said.

Yes, God is still in the picture. God is not mocked. Today, the day of this so great news, God made a madman dance and talk, who had not spoken for twenty years. God sent a typhoon to damage the carrier *Hornet*. God permitted a fog to obscure vision and a bomber crashed into the Empire State Building. God permits these things. We have to remember it. We are held in God's hands, all of us, and President Truman too, and these scientists who have created death, but will use it for good. He, God, holds our life and our happiness, our sanity and our health; our lives are in His hands.

He is our Creator. Creator.

...And I think, as I think on these things, that while here in the western hemisphere, we went in for precision bombing (what chance of *precision* bombing now?), while we went in for obliteration bombing, Russia was very careful not to bomb cities, to wipe out civilian populations. Perhaps she was thinking of the poor, of the workers, as brothers.

I remember, too, that many stories have come out of Russia of her pride in scientific discoveries and of how eagerly and pridefully they were trying to discover the secret of life – how to create life (not death).

Exalted pride, yes, but I wonder which will be easier to forgive?...

Everyone says, "I wonder what the Pope thinks of it." How everyone turns to the Vatican for judgment, even though they do not seem to listen to the voice there! But our Lord Himself has already pronounced judgment on the atomic bomb. When James and John (John the beloved) wished to call down fire from heaven on their enemies, Jesus said:

"You know not of what spirit you are. The Son of Man came not to destroy souls but to save." He said also, "What you do unto the least of these my brethren, you do unto me."

ROBERT LUDLOW

Born in Scranton, PA, into a family of coal miners, Ludlow converted to Catholicism after hearing a lecture by Dorothy Day and Peter

Maurin in 1937. Fired from his high-school teaching job for criticizing U.S. foreign policy, he became a librarian at Catholic University until 1942. During World War II Ludlow had served as a CO in the Rosewood Training School and after this release in 1947 he went to St. Joseph's House in New York, became associate editor of the *Catholic Worker*, and began to write the "PAX" column. He remained on the paper and actively involved in the Worker community until 1954, when he left the movement.

Ludlow was the first Catholic intellectual to really absorb and interpret Gandhi's nonviolence. Through the 1940s and 1950s he broadened the direction already charted by Paul Hanly Furfey [356] and developed these influences into a full-fledged Catholic theology of nonviolence. Rejecting the passivity and individualism that people often associated with pacifism, he took up the idea of *satyagraha* as "a new *Christian* way of social change." Ludlow urged Catholic pacifists to move forward from their individual opposition to violence to a social effort, first to move the church toward a commitment to peace, and then to transform American life.

Like much of the Catholic Worker movement then and today, Ludlow shares a deep Catholic conservatism, here expressed through an essentially hierarchical view of existence and an open hostility to modern civil and secular society. Yet many of the key elements of much current discourse can be found in Ludlow's thought: the priority of conscience and the rejection of state attempts to define its limits, his obvious reliance upon a gospel model of nonviolent revolution. The Gospel is not a "counsel to perfection" but a requirement of Christian life. Ludlow also offers an early critique of the nation-state and its idolatrous ideology long before the analysis of the National Security State by Latin American liberation theologians [333-334], and a realization that conscription and militarism oppress most heavily the poor and people of color. Ludlow was also a generation ahead of his time in attacking the very basis of the conscription system of compulsion, even when no military draft exists: registration.

At the same time that Ludlow's question "what would happen if we are all pacifist" looks back to Origen [59], it also looks forward to the thought of Gene Sharp and his students on the possibilities of nonviolent national defense.

The following selection is taken from the Pax Column in *The Catholic Worker* 15.5 (July-August 1948): 7

362. Robert Ludlow, The Draft, Christian Anarchism, and the State

With the new registration act we now have it written into the law of the land that the State is at liberty to violate conscience. This occurs in the provisions regarding conscientious objectors which states, "Nothing contained in this act shall be construed to require any person to be subject to combat service which for the purpose hereof includes training for combat duties in the armed forces of the United States who by reason of religious training and belief is conscientiously opposed to participation in war in any form. Religious training and belief in this connection means an individual's belief in a relation to a Supreme Being involving duties superior to those arising from any human relation but does not include essentially sociological or philosophical views or a merely personal moral code."

As Henry VIII [of England, 1509-47, see **212**] arrogated to himself the role of Vicar of Christ and made theological decisions by State authority so today we are handing over to the State not only such authority but the very right to define what religion is. It does not matter whether the State's definition of religion is correct or not – the point is that we have conceded the right of the State to make such decisions and to deny validity of conscience to those who may not agree with it. In the present draft law the State denies the right of a personal moral code. Conscience is thus made the sole prerogative of those who happen to belong to an organized *pacifist* Church or who base their opinion on consciously accepted religious grounds. It is, in effect, a denial of the existence of conscience in man as such. It makes of conscience a purely sociological phenomenon. It is a sociological relativism. It subjects conscience to the State just as firmly as does any professedly atheist State. National States have been and are for all practical purposes atheistic. For they use religion for the utility of the State....

Political Means

And this is why it is so futile to expect anything from political means. For once power is attained the temptation to defend and increase it by any means available has proven too strong for most political leaders. The bankruptcy of the left comes from this reliance on political means and

733

the consequent use of force to maintain regimes which should, if Marxist theories were valid, look forward to their own cessation from power. And that is why there is such a strong case for Christian anarchism. Why there is so great a need today to place the emphasis on freedom, on the liberty of the sons of God. There should be no insurmountable difficulty in the use of this terminology – in the advocacy of Christian anarchism. Since it is Christian it is obviously not atheistic. For the Catholic there would be no denial of original sin or the consequences that flow from it and which means that, taking man as he is, there will in all probability be need for some government. But the Christian anarchist contention is that the State as we know it, the State of history, the State which is nationalist and centralized has in the past and does today work against the Christian concept of the brotherhood of all men, that it leads to hatreds and wars and such manifold injustices that we should work against the State, that we should advocate instead a decentralized and democratic workers economy. And that precisely as we become more Christian so do we approach as nearly as possible in this life towards a governmentless society. For as we become bound by love rather than by law do we realize in concrete society that liberty of which St. Paul is so eloquent. That liberty which becomes possible as man utilizes the possibilities of deification, of living personally and socially above the plane of the natural.

A successful revolution will be one that has a transcendental basis, the radical today (as always) is he whose values come from the Absolute, whose conscience is responsive to concepts which depend for their validity not on cultural patterns but on faith in the supernatural. But it will be a faith freely accepted, freely propagandized. It will not proceed with eyes closed to the world as we know it and consequently it will reject theocratic government because it will be realized that such a regime could only be realized within the confines of temporal history at the expense of freedom. Clerical administration of temporal affairs, even by proxy, has not tended towards that freedom which is the necessary requisite for meritorious faith.

The Church

The Catholic who advocates a Christian anarchist position in nowise separates himself from the common acceptance of the governance of the Church, the hierarchical character of it. For he realizes that Christ spoke with authority, that we accept supernatural truth on the basis of authority that it could not be otherwise. And that it is as foolish to attempt settlement of theological questions by reason alone as it would be to settle philosophical questions by authority. The revolution we speak of will be one that informs the temporal order with the supernatural, transcendental values will motivate those who work for its fulfillment. But it will not transpose the hierarchical set-up of the Church into the temporal order, it will keep always in mind that Christ's Kingdom is not of this world, that the ultimate realization of our end transcends the temporal order and finds its terminal point in God. Christian values will find visible expression more in a workers democracy than in any form of authoritarianism known in history, for there will be realized to a greater degree than we have known the realization of that greatest of all commands, the commandment of love, which if it be not fulfilled makes all else of no account.

Refuse to Register

Our definite problem now becomes one of disobedience to the State. For the State as we know it is the visible representation of those values which proceed from the spirit of the world and the flesh and the devil. We see how it has invaded the realm of conscience, we see how it has destroyed human brotherhood. We know there can be no collaboration. So we must refuse to register under this draft act, and we must be prepared for whatever consequences come of this refusal. Registration is an acknowledgment of the government's right to conscript. To conscript means to conscript for war. And war is not possible for those who would follow the teachings of the Sermon on the Mount. And the Sermon on the Mount was addressed to ALL.

What will happen then if we are all pacifist? We will be in danger of invasion. We are in danger of such Invasion anyway and it is far better that we perish in defense of Negroes; not to register because discrimination is enforced in the army. And it is good that Negroes and whites should refuse to register for this reason. It is another protest against the State. But it should not rest there. A democratic army is an impossibility from the very nature of a military set-up. And if you eliminate racial discrimination there will still remain the concrete evil of the army, the sin that is its existence. Perhaps those who object to the army on the score of this discrimination will go further and realize that it is impossible to have any democracy at all as long as there exists a military. That we must press for absolute disarmament, that it will have to start as a unilateral affair, and that what happens tomorrow is not at all as important as what we do today. For if today we proceed in any other spirit than that of Christ our tomorrow will already be assured, it will remain the same grim world, and there will remain all the rivalries, all the distrust and hatred, all the injustice that have made for a world in which we live as though in armed fortresses.

AMMON HENNACY

More than any other single individual, Ammon Hennacy was responsible for bringing the Catholic Worker out of the shock of the post-war years and for developing an activist practice of nonviolence and civil disobedience that matched Ludlow's vision. Born in 1893, the son of a Quaker and Abolitionist family, by 1916 Hennacy was a socialist organizer. In 1917 he was sentenced to five years in Federal prison for resisting the draft, and by 1918 had fully embraced anarchism. Confined to solitary in prison, he converted to Christianity, and by 1937 had been attracted to the Catholic Worker house in Milwaukee and there met both Day and Maurin. With Pearl Harbor, Hennacy wrote to the IRS announcing his intention to refuse war taxes, and when Dorothy Day endorsed his action, he wrote to thank her and began contributing articles to the *Catholic Worker.*

Throughout the 1940s Hennacy maintained his tax protest, living as a farm worker in the Southwest and among the Hopi Indians, writing, and spreading the influence of Gandhi and, later, of Danilo Dolci [304-305] in the United States. By 1952 he had come to the Chrystie Street House in New York, converted to Catholicism, and joined the Catholic Worker movement.

Ammon Hennacy's best known achievement was his resistance to the annual Civil Defense drills that marked life throughout the 1950s. Designed to beef up American resolve and preparedness to atomic war, every year the drills summoned all U.S. citizens in major cities to underground shelters, basements, and subways, commanded students to cower beneath desks or in darkened hallways as hundreds of air-raid sirens wailed the coming of nuclear destruction. Most Americans over 40 today will recall the silent terror that the sirens inspired with chilling regularity. In 1955 the program was made compulsory across the country, and in New York the State Defense Emergency Act punished failure to run underground with one year in prison and a $500 fine.

In 1953 and 1954 Hennacy picketed against the drills, alone and unnoticed. In 1955, however, with defiance now illegal, he and twentyeight people, including ten Catholic Workers, stood outside City Hall in New York City and refused to take shelter as the sirens wailed. In 1956 Hennacy, Day, and twenty others were arrested. By 1960 a wellpublicized protest drew 1,000; the police, unaccustomed to such massive peaceful demonstrations, arrested only 27 and ignored the leaders. In 1961 A.J. Muste's Committee for Nonviolent Action joined the Catholic Workers as 2,500 people demonstrated throughout New York City, and many other groups joined them across the country. Embarrassed by the pacifists' success, in 1962 the Kennedy administration cancelled the drills.

Hennacy continued planting the seeds of nonviolence throughout the country. In 1957 he joined Muste's CNVA to successfully stop an Atomic Energy Commission hydrogen bomb test near Las Vegas; he was arrested for protests in Washington, D.C., in Florida, and outside Strategic Air Command headquarters in Omaha in 1959. After serving in Federal prison, he returned to the Catholic Worker in New York in 1960, departed for for Salt Lake City in 1961, and finally left the Catholic Worker and the Catholic church in 1962. In Salt Lake he founded his own Joe Hill House of Hospitality and died there in January 1970.

The following selections are taken from Ammon Hennacy, *The Book of Ammon Hennacy*, Salt Lake City, 1964, pp. 262-65, 286-89.

363. Ammon Hennacy, Autobiography

I Become a Catholic September 21 to November 17, 1952

"When will Ammon join the Church?" asked a friend, of Father George.

"When it gets underground, I suppose," he answered.

I felt that in ten years or more the capitalist or the Communist dictatorship might have all of us radicals in jail, and then would be time enough for joining a church. I had always said that a priest or preacher who blest war could not bless me.

When picketing that Wednesday in August of 1950, I had momentarily been drawn to the Church. Also for a moment at Fr. Casey's retreat at Mary Farm in August of 1952 I felt that there might be something inside the Church that I ought to have, but that was only for a second and I thought of it no more. I attended mass daily after that retreat because I was at the CW and loved them all. So when Bob Ludlow [362] went to Uniate mass at the Ukrainian church, each morning I got up early and went with him. If I was at Peter Maurin Farm I went to mass there. I did not understand much of it and it did not mean much to me. I was busy writing on this book, speaking to all kinds of radicals, and answering letters that came to the CW. Father Casey had left for Minnesota and I was glad to have met him. I told him that if I ever joined the Church he would be the one to baptize me, but I felt no reason to even think of joining it now. Dorothy had said not to join the Church because I loved her and the CW, so if, in addition, I loved Fr. Casey, the first anarchist priest I had met, this only meant that I had fine radical friends who were Catholic. The Church which upheld the rich landlords in every country when it was in the majority and who still blessed Franco and Peron, and still blest war – that was the Church that people thought of when the name Catholic was mentioned, and not the Catholic Worker.

It was Saturday the 20th of September when Dorothy mentioned that she had to talk to a Communion Breakfast at the Hotel Biltmore the next morning to 600 employees of Gimbels [the department store, as famous as Macy's in its time]. I knew what those confabs consisted of: they all got together and said: "God, Jesus, Gimbels! God, Jesus, Gimbels!" Pretty soon they were saying "Gimbels, Jesus, God," and finally ending up with only the word, "Gimbels." It was the old Pie in the Sky racket. As the old I.W.W. [Industrial Workers of the World], song went:

Long haired preachers come out every night;
Try to tell you what's wrong and what's right
But when asked how 'bout something to eat,
They will answer in voices so sweet:
You will eat
Bye and Bye
In that beautiful land
Above the Sky.
Work and Pray;
Live on hay;

Chapter 7: Catholic Peacemaking in the USA

You'll get pie in the sky
When you die.

Around 9 p.m. I was typing in the office when Dorothy stopped on her way to the church. She said she did not know what to say to such a crowd so she would have to pray about it and ask for guidance. She came back in a couple of hours.

We all wished her good luck as she went, as the saying was, into the jaws of the lion next morning. In the afternoon Tom was called to the phone and received the message that I was to accompany Florence Quinn, who did secretarial work for Dorothy at times, and who had questioned me about "Rendering unto Caesar" at my first talk at the CW, to some free opera down in the village. Dorothy had mentioned about going there and I told her I didn't care about such things. Florence had tried to get reserved seats but only got a number to call to wait in line. I thought that as long as I was there I might as well stay for we could just as easily get 3 seats as 2. While we were talking about it Dorothy came up. She had been to see her sister Della after the talk at the Hotel Biltmore. She described how the big shots from the store and the chancery office breathed hard when she commenced her voluntary poverty, reliance upon God rather than insurance companies and capitalist effort, non-payment of taxes for war and Atom Bombs, etc. She described going to mass in the big church nearby, and that right after Communion without any reason or warning the big organ burst forth with the blasphemy of the Star Spangled Banner. This was a most holy moment after partaking of the body of Christ and it was broken up by this war-mongering. Everyone stood up in honor of this God of Battles. Dorothy did that thing which only St. Francis or Gandhi would have had the spiritual insight to do: *she knelt and prayed.*

Hearing her tell of this gave me the one positive jolt of my life since I knew in solitary in Atlanta that I loved my enemy the warden. Here was I, brave and boastful about my great One Man Revolution. I had faced the taunts of crowds and of the police, had felt nearly alone in opposing the draft in two wars. I was making a good fight. I remembered right then of my debate with the head of the American Legion in Milwaukee, Sam Corr, at the Grand Avenue Congregational Church in 1941, before Pearl Harbor. The flustered assistant minister stood between Sam and me on the platform before the crowd, saying "Now what song will we sing? Oh, Onward Christian Soldiers, with your permission Mr. Hennacy." "You fellows can sing it. I won't," I replied. Accordingly I sat stubbornly in front of them all while they stood and sang. I felt mean and I expect I looked mean. And they glowered at me. I was the first to speak. I said, "I suppose you folks will wonder why I did not have the courtesy to arise and sing with you. I wouldn't sing such a song in prison and stood the chance of going to solitary many times. One young fellow walked out of prison chapel when they sang it and did a month in solitary. So I'll be damned if I'll stand up for such a war-mongering song on the outside." The next day the Milwaukee *Journal* commented on my stubbornness.

Now all this came back to me. I called myself a non-church Christian. I was just a stubborn smart-aleck – perhaps with more knowledge than many others I met, but still moving along with a handicap of lack of spirituality. Now I knew my lack of it. How was I going to get it and where? I did not dare admit to myself out-loud that I was slipping, but I did say then with tears in my eyes to Dorothy, "You have shown me a great light; you have made me ashamed of myself. This is the biggest jolt that I have received in my life. Where it will lead I don't know, but from now on life is going…to be different for me."…

[One evening the next week] Dorothy went upstairs at once to read and write and I went towards the barn, where I slept upstairs, above Fr. Duffy's room. It was quite dark. Without any conscious intention it seemed I walked into the chapel instead of going upstairs. There was a candle burning by the Little Flower. (I didn't know what the Little Flower was. I had always bought Carmen and Sharon a red rose every day or two and had brought one for Dorothy when I could get one. I did not know how I was "working against my stubborn self," for Dorothy had put a rose by the Little Flower and it was there while I prayed and meditated for an hour or more.) I had always prayed for grace and wisdom when in a Catholic Church, and I did so now. Much of the time I was just quiet and did not say any prayers. I did not hear any "voices" but there came to me a clear assurance that the Catholic Church was the true Church, that whatever I did not understand would be explained to me, that I was not hurting the Church by remaining outside: I was only hurting myself. For I needed this spiritual insight that Dorothy had when she knelt and the main thing now in my life was to work toward getting it.…

Chapter 7: Catholic Peacemaking in the USA

June 15, 1955, Air Raid Drills

In the spring of 1955 I saw in the paper that there would be an air raid drill on June 15 and all were supposed to take part or suffer a penalty up to a year in jail and $500 fine, this being a state law. I told Dorothy and said we must get ready to disobey this foolish law. I contacted Ralph DeGia of the War Resisters League and he got in touch with others, F.O.R. [Fellowship of Reconciliation, the interfaith peace organization], American F.S.C. [Friends Service Committee, the Quaker peace and justice organization] & W.I.L. and so accordingly when the time came we had a whole group in City Hall Park ready to disobey when the whistles blew. The television men were there and asked Dorothy to tell why we were acting as we did, but she asked me to speak as my voice would be louder so I told them that if a bomb dropped there would be no police left to arrest us and that the whole thing was a farce. Robert Fisher, a young man uptown who was working as a social worker in lieu of going to the army heard me on television and took a taxi and came down and went to jail with us. He is a Unitarian. Just before the whistles blew we gathered at the War Resisters Office at 5 Beekman Street where Bayard Rustin advised all of us not to refuse shelter unless we were ready to take the consequences of perhaps a year in jail and $500 fine. There were some who handed out leaflets until the last minute and then took shelter. Dorothy and I had signed a leaflet which was well printed by Dave Dellinger [a major figure in the 1960s peace movement] which we distributed. It began "In the name of Jesus who is God, who is Love, we will not obey this order to pretend, to evacuate, to hide...we will not be drilled into fear.... We do not have faith in God if we depend upon the Atom Bomb"...ending up with our pacifist anarchist idea of refusal in every way to support war and governments.

We were ordered to take shelter and refused to do so. We were packed into vans and when we were waiting to be booked at Elizabeth Street station we noticed an elderly man with a badge on his cap whom we thought might be an attendant. I gave him one of our leaflets and it was not until later when our indictment was read in court that we discovered that he was Rocco Parelli, a bootblack, who had been sitting in the park knowing nothing about the air-raid drill, who happened to be the first one arrested. Our indictment thus read: "Rocco Parelli and 28 others willfully refused to take shelter." It was entirely fitting that this common

741

man, not a scholar, intellectual or radical, should symbolically head the list, representative of the workers of the world we were trying to awaken. There were ten of us from the CW: Dorothy and I; Carol Perry, a tax refuser from San Francisco; Patricia Rusk, Mary Ann McCoy; Eileen Fantino and Helen Russell of the group who work with Puerto Rico children in Harlem. Mary Roberts, an artist, Stanley Borowski who has helped in selling CW's and picketing, and Michael Kovalak, who with others had picketed the [Catholic archbishop's] Chancery office at the time of the graveyard strike in 1949. A.J. Muste, Ralph DeGia, and Bayard Rustin were old time War Resisters. Jackson MacLow, our atheist anarchist friend; Bob Berk, a young radical I had known in Tucson, and Dale Brotherington, a Quaker who had corresponded with me from Florida. Andy Osgood, a War Resister who had visited me in Phoenix and Hugh Corbin of the same group who had picketed with us in Washington, D.C. Also Edith Horwitz whose husband had been a CO, and Jim Peck, an old time CO. I had not met Henry Babcock, an elderly Quaker, or Henry Maiden, a Quaker with whom I celled. Kent Larrabee, head of the New York City Fellowship of Reconciliation. Orie Pell of the Women's International League for Peace and Freedom, but the Queen of us all was Judith [Malina] Beck, the actress who was supposed to be playing Phaedra in The Living Theatre that night but who went to jail with us....

By chance we fellows had sandwiches but the women did not have anything to eat all day. Around 11 p.m. we appeared before Judge Louis Kaplan. As our names were read out the Irish clerk it seemed did not wish to admit that an Irishman by the name of Hennacy could possibly be among these radicals so he persisted in pronouncing my name as "Hennacky." Some of the girls laughed lightly at this and the judge pounded his gavel and wanted to know what was the matter. Judith answered pertly that she had had nothing to eat and was giddy. The judge asked her to step up and she did quickly, and not demurely. He told her to stand back and shouted angrily, asking her name, where she had been born, and who paid her rent. She answered without the customary "your honor" with which these dignitaries inflate their ego. This enraged him all the more and he wanted to know if she had ever been in a mental institution. *"No, have you?"* was her classic answer which will reverberate through these musty halls until the time when courts and prisons will cease to exist. The audience laughed and the judge shouted

Chapter 7: Catholic Peacemaking in the USA

"Take her for observation to Bellevue psychiatric ward." Judith screamed dramatically and her husband who was one of the audience in the court-room, a Yale graduate, stood up and shouted "You can't do this." The place was in an uproar. The judge ordered the courtroom cleared by the riot squad and we were all put back in our cells. Later he had us brought in and read off a written statement saying, "Theoretically three million people have been killed in this air raid and you are the murderers." He placed our bail at the unheard of sum of $1500 each.

At that time we of the CW had not discussed the matter of bail so we accepted it after being held for 24 hours. I had thought to plead not guilty with the others to show our solidarity with them, but Dorothy being a better basic radical than I am persuaded me to plead guilty on the anarchist principle of "we did it once and we will do it again; and no legal quibbling." So Dorothy and I, Carol, Mary, Stanley, Dick Kern and Judith pled guilty but Judge Bushel deferred our sentence until those pleading not guilty should have their trial.

After our arrest the diocesan paper, *The Catholic News*, N.Y. City, felt that we were presumptuous in our "private interpretation" when the Church always upheld obedience to duly constituted authority. On the other hand the *Commonweal* in a long editorial praised our stand: "The saint and the radical (and they are often the one and the same) share a common, ironic destiny, honored by posterity, they are usually perse-cuted during their life times.... We honor the saint and the radical – dead; alive we find them too uncomfortable for our tribute.... A society without its radical is a dead society, just as a Church without its saints is a blighted Church...we need them to remind us of uncomfortable truths, to rebuke our slothfulness and ease."...

Fritz Eichenberg, who had been in court, provided us with a sketch for the front page of the July-August CW. The case dragged on and on and finally on Dec. 22 we were all found guilty and sentence suspended. We had all expected to get time and when I came home Tom Caine had prepared a card wreathed in black on my desk, "To express our sincerest condolence on this sad occasion." Opening it I saw in big letters: "So Sorry! NO JAIL!"

The anti-nuclear movement soon began attracting a younger gen-eration who would soon become the leaders of the peace movement of the 1960s. One of these was the writer, organizer, and activist Thomas

Cornell. He was born on April 11, 1934 in Bridgeport, CT and attended Bridgeport public schools and Fairfield Prep. He earned a BA from the Jesuit Fairfield College in Connecticut in 1956. While at Fairfield Cornell was first attracted to the Catholic Worker by reading Dorothy Day's autobiography. He joined the movement in 1953. By 1962 he had become associate editor of the *Catholic Worker*. In November 1965 he became one of the first open draft resisters and a founder of the Catholic Peace Fellowship [CPF, 372]. Upon his release from prison in 1968 for burning his draft card, Cornell became a representative to the UN's Non-Governmental Organizations Disarmament Committee, while remaining head of the CPF, maintaining the deeply religious spirit of the Catholic Worker's nonviolence within the organization and continuing the CPF's emphasis upon the draft. At the same time Cornell was deeply involved in the civil-rights movement, first participating in an NAACP campaign in Bridgeport in 1953 and maintaining his commitment through the 1960s and 1970s. He was one of the founders of Pax Christi/USA in its first incarnation in 1972, and – ironically – it was the rapid growth of Pax Christi as a more broad-based and institutionally linked organization that soon made Cornell's CPF irrelevant to many Catholics.

In September 1979 Cornell lost his post at the FOR due to restructuring and the emergence of a new generation of peace leadership, but continued his organizing work, especially against registration and the draft. He has served as a consultant to the U.S. bishops on the draft and on the pastoral letter The Challenge of Peace [389], on the executive committees of the War Resisters League, the Central Committee for Conscientious Objectors, the National Interreligious Board for Conscientious Objectors and others. In 1981 he finally left his active role in the CPF to accept a position with the World Council of Churches. In 1982 he established a soup kitchen in Waterbury, CT in cooperation with the NAACP and PRIDE and served as its director until 1992. In 1988 Cornell was ordained as a deacon and assigned to St. Thomas Parish in Waterbury and in the 1990s began studies toward the priesthood at St. Joseph College. He remains affiliated with the CPF as national secretary. Cornell has published dozens of articles in various peace and religious journals and is co-editor of the collection of Catholic Worker articles, *A Penny a Copy*, cited frequently in this book.

Chapter 7: Catholic Peacemaking in the USA

The following excerpt is taken from Tom Cornell, "The Catholic Church and Witness Against War," in Thomas A. Shannon, ed., *War or Peace? The Search for New Answers,* Maryknoll, NY: Orbis Books, 1980, pp. 200-213.

364. Tom Cornell, The Nuclear Air-Raid Protests

...Nonviolent group civil disobedience wasn't in the political lexicon in the immediate postwar period. Since the days of labor militancy in the late 1930s there had not been any advance in the technique. But in 1955 the National Civil Defense program was in high gear. Its principal reason for existence, so Catholic Workers were convinced, was to make the idea of nuclear war "thinkable," to prepare, psychologically, for war with the Soviet Union. Civil Defense units were organized on a local basis, and although they sometimes performed worthily in "normal" disaster situations such as floods and the like, many operated as vigilante squads, maintaining dossiers on suspect persons in local communities and intimidating local meetings where anything that local C.D. leaders considered subversive might be said. An annual mock drill in case of nuclear attack was instituted on a nationwide basis. The individual states were left to determine the degree of compulsion upon citizens to participate. New York State decided to make mandatory the taking of shelter in subway tunnels and designated buildings during the spring mock attacks. The first was in the spring of 1955....

By chance I happened to be driving from New Haven to the Bowery that day, proselytizing a group of Yale students who were interested in the CW movement. While listening to the news on the car radio, we learned that a group of pacifists had just been arrested in City Hall Park for refusing shelter during the drill. The thought crossed my mind that the Yalees might be in for a more exciting day than I could have planned for them because some of my friends would be likely to have participated in the demonstration. So it was. The Chrystie Street St. Joseph House of Hospitality was bedlam, the telephone ringing off the wall. Friends of the Worker, priests and bishops were calling one after the other to inquire. It was true: Dorothy, Ammon, Eileen Fantino, Pat Rus[k], and Mary Ann McCoy were in jail, Dorothy for the first time since the 1920s when she was caught in a raid on an IWW house and charged with prostitution, the other women for the first time. (Ammon had the longest arrest record in the movement, any movement almost.) When a telephone call came in announcing that Dorothy and the women were released pending a hearing, most of us decided to celebrate at the White Horse Tavern in Greenwich Village, where we discussed Eric Gill's theory of aesthetics.

The next spring many of the same people sat in City Hall Park, and the next year, and the next. Jail sentences ranged from 30 days to suspended terms. One judge gave tickets to the reviewing stand for the St. Patrick's Day parade to the Catholics. But even her most fervent admirers were beginning to show signs of irritation at Dorothy's insistence on her annual pilgrimage to jail. "Why does she bother? She's made her point! Why go through this over and over again?" "Upsetting our consciences," they might have added.

The band of civil disobedients became smaller [sic] each year, until the absurdity of the Civil Defense program became more evident to more people, and the political potential for mass civil disobedience began to dawn on people. In 1961 the demonstration was well prepared for. An estimated 2,000 people showed up at City Hall Park on Civil Defense Day, too many to arrest. The police nabbed 52 apparent leaders. Similar demonstrations were mounted at campuses around the city, involving perhaps another 2,000. Not only was the state law requiring participation nullified, but the national program was drastically curtailed and no more nationwide drills were conducted.

The demonstration begun so casually by the CW in 1953 can now be seen as a watershed. Civil disobedience on a mass scale was not new, but as a manifestation consciously rooted in a philosophy of nonviolence it was new to the U.S. Martin Luther King in 1956-1957 led a mass legal nonviolent boycott of the Montgomery bus system. In 1959 A.J. Muste and a small group including Carl Meyer of the Chicago CW House climbed over a small fence bordering the Strategic Air Command Headquarters outside Omaha, Nebraska, in an act of civil disobedience. In these three actions the movement of nonviolent mass civil disobedience was launched....

THE NEVADA ATOM-BOMB PROTESTS

While the issues of nuclear weaponry and testing came to the center stage of American politics only with the 1980s and the Nuclear Freeze movement, Catholic peacemakers had been at the forefront of the antinuclear movement since Dorothy Day's first condemnation of the Hiroshima and Nagasaki bombings [361]. In 1957 Ammon Hennacy had launched a new form of protest in the deserts of Nevada, where just north of Las Vegas at Yuca Mountain the U.S. government has maintained a testing ground for nuclear weaponry since the 1940s.

Here, for the past fifty years, in a interdenominational movement that has come to call itself the Nevada Desert Experience, many in the peace community have participated in what has been a strange, mysterious and moving ritual. Arriving from all across the United States, peacemakers soon leave behind the magical theater of Las Vegas for the even deeper magic of the desert to camp, form a community, and make peace within eyesight of the nuclear-test range. After a period of spiritual and physical preparation – and in total openness with the authorities – participants join in various levels of protest and civil disobedience. Some flank the gates of the test site to silently witness as workers – many very highly paid – buzz in and out in expensive new cars; some hand out leaflets to visitors or attempt to engage workers in dialog, some then openly cross over the "cattle guard" that marks the boundary of the test range to be met by local police and arrested for trespass. Others camp and hike to more remote sections of the site to cross the barbed-wire fences. Some turn themselves in for arrest immediately to stand trial as a protest against the crimes of nuclear preparation; others – seasoned in survival and outdoor skills – penetrate either to Ground Zero itself or to testing facilities, there to be arrested not only as a witness for nonviolence but also to dramatize the futility of government security measures against a people determined to exercise their own will.

The variety of witness – and of motive – is wide, and the "effectiveness" of such action has been debated since the beginning of these actions, and it continues to be debated both by participants on the site and by many in the peace movement. Yet the mystery and grace of individuals coming together to challenge the darkest powers humanity has yet invented, in the middle of the desert, inevitably brings comparison to Jesus's own wandering and temptations to power in the desert [30] and looks forward to ever more inventive action.

The following is taken from Charles Butterworth's first-hand account of his own desert experience. Butterworth was an attorney who practiced in Philadelphia and became active in the CW movement in the late 1950s, writing the *Catholic Worker's* "Chrystie Street" column in the 1960s, reporting on Worker houses around the country, engaging in acts of nonviolence, and contributing articles and book reviews to the paper until his death in 1978. He was an advocate of prisoners rights and an outspoken critic of the Vietnam war and a signer of the Catholic Peace Fellowship's open letter against the war in 1966 [372].

His account was reported in *The Catholic Worker* 24.2 (September, 1957): 5.

365. Charles Butterworth, Nonviolence in Nevada

One thing that helps my thinking about what man really is, is to remember that we are members of one family with God as our Father. Heredity, history, and economic environment affect us, but it's much more important that we are children of one living God. Our Faith explains why this is really true in spite of appearances. It follows that we ought not to drop atomic bombs on each other.

That is one of the reasons, I expect, that brought this group of Quakers and others to Nevada to protest the continued testing of atomic weapons by our government. The idea was simple. On August 6, Hiroshima day, a group of people would have a prayer and meditation meeting in front of the test site which is about 70 miles NW of Las Vegas. Then some from the group would rise, approach the gate, cross the line, and submit to arrest. It was hoped that this speaking with the body would give voice to the many people here and all over the world who want to say no to war in a more effective way.

Two of our leaders paid a personal visit to the Atomic Energy Commission representatives in Las Vegas, who were friendly and seemed to know all about us. They offered the use of their cool water at the test site and warned us not to watch the blast. It can cause blindness for a week. They had discussed letting us present our case to the test site employees in their auditorium, but decided that there had been enough publicity already for people to understand.

The state highway police were also visited. When a patrolman there heard that the witness was to be fully peaceful he was very grateful. "Well," he exclaimed, with a sigh of relief, "I'm so glad there's to be no uprising."

The purpose of these visits was to tell the government just what we planned to do. In war truth may be the desired end, but secrecy and half truths are the means. In nonviolent conflict truth is end and means. Win or lose in war, truth suffers. Win or lose in nonviolence, truth is stronger. Ends don't justify means, means determine ends.

About 10 AM Tuesday morning the first group of three arose to cross the line. Eleven in all were to cross and there were nineteen in the prayer vigil. The three approached the gate slow and steady. Their wide brim hats and camping clothes added to the western flavor of the scene. A big crowd of reporters, camera men, and sightseers at the gate swallowed them out of our sight. There was conversation for about five minutes, the line was crossed, and the arrests made.

Lawrence Scott, coordinator of the project, later told us that there was a certain exhilaration in stepping across the line. He was the first and his arm was held so tight by the officer that he couldn't turn toward his companions. But his thoughts were with them only, not on himself at all. The great gift of a moment of total selflessness was given him.

The trial of the eleven who crossed the line was in the local county court Tuesday afternoon on the basis of trespassing. They stated to the judge that they thought they had done right and he construed this as a plea of not guilty. He suspended sentence for a year and released them. That means that if there is no new trespass for a year, then there is no requirement to appear again, no sentence, and no record kept. The group did not make any agreement or promises to the court.

Several incidents showed us that beneath people's outward calm is often great fear and distrust. We learned afterwards that no one had wanted to be the guard on duty at the gate Tuesday morning. In their view anything could happen and there might be some trick.

But the clearest incident of distrust took place Tuesday evening when we had decided to continue the prayer vigil through the night. There was to be a test blast in the morning at 5:20 AM and the guard felt it was his duty to put up strings around our group. Lawrence Scott said no one would wander and no guarding was needed. But the lines went up anyway. Cars were stationed at the corners with their lights shining along the strings. A guard sat up all night in each car to see that no one passed these lighted lines. One reporter joined a guard, but decided nothing was going to happen and so went off to sleep.

As far as I can see this was just an ordinary precaution taken in line of duty. When we stop watching God with confidence we have to start watching everyone else with suspicion. And it gets more complicated all the time,

Wednesday morning after the test blast the question of going back over the line was taken up. One said he was ready, but he felt his family wasn't yet. Another thought that our relations with the AEC were friendly and now a further crossing would strain them too much. A third felt that the line should be crossed again, that the price hadn't been paid.

After a time Lawrence Scott expressed what I believe was the sense of the meeting. He said, "I have gone as far as I am led," and there was no uneasiness in the way he said it. He sensed that a first step had been completed and he was at peace. Now it was time to go home and help people in the community understand what had been done. Time and discussion would clarify what further step should be made next year in Nevada.

THOMAS MERTON

Along with Dorothy Day, Thomas Merton (1915-1968) personified the potentials of the Catholic peace tradition in America and stands out as one of the most brilliant peacemakers in the entire Catholic tradition. He was born in Praedes, France in January 1915, the son of painters. His mother was also a Quaker. After studying at Cambridge for a year, he came to the United States and completed an M.A. in English at Columbia University. During his studies a Hindu monk had recommended Augustine and the Early Fathers to him, and his extensive readings in these, in Blake's mystical poetry, and his frequent attendance at Catholic services produced his conversion to Catholicism in 1938, a process recounted in his immensely popular *Seven Story Mountain* (New York: Harcourt, Brace, 1948).

By 1940 Merton had decided on the priesthood, was rejected by the Franciscans, and finally applied for the Trappists in 1942 in Gethsemani, Kentucky. By that time World War II was in full swing, and Merton applied for CO status as a "modified pacifist" but was accepted by the monastery before being drafted. His years at Gethsemani fall into three more or less distinct periods. The first from 1938 to 1949 reflected his ascetic flight from the world, an intransigent and apocalyptic spirituality. The next period, 1949 to 1959, showed Merton's deepening concerns to integrate his monastic vocation with the larger concerns of Catholicism and the world. During these years he read widely in psychology, Zen Buddhism, and existentialism. Finally, from roughly 1959, Merton confronted the central issues of his time and faith: war and peace, social justice, morality and power, conversion and Christian love.

Merton's monastic journey thus reflects the historical mission of the monastic life since its origins in the third century: a flight to the desert both to purify the individual, a rediscovery of his ties with God and the world, and a final commitment to confront the injustices and evils of the world from the spiritual citadel of the monastery [see 87-93, 114-120]. Despite his problems with censorship, temptations to leave the order, and the strict discipline of the Trappist routine, by the 1960s Merton had come to see the monastery as the model of the nonviolent Christian life of community, conscience, and witness.

Merton came gradually to surpass this monastic rejection and prophetic protest with a positive building, an affirmative theology of peace in an eschatological age. His journey took several stages, from his first denunciations of nuclear terror in a post-Christian age, to his scepticism of the justice of all wars in the modern age, his rejection of the pacifism of passive retreat, and finally his emergence as the spokesman for a new nonviolent Catholic activism aimed at rebuilding the world.

Merton never fully embraced pacifism and, like Thomas More [213-215] and Erasmus [217-222], continued to believe in the theoretical applicability of the just war. Yet, like the Renaissance humanists, he looked at the horrors of contemporary warfare and concluded that the just war had been made irrelevant in practice. He was, in fact, one of the first "nuclear pacifists." Merton viewed the rationality that emerged from World War II that could reduce the ovens of Auschwitz, the firebombing of Dresden, and the nuclear attacks on Hiroshima and Nagasaki to the cold calculations of men in power as a supreme evil and a madness shared by both capitalist and communist ideologies.

Individual Christians therefore face a real dilemma. They can consent to this mass destruction, lost in numbness, or they can choose peace. Yet the choice is not the traditional Catholic piety of seeking inner flight from the world. The Christian can no longer afford to retreat from concrete reality but must embrace the world and actively make peace and justice, protesting abuses of power and brute force. The Christian must imitate the Old Testament prophets and Christ himself to create a new Christian peace, not a Pax Romana built on terror and power.

751

For this reason Merton actively rejected the label "pacifist," which he saw as too closely tied to "passiveness" and nonresistance to evil. Nevertheless, in reality pacifism is not to be rejected: it is neither a luxury nor the end of Christian action but an obligation and the beginning point. True peace must begin with this basic change of heart to peace but must go on from there to attempt to change the world.

Merton's theology of peace therefore begins with the conversion of the individual heart. For American Catholics this means healing the American disease of belligerency. American Catholics must demythologize the glory of war for their fellow Americans and turn back the hopelessness that dominates the American climate of opinion, its nihilism, and its mad rush to destruction preached by hateful leaders and a media addicted to violence. Merton therefore espoused an anthropology of mutual aid and community much like that of Erasmus and other Renaissance humanists. He also called for a new "theology of resistance" that would confront the violence of the state, Augustine's "great band of robbers" [86]. He condemned a theology that counsels the poor and the oppressed to accept their lot passively and decries their isolated crime while society at large daily produces more and better methods of mass technological murder and maintains poverty and oppression by force, and therefore encouraged strong links between the peace and civil-rights movements.

Merton was convinced that only when individuals have undergone an inner conversion can a new age come. Their witness to Christian truth and nonviolent resistance to evil and injustice will earn them nothing but opposition and persecution, but only through the sufferings of true Christians can the new age, the eschaton of God's kingdom, arrive. Merton's revolution thus continues the long Catholic tradition of nonviolent apocalyptic [46, 162-168, 176-178].

Merton began writing on peace as an isolated prophet condemning modern Catholicism's alliance with the powers of the world. By the time he had begun to develop his theology of peace his voice had been joined by John XXIII and Vatican II [297-301]. By the time of his unexpected death in 1968 by an accidental electrocution while at an ecumenical conference in Bangkok, Thailand, his prophesy had become the major impetus in the Catholic struggle against the American war in Vietnam.

Chapter 7: Catholic Peacemaking in the USA

The following excerpts are taken from James H. Forest, *Thomas Merton's Struggle with Peacemaking*, Erie, PA: Benet Press, n.d.

366. Thomas Merton, From the Author's Preface to the Japanese Translation of The Seven Story Mountain (Tokyo: Chou Shuppansha, 1966)

...I have learned...to look back into (the) world with greater compassion, seeing those in it not as alien to myself, not as peculiar and deluded strangers, but as identified with myself. In freeing myself from their delusions and preoccupations I have identified myself, none the less, with their struggles and their blind, desperate hope of happiness.

But precisely because I am identified with them, I must refuse all the more definitely to make their delusions my own. I must refuse their ideology of matter, power, quantity, movement, activism and force. I reject this because I see it to be the source and expression of the spiritual hell which man has made of his world: the hell which has burst into flame in two total wars of incredible horror, the hell of spiritual emptiness and sub-human fury which has resulted in crimes like Auschwitz or Hiroshima. This I can and must reject with all the power of my being. This all sane men seek to reject. But the question is: how can one sincerely reject the effect if he continues to embrace the cause?...

...the monastery is not an "escape from the world." On the contrary, by being in the monastery I take my true part in all the struggles and sufferings of the world. To adopt a life that is essentially non-assertive, nonviolent, a life of humility and peace is in itself a statement of one's position. But each one in such a life can, by the personal modality of his decision, give his whole life a special orientation. It is my intention to make my entire life a rejection of, a protest against the crimes and injustices of war and political tyranny which threaten to destroy the whole race of man and the world with him. By my monastic life and vows I am saying *No* to all the concentration camps, the aerial bombardments, the staged political trials, the judicial murders, the racial injustices, the economic tyrannies, and the whole socio-economic apparatus which seems geared for nothing but global destruction in spite of all its fair words in favor of peace. I make monastic silence a protest against the lies of politicians, propagandists and agitators, and when I speak it is to deny that my faith and my Church can ever seriously be aligned with these forces of injustice and destruction.... My life must, then, be a protest against these also, and perhaps against these most of all....

The following selection is taken from Thomas Merton, *The Nonviolent Alternative,* Gordon C. Zahn, ed., New York: Farrar, Straus, Giroux, 1980, pp. 70-75.

367. Thomas Merton, Peace and Revolution: A Footnote from Ulysses

The Language of Action

One of the main themes of [James Joyce's novel] *Ulysses* is the breakdown of language and of communication as part of the disruption of Western culture. The extraordinary linguistic richness of the book – which however comes out mostly in parody – only reminds us more forcefully how much further the breakdown has gone in the last fifty years. Pacifism and nonviolence are fully and consciously involved in this question of language. Nonviolence, as Gandhi conceived it, is in fact a kind of language. The real dynamic of nonviolence can be considered as a purification of language, a restoration of true communication on a human level, when language has been emptied of meaning by misuse and corruption. Nonviolence is meant to communicate love not in word but in act. Above all, nonviolence is meant to convey and to defend truth which has been obscured and defiled by political double-talk.

The real lesson for us is this: we must clearly understand the function of nonviolence against the background of the collapse of language. It is no accident that Noam Chomsky, a leader in the Draft Resistance movement, is also an expert in the study of language. The special force of the Cyclops episode in *Ulysses* is that it shows how the language of pacifism and the language of force can both fit with equal readiness into a context of linguistic corruption. We have to be terribly aware of the fact that our pacifism and nonviolence can easily be nothing more than parodies of themselves. We must recognize the temptation to be quite content with this – to be content to express our weak convictions in weak and provisional terms, meanwhile waiting for an opportunity to abandon nonviolence altogether and go over to the side of force, on the ground that we have tried nonviolence and found it wanting.

Has nonviolence been found wanting? Yes and No. It has been found wanting wherever it has been the nonviolence of the weak. It has not been found so when it has been the nonviolence of the strong. What is the difference? It is a difference of language. The language of spurious nonviolence is merely another, more equivocal form of the language of power. It is a different method of expressing one's will to power. It is used and conceived pragmatically, in reference to the seizure of power. But that is not what nonviolence is about. Nonviolence is not for power but for truth. It is not pragmatic but prophetic. It is not aimed at immediate political results, but at the manifestation of fundamental and crucially important truth. Nonviolence is not primarily the language of efficacy, but the language of *kairos*. It does not say "We shall overcome" so much as "This is the day of the Lord, and whatever may happen to us *He* shall overcome."...

The following is from Merton, *Nonviolent Alternative,* pp. 111-14.

368. Thomas Merton, Peace: A Religious Responsibility

2. The Christian as Peacemaker

...The Christian is and must be by his very adoption as a son of God in Christ, a peacemaker [Mt. 5:9]. He is bound to imitate the Savior who, instead of defending Himself with twelve legions of angels [Mt. 26:55], allowed Himself to be nailed to the Cross and died praying for His executioners. The Christian is one whose life has sprung from a particular spiritual seed: the blood of the martyrs who without offering forcible resistance, laid down their lives rather than submit to the unjust laws that demanded an official religious cult of the emperor as God. That is to say, the Christian is bound, like the martyrs, to obey God rather than the state whenever the state tries to usurp powers that do not and cannot belong to it. We have repeatedly seen Christians in our time fulfilling this obligation in a heroic manner by their resistance to dictatorships that strove to interfere with the rights of their conscience and their religion.

Hence it must be stated quite clearly and without any compromise that the duty of the Christian as a peacemaker is not to be confused with a kind of quietistic inertia which is indifferent to injustice, accepts any kind of disorder, compromises with error and with evil, and gives in to every pressure in order to maintain "peace at any price." The Christian knows well, or should know well, that peace is not possible on such terms. Peace demands the most heroic labor and the most difficult sacrifice. It demands greater heroism than war. It demands greater fidelity to the truth and a much more perfect purity of conscience. The Christian fight for peace is not to be confused with defeatism. This has to be made clear because there is a certain complacent sophistry, given free currency by the theologians who want to justify war too easily, and who like to treat anyone who disagrees with them as if he were a practical apostate from the faith who had already surrendered implicitly to Communism by refusing to accept the morality of an all-out nuclear war. This, as any one can easily see, is simply begging the question. And one feels that those who yield to this temptation are perhaps a little too much influenced by the pragmatism and opportunism of our affluent society.

There is a lot of talk, among some of the clergy, about the relative danger of nuclear war and a "Communist takeover." It is assumed, quite gratuitously, that the Communist is at the gates, and is just about to take over the United States, close all the churches, and brainwash all the good Catholics. Once this spectral assessment of the situation is accepted, then one is urged to agree that there is only one solution: to let the Reds have it before they get our government and our universities thoroughly infiltrated. This means a preemptive strike, based not on the fact that we ourselves are actually under military attack, but that we are so "provoked" and so "threatened" that even the most drastic measures are justified.

If it is argued that there can be no proportion between the awful destruction wrought by nuclear war and the good achieved by exorcising this specter of Communist domination, the argument comes back: "better dead than Red." And this, in turn, is justified by the contention that the destruction of cities, nations, populations is "only a physical evil" while Communist domination would be a "moral evil."

It must be said at once that this has no basis in logic, ethics, politics or sound moral theology....

This selection is from Merton, *Nonviolent Alternative,* pp. 168-71.

369. Thomas Merton, Man is a Gorilla with a Gun: Reflections on a Best-Seller

...On the basis of the possibility that there were, in Africa, perhaps a million years ago, tool-and-weapon-using anthropoids, Mr. Ardrey [Robert Ardrey, author of the then best-selling *African Genesis,* New York: Atheneum, 1961] delivers a very aggressive homily on atheistic evolutionism. He attacks not only the traditional Christian world view but also, much more radically, the world views of Marx, Freud, Darwin and practically everyone else you can think of. One theory of man after another is tossed out the window with glorious enthusiasm: and all because some ape picked up the leg bone of an antelope and used it to crack the skull of one of his fellows. This is all we need in order to entirely reconstruct all social philosophy, all history, all anthropology, all psychology, all economics. For Mr. Ardrey, this one monumental act of violence explains everything.

Homo sapiens (including modern man) is the direct "legitimate" descendent of a transitional, carnivorous, erect-walking and weapon-using anthropoid. Because this ape was no ordinary mild-mannered vegetarian ape, but a ruthless "killer ape," man emerged. Man is, according to Ardrey, the child not only of the ape but of the weapon. It was "the weapon that fathered man." The consequence follows immediately. Man is by his very nature an inventor and user of weapons. The essence of human nature is therefore not so much rationality as trigger-happiness, or at least club-happiness. Even sex is set aside as a secondary, relatively meaningless urge compared with man's essential drive to beat anything and anyone that threatens to invade his "territory." Yes, "territory" is very important here, crucially important. Man is not really interested in woman, in love, in the warmth of satisfied yearning (as Freud may have thought). Man is not so deeply engaged in making a living that his very existence is shaped and dominated by the system of production (according to Marxian dogma). Man is an ape that goes berserk when he thinks he is running out of *lebensraum,* and I must admit that Mr. Ardrey's description of two rival teams of howling monkeys trying to jam each other's broadcasts is very suggestive of modern political life.

The chief contention of Robert Ardrey's high-powered social message is that any philosophy, religious or otherwise, which takes an optimistic view of man, regards him as basically rational and progressive, and postulates that he can better himself by improving his social system, is basically a "romantic illusion." It is absurd, says Mr. Ardrey, to hope that man can some day reach the point where he will settle his difference over "territory" by means of arbitration rather than by bombs. It is fortunate that some members of the human race are still capable of thinking otherwise (for instance Pope John XXIII in his encyclical *Pacem in Terris).*

Quite apart from religious faith and Christian hope, it seems to me that Mr. Ardrey's thesis negates any real value there may be in evolutionism. After all, the theory of natural selection postulates that a species is able to survive by progressive adaptation to new and more difficult conditions. We armed gorillas have now reached a rather crucial point in our evolutionary development in which it would seem that if we cannot get beyond the stage where we were a million years ago, in other words, if we cannot settle our problems by reason instead of with clubs, we are soon going to be as extinct as any dinosaur. The amusing thing about all this is that we are a species that has been given the *choice* of survival or non-survival. We have very large skulls and, presuming there is still something inside of them, it is up to us to make use of them for something besides inventing ways to blow ourselves up.

And that is what one regrets about a book like this. The author has a great deal of imagination and yet not quite enough. He is totally and slavishly committed to a philosophy of ironbound determinism which is dominated by one inexorable obsession: that ape with the club. *Because* man descended in a direct line from an ape with a club, then he is predetermined to be a killer, he is before all else a killer, and it is folly to even consider him being anything else. Mr. Ardrey confesses himself to be firmly convinced of "man's pristine depravity." Thus he is committed to a world view in which violence, barbarism, murder, and every form of depravity are bound to prevail. As a priest I am prompted to reflect that this is where you end up when you lose your grasp on the real import of the higher religions. No man can really exist completely without religion. If he gets rid of a good one, he will unconsciously exchange it for a bad one. If he is impatient of "myth" in higher religion then he will end up fabricating a myth of his own, and organizing his own crude fantasies into another homemade "system" which pleases him better – perhaps with unfortunate consequences.

Now Mr. Ardrey's exploits in myth-making are not hard to observe. They are evident on every page of his book. To take just one example: on page twenty-one, he wants to give a brief description of Lake Victoria, as the spot near which man came into existence. There are innumerable ways in which one could describe Lake Victoria. Out of several hundred possible qualifiers Mr. Ardrey, characteristically, selects the following: "A hundred miles to the east spreads *sprawling* and *enormous* the *cynically smiling* face of Lake Victoria, *poisonous with disease, crawling with crocodiles,* the probable focus of our earliest human experience." I submit that people who read books like this need a little elementary training in semantics, in the interests of their basic mental and spiritual hygiene. Such a sentence (and there are hundreds like it in the book), has one function above all others: it bludgeons the reader into emotional submission, and subjects him to a crude impression of violence and evil, so that his intelligence raises no objections to the author's thesis. The author pressures the reader into an emotional acceptance of man's pristine depravity by suggesting that the very place where man came into being was itself sinister and depraved.

This kind of thinking is all too common in the twentieth century. It abounded in the Europe of Mussolini, of Hitler, of Goebbels. The Second World War was the direct consequence of this kind of high-powered emotional conditioning. The Nazi dogma of race, blood and land developed an ideology of war and conquest out of just this kind of emotionally loaded anthropology. Everyone is aware that Hitler's thought was, in part, simply a crudely misunderstood mishmash of popular evolutionism.

Nothing can better dispose us for a third world war than the conviction that we are doomed to fight anyway, that our enemies are all well-armed gorillas too, and the only smart thing to do is to let them have it before they ambush us. In the chaotic atmosphere of a nation torn by race riots, deafened by the stridency of hate groups and of fanatics, it is understandable that readers may derive a kind of comfort from this mythology – made to order for readers of Ayn Rand....

These excerpts are from Merton, *Nonviolent Alternative*, pp. 208-18.

370. Thomas Merton, Blessed Are the Meek: The Christian Roots of Nonviolence

It would be a serious mistake to regard Christian nonviolence simply as a novel tactic which is at once efficacious and even edifying, and which enables the sensitive man to participate in the struggles of the world without being dirtied with blood. Nonviolence is not simply a way of proving one's point and getting what one wants without being involved in behavior that one considers ugly and evil. Nor is it, for that matter, a means which anyone legitimately can make use of according to his fancy for any purpose whatever. To practice nonviolence for a purely selfish or arbitrary end would in fact discredit and distort the truth of nonviolent resistance.

Nonviolence is perhaps the most exacting of all forms of struggle, not only because it demands first of all that one be ready to suffer evil and even face the threat of death without violent retaliation, but because it excludes mere transient self-interest from its considerations. In a very real sense, he who practices nonviolent resistance must commit himself not to the defense of his own interests or even those of a particular group: he must commit himself to the defense of objective truth and right and above all of *man*. His aim is then not simply to "prevail" or to prove that he is right and the adversary wrong, or to make the adversary give in and yield what is demanded of him.

Nor should the nonviolent resister be content to prove to *himself* that *he* is virtuous and right, and that *his* hands and heart are pure even though the adversary's may be evil and defiled. Still less should he seek for himself the psychological gratification of upsetting the adversary's conscience and perhaps driving him to an act of bad faith and refusal of the truth. We know that our unconscious motives may, at times, make our nonviolence a form of moral aggression and even a subtle provocation designed (without our awareness) to bring out the evil we hope to find in the adversary, and thus to justify ourselves in our own eyes and in the eyes of "decent people." Wherever there is a high moral ideal there is an attendant risk of pharisaism, and nonviolence is no exception. The basis of pharisaism is division: on one hand this morally or socially privileged self and the elite to which it belongs. On the other hand, the "others," the wicked, the unenlightened, whoever they may be, Communists, capitalists, colonialists, traitors, international Jewry, racists, etc.

Christian nonviolence is not built on a presupposed division, but on the basic unity of man. It is not out for the conversion of the wicked to the ideas of the good, but for the healing and reconciliation of man with himself, man the person and man the human family.

The nonviolent resister is not fighting simply for "his" truth or for "his" pure conscience, or for the right that is on "his side." On the contrary both his strength and his weakness come from the fact that he is fighting for *the* truth, common to him and to the adversary, *the* right which is objective and universal. He is fighting for *everybody*.

For this very reason, as Gandhi saw, the fully consistent practice of nonviolence demands a solid metaphysical and religious basis both in being and in God. This comes *before* subjective good intentions and sincerity. For the Hindu this metaphysical basis was provided by the Vedantist doctrine of the Atman, the true transcendent Self which alone is absolutely real, and before which the empirical self of the individual must be effaced in the faithful practice of *dharma*. For the Christian, the basis of nonviolence is the Gospel message of salvation for *all men* and of the Kingdom of God to which *all* are summoned. The disciple of Christ, he who has heard the good news, the announcement of the Lord's coming and of His victory, and is aware of the definitive establishment of the Kingdom, proves his faith by the gift of his whole self to the Lord in order that *all* may enter the Kingdom. This Christian discipleship entails a certain way of acting, a *politeia*, a *conservatio*, which is proper to the Kingdom....

...Let us however seriously consider at least the *conditions* for relative honesty in the practice of Christian nonviolence.

(1) Nonviolence must be aimed above all at the transformation of the present state of the world, and it must therefore be free from all occult, unconscious connivance with an unjust use of power. This poses enormous problems – for if nonviolence is too political it becomes drawn into the power struggle and identified with one side or another in that struggle, while if it is totally apolitical it runs the risk of being ineffective or at best merely symbolic.

(2) The nonviolent resistance of the Christian who belongs to one of the powerful nations and who is himself in some sense a privileged member of world society will have to be clearly not *for himself* but *for others*, that is for the poor and underprivileged. (Obviously in the case of Negroes in the United States, though they may be citizens of a privileged nation, their case is different. They are clearly entitled to wage a nonviolent struggle for their rights, but even for them this struggle should be primarily for *truth itself* – this being the source of their power.)

(3) In the case of nonviolent struggle for peace – the threat of nuclear war abolishes all privileges. Under the bomb there is not much distinction between rich and poor. In fact the richest nations are usually the most threatened. Nonviolence must simply avoid the ambiguity of an unclear and *confusing protest* that hardens the warmakers in their self-righteous blindness. This means in fact that *in this case above all nonviolence must avoid a facile and fanatical self-righteousness*, and refrain from being satisfied with dramatic self-justifying gestures.

(4) Perhaps the most insidious temptation to be avoided is one which is characteristic of the power structure itself: this fetishism of immediate visible results. Modern society understands "possibilities" and "results" in terms of a superficial and quantitative idea of efficacy. One of the mis-

761

sions of Christian nonviolence is to restore a different standard of practical judgment in social conflicts. This means that the Christian humility of nonviolent action must establish itself in the minds and memories of modern man not only as *conceivable* and *possible,* but as *a desirable alternative* to what he now considers the only realistic possibility: namely political technique backed by force. Here the human dignity of nonviolence must manifest itself clearly in terms of a freedom and a nobility which are able to resist political manipulation and brute force and show them up as arbitrary, barbarous and irrational. This will not be easy. The temptation to get publicity and quick results by spectacular tricks or by forms of protest that are merely odd and provocative but whose human meaning is not clear may defeat this purpose.

The realism of nonviolence must be made evident by humility and self-restraint which clearly show frankness and open-mindedness and invite the adversary to serious and reasonable discussion....

(5) Christian nonviolence, therefore, is convinced that the manner in which the conflict for truth is waged will itself manifest or obscure the truth. To fight for truth by dishonest, violent, inhuman, or unreasonable means would simply betray the truth one is trying to vindicate. The absolute refusal of evil or suspect means is a necessary element in the witness of nonviolence....

(6) A test of our sincerity in the practice of nonviolence is this: are we willing to *learn something from the adversary?* If a *new truth* is made known to us by him or through him, will we accept it? Are we willing to admit that he is not totally inhumane, wrong, unreasonable, cruel, etc.? This is important. If he sees that we are completely incapable of listening to him with an open mind, our nonviolence will have nothing to say to him except that we distrust him and seek to outwit him....

Our willingness to take *an alternative approach* to a problem will perhaps relax the obsessive fixation of the adversary on his view, which he believes is the only reasonable possibility and which he is determined to impose on everyone else by coercion.

It is the refusal of alternatives – a compulsive state of mind which one might call the "ultimatum complex" – which makes wars in order to force the unconditional acceptance of one oversimplified interpretation of reality. This mission of Christian humility in social life is not merely to edify, but to *keep minds open to many alternatives.* The rigidity of a certain type of Christian thought has seriously impaired this capacity, which nonviolence must recover.

Needless to say, Christian humility must not be confused with a mere desire to win approval and to find reassurance by conciliating others superficially.

(7) Christian hope and Christian humility are inseparable. The quality of nonviolence is decided largely by the purity of the Christian hope behind it. In its insistence on certain human values, the Second Vatican Council, following *Pacem in Terris,* displayed a basically optimistic trust in *man himself.* Not that there is not wickedness in the world, but today trust in God cannot be completely divorced from a certain trust in man. The Christian knows that there are radically sound possibilities in every man, and he believes that love and grace always have the power to bring out those possibilities at the most unexpected moments. Therefore if he has hopes that God will grant peace to the world it is because he also trusts that man, God's creature, is not basically evil: that there is in man a potentiality for peace and order which can be realized provided the right conditions are there. The Christian will do his part in creating these conditions by preferring love and trust to hate and suspiciousness. Obviously, once again, this "hope in man" must not be naive. But experience itself has shown, in the last few years, how much an attitude of simplicity and openness can do to break down barriers of suspicion that had divided men for centuries....

THE 1960s: VATICAN II AND VIETNAM

U.S. PACIFISTS AT VATICAN II

The impact of Vatican II on America was profound. The political debate between the American bishops and lobbying groups at Vatican II was a microcosm of the dialogue at work within the American church as a whole since the 1940s. Chief among the issues debated under Schema XIII, which eventually resulted in the *Pastoral Constitution,* were the morality of nuclear war and the provisions for conscientious objection.

Many of the progressive bishops at the council, including the French, Spanish, and Canadians, sought a complete ban and condemnation of nuclear weapons as a clear violation of Christian morality. With the exception of Joseph Cardinal Ritter, who even sought a condemnation of the *possession* of nuclear weapons, the American delegation, along with the British, opposed any "ban the bomb" movement as "unrealistic." Chief among the opponents were Francis Cardinal Spellman of New York, Lawrence Cardinal Sheehan of Baltimore, and Bishop Patrick O'Boyle of Washington, DC. These bishops were aided by Harry W. Flannery of CAIP, whose members on the subcommittee on arms vigorously opposed the "European pacifists." They defended nuclear war both on the grounds of the just-war theory and through their diehard Americanism, the complete association of Catholic church interests with the interests of the American nation, and a commitment to defend the American military position as the best path to world stability.

America may well have stood unanimously against the council's eventual condemnation of war in the nuclear age were it not for the intervention of a delegation of American pacifists sent to Rome by the Catholic Worker and PAX. Among those present were Dorothy Day and James Douglass, a Catholic theologian and critic of the just-war tradition, Philip Scharper, a noted journalist, Eileen Egan [379], and Gordon Zahn [358]. They were supported from home by Thomas Merton who sent an "open letter" to the council calling for the explicit condemnation of nuclear war and clear provisions for conscientious objection. The Americans matched their lobbying behind the scenes with dramatic fasts in Rome by Dorothy Day, Eileen Egan, Chantarelle and other women from Lanza del Vasto's Ark [303]. With the help of Bishop John Taylor the pacifists eventually had their opinions brought to the floor of the council and won the support of others American bishops like Fulton J. Sheen, who adopted Cardinal Ottaviani's position outlawing all modern war.

On the issue of conscientious objection the American pacifists were even more successful. Once again the chief opposition to the provision in Schema XIII came from Cardinal Spellman, also head of the U.S. Military Vicariate. Spellman actually sought to have the church call for obligatory military service for all Catholics, declaring that "individuals cannot refuse their obedience to the state." Here Thomas Merton's moral authority and the intervention of Archbishop Roberts assured the council's call for conscientious objection as a legitimate and praiseworthy Catholic response to war.

The following selection describes the daily life of the peace fasters and is taken from Dorothy Day, "A Prayer for Peace," in her *By Little and Little. Selected Writings,* Robert Ellsberg, ed., New York: Alfred A. Knopf, 1983, pp. 331-33.

371. Dorothy Day, The Fast for Peace at Vatican II, November 1965

Rome. The fast of the twenty women, which I had come to join and which was the primary reason for my visit to Rome during the final session of the Council, began on October 1, a Friday. That morning I checked out of my hotel and proceeded to the great square in front of St. Peter's to wait for Barbara Wall and Eileen Egan at the end of the Colonnade. We were going to Mass together on that First Friday morning....

The Mass that morning was in the Syriac rite and was sung, so it was not until ten that I arrived at the Cenacle on Piazza Pricilla on the other side of Rome. There we gathered in the garden, twenty women, and a few of the male members of the Community of the Ark, including Lanza del Vasto, whose wife, Chanterelle, had initiated the fast. He led us in the prayers that we would say each morning as we gathered together after Mass: the our Father, the peace prayer of St. Francis and the Beatitudes. Afterward, the trained members of the community sang. Then we went to our rooms, which were on the third floor of the old convent, looking out on gardens and sky.

Each day we followed a schedule. There was Mass at seven-fifteen and then prayer together. From nine to twelve we kept to our rooms in silence, reading, writing, or praying. During the day and night there was always one of us keeping vigil. At noon we went to the garden and read together. Readings included a book by Martin Luther King and an account of the work of Father Paul Gauthier, who founded the Companions of Jesus the Carpenter, in Nazareth. Most of us had some sewing or knitting to do. The wicker chairs were comfortable, the garden smelled of pine trees and eucalyptus and sweet herbs, and every day the sun was warm. Other members of the Ark, who were running an exhibit on non-violence, came and told us news of the visitors to the exhibit and of the Fathers of the Council they had talked to.

At four in the afternoon there were lectures by priests, and at six a French doctor came daily to see how everyone was getting along. Two of the women were ill during the fast and had to keep to their beds, so the lectures were held in Chanterelle's room. Prayers again at seven or eight, and then silence and sleep – for those who could sleep.

As for me, I did not suffer at all from the hunger or headache or nausea which usually accompany the first few days of a fast, but I had offered my fast in part for the victims of famine all over the world, and it seemed to me that I had very special pains....

But these pains which went with the fast seemed to reach into my very bones, and I could only feel that I had been given some little intimation of the hunger of the world. God help us, living as we do, in the richest country in the world and so far from approaching the voluntary poverty we esteem and reach toward.

On the night of the 10th of October, the fast, those ten days when nothing but water passed our lips, was finished. Hard though it was, it was but a token fast, considering the problems of the world we live in. It is a small offering of sacrifice, a widow's mite, a few loaves and fishes. May we try harder to do more in the future....

November 1965

VIETNAM

A long, slow struggle over war and peace had begun within the Catholic church. On one side the institutional church sought to maintain its alliance with power and influence and to impose order from the top on an obedient and unquestioning Catholic laity. On the other a new movement for peace started from below with the people themselves. The Catholic Worker, Catholic Peace Fellowship, PAX, campus groups, and thousands of Catholic individuals began to respond to the new call of Vatican II and a new awareness of the strength of the Catholic peace tradition. Where there were only four Catholics among the 3,989 conscientious objectors to World War I, and only 135 among the 11,887 COs classified as IV-E during World War II, by 1969, 2,494 Catholics had received CO status among the 34,255 so classified, the single largest percentage of all American religious bodies.

Yet the witness of the Catholic pacifist was not easy. Not only had the Catholic objector to convince a skeptical draft board of his sincerity, but he had to do so without the sanction of his own church, even in the face of repeated hierarchical condemnation or indifference. In addition, even those Catholics who convinced draft boards of their sincerity had to consciously renounce what many, both Catholic and Protestant, saw as the crusade and just-war heritage of the Catholic church.

766

Left isolated by their tradition and their present church, many Catholic pacifists were forced to turn to the traditional peace churches for advice and counseling, to seek out examples of isolated figures from the Catholic past. In many cases the Catholic pacifists had to accept their own dissent and the truth of their Catholic tradition on complete faith. In many others Catholics rejected their supposed Catholic militarism for a more biblical pacifism.

On the other hand, Catholic support for war, including the Vietnam War, was only too well known. Francis Cardinal Spellman epitomized official Catholic support for the war effort. In his Christmas 1966 visit to Vietnam as both the head of the U.S. Military Vicariate and as the most influential American Catholic prelate, Spellman comforted Conservatives like William F. Buckley and outraged liberals in a series of symbolic gestures and statements. He consciously discarded the Catholic moral tradition by proclaiming his unswerving support of "my country right or wrong." He toured the front, blessing the Army's canons and calling for victory, describing the U.S. intervention "a war for the defense of Civilization," claiming that "any solution other than victory was inconceivable." By the time it was over this war for civilization had left over 58,000 U.S.; 200,000 South Vietnamese military; and 1 million Vietnamese civilian dead; and it had created over 6.5 million refugees.

THE CATHOLIC PEACE FELLOWSHIP

The impact of Vatican II on American Catholics was immediate and far-reaching. As early as 1962 a dozen Catholic Workers proposed founding a Catholic Peace Fellowship as an affiliate of the Fellowship of Reconciliation. In November 1964 a retreat under Thomas Merton at Gethsemani brought together social activists Daniel and Philip Berrigan, James Forest, and Tom Cornell along with John Heidbrink from FOR and several leading Protestant peace activists, including A.J. Muste, John Yoder, and W.H. Ferry. The result was the actual founding of the Catholic Peace Fellowship (CPF) with Cornell and Forest as full-time staffers and Daniel Berrigan and Merton as directors.

Unlike the institutional approach of PAX, the CPF became the chief outlet of individual Catholic radicalism of the 1960s as the Gulf of Tonkin Resolution and increased U.S. involvement in Vietnam shifted

Catholic attention away from the nuclear issue and to full resistance to the war. Already in November 1962 Tom Cornell had publically burned his draft card at an anti-Vietnam war rally in Union Square, New York City. In May 1964 Cornell burned his card again along with Christopher Kearnes, another Catholic Worker. Further draft-card burnings in August 1965 in Washington, in which 32 Catholic Workers participated, led to the hasty Congressional passage of the Rivers Act, which made draft-card burning a Federal offense.

By 1965 the Catholic Worker was again at the center of Catholic peacemaking in America as the paper's circulation rose dramatically to 65,000 and it actively participated in civil rights and anti-Vietnam war coalitions. Its theology of peace and theory of nonviolent resistance gave form to much of the protest against the war. On October 15, therefore, David Miller, a Catholic Worker, publically burned his card before cameras and the FBI. He was promptly arrested, tried, convicted, and imprisoned; Miller's offense became the test case of the Rivers Act. On November 6, 150,000 people gathered outside the Federal Court House in New York City as Dorothy Day and A.J. Muste introduced five more card burners, three of whom were Catholic Workers. By the end of 1965 Catholic criticism of the war had become vocal, organized, and squarely based on current church teachings of war, peace, the sanctity of life and the sacramental role of nature itself. Such themes set the tone for religious protest against the war for the next decade and were to become the foundations for much of the peacemaking of the next generation.

The following is an ad taken by the Catholic Peace Fellowship on December 10, 1965 in *Commonweal.*

372. Catholic Peace Fellowship, Peace on Earth, Peace in Vietnam

"The right of every man to life is correlative with the duty to preserve it." – Pope John XXIII, *Pacem in Terris*

During the two years which have passed since the Holy Father's [John XXIII's] death, the United States has become increasingly involved in a war in Southeast Asia, a war in which many thousands have died, in which the buildup of troops and arms continues, a war in which the threat of total destruction, even nuclear war, grows apace.

As Catholics and Americans, we, the signers of this appeal, can no

longer remain silent before the part our nation is playing in this fratricidal war. We therefore state, without questioning the sincerity of our
government leaders, that we believe this war to be morally unjustifiable,
an objective violation of the law of God and a betrayal of our national
tradition of respect for democratic process.

Our specific objections to the war in Vietnam stem from three sources:
1) the character of the governments we have sponsored there, 2) our
failure to explore peaceful means of settlement, and 3) the conduct of the
war itself.

South Vietnam Government Failure

Guarantee of the basic social rights of man is binding upon governments, both in times of war and of peace. Among these rights must be
included the right of citizens to express political opinions, the right of
fair trial, and the right of free assembly and association. Such rights are
granted, not by society, but by God; no human authority, therefore, can
be permitted to abrogate them. Pope John wrote in *Pacem in Terris,* "If
any government does not acknowledge the rights of man or violates them,
it not only fails in its duty, but its orders actually lack juridical force."

As the government of South Vietnam has denied these rights in practice, we question its moral legitimacy. We also question the assumption
that when such rights are abrogated, anti-communism can be considered an acceptable basis for the establishment of military alliances with
such governments.

Failure to Explore a Peaceful Settlement

For centuries, Catholic teaching has maintained that violence can be
sanctioned only when all peaceful means of settlement are exhausted.
Even when war has broken out, governments are not excused from the
obligation to pursue every possibility of reasonable settlement.

In spite of this tradition, whose application is rendered most urgent
by the danger of nuclear war, our government has consistently ignored
the possibility of a peaceful settlement in Vietnam. Among these possibilities must be mentioned the Election Mandate of the 1954 Geneva
Agreements. Former President Dwight Eisenhower has written that, if
elections had been held in 1954, "possibly 80 percent of the population
would have voted for the communist Ho Chi Minh as their leader."
(Mandate for Change)

Again, our government has repeatedly stated that this nation welcomes "unconditional negotiations." In spite of this, our government has thus far refused to negotiate directly with the National Liberation Front (the Vietcong). Whatever the merits of the view that the N.L.F. is an arm of North Vietnamese aggression, it remains true that the danger of total war, and the injustice of the present war, nullify any objection against seeking a peaceful settlement with our enemies.

Failure in Just Conduct of the War

Minimal human justice requires that during war the innocent and non-combatants be protected, and that the least possible violence be inflicted on the enemy.

These basic moral principles are consistently violated in the war in Vietnam. Entire families are incinerated, prisoners of war are tortured, indiscriminate bombings erase all distinction between the innocent and the guilty. Moreover, large numbers of people have been forced into "strategic hamlets," without respect to their wishes or rights. Crops have been chemically defoliated or put to the torch. Under suspicion of collaboration or sympathy with the enemy, men have been condemned to death and publicly executed without trial.

The war in Vietnam has thus unleashed weapons and tactics which are in violation of natural law and of the Gospel. We believe that men of conscience can therefore neither defend nor support such a war.

Appeals of the Pope

Recalling Pope Paul's recent letter, *Mense Maio,* we condemn the tactics both of the American forces and of the Vietcong. In his letter, the Pope stated, "Populations of entire nations are subjected to unspeakable sufferings caused by agitation, guerrilla warfare, acts of war…which could at any moment produce the spark for a terrible fresh conflict…. All these outrages can block the paths still open to mutual good will, or can at least render more difficult the negotiations which, if conducted with openness and fairness, could lead to a reasonable settlement."

Again, on June 24, 1966, the Pope said, "Our heart suffers bitterly for the bloody and ruinous struggle that is causing so much suffering to the people of Vietnam. We wish to say to reasonable men, 'It is necessary to stop while there is still time. The spark that is not extinguished can provoke a fire of proportions that appall the imagination.'"

Chapter 7: Catholic Peacemaking in the USA

Basic Proposals

§ According to Church teaching, individuals are obliged to refuse to serve in wars which they judge unjust [see **194-207, 253**]. A growing number of Catholics is reaching this conclusion with regard to the Vietnam war. We declare our solidarity with them, and our determination to aid them in every possible way.

§ We call for determined, courageous efforts to bring the war to an end. We invite all men of good will, and especially our fellow Catholics and the American Catholic Bishops, to lend their moral support to efforts of peace.

§ We ask that the National Liberation Front be considered a legitimate and necessary party to negotiations. Such a request, it goes without saying, is not an endorsement of the political objectives of the N.L.F., nor of the means it has used to obtain them.

§ We ask that the United Nations be formally requested to intervene and to mediate in the area of dispute, and to chart an independent, militarily unaligned and independent Vietnam, as was sought under the 1954 Geneva Agreements.

§ We ask an immediate end of all bombing raids against both North and South Vietnam.

§ We ask that the United States make clear its responsibility toward both the refugees from North Vietnam, and toward those who have allied themselves with the various Saigon regimes. With vigor and imagination, the ravaged countryside must be restored, responsible political and social structures established, and the security of unprotected and innocent victims of war be guaranteed.

Finally, we call upon American Catholics to respond fully to the words of Pope John in *Pacem in Terris* – words of political maturity, altruism and sacrifice. "There is an immense task incumbent on all men of good will, namely the task of restoring the relations of the human family in truth, in justice, in love and in freedom.... May God banish from the hearts of men whatever might endanger peace. May He transform men into witnesses of truth, justice and brotherly love."

The Catholic Peace Fellowship
of the Fellowship of Reconciliation

[There follow the signatures of 70 Catholic clergy, academics, artists, journalists, publishers, and other professionals.]

U.S. BISHOPS CONFERENCE

Through most of the 1950s and 1960s the U.S. bishops' letters on war and peace had a decidedly anti-Soviet slant and sought to warn the U.S. against cooperation with communism; yet their critical tone was clearly leveled against U.S. policy as well and showed a growing willingness to speak out against the government in prophetic form, regardless of political allegiance. This tone dominated their last pastoral of the 1950s, *Freedom and Peace.*

While the letter is clearly a Cold-War document and warns of the dangers of atheistic communism, it links this threat to other, equally pressing, dangers. These include an excessive nationalism that blinds Americans to the basic unity of all peoples and the abject "poverty, hunger, disease and bitterness engendered by social injustice" that communist aggression only exploits. Before it can accept the challenge of injustice in the Third World, however, America must undergo a conversion of its own, abandoning the materialism that characterizes American life and, paradoxically, leaves "the communists to capture the minds of men."

By 1960 the Catholic hierarchy, while still firmly allied with American national interests, had begun to prod the government in significant ways and to openly question many of the fundamental assumptions of American life and its power in the world. In November of that year the Catholic bishops' pastoral, *Personal Responsibility,* began to repudiate the old Constantinian alliance, noting that too much responsibility for peace had been entrusted to international bodies and not enough to individuals. The letter departed from the model of peace as order imposed from above that had dominated American Catholic thought since World War I. In this the American church reflected the changes in papal thought that John XXIII was introducing and prepared the way for the next wave of Catholic peacemaking from the bottom up.

At the beginning of the Vietnam War the U.S. Bishops' Conference largely agreed with Cardinal Spellman's ultra-nationalism. Despite the Catholic Peace Fellowship's public call for the bishops to condemn the war, in November 1966 the bishops issued their pastoral *Peace and Vietnam,* in which they used Vatican II to support the conclusion that "it is reasonable to argue that our presence in Vietnam is justified."

Ironically the pastoral letter's title recalls that of the Catholic "radicals" who only a year before had shocked the church by calling for peace in the *Commonweal* advertisement [372]. The letter and the ad, in fact, represent two lines of convergence within the Catholic church that quickly merged during the Vietnam war to form the new consensus on peace and justice of the 1970 and 1980s.

Under paragraph 10, the bishops call to the American people to judge U.S. involvement is nothing radical, but is as old as the medieval canon-law tradition of how consensus concerning the justice of a war is to be determined by open and responsible public discussion. [See 194-207, 253]

The following is taken from Nolan, *Pastoral Letters,* pp. 604-7.

373. U.S. Catholic Conference, Peace and Vietnam, November 18, 1966

(1) Our common humanity demands that all people live in peace and harmony with one another. This peace will exist only if the right order established by God is observed, an order which is based on the requirements of human dignity. Everyone, therefore, must be vitally and personally concerned about correcting the grave disorders which today threaten peace. As Catholics we are members of the Church that Pope Paul has called a "messenger of peace."

(2) We, the Catholic Bishops of the United States, consider it our duty to help magnify the moral voice of our nation....

(3) While we cannot resolve all the issues involved in the Vietnam conflict, it is clearly our duty to insist that they be kept under constant moral scrutiny. No one is free to evade his personal responsibility by leaving it entirely to others to make moral judgments. In this connection, the Vatican Council warns that "men should take heed not to entrust themselves only to the efforts of others, while remaining careless about their own attitudes. For government officials, who must simultaneously guarantee the good of their own people and promote the universal good, depend on public opinion and feeling to the greatest possible extent" [*Gaudium et Spes* II.5.1, *Documents of Vatican II,* p. 296].

Peace and Modern Warfare

(4) While it is not possible in this brief statement to give a detailed analysis of the Church's total teaching on war and peace, it seems necessary to review certain basic principles if the present crisis is to be put in its proper moral perspectives.

(5) We reaffirmed at the Council the legitimate role of patriotism for the well-being of a nation, but a clear distinction was made between true and *false* patriotism: "Citizens should develop a generous and loyal devotion to their country, but without any narrowing of mind. In other words, they must always look simultaneously to the welfare of the whole human family, which is tied together by the manifold bonds linking races, peoples and nations" [Ibid, p. 286].

(6) But these limits on patriotism do not rule out a country's right to legitimate self-defense....

(7) In the conduct of any war, there must be moral limits....

(8) While the stockpiling of scientific weapons serves, for the present, as a deterrent to aggression, the Council has warned us that "the arms race in which so many countries are engaged is not a safe way to preserve a steady peace" [Ibid, p. 295]....

(9) The Council commended those citizens who defend their nation against aggression. They are "instruments of security and freedom on behalf of their people. As long as they fulfill this role properly, they are making a genuine contribution to the establishment of peace" [Ibid, p. 293].

At the same time, however, it pointed out that some provision should be made for those who conscientiously object to bearing arms: "It seems right that laws make humane provisions for the care of those who for reasons of conscience refuse to bear arms; provided, however, that they accept some other form of service to the human community" [Ibid].

Principles Put to Work

(10) In the light of these principles, how are we as Americans to judge the involvement of the United States in Vietnam? What can we do to promote peace?

(11) Americans can have confidence in the sincerity of their leaders as long as they work for a just peace in Vietnam. Their efforts to find a solution to the present impasse are well known. We realize that citizens of all faiths and of differing political loyalties honestly differ among them-

selves over the moral issues involved in this tragic conflict. While we do not claim to be able to resolve these issues authoritatively, in the light of the facts as they are known to us, it is reasonable to argue that our presence in Vietnam is justified. We share the anguish of our government officials in their awesome responsibility of making life-and-death decisions about our national policy in Vietnam. We commend the valor of our men in the armed forces, and we express to them our debt of gratitude. In our time, thousands of men have given their lives in war. To those who loved them, we express our sorrow at their loss and promise our constant prayer.

(12) But we cannot stop here. While we can conscientiously support the position of our country in the present circumstances, it is the duty of everyone to search for other alternatives. And everyone – government leaders and citizens alike – must be prepared to change our course whenever a change in circumstances warrants it.

(13) This can be done effectively only if we know the facts and issues involved. Within the limits imposed by our national security, therefore, we must always insist that these facts and issues be made known to the public so that they can be considered in their moral context.

(14) On the basis of our knowledge and understanding of the current situation, we are also bound always to make sure that our Government does, in fact, pursue every possibility which offers even the slightest hope of a peaceful settlement. And we must clearly protest whenever there is a danger that the conflict will be escalated beyond morally acceptable limits.

(15) On a broader level, we must support our government in its efforts to negotiate a workable formula for disarmament....

(16) Moreover, we must use every resource available, as a nation, to help alleviate the basic causes of war. If the God-given human dignity of the people of poorer nations is not to become an illusion, these nations must be able to provide for the spiritual and material needs of their citizens....

'The Second Mile'

(17) There is a grave danger that the circumstances of the present war in Vietnam may, in time, diminish our moral sensitivity to its evils. Every means at our disposal, therefore, must be used to create a climate of peace. In this climate, prayer, personal example, study, discussion and lectures can strengthen the will for peace. We must advocate what we

believe are the best methods of promoting peace: mutual agreements, safeguards and inspection; the creation of an international public authority to negotiate toward peace. Above all, in its peace-making efforts, we must support the work of the United Nations which, in the words of Pope Paul, marks "a stage in the development of mankind, from which retreat must never be admitted, but from which it is necessary that advance be made" [*Address to the UN*, Oct. 4, 1965].

(18) We ask every person of good will to support with prayer the Holy Father's plea for a Christmas cease-fire. May it open the way to lasting peace. In the spirit of Christ, the Christian must be the persistent seeker in the Gospel, the man willing to walk the second mile [cf. Mt. 5:42]. He walks prudently, but he walks generously and he asks that all men do the same.

(19) As Catholics we walk in good company. Pope Paul, in his recent encyclical on peace, cried out, in God's name, to stop war. We pray God that the sacrifices of us all, our prayers as well as our faltering efforts toward peace, will hasten the day when the whole world will echo Pope Paul's historic words: "No more war, war never again!" [*Address to the UN*, Oct. 4, 1965].

HUMAN LIFE

As early as June 1966 Lawrence Cardinal Sheehan of Baltimore had issued a pastoral letter instructing Catholics that Vatican II had legitimized both just defense *and* conscientious objection. Conscience, in fact, was the key to deciding on the legitimacy of the war and to limiting its violence. Sheehan's position was reflected in the bishops' next pastoral, the *Resolution on Peace* of Nov. 16, 1967, which criticized the extremism of both left and right but acknowledged that the anti-war protestors represented "responsible segments of our society." The bishops also refused to repeat their 1966 endorsement of the war as just.

By 1967/68 events in Vietnam itself and the pressures of the Catholic left had brought great changes in the hierarchy's attitudes. The majority of Catholic bishops themselves had moved clearly toward neutrality on the war, while the number of dissenting bishops steadily grew. Finally in November 1968 the bishops issued their pastoral *Human Life in Our Day*, the American reply to Paul VI's *Humanae Vitae*.

The letter tackled two divisive issues in the America of 1968. After discussing the church's position on birth control, the bishops addressed themselves to issues of war and peace. Recalling the declarations of Vatican II to "evaluate war with an entirely new attitude," the bishops went on to explicitly condemn all aggressive wars and all total war. While asserting that the soldier also contributes to peace by ensuring order, the bishops reminded Catholics that "in the Christian message peace is not merely the absence of war or the balance of power." Charity and justice are true peace, and these are achieved not by support of dictatorships but by true development as defined by Paul VI. Turning to the issue of America's nuclear capability, the bishops repeated the message of the *Pastoral Constitution* condemning the "indiscriminate destruction of whole cities or vast areas with their inhabitants [as] a crime against God and man." They endorsed the Partial Test-Ban Treaty and the Non-Proliferation treaty, condemned the ABM and the doctrine of nuclear superiority and escalation, describing the arms race as "an utterly treacherous trap for humanity, and which ensnares the poor to an intolerable degree."

Finally, turning to Vietnam, the bishops then declared their opposition to the peacetime draft, an institution that only contributes to future wars, a position, they noted, already taken by Benedict XV. Finally the bishops posed several questions about the war in Vietnam: has the U.S. already crossed the point of proportionality that makes the war unjust? Can the U.S. now withdraw? Are the billions now being spent on killing better used on hospitals, schools, poverty programs, and positive works of social justice [§137-§138]? The bishops concluded that these are all valid moral questions and that Vietnam was providing several moral lessons and then turned to the responsibility of American Catholics to make peace.

They declared, for the first time in American history, that conscientious objectors, even selective conscientious objectors who refuse to fight because of the injustice of a particular war, have a basis in modern Catholic teaching, especially after Vatican II [§144-45, 150-51], and that unquestioning obedience "is not necessarily in conformity with the mind and heart of the Church" [§147]. The prelates therefore declared that the Selective Service System must modify the draft law to include selective objection against particular wars considered unjust or immoral [§152], and that even if the SSS refuses to act, Catholics must follow their consciences in refusing to serve [§153], a radical call for obedience to God above that to human laws. They concluded that "the hour has indeed struck for 'conversion,' for personal transformation, for interior renewal" [§155].

The following selections are taken from O'Brien and Shannon, *Renewing the Earth*, pp. 451-67.

374. U.S. Catholic Conference, Human Life in Our Day

Chapter II: The Family of Nations

...Vietnam

(135) In a previous statement we ventured a tentative judgment that, on balance, the U.S. presence in Vietnam was useful and justified.

(136) Since then American Catholics have entered vigorously into the national debate on this question, which, explicitly or implicitly, is going deeply into the moral aspects of our involvement in Vietnam. In this debate, opinions among Catholics appear as varied as in our society as a whole; one cannot accuse Catholics of either being partisans of any one point of view or of being unconcerned. In our democratic system the fundamental right of political dissent cannot be denied, nor is rational debate on public policy decisions of government in the light of moral and political principles to be discouraged. It is the duty of the governed to analyze responsibly the concrete issues of public policy.

(137) In assessing our country's involvement in Vietnam we must ask: Have we already reached, or passed, the point where the principle of proportionality becomes decisive? How much more of our resources in men and money should we commit to this struggle, assuming an acceptable cause or intention? Has the conflict in Vietnam provoked inhuman dimensions of suffering? Would not an untimely withdrawal be equally disastrous?

(138) Granted that financial considerations are necessarily subordinate to ethical values in any moral question, nonetheless many wonder if perhaps a measure of the proportions in this, as in any modern war, may be reflected in the amounts inevitably lost to education, poverty-relief and positive works of social justice at home and abroad (including Southeast Asia) as a result of the mounting budgets for this and like military operations. This point has frequently been raised by the Popes, notably by Pope Pius XII, who invoked the principle of proportionality in his

analysis of the morality even of defensive wars, particularly when these involve A.B.C. elements (atomic, biological, chemical) and losses disproportionate to the "injustice tolerated" [*Address to Military Doctors*, Oct. 19, 1953].

(139) While it would be beyond our competence to propose any technical formulas for bringing the Vietnam War to an end, we welcome the bombing halt and pray for the success of the negotiations now underway.

(140) Meanwhile there are moral lessons to be learned from our involvement in Vietnam that will apply to future cases. One might be that military power and technology do not suffice, even with the strongest resolve, to restore order or accomplish peace. As a rule, internal political conflicts are too complicated to be solved by the external application of force and technology.

(141) Another might be the realization that some evils existing in the world, evils such as undernutrition, economic frustration, social stagnation and political injustices, may be more readily attacked and corrected through non-military means than by military efforts to counteract the subversive forces bent on their exploitation.

(142) In addition, may we not hope that violence will be universally discredited as a means of remedying human ills, and that the spirit of love "may overcome the barriers that divide, cherish the bonds of mutual charity, understand others and pardon those who have done them wrong?" [*Pacem in Terris*, §171.]

The Role of Conscience

(143) The war in Vietnam typifies the issues which present and future generations will be less willing to leave entirely to the normal political and bureaucratic processes of national decision-making. It is not surprising that those who are most critical, even intemperate in their discussion of war as an instrument of national policy or as a ready means to the settling even of wrongs, are among the young; the burden of killing and dying falls principally on them.

(144) There is sometimes ground for question as to whether the attitudes of some toward military duty do not spring from cowardice. In this problem, as in all crises which test generosity and heroism, cases of moral as well as physical cowardice doubtless occur. But a blanket charge of this kind would be unfair to those young people who are clearly willing to

suffer social ostracism and even prison terms because of their opposition to a particular war. One must conclude that for many of our youthful protesters, the motives spring honestly from a principled opposition to a given war as pointless or immoral.

(145) Nor can it be said that such conscientious objection to war, as war is waged in our times, is entirely the result of subjective considerations and without reference to the message of the Gospel and the teaching of the Church; quite the contrary, frequently conscientious dissent reflects the influence of the principles which inform modern papal teaching, the *Pastoral Constitution* and a classical tradition of moral doctrine in the Church, including, in fact, the norms for the moral evaluation of a theoretically just war.

(146) The enthusiasm of many young people for new programs of service to fellow humans in need may be proof that some traditional forms of patriotism are in process of being supplemented by a new spirit of dedication to humanity and to the moral prestige of one's own nation. This new spirit must be taken seriously; it may not always match the heroism of the missionaries and the full measure of the life of faith, but it is not contradictory to these and may open up new forms of Christian apostolate.

(147) As witnesses to a spiritual tradition which accepts enlightened conscience, even when honestly mistaken, as the immediate arbiter of moral decisions, we can only feel reassured by this evidence of individual responsibility and the decline of uncritical conformism to patterns some of which included strong moral elements, to be sure, but also include political, social, cultural and like controls not necessarily in conformity with the mind and heart of the Church.

(148) If war is ever to be outlawed, and replaced by more humane and enlightened institutions to regulate conflicts among nations, institutions rooted in the notion of universal common good, it will be because the citizens of this and other nations have rejected the tenets of exaggerated nationalism and insisted on principles of non-violent political and civic action in both the domestic and international spheres.

(149) We therefore join with the Council Fathers in praising "those who renounce the use of violence in the vindication of their rights and who resort to methods of defense which are otherwise available to weaker parties, provided that this can be done without injury to the rights and duties of others or of the community itself" [*Gaudium et Spes,* §78].

(150) It is in this light that we seek to interpret and apply to our own situation the advice of the Vatican Council on the treatment of conscientious objectors. The Council endorsed laws that "make humane provision for the care of those who for reasons of conscience refuse to bear arms, provided, however, that they accept some other form of service to the human community" [§79].

(151) The present laws of this country, however, provide only for those whose reasons of conscience are grounded in a total rejection of the use of military force. This form of conscientious objection deserves the legal provision made for it, but we consider that the time has come to urge that similar consideration be given those whose reasons of conscience are more personal and specific.

(152) We therefore recommend a modification of the Selective Service Act making it possible, although not easy, for so-called selective conscientious objectors to refuse – without fear of imprisonment or loss of citizenship – to serve in wars which they consider unjust or in branches of service (e.g., the strategic nuclear forces) which would subject them to the performance of actions contrary to deeply held moral convictions about indiscriminate killing. Some other form of service to the human community should be required of those so exempted.

(153) Whether or not such modifications in our laws are in fact made, we continue to hope that, in the all-important issue of war and peace, all men will follow their consciences. We can do no better than to recall, as did the Vatican Council, "the permanent binding force of universal natural law and its all-embracing principles," to which "man's conscience itself gives ever more emphatic voice."

(154) In calling so persistently in this Pastoral for studies on the application of sound moral principles to new dimensions of changes in the problems of war and peace, we are mindful of our own responsibility to proclaim the Gospel of peace and to teach the precepts of both natural and revealed divine law concerning the establishing of peace everywhere on earth [§79]. We therefore make our own the Council's judgment on "the deeper causes of war," sins like envy, mistrust and egoism. We echo the warning given by Pope Paul at the United Nations: "Today as never before, in an era marked by such human progress, there is need for an appeal to the moral conscience of man. For the danger comes not from progress, nor from science – on the contrary, if properly utilized these could resolve many of the grave problems which beset mankind. The

781

real danger comes from man himself, who has at his disposal ever more powerful instruments, which can be used as well for destruction as for the loftiest conquests."

(155) The hour has indeed struck for "conversion," for personal transformation, for interior renewal. We must once again begin to think of man in a new way, and of human life with a new appreciation of its worth, its dignity and its call to elevation to the level of the life of God Himself. All this requires that, with refreshed purpose and deepened faith we follow the urging of St. Paul that we "put on the new man, which has been created according to God in justice and holiness of truth" [Eph. 4:23]....

Official Catholic thought continued to evolve under both the influence of papal teaching since Vatican II and under the pressure of the Catholic laity, who were increasingly taking the lead in the religious anti-Vietnam war movement. By 1971 these trends had led the bishops to clarify Cathoic teaching on conscientious objection.

The following is taken from the USCC Publication B-55.

375. U.S. Catholic Conference, Declaration on Conscientious Objection and Selective Conscientious Objection, October 21, 1971

...Although a Catholic may take advantage of the law providing exemption from military service because of conscientious opposition to all war, there often arises a practical problem at the local level when those who exercise civil authority are of the opinion that a Catholic cannot under any circumstances be a conscientious objector because of religious training and belief. This confusion, in some cases, is the result of a mistaken notion that a person cannot be a conscientious objector unless the individual is a member of one of the traditional pacifist churches (for example, a Quaker).

In the light of the Gospel and from an analysis of the Church's teaching on conscience, it is clear that a Catholic can be a conscientious objector to war in general or to a particular war "because of religious training and belief." It is not enough, however, simply to declare that a Catholic can be a conscientious objector or a selective conscientious objector. Efforts must be made to help Catholics form a correct conscience in the matter, to discuss with them the duties of citizenship, and to provide them with adequate draft counseling and information services in order to give them the full advantage of the law protecting their rights. Catholic organizations which could qualify as alternative service agencies should be encouraged to support and provide meaningful employment for the conscientious objector. As we hold individuals in high esteem who conscientiously serve in the armed forces, so also we should regard conscientious objection and selective conscientious objection as positive indicators within the Church of a sound moral awareness and respect for human life.

The status of the selective conscientious objector is complicated by the fact that the present law does not provide an exemption for this type of conscientious objection. We recognize the very complex procedural problems which selective conscientious objection poses for the civil community; we call upon moralists, lawyers and civil servants to work cooperatively toward a policy which can reconcile the demands of the moral and civic order concerning this issue. We reaffirm the recommendation on this subject contained in our November 1968 pastoral letter, "Human Life in Our Day":

> (1) a modification of the Selective Service Act making it possible for selective conscientious objectors to refuse to serve in wars they consider unjust, without fear of imprisonment or loss of citizenship, provided they perform some other service to the human community; and
>
> (2) an end to peacetime conscription.

In restating these recommendations, we are aware that a number of young men have left the country or have been imprisoned because of their opposition to compulsory military conscription. It is possible that in some cases this was done for unworthy motives, but in general we must presume sincere objections of conscience, especially on the part of those ready to suffer for their convictions. Since we have a pastoral concern for their welfare, we urge civil officials in revising the law to consider granting amnesty to those who have been imprisoned as selective conscientious objectors, and giving those who have emigrated an opportunity to return to the country to show responsibility for their conduct and to be ready to serve in other ways to show that they are sincere objectors.

The war in Vietnam ended only in April 1975. For many years before that Catholic opposition to the war had become the most vocal in the nation. In 1967 Catholics ranked only below Jews in their oppo-

sition to Vietnam. They averaged 27% opposed, Jews 48%, and Western European Protestants 17%. By 1970 Catholics far surpassed Protestants in their call for withdrawal from Vietnam. Given a choice of withdrawal/victory in Vietnam, Anglo-Saxon Protestants recorded 40/ 36, and Catholics an average of 51/30, with Catholic white-collar groups the most consistently opposed to the war. Northern, white opposition divided along the following lines, Protestant/Catholic: blue collar 50%/ 47%, clerical 32%/38%, professional 39%/52%.

The bishop's stance followed Catholic opinion closely; and by November 1971 they had moved to open and complete condemnation of the war as immoral: the evil perpetrated by U.S. involvement far out of proportion to any good the nation could hope to achieve there.

The following is taken from the U.S. Catholic Conference, *In the Name of Peace: Collective Statements of the United States Bishops on War and Peace, 1919-1980,* Washington, DC: USCC, 1983, pp. 59-62.

376. U.S. Catholic Conference, Resolution on Southeast Asia, November 1971

In light of the urgent appeal for justice in the world pronounced by the recent Synod in Rome, we Bishops of the United States address ourselves again to the agonizing issue of the American involvement in Southeast Asia. And we feel compelled to make some positive recommendations concerning the long journey ahead to peace with justice in our world.

I. The American Involvement in Southeast Asia

Three years ago, in our Pastoral Letter *Human Life in Our Day* [**374**], we raised some basic moral questions concerning the Vietnam War:

> In assessing our country's involvement in Vietnam we must ask: Have we already reached, or passed, the point where the principle of proportionality becomes decisive? How much more of our resources of men and money should we commit to this struggle, assuming an acceptable cause and intention? Has the conflict in Vietnam provoked inhuman dimensions of suffering?

At this point in history it seems clear to us that whatever good we hope to achieve through continued involvement in this war is now outweighed by the destruction of human life and of moral values which it inflicts. It is our firm conviction, therefore, that the speedy ending of this war is a moral imperative of the highest priority. Hence, we feel a moral obligation to appeal urgently to our nation's leaders and indeed to the leaders of all the nations involved in this tragic conflict to bring the war to an end with no further delay.

II. The Journey Ahead to Peace with Justice in Our World

It is our prayerful hope that we in America will have learned from the tragedy of Vietnam important lessons for reconstructing a world with justice and a world at peace.

First, we must be determined as never before to "undertake an evaluation of war with an entirely new attitude" [*Gaudium et Spes*, §80, see **299**]. And we reach this attitude by attending more carefully to the spirit of the Gospel and heeding the pleas of recent Popes: "Nothing is lost by peace; everything may be lost by war" [Pius XII, Radio Broadcast of 24 August 1939]; in this age of ours which prides itself on atomic power, it is irrational to believe that war is still an apt means of vindicating violated rights" [John XXIII, *Pacem in Terris*, §127, see **298**]; "No more war, war never again" [Paul VI, *Address to the United Nations*, 4 October 1965].

Secondly, we realize that "peace is not merely the absence of war but an enterprise of justice" [*Gaudium et Spes*, §78]. In this vein we recognize our nation's moral obligation, together with other nations, to contribute mightily to the restoration and development of Southeast Asia. After World War II our country launched an unprecedented program of economic assistance and social reconstruction of war-torn countries. Certainly we can do no less now.

Thirdly, we are convinced that the United Nations must become more effective in the promotion of world justice and peace. In saying this we echo the words of Pope Paul VI that "the people of the earth turn to the United Nations as the last hope of concord and peace" and we recognize with the Holy Father that the United Nations "must be perfected and made equal to the needs which world history will present" [*Address to the United Nations*, 4 October 1965]. Only by strengthening the United Nations as an international forum for peace and as a multilateral instrument for peace-keeping can future Vietnams be averted.

Finally, we recognize a clear need at this point in history to urge upon all Americans a spirit of forgiveness and reconciliation. We recall that at a similarly critical moment in American history, Abraham Lincoln urged his countrymen to act "with malice towards none, with charity towards all." We invite our fellow Americans to let these words guide new efforts to heal wounds in our divided society and to unite our country in the years after the war in Southeast Asia.

We speak with special concern for those who have borne the heaviest burden of this war: the young men who chose conscientiously to serve in the Armed Forces, many of whom lost life or limb in this conflict. We wish to express our profound sympathy to the wives and families of the soldiers who have died in Southeast Asia. We express our profound concern for our prisoners of war and their families and promise our prayers for the prisoners' welfare and release. And on behalf of the returning veterans we urge strongly that the Government increase the present benefits and educational opportunities afforded by the GI Bill, and that it create new programs of drug rehabilitation, vocational training and job placement wherever necessary.

Those who in good conscience resisted this war are also subjects of our genuine pastoral concern. They too must be reintegrated as fully as possible into our society and invited to share the opportunities and responsibilities of building a better nation. Hence we repeat our plea of October 21, 1971 that the civil authorities grant generous pardon of convictions incurred under the Selective Service Act, with the understanding that sincere conscientious objectors should remain open in principle to some form of service to the community. Surely a country which showed compassion by offering amnesty after the Civil War will want to exercise no less compassion today....

TRIAL OF THE CATONSVILLE NINE: DANIEL BERRIGAN

On May 17, 1968 a group of nine Catholic activists, including Daniel and Philip Berrigan, David Darst, Thomas and Marjorie Melville, George Mische, Mary Moylan, John Hogan, and Thomas Lewis, entered the Selective Service headquarters at Catonsville, Maryland, brought draft files outside, and burned them with napalm. The police waited until the nine had completed the Lord's Prayer and then hand-cuffed and led them away. The action, arrest, trial, and conviction of the Catonsville Nine issued in a new era in American and Catholic peace history. In October 1967 Philip Berrigan had led a similar raid on the draft offices in the Baltimore Customs' House, symbolically pouring blood on draft records as a dramatic means of confronting the Pentagon and the American people with their own war guilt. The Baltimore action had also resulted in arrest, but the Catonsville case raised new issues and concerns among all Americans.

Daniel Berrigan, SJ was born on May 9, 1921 in Virginia, Minnesota, the son of an Irish-American union organizer and a German-American mother who devoted her life to the works of charity: offering hospitality and food to the homeless and unemployed of the Great Depression. In 1926 the Berrigans moved to Syracuse, New York, where Daniel attended St. John the Baptist Academy. He entered the Jesuit seminary in Poughkeepsie, NY in 1939 and taught at St. Peter's Prep in Jersey City from 1946 to 1949. Berrigan was ordained a priest in June 1952, having published his first work, a poem in *America* magazine in 1942. After studying in France from 1953 to 1954 and serving briefly as a military chaplian in Germany, Berrigan returned to the USA and began his long career of writing both poetry and religous works while teaching at Brooklyn Prep, a Jesuit high school, from 1954 to 1957 and at Le Moyne College from 1957 to 1962.

With the 1960s came Berrigan's involvement in peace and justice issues. In 1964 he was one of the founders of the Catholic Peace Fellowship, and in 1965 of the Clergy Concerned About Vietnam. In November 1965, following his antiwar statement at the funeral of Roger La Porte, a young Catholic Worker who had burned himself to death in protest against the Vietnam War, Berrigan was transferred to Latin America by the New York archdiocese. Cardinal Spellman's attempt to silence the young Jesuit sparked a wave of protest from Catholic laity and clergy, making him a symbol of the new Catholic peace movement. Recalled in 1966, Berrigan became a recognized leader of the Catholic anti-war effort of the late 1960 and 1970s, culminating for many in the Catonsville raid of 1968.

The Catonsville Nine took every precaution to avoid human injury, had made their protest open, and had not resisted arrest but had made it a form of nonviolent witness; yet their illegal break-in and their theft and destruction of property were seen as forms of nonviolence that stretched the definition. Thomas Merton himself, while fully in accord with the idea of an active resistance, wondered whether the Catonsville Nine had crossed the line but concluded that they had not.

Despite the Catonsville Nine's eventual conviction for interfering with operations of the Selective Service and destroying Selective Service and Federal property, other actions quickly followed in Milwaukee and Chicago, and the media soon turned on to the new "Catholic Left." By 1969 Catholic resisters had staged similar actions against private corporations in secret night actions, only later surfacing to face arrest. In April 1970 Daniel Berrigan went underground to avoid arrest, emerging sporadically to give interviews, embarrass the FBI, or to celebrate mass with supporters, until his final arrest in August.

The tactics produced bitter splits within Catholic peace circles. Many condemned them as a serious departure from Gandhian openness and truth, closely approaching the "just revolution," bringing harsh repression from the Nixon administration that far exceeded the intentions of the actions, and deviating from the commitment to nonviolence already laid out by Dorothy Day and the *Catholic Worker* and such Catholic intellectuals as Gordon Zahn and James Douglass. The Berrigans and the others involved in the actions claimed that their tactics were the only form of nonviolent witness to the horrors of mass destruction and sanitized madness that an American people immunized to every sight of brutality and destruction could respond to. The symbolism of the actions was certainly not lost on the Pentagon or the U.S. administration, which reacted in shock and outrage to every ounce of blood poured with an almost ritual understanding of the actions' true witness. With the subsequent arraignment, trial, and acquittal of Philip Berrigan, Sister Elizabeth McAlister and five others for conspiracy in what was to become known as the Harrisburg Seven Trial, Catholic resistance and government repression reached levels that exhausted the Catholic peace movement amid doubts over aims, tactics, and effectiveness.

Berrigan's play based on the events, *The Trial of the Catonsville Nine,* appeared in 1970 and won an Obie Drama Award in New York in 1971. Its court testimony is written in the form of poetic dialogue. The following selection is taken from Daniel Berrigan, *Poetry, Drama, Prose,* Michael True, ed., Maryknoll, NY: Orbis Books, 1988, pp. 247-51.

377. Daniel Berrigan, The Trial of the Catonsville Nine

...On my return to America [from Vietnam in 1968]
another event
helped me understand

the way I must go
It was the self-immolation
of a high school student [Roger La Porte]
in Syracuse New York
in the spring of 1968
This boy had come to a point of despair
about the war   He had gone
into the Catholic cathedral
drenched himself with kerosene
and immolated himself in the street
He was still living a month later
I was able to gain access to him
I smelled the odor
of burning flesh
And I understood anew
what I had seen in North Vietnam
The boy was dying in torment
his body like a piece of meat
cast upon a grille He died shortly thereafter
I felt that my senses
had been invaded in a new way
I had understood
the power of death in the modern world
I knew I must speak and act
against death
because this boy's death
was being multiplied
a thousandfold
in the Land of Burning Children
So I went to Catonsville and burned some papers   because
the burning of children
is inhuman and unbearable
I went to Catonsville
because I had gone to Hanoi
because my brother was a man
and I must be a man
and because
I knew at length

I could not announce the gospel
from a pedestal
I must act as a Christian
sharing the risks and burdens and anguish
of those whose lives were placed
in the breach by us
I saw suddenly   and it struck with the force of lightning
that my position was false
I was threatened with verbalizing
my moral substance out of existence
I was placing upon young shoulders
a filthy burden   the original sin of war
I was asking them to enter a ceremony of death
Although I was too old
to carry a draft card   there were other ways
of getting in trouble with a state
that seemed determined upon multiplying the dead
totally intent upon a war
the meaning of which   no sane man could tell
So I went to Hanoi
and then to Catonsville
and that is why I am here

Defense Did you not write a meditation to accompany the statement
issued by the nine defendants at Catonsville?

Daniel Berrigan
Yes sir

Defense
Would you read the meditation?

Daniel Berrigan Certainly
"Some ten or twelve of us (the number is still uncertain)
will if all goes well (ill?) take our religious bodies
during this week
to a draft center in or near Baltimore
There we shall   of purpose and forethought
remove the I-A files   sprinkle them in the public street
with home-made napalm   and set them afire

790

For which act we shall beyond doubt
be placed behind bars for some portion of our natural lives
in consequence of our inability
to live and die content in the plagued city
to say 'peace peace' when there is no peace
to keep the poor poor
the thirsty and hungry thirsty and hungry
Our apologies   good friends
for the fracture of good order   the burning of paper
instead of children   the angering of the orderlies
in the front parlor of the charnel house
We could not   so help us God   do otherwise
For we are sick at heart   our hearts
give us no rest for thinking of the Land of Burning Children
and for thinking of that other Child of whom
the poet Luke speaks   The infant was taken up
in the arms of an old man whose tongue
grew resonant and vatic at the touch of that beauty
And the old man spoke: this child is set
for the fall and rise of many in Israel
a sign that is spoken against
Small consolation   a child born to make trouble
and to die for it   the First Jew (not the last)
to be subject of a 'definitive solution'
And so we stretch out our hands
to our brothers and sisters throughout the world
We who are priests to our fellow priests
All of us who act against the law
turn to the poor of the world   to the Vietnamese
to the victims   to the soldiers who kill and die
for the wrong reasons for no reason at all
because they were so ordered by the authorities
of that public order which is in effect
a massive institutionalized disorder
We say: killing is disorder
life and gentleness and community and unselfishness
is the only order we recognize
For the sake of that order

we risk our liberty   our good name
The time is past when good men and women may be silent
when obedience
can segregate people from public risk
when the poor can die without defense
How many indeed must die
before our voices are heard
how many must be tortured dislocated
starved maddened?
How long must the world's resources
be raped in the service of legalized murder?
When at what point will you say no to this war?
We have chosen to say
with the gift of our liberty
if necessary our lives:
the violence stops here
the death stops here
the suppression of the truth stops here
this war stops here
Redeem the times!
The times are inexpressibly evil
Christians pay conscious   indeed religious tribute
to Caesar and Mars
by the approval of overkill tactics   by brinkmanship
by nuclear liturgies   by racism   by support of genocide
They embrace their society with all their heart
and abandon the cross
They pay lip service to Christ
and military service to the powers of death
And yet   and yet   the times are inexhaustibly good
solaced by the courage and hope of many
The truth rules   Christ is not forsaken
In a time of death some men and women
the resisters   those who work hardily for social change
those who preach and embrace the truth
such men and women overcome death
their lives are bathed in the light of the resurrection
the truth has set them free

In the jaws of death
they proclaim their love of the neighbor
We think of such men and women
in the world   in our nation   in the churches
and the stone in our breast is dissolved
we take heart once more"

Defense
Nothing further.

AFTER VIETNAM:
TOWARD A THEOLOGY OF PEACEMAKING

The end of the Vietnam War in 1975 saw American Catholics at the forefront of the peace movement. Not only had they retained a consistently religious stance toward the conflict, but they had also deepened the insights of church councils, papal letters, and theological reflection by long years of praxis. By the mid-1970s therefore Catholic peacemaking in America had forged a new synthesis of lay action and analysis with the growing consensus of the hierarchy and clergy for a commitment to the works of peace and justice. The following selections offer a sampling of the richness of this peacemaking in the 1970s and 1980s.

JOSEPH FAHEY

Joseph Fahey was born in the Bronx, New York on January 8, 1940 and educated in Catholic elementary and high schools. He earned a BA from Maryknoll Seminary in philosophy and social sciences in 1962, an MA in theology from Maryknoll in 1966, and a doctorate in religion and social ethics from New York University in 1974. He has taught at Manhattan College in New York City since 1966 where he is now a professor of religious studies and the director of the Peace Studies Program.

Instrumental in the founding of the U.S. branch of Pax Christi, Fahey served as its general secretary and chair from 1973 to 1980. He was a member of the executive committee of Pax Christi International from 1974 to 1978 and of its International Disarmament and Theological Commission from 1977 to 1985. From 1983 to 1986 he chaired the personnel committee of the Fellowship of Reconciliation. Fahey has been actively involved in issues of peace education, arbitration and international order. On behalf of Pax Christi he wrote the Carter administration urging an end to U.S. support of the Somoza regime in Nicaragua, thus signalling the close ties that would emerge in the 1980s between the churches of North and Central America over issues of peace and justice. Along with Thomas Gumbleton [392], and Gerald Vanderhaar, he brought Pax Christi to oppose the Salt II Treaty in favor of the more far-reaching moratorium. In 1982 Fahey authored Pax Christi/USA's position paper on nuclear arms for the UN Special Session on Disarmament. In it he framed the group's "nuclear pacifist" stance that would ultimately be rejected by Pope John Paul II in favor of bilateral "freeze" and by the U.S. bishops in their *Challenge of Peace* [389] in favor of continued nuclear deterrence.

Fahey is the author of dozens of articles and co-editor of *A Peace Reader: Essential Readings on War, Justice, Non-Violence and World Order* (rev. ed. 1992). He has consistently provided an enlightened *lay*, and broad-based view of peacemaking that finds its primary instrument – as for Erasmus – in education. In his May 1971 essay in *Catholic World* entitled "Toward a Theology of Peace," Fahey summarized the insights and gains of Catholic peacemaking over the past fifty years as a positive alternative to the theories and theologies that underpin the waging of war.

Our selection is taken from *Catholic World* 213 (May 1971): 64-68.

378. Joseph Fahey, Toward a Theology of Peace

To speak of Christian peace today is to offer a sign of contradiction to our world. In our century Christianity finds itself with a world that spends more money on destroying people than keeping them alive. The so-called civilized nations of our globe spend over 150 billion dollars on arms while under seven billion dollars is spent on aid of all types to the destitute of our earth. It is estimated that in the past seventy years over 100 million people have lost their lives through warfare – most of them civilians. At this present moment there are some 15,000 tons of dynamite for each person on the face of the earth. Since 1945 more than forty savage wars have been and are being fought around us and the voices of reconciliation are few and weak.

The many Christians who favor such a situation are not only potent threats to human survival but are also the greatest enemies to the Gospel of Peace. In our age Christian theologians must stop providing a theoretical basis for such a state of affairs by continuing to elaborate conditions in which a just war may be fought in this age of total war. We are in desperate need of a theology of peace which can speak to our world with a realistic message of hope and reconciliation. This article is an attempt to elaborate some elements of such a theology.

The first element of a theology of peace must deal with the Christian conception of God. Men have done all sorts of things with God when it comes to war. Some have dressed Him in khaki, others have claimed that He is on "our" side; while still others have turned Him into the super-patriot. The Christian God is first and foremost a God of love. He created this world out of love and intends nothing but the best for it. He can hardly be on the side of hate and destruction although men have said He is.

The Christian God is not a nationalistic God. He transcends political or economic persuasions considering all men of every nation to be His children. Abraham Lincoln once advised us to pray not that God be on our side, but rather that we be on God's side. God is on the side of people and their survival; He serves the cause of life – not death. Today's Christian who would be on God's side must not associate God with any one nation-state. What must survive is not governments but people; God gave this world not to some or a few chosen, but for the benefit of all.

The Gospels do not speak of peace in terms of arms or preparation for war. The basic message is reconciliation. Jesus told His followers that those who may be called "sons of God" must be peacemakers [Mt. 5:9, see **31**]....

The second element of a theology of peace should deal with our concept of man. Is man basically evil and corrupt? If so, then we will agree with Thomas Hobbes who argued that only the "sword" will keep him in his place. Is man good with no proclivity to evil? Then how do we explain the obvious injustice and inhumanity about and within us? Obviously the answer, if there is one, lies somewhere in between. For we know that man has cured polio and walked on the moon and has also invented and used nuclear weapons.

...Human nature has the ability to be both good and evil: man can save life or destroy it. Nevertheless it appears that man is basically good since his most fundamental drive is a healthy one: to survive. Other drives naturally flow from this desire: food, shelter, territoriality, and, on a more sophisticated level: freedom, independence, knowledge, etc. Man's desire to survive is by definition communal in that man by nature seeks to be with others and to work with others for their common existence....

We have been speaking here about life as if it were essentially a choice between good and evil and indeed it often is. But there are times when man's only choice may be between a lesser and a greater evil. In short the reality of self-defense cannot be excluded from man's ethical alternatives. The drive to defend territory (of all types) is basic to man and there may be times when man has no alternative but to use violence. These words should not be interpreted as a "cop-out" as they mean simply to describe man's present state of moral evolution in which violence is considered by some as the only means to insure human existence. It becomes the role of the Christian in this area to remind man by the witness of his life that there are superior alternatives to violence: the nonviolence of early Christianity [see 48-88], Gandhi, [Martin Luther] King and [Cesar] Chavez [see **385**] must become the norm for man rather than the exception.

This leads us to the third element of a theology of peace, which is nonviolence. It is the task of nonviolence to seriously challenge the view that man's basic ethical choice regarding war is between two evils. Cicero once stated that "discussion and force are the main ways of setting quarrels, the former of which are peculiar to man, the latter to brute beasts." In this statement Cicero is implicitly stating that nonviolence is more proper to man than is violence. Unfortunately, there have been all too few witnesses to nonviolence in human history. But there are men who have tried it, and for whom nonviolence has "worked."

...One of the chief objections to nonviolence is that it takes so long to achieve its goal. Better, some argue, to opt for violence since results will be more immediate. One cannot really dispute this argument: nonviolence is the only truly effective weapon for long-range social evolution since violence, while achieving some immediate minor gains, leads ultimately only to further violence and repression. It is nonviolence that aims toward reconciliation while violence aims at destruction; nonviolence is the weapon of love, while violence is the child of hate.

It is very difficult to ask the poor and oppressed to look to long-range social change since violence seems so appealing and satisfying. But the central question that those who use or threaten violence (including the Pentagon, Black Panthers, and Weathermen) must ask themselves is whether the use of physical violence will bring about true liberation for our world. We are living in an age and society in which violence has become a practical impossibility; only nonviolent love has a true chance of working. He who believes in nonviolence believes in the future of man; violence is a pronounced threat to that very future. Despite his critics, Dr. King is quite correct in maintaining that: "The choice today is no longer between violence and nonviolence. It is between nonviolence and nonexistence."

It should be noted here that nonviolence does not mean nonresistance just as pacifism does not mean "passivity." Jesus' counsel to "resist not evildoers" means that evildoers should not be resisted with the methods of the Zealots (physical violence), but they should nevertheless be resisted. The use of the strike, noncooperation, civil disobedience, and vocal protest in the political realm are all nonviolent techniques and they can hardly be accused of offering no resistance. The Christian spirit stands on the side of nonviolence; it is time that Christians asked where they stood.

A theology of peace, then, must by definition be a theology of nonviolence. Nonviolence needs to be studied in much greater depth for we have only begun to realize its power for good. We need courses on peace in our schools, parishes, and universities. It is not too late in our own nation's history to establish a cabinet-level Department of Peace and a United States Peace Academy to train young citizens, to resolve man's conflicts through understanding, reconciliation and development.

The fourth element of a Theology of Peace is international development. Paul VI in *Populorum Progressio* [see **301**] has stated that the modern word for peace is "development." If the majority of man's problems are primarily environmental in nature, then Paul is correct in pursuing development as a means to peace. But if they flow from the corrupt unchangeable nature of man, then the Pope is mistaken. Better in this case to argue for a continued arms buildup. But Paul links peace with development and consequently provides an alternative to violent revolution and war....

Major global confrontations can be avoided in the future if the "rich" nations of our earth will realize their human responsibilities to the wretched of our world. They will hardly do it by systematically destroying these people: there are no short cuts for human history, and it will progress even if the rich bury their heads in the sand. Development seeks to eliminate the basic causes of physical violence by significantly altering man's environment so that he can vent his aggressive drive toward bettering his life instead of striking out in frustration, which can only make his condition worse.

In short, the rich nations must participate in and facilitate the revolutions of the poor nations and this can only be done through an equitable distribution of the goods of the earth (of all types) to those who have a right to them as human beings. The rich will have to suffer in this sharing, but this suffering will be minor compared to what they will receive if they continue to defend their selfishness with billions of dollars that rightly belong to their destitute brothers who inhabit our earth.

None of the above can be accomplished without the awakening of compassion in man. Compassion reminds us that we must suffer with our brothers for their total human development; compassion tells us that people are not statistics or numbers but human beings. A compassionate person is not one who engages in the self-defeating activity of caring only for himself, rather, he is a person who sees interests wider than his own and who has the basic human warmth and sensitivity to act in the common interest of human development.

The above thoughts by no means exhaust what would constitute a Theology of Peace. Many elements need to be added and those mentioned must be examined in far greater depth. In summary then, let us say that a Theology of Peace may be called a theology of a loving God who calls upon men to respond in hope, compassion, service, and nonviolence to the legitimate needs of their fellow men. This response of man to his brothers is a precondition to and is ultimately constitutive of what may be called "peace."...

Eileen Egan

Eileen Egan has long been central to American Catholic peacemaking, both as an associate of Dorothy Day in the Catholic Worker and as one of the guiding forces behind the creation of PAX and Pax Christi/USA [380]. Born in Wales on the brink of World War I, she emigrated to the United States as a teenager. Her mother was a nonviolent Irish nationalist, and this commitment was to have a great influence upon the younger Egan. After graduation from Hunter College in New York City, she went on to join Catholic Relief Services in 1943, the year of its birth. In 1955, as director of the CRS in India, she met and befriended Mother Teresa, an association that was to last a lifetime. Equally as important was Egan's close friendship with Dorothy Day and her central role in the Catholic Worker movement. She began writing for the paper in 1964, arranging lecture tours for Day, becoming associate editor of the paper, while continuing her position for the CRS and her own writing and organizing work.

In 1962 Egan helped found and then headed PAX, the lay Catholic peace group, and edited its newsletter, *Peace*. She was able to assemble a remarkable group of sponsors, including Thomas Merton [366-370], Gordon Zahn [358], Dorothy Day [354-355, 361-371], Anne Taillefer [393], Rosemary Sheed, and Arthur Sheehan. Perhaps the organization's most important contribution to the history of Catholic peacemaking was its sending a delegation to Vatican II. While Dorothy Day participated in Chanterelle's fast and vigil [371], Egan, along with Gordon Zahn and James Douglass [403] lobbied for the adoption of nonviolence in the council's Schema XIII, what was later to become the *Pastoral Constitution*. [299]. The relative success of their efforts pointed not only to changing attitudes within the church hierarchy during John XXIII's pontificate, but also to the growth of Catholic peacemaking in America.

Egan's work for the Catholic Relief Services sometimes put her into conflict with her friends and colleagues in the peace movement, especially over the revelation of CRS's relief efforts on behalf of South Vietnam's military in 1967. In April 1972 Egan proposed to the Pax Christi International Council that PAX become the basis for a Pax Christi/USA. The proposal was approved, and Egan set to work forming the American peace group. At Oakridge, NJ in June 1972 she brought together leading Catholic peacemakers and won approval for her idea that Pax Christi should become as broad-based as possible, including both pacifists of the CPF persuasion, and more moderate Catholics. After some initial setbacks, she, Gordon Zahn, and Bishop Carroll T. Dozier of Memphis, TN saw the final launching of Pax Christi/USA in 1975.

Egan has remained central to Catholic peacemaking, retaining her personal commitment to nonviolence and the rights of conscientious objection while remaining a voice of moderation within Catholic peace circles. She is the author of eight books, editor of several others, and author and co-author of dozens of articles. Her books include *The Works of Peace* (1965); *Dorothy Day and the Permanent Revolution* (1984); *Such a Vision of the Street: Mother Teresa, The Spirit and the Work* (1985), which won the Christopher Award; and most recently, *For Whom There is no Room: Scenes from the Refugee World* (1995).

The following excerpts are taken from Eileen Egan, "The Right to Refuse to Kill," *Worldview* (Dec. 1974): 19-27.

379. Eileen Egan, Making Conscientious Objection a Human Right

In a century called "the century of total war" more than 69,000,000 human beings met death in two World Wars. These figures do not include people killed in conflicts such as those in Korea, Vietnam, and the Middle East. The striking difference between the First and Second World Wars was the number of estimated deaths among noncombatants: 5 per cent in the First and 48 per cent in the Second.

In the lesser conflicts the incidence of noncombatant deaths rose to previously unheard-of proportions; in the Korean hostilities, over 80 per cent of the casualties are estimated to have been civilians.

No figures have been forthcoming about the long drawn-out carnage in Vietnam, but it is generally believed that the proportion of noncombatant deaths will be higher than that in Korea. This likelihood stems from the nature of the conflict in which each side, claiming either "military" or "liberation" strategy, destroyed entire villages.

In the sixties and seventies general revulsion against war, particularly among young people, the right not to kill, not to take part in organized slaughter, entered the public consciousness through demonstrations, desertion, the frequent choice of prison or exile, and an extensive literature in many languages. Recognition of this right might be expected at the United Nations, the organization of the world's peoples dedicated to a world without war. However, when the right to be a conscientious objector to military service and war first surfaced at the U.N. in its twenty-fifth year, it brought forth not a welcome but an explosive collision of worldviews.

It had become dreadfully clear by World War II that the obedience of the young was abused when they carried out orders for mass destruction of human beings – whether this was achieved through air strikes or liquidation camps. Millions of young men, drafted into the military, were given little choice but to submit to induction and, after that, to follow orders. Yet in the wake of the Second World War the ultimate responsibility of the individual was asserted, even though that individual had been part of a military machine oiled by the principle of unquestioning obedience.

The international tribunal at Nuremberg refused to accept the argument from obedience as exoneration for individuals who had carried out the legal but lethal commands of their superiors – when these commands called for the commission of crimes against humanity. The "Nuremberg principle" – first applied only by the victors to those among the vanquished adjudged guilty of such crimes – was seized on by peace activists as a principle capable of a wider, general application.

The subject of conscientious objection to military service was one of the absolute taboos at the United Nations since its founding. When the taboo was finally broken and the question surfaced as a human right on the U.N. agenda, some member states saw it as so great a threat to their sovereignty that they tried to expunge it from consideration by every available means....

...Until the taboo on even the mention of conscientious objection was broken when I raised it publicly in 1970, the question had never actually surfaced at the U.N., although it was mentioned in a report of a U.N. sub-commission, the Sub-Commission on the Prevention of Discrimination and the Protection of Minorities. And I was able to raise it in 1970 only because of some recent actions.

During the U.N. International Year for Human Rights in 1970 the U.N. held a conference in Teheran dealing with the promotion of human rights. A resolution was passed there urging that the education of youth in respect for human rights be a subject for discussion and study by the United Nations. At the same time Devi Prasad, Chairman of War Resisters International (WRI), deliberately chose that year to launch a World Appeal for U.N. Recognition of Conscientious Objection to Military Service as a Human Right. Prasad worked to collect signatures around the globe, and chiefly during the Gandhi centenary year of 1969 gathered over forty thousand signatures. The petition stated simply: "We the undersigned call upon the Commission on Human Rights to recognize conscientious objection to military service as a human right." Three Nobel Prize winners gave their support to the petition: Max Born, Alfred Kastler, and Abbé Pierre. Other noted signers included Dr. Benjamin Spock, Josue de Castro of Brazil, Danilo Dolci of Italy [see **304-305**],

Martin Niemoller of Germany, Jayaprakash Narayan of India, and Vo Van Ai, exiled Buddhist peace leader from Vietnam.

On January 30, 1970, Igal Roodenko of the War Resisters League, U.S. affiliate of WRI, lodged the signatures with the Division of Human Rights at U.N. Headquarters. Roodenko deposited the fifteen-pound carton of signed petitions along with a letter of transmittal. He asked that the petition be transmitted to the Commission so that the question could be taken up "with the urgency demanded by the evils and carnages of our time."...

Within three months after those signatures were deposited, however, I was able to resurrect the petition before the members of the Human Rights Commission, and I cited the World Appeal for recognition of conscientious objection as a human right. I was able to raise the question as representative of Pax Romana, an international, multiracial movement of Catholic students and graduates. *The Church in the Modern World,* [*Gaudium et Spes,* **see 299**] which the Catholic Bishops of the world accepted at the Second Vatican Council in 1965, contained not only support for conscientious objection but a hope that nations would "make humane provision" for the conscientious objector through some form of alternative service. This was associated with a statement of the World Council of Churches and the great spiritual traditions of Hinduism and Buddhism and Islam.

The day after the circulation of the statement, the question of conscientious objection leapt across the table, from the NGO [Non-Governmental Organization] side to the government side, when two delegations spoke up for conscientious objection in the context of a human right. Klaus Tornudd of Finland asserted "My delegation would without hesitation consider conscientious objection to military service as a human right." Felix Ermacora of Austria agreed that the question was of special concern to youth and should be a matter of concern for discussion in the United Nations. *Conscientious objection had at last been publicly mentioned by U.N. member states.*

The question was raised in discussion once more when I was given the floor at a night session to add some data to the written statement. I began by stating that youth seemed ahead of its elders in respect for life and that for many young people a commitment to the U.N. aim of a "warless world" began with their commitment not to take life.

In an effort to speak for as large a spectrum of youth as possible, I said that there were many young people around the globe who considered that military service was a privilege of citizenship and a sacred duty. I explained that I was raising my voice for others who felt that even the so-called "just wars" might be questionable in their means. They therefore would wish to serve their country by some means other than the military. I referred to still others whose religious or ethical beliefs enjoined them from the intention to injure or kill another person for any reason whatsoever. I asked if a person could be free if he were not free to choose the means whereby he filled his duty to his country and to mankind....

A far more comprehensive study of conscientious abjection was published in the December 1972 issue of *The Review,* publication of the International Commission of Jurists. It covered legislation and C.O. practices in 150 countries around the world and had been prepared by a husband-and-wife team, David Weissbrodt and Patricia Schaffer. Their article, entitled "Conscientious Objection to Military Service as a Human Right," was far more revealing than the [1973] U.N. study, since it relied on facts gathered by disinterested observers rather than on what governments had to say about themselves. It also carried material on countries which for reasons of their own did not reply to the Secretary-General's letter.

The article listed eighty-four countries as maintaining conscription, of which twenty-four allowed at least partial recognition of conscientious objection. Another twelve countries were known to have made administrative arrangements for dealing with conscientious objectors, often on an ad hoc basis. In the latter group were Bulgaria, the German Democratic Republic, and Hungary. Research had revealed that in the USSR local army commanders had responded to the claims of conscientious objectors by assigning them to nonmilitary posts in hospitals – or merely sending the C.O.'s back home and ignoring them. If these commanders had adhered to the letter of the law they would have referred the objecting recruits for prosecution with possible penalties of one to three years' imprisonment in peacetime. Schaffer and Weissbrodt gathered evidence of persons claiming the right of conscientious objection in forty-eight countries of the world which had no provision for conscientious objection. Of these claims, eighteen occurred in developing countries, nine in Eastern Europe, ten in the Americas, eight in Africa and the Middle East, and the remaining twenty-one in Western Europe, Australia, and the Pacific....

Following the 1973 session I boarded a plane at the Geneva airport to return to New York. Thinking back on our struggle for the rights of conscience, I found that Thoreau's pithy question kept running through my mind: "What is each man given a conscience for if he is not to use it?"...

PAX CHRISTI

With the end of the Vietnam War the Catholic Worker and the CPF had returned to their traditional peace and justice work. They were soon joined by another Catholic peace group, Pax Christi. Born at the end of World War II out of the desire of several French Catholics for reconciliation with their former German enemies, Pax Christi soon gained the enthusiastic leadership of Bishop Pierre-Marie Theas of Lourdes. Endorsed by Pius XII by 1948, it quickly spread all over Europe and to Australia. Closely aligned with the Catholic hierarchy, Pax Christi emerged as a Catholic internationalist organization that concentrated on disarmament, peace education, contacts with the Eastern Bloc, the arms race, and the arms trade. While not specifically pacifist, the group also reflected the church's gradual abandonment of the just war since World War II.

On his return from a European meeting of Pax Christi in 1957, Gordon Zahn attempted to found a chapter of the group in the United States. The American hierarchy, however, preferred to retain its own internationalist group, CAIP. With the ending of the Vietnam War, however, and the transformation of British PAX into an affiliate of Pax Christi International, American PAX under Eileen Egan decided to make the same move and to affiliate itself with the international group. By then CAIP was well dead, smothered by its own embrace of U.S. policy in Vietnam and discredited by its diehard adherence to the just war in the nuclear age. It was dissolved in 1967 when its functions were absorbed into the Commission for World Justice and Peace of the U.S. Catholic Conference.

Two bishops, Carroll T. Dozier of Memphis and Thomas J. Gumbleton of Detroit, agreed to act as "moderators" for Pax Christi/ USA, an arrangement that avoided the hierarchical control that characterized the European chapters and had proven so compromising for CAIP. The group got started in October 1973, but staff and communications problems soon brought its suspension. In May 1975, however, at a meeting at Manhattan College in New York, Joseph Fahey, Dorothy Day, Tom Cornell, Eileen Egan, Gordon Zahn, and others reformed Pax Christi. This was followed by a well-publicized national meeting in Dayton, Ohio in November 1975.

Since then Pax Christi's goals have remained consistent: they range from continuing Vatican II's commitment to look at war with an entirely new attitude, to ally with all other groups committed to nonviolent peacemaking, and to maintain an alliance between pacifists and just warriors on certain key issues. These include supporting the U.N. and all efforts for a viable world government; critically examining nuclear arms, the Federal budget, arms traffic, and disarmament; working for recognition of conscientious objection and selective conscientious objection; and furthering the role of women and the local community in making peace. It has placed great emphasis on peace education for alternatives to violence on all levels and condemned ROTC and Junior ROTC as clearly against Catholic principles.

While attempting to maintain a fragile balance between all segments of the Catholic peace movement in America, Pax Christi/USA has gradually moved away from the just war and toward gospel nonviolence as the only viable Catholic attitude. By the October 1981 Pax Christi conference in Richmond, Virginia the group had 5,000 members, 46 of whom were bishops, and had openly begun its criticism of U.S. nuclear and conventional militarism. Throughout the 1980s it maintained its campaign against the draft and registration, the death penalty, and nuclear weapons. It also served as a focal point for Catholic resistance to the war in Nicaragua, the U.S. role in El Salvador, and the unprecedented arms buildup under the Reagan administration. During the Persian Gulf War of 1990-91 it remained the most outspoken and best organized of all Catholic peace groups, maintaining its gospel message of nonviolence and reconciliation. Through its Pax Christi Book Awards the organization has also sought to encourage a Catholic intellectual discourse on war and peace and to bring much needed public attention to topics of peace and justice.

The following is taken from the Pax Christi Pamphlet, *Conscience and War*, Cambridge, MA: Pax Christi USA Center on Conscience and War, n.d (1984).

380. Pax Christi: The Role of Conscience

...Every person faces many choices throughout his or her entire lifetime. Some are minor; others crucial in their importance. All call for decisions guided by conscience in the light of one's responsibilities to family, friends, neighbors, community, nation – finally and most important of all – to humanity itself. To the believer, of course, the greatest responsibility is that owed to God. At times these responsibilities may seem to compete, even conflict, with one another. It is the task of a properly informed conscience to tell the individual what his or her responsibilities are in any given situation and, when necessary, to recognize which take precedence over the others.

So what do we mean by "conscience?"... Conscience, according to the Second Vatican Council, is the "most secret core and sanctuary" where "one is alone with God." It enables us to know and obey the Law of God which is written on every human heart and which summons us to seek the good and avoid evil in everything we do....

To the believer, of course, each person is created in the image of God and has an unique relationship with God. The exercise of religion consists, before all else, in those internal voluntary and free acts whereby a person sets the course of one's life toward God. In these internal acts, such as prayer and contemplation or even having "second thoughts" about decisions already reached, a person is obliged to seek the truth from his or her conscience in order not to offend against the personal sense of right and wrong. To violate one's conscience by doing something known in the heart to be wrong or to fail to do something known to be right, is to fail to live up to one's responsibility to oneself and to God. Being true to one's conscience is seldom easy. Often it is difficult and costly.

Of the many difficult decisions of conscience, few are as crucial as those relating to war, peace, and participation in the military. In this age of nuclear weapons and modern warfare, they became more crucial than ever before....

In our day when nuclear weapons and modern warfare threaten the sudden mass murder of millions of innocent people, the obligation of Christians to search deeply into their consciences and to obey God's call, whatever the cost, is of utmost importance....

The military poses special problems for the conscience. The insistence upon strict discipline and almost automatic obedience to superior officers limits the freedom and power of the individual man or woman in uniform to make personally responsible decisions....

Creating and encouraging the capacity to completely disregard conscience and blindly obey human authority leads to tragic consequences. The pilot who flew the mission over Hiroshima on August 6, 1945, was asked years later if he felt guilty about his role in the nuclear destruction of that city and its inhabitants. His reply was that he did not feel responsible for what happened: "I did not have any authority to decide. I have been trained to follow orders by competent authority...I have no regrets."

It is because of this that many decide, for reasons of conscience, that they cannot participate at all in the armed forces or take any part in war. To them it is simply too radical a departure from Christ's command. In their pastoral letter, *The Challenge of Peace* [389], the U.S. Bishops reaffirmed the rights of those who are conscientiously opposed to war and military service and praised those who devote themselves to a life of nonviolence.

Men and women who do join the military may decide, once they are in, that they cannot obey all the commands of their superior officers. During the Vietnam War, many American soldiers actively opposed what they believed to be a morally unjust war. Many refused orders and would not fight in the field; some even felt obliged to choose "conscientious desertion." Military personnel published newspapers expressing opposition to the war and support for the resistance. Many petitioned to the courts and asked Congress to stop the war. Such actions, joined with those of the peace movement at home, helped pressure the government into ending the war earlier than would otherwise have been the case....

It is not unpatriotic to be a conscientious objector or to oppose the nation's foreign and military policies. Our responsibilities as Christians and as citizens of a democracy might actually *realize* that we do so. As Thomas Merton wrote, "It is no longer reasonable or right to leave all decisions to a largely anonymous power elite that is driving us all, in our passivity, towards ruin. We have to make ourselves heard."

Letting conscience be our guide means more than just "doing your own thing" or considering only what seems best or safest in any given situation. It means deliberately guiding one's actions and making personal choices according to higher standards – such as Christian morality, humanitarian values or, if nothing else, a sense of personal integrity and responsibility to others. Following your conscience may mean, and usually will, that you must be ready to sacrifice personal convenience and sometimes much more for doing what you "know in your heart" is right or refusing to do what you believe is wrong.

In a world where more than four billion people are held as nuclear hostages by the superpowers; where human and natural resources are squandered upon new and ever more destructive weapons – while 50,000 die each day of poverty and starvation – in such a world Christians should feel obliged to recognize and acknowledge God's law. In Christ's world each of us is called upon to love one another "as I have loved you" [John 15:12]. This must become more than just a pious abstraction. It must be put into practice in our lives.

The survival of humanity depends upon whether Christians and other people of goodwill decide, in their "secret core and sanctuary" that it can *never* be permissible to take part in, or cooperate with, actions leading to the annihilation of the world and all who inhabit it. Democracy, national security, patriotism etc. are all important values, but they cannot be the ultimate value for the Christian. After all, if it avails us not to gain the whole world at the cost of our immortal souls, gaining or preserving our small part of it could never justify paying that price....

JAMES H. FOREST

James Forest grew up in a highly political family; his father was an important official in the American Communist Party. Partly out of a teenage rebellion now familiar to many parents of the baby-boom generation, Forest joined the U.S. Navy and served as an intelligence officer. In 1960, however, he experienced a religious conversion to Catholicism and was granted a discharge as a conscientious objector. He joined the Catholic Worker immediately after his discharge, began writing for the paper in 1961, and continued into the 1980s.

Forest maintained an on-going correspondence with many Catholic peacemakers, including Thomas Merton [366-370] and Daniel Berrigan [377, 382]. In 1964, along with Daniel and Philip Berrigan [384], Tom Cornell [364], Robert Cunnane, and John Peter Grady, Forest attended a retreat under Thomas Merton on the "Spiritual Roots of Protest," an encounter that was to crystallize the theory of Catholic nonviolence. In 1965 he was one of the founders of the Catholic Peace

Fellowship. In 1966, while still heading the CPF, he accepted an offer to become special projects coordinator of the Fellowship of Reconciliation, thus signaling – at least on the level of deep religious commitment – the Catholic entry into the mainstream of American peacemaking. In 1969, however, he was imprisoned for his part in the burning of draft records in Milwaukee, but resumed his work for FOR as editor of *Fellowship* magazine in 1971, and was instrumental in the initial groups that founded Pax Christi in the early 1970s. While it is always inaccurate to classify, one might say that Forest has always taken the role of the independent intellectual for the Catholic peace movement. Forest irked many in the peace community, for example, by criticizing FOR for its bureaucratic approach, breaking with Dorothy Day over his divorce and remarriage, and defending Daniel Berrigan for his criticisms of Israel in 1974.

Forest continued to run the CPF through the 1970s until his departure for Holland to become general secretary of the international FOR. In the 1980s he made several trips to the former Soviet Union and the Eastern Bloc nations and converted to Russian Orthodoxy. He has authored many articles and several books, including *Living with Wisdom*, a life of Thomas Merton, and *Love is the Measure*, a biography of Dorothy Day. Most recently, with Tom Cornell and Robert Ellsberg, he coedited the new edition of *A Penny a Copy*, cited frequently in this chapter.

The following is taken from Forest's *The Catholic Conscientious Objector*, New York: Catholic Peace Fellowship, 1965, rev. ed. 1981.

381. James H. Forest, *The Catholic Conscientious Objector*

We live in the century of Auschwitz and Hiroshima, places on opposite sides of the globe whose names suggest the dark side of our God-given freedom. We are as free to choose death as life, free even to choose the death of entire cities and whole peoples, free to choose even our own extinction.

At Auschwitz and similar concentration camps in the Hitler period killing was a daily task of ordinary men and women who were simply following orders and trying to survive. Still other normal, everyday people were involved in destroying Hiroshima on the sixth of August, 1945, the day an era began in which it became possible to kill hundreds of millions of people in a single day.

Auschwitz and Hiroshima bear painful witness to our ability not only to kill one another but to rationalize the mass killing of innocent people we find undesirable. As a result we find ourselves today prepared to kill whole nations of strangers no more wicked than ourselves and who, in the Soviet sphere, are even less responsible for their government's policies than we are for ours.

The means of total destruction are, as Pope John XXIII observed in his encyclical, *Pacem in Terris* [298], readily at hand. The American President is always accompanied by a military aide whose attaché case contains "the button," a device through which the coded message can be transmitted which would initiate a nuclear holocaust. We can assume the Soviet Premier has a similar companion. Should the order be given, in *fifteen minutes* the initial burst of missiles would have reached target. In a flash more lives would have been consumed than in all the wars in human history combined.

But Auschwitz and Hiroshima do not necessarily condemn the human race to such self-inflicted disaster. They can also be experienced as birthplaces of the will to disarm ourselves and our governments, and to commit our lives to the nonviolent resolution of conflict. While Auschwitz and Hiroshima can numb the mind and soul with their evidence of the human capacity for evil, they can also teach a life-giving lesson at the core of the Gospel. As Pope John Paul II put that lesson when visiting Auschwitz in 1979, "One must never pursue one's selfish interest at the other's expense, at the cost of enslavement of the other, at the cost of conquest, exploitation or death." He went on to stress the duty of ordinary citizens to join in the work of overcoming war, for it is "not only those who directly bring wars about who are responsible for them, but also those who fail to do all they can to prevent them."

The prevention of war, then, is not to be left to political and military leaders. It has to do with each of us and how we live our lives and choose our work, no matter how young we are, no matter how inexperienced. We cannot expect others to live by the Commandment, "You shall not kill,' when even we who call ourselves Christians refuse to do so....

Forming Your Own Conscience

"It wasn't I who persecuted the Jews," said Adolf Eichman at his trial in Jerusalem. "That was done by the government." The architect of the Nazi death camps saw himself as simply a high-level civil servant obediently doing what he was ordered to do. "Obedience has always been praised as a virtue," he said. "I accuse the rulers of abusing my obedience." Though the structure he had supervised had killed millions of defenseless and innocent men, women and children, psychiatrists found him to be a sane man. Nor should that judgment surprise us when we consider that there are many respected and apparently sane people today ready, under certain circumstances, to order and carry out the cremation in a single day of far more innocent people than Eichman's ovens could have burned in a century.

But there is another kind of sanity for those seeking to shape their lives according to the example and the teaching of Jesus. It is a sanity that treasures creation and condemns as irrational the intentional killing of defenseless and innocent people. One of the guidelines of a God-centered sanity is a deep reverence for life. It is this sanity that permeates the New Testament and the social encyclicals of the Popes in this century. It is from this vantage of caring common sense that Pope John XXIII made his simple, often quoted declaration in *Pacem in Terris*, "In this age of ours which prides itself on its atomic power, it is irrational to believe that war is still an apt means of vindicating violated rights" [§127].

Nearly two decades later, what was clear to Pope John has become even more obvious. For those aspiring to a sanity and responsibility that recognizes the right to life as the indispensable basis of all other human rights and duties, it is clear that none of us is free to ignore the crisis of violence in our time. Whatever our gifts, vocation, nationality, or state in life, certain questions are raised over and over again each day:

How to build up a greater reverence for life within myself and those around me?

How to let the love of God inform my life rather than the fear and hatred of destructive ideologies, movements or parties?

How to develop non-destructive, reconciling ways of dealing with the conflicts that are inevitable in social relationships?

How to become, as St. Francis prayed, "an instrument of Christ's peace?"

These questions are most difficult and urgent when we consider military service. In trying to answer them one has to look closely at the New Testament and the social teaching of the Church. This means careful study and reflection. It also means prayer, prayer for God's help not only in understanding the way to take in one's own life, but prayer for the courage to follow God's lead.

No amount of study and reflection can lead to certainty in every matter that confronts us. And yet we can be certain that we are called to love God and our fellow humans....

Choosing a Path

Peacemaking is a dimension of any Christian vocation. There is no single norm. Nor can those who choose to renounce violence claim there is an automatic sanctity in that by itself. It may happen that a soldier at war is in reality more compassionate, more self-giving, more courageous in seeking to hear God's voice, more willing to lay down his life for others than someone who refuses to bear weapons but who takes pride in his own ideas and risks very little. But for those who see the refusal of violence or war as God's will for them, or who are troubled by the moral implications of modern war, and who may be subject to the military draft, there are several alternatives that must be considered.

In the United States as in many countries, there is a traditional recognition of *conscientious objection* to war and military service. U.S. law [as of 1981] requires that a conscientious objector oppose participation in "war in any form," that is, any kind of war, and that his opposition be based upon religious or ethical principle deeply and firmly held. Conscientious objectors may accept military service as non-combatants, or they may object to military service altogether and seek *alternative service* under civilian authority.

Alternative service is often performed in hospitals or other community agencies. It may involve forestry projects or agricultural experimentation. During the Vietnam war many Catholic agencies offered employment to conscientious objectors doing alternative service. While it is hoped that U.S. law will come to respect the objector to a *particular* war, to date it has not done so. Nevertheless, during the Vietnam period many local draft boards treated such persons as they did those who were opposed to all wars.

Noncombatant military service has most often been performed in medical units, though any assignment is possible as long as the use of weapons is not required. It should be kept in mind, however, that noncombatant personnel share in overall military goals. According to the Army Field Manual, "The primary duty of medical troops, as of all other troops, is to contribute their utmost to the success of the command of which they are a part" [FM 8-40, p. 195].

Many do not think seriously about the question of war, peace and personal responsibility until actually in the armed forces. For those who become conscientious objectors while in uniform, there are provisions either for discharge or for reassignment, according to the individual conscience.

Some are opposed in principle to conscription whether for military or civilian purposes and refuse either to register with Selective Service or to request or perform alternative civilian or non-combatant military service. This position of *draft resistance* or *total non-cooperation* must be approached with great caution. For those who refuse cooperation with conscription or whose conscientious objection is not recognized, there are several possibilities: some try to live "underground," moving where they aren't known, finding employment under assumed names, trying not to be noticed; some move to countries where there is no draft; some are imprisoned.

The underground life is itself a kind of imprisonment. Yet it has known its saints. St. John Vianney [1786-1859] has already been mentioned.

Leaving one's homeland is also painful, often more so than those who consider it imagine. It is no small thing to leave one's family and friends and culture behind. It is advisable only if one really wants to live in the country of destination. But this is also an historically honored choice. A great many American families were founded by immigrants fleeing military conscription.

Going to prison for conscience also has a long and highly regarded tradition not unknown to Christians. It has often been a place of spiritual growth and service to others, of prayer and real sacrifice. But its dangers should not be underestimated or romanticized....

THE PLOWSHARES MOVEMENT

By the 1980s renewed concern over the immorality and apocalyptic destructiveness of nuclear weaponry had led the Berrigans to take literally the call of the prophets Isaiah and Micah: "They shall beat their swords into plowshares and their spears into pruning hooks" [Is. 2:4; Mi. 4:3, see 25]. On September 9, 1980, eight people, including

Daniel and Philip Berrigan and Sister Ann Montgomery, entered the General Electric nuclear warhead plant in King of Prussia, Pennsylvania and "disarmed" Mark 12A warheads. There followed a series of "Plowshares" actions: ramming and "disarming" nuclear submarines in Groton, Connecticut, pouring blood in a GE nuclear warhead plant, "disarming" components of Cruise, Pershing, and MX missiles at the AVCO plant in Wilmington, Delaware. Elizabeth McAlister and others hammered and poured blood on a B-52 bomber armed with Cruise missiles at Griffiss Air Force Base on Thanksgiving Day 1983, and on Easter 1984 members of Plowshares poured blood and hammered on Pershing II components at the Martin Marietta plant in Orlando, Florida.

Clearly repudiating the secret tactics of the Vietnam era, the "Plowshares" offered themselves for arrest without resistance and affirmed their commitment to nonviolence. For them the outrage expressed by government officials at their hammering on warheads symbolizes the twin American evils: love of material things and the love of death. They have dismissed charges that they have broken the law by destroying private property as absurd since property in Catholic tradition is something that enhances life and contributes to the common good. According to the Plowshares, it is the Pentagon and the arms producers who destroy property by misusing "the resources of God's earth" to create tools of destruction.

The Plowshares' actions have continued into the 1990s, with most participants facing prison sentences of decades. They have compared their acts to those of Old Testament prophets, smashing the false gods and idols, the "gods of metal" [Exod. 34:17] that America has made of nuclear warheads and missiles. The selections below attempt to present a representative sampling of the thought and spirituality of the Plowshares movement, first with a classic restatement of Catholic nonviolence from Daniel Berrigan, then a personal account of the Plowshares from Elizabeth McAlister, and finally, a very recent assessment of North America's need for conversion by Philip Berrigan.

DANIEL BERRIGAN

With his release from Danbutry federal prison in February 1972 and the end of the Vietnam War, Daniel Berrigan continued to write, to do pastoral work for cancer and AIDS patients, to teach, and to engage in acts of civil disobedience. As we have already seen [343] in 1966 Ernesto Cardenal had helped establish a Christian community on Solentiname Island in Nicaragua. In 1977 some members later joined the Sandinista armed resistance to Somoza, and Cardenal issued a declaration of his support for them and the Sandinista Front that takes up the theme of the "just revolution." Berrigan, an old friend of Cardenal – fellow priest, poet, and peacemaker – writes to his dear friend and offers a frank and classic statement of Catholic nonviolence.

The following excerpts are taken from Berrigan, *Poetry, Drama, Prose*, pp. 166-70.

382. Daniel Berrigan, Letter to Ernesto Cardenal: Guns Don't Work, National Catholic Reporter, May 5, 1978

Dear Brother Ernesto Cardenal,

Your account of events in your community of Solentiname has been widely distributed in the United States, especially by the religious press. One translation appended a word: "It is important for us in this country to be able to listen and not to judge this."

Indeed. But at least we can talk together. Please consider what follows, then, as a continuing reflection on matters you have had the courage to open up, and indeed, to act on....

I hope I am inching toward the contents of your letter. You discuss quite freely and approvingly the violence of a violated people, yourselves. You align yourself with that violence, regretfully but firmly, irrevocably.

I am sobered and saddened by this. I think of the consequences of your choice, within Nicaragua and far beyond. I sense how the web of violence spins another thread, draws you in, and so many others for whom your example is primary, who do not think for themselves, judging that a priest and poet will lead them in the true way.

I think how fatally easy it is, in a world demented and enchanted with the myth of short cuts and definitive solutions, when nonviolence appears increasingly naive, old hat, freakish – how easy it is to cross over, to seize the gun. How easy to conclude: the deck is stacked, first card to last, in favor of the Big Sharks; the outcome of the game, of life itself, is settled before the cards are dealt. Why then isn't taking a few lives (of dubious value at best, torturers, lackeys, police) preferable to the taking of many lives of great value, students, the poor, the victimized and defenseless, the conscientious, those easily identifiable as gospel brothers and sisters? There is, after all, a long tradition of legitimate self-defense.

It may be true, as you say, that "Gandhi would agree with us." Or it may not be true. It may be true, as you imply, that Merton would agree with you. It may be true that Christ would agree with you. I do not believe he would, but I am willing to concede your argument, for the sake of argument.

You may be correct in reporting that "those young Christians fought without hate...and especially without hate for the guards" they shortly killed (though this must be cold comfort to the dead). Your vision may one day be verified of a Nicaragua free of "campesino guards killing other campesinos...." The utopia you ache for may one day be realized in Nicaragua: "...an abundance of schools, child-care centers, hospitals and clinics for everyone...and most importantly, love between everyone." This may all be true; the guns may bring on the kingdom.

But I do not believe it.

One religious paper here published your words under the following headline: "When they take up arms for love of the kingdom of God." How sublime, I thought, how ironic. We have had "just" wars of the Right, a long history of blood, the blood of colonials and natives and slaves and workers and peasants. But we are through with all that. Now we are enlightened. We are to have "just" wars of the Left!

So the young men of Solentiname resolved to take up arms. They did it for one reason: "on account of their love for the kingdom of God." Now here we certainly speak within a tradition! In every crusade that ever marched across Christendom, murder – the most secular of undertakings, the most worldly, the one that enlists and rewards us along with the other enlistees of Caesar – this undertaking is invariably baptized in religious ideology: the kingdom of God.

The power of such language we know too well. Religious battle cries induct hearts and minds as no secular slogans can. Religious ideology raises its flag in every nation, even as it denies the final authority of every nation. It offers to transcendent longings a task that is simple and forthright: kill. It offers a slogan that is as immediately tactile and hot as a fired gun: kill for the kingdom. And perhaps most important of all, it offers a way out: out of anger, out of frustration, out of poverty, out of political stagnation, out of the harsh and dreadful necessity of love. God wills it! The kingdom requires it!

Chapter 7: Catholic Peacemaking in the USA

Blood and iron, nukes and rifles. The leftists kill the rightists, the rightists kill the leftists, both, given time and occasion, kill the children, the aged, the ill, the suspects. Given time and occasion, both torture prisoners. Always, you understand, inadvertently, regretfully. Both sides, moreover, have excellent intentions, and call on God to witness them. And some god or other does witness them, if we can take the word of whatever bewitched church.

And of course nothing changes. Nothing changes in Beirut, in Belfast, or in Galilee, as I have seen. Except that the living die. And that old, revered distinction between combatant and noncombatant, which was supposed to protect the innocent and helpless, goes down the nearest drain; along with the indistinguishable blood of any and all.

Alas, I have never seen anyone morally improved by killing; neither the one who aimed the bullet, nor the one who received it in his or her flesh.

Of course we have choices, of course we must decide. When all is said, we find that the gospel makes sense, that it strikes against our motives and actions or it does not. Can that word make sense at all today, can it be something more than utopian or extravagant? The gospel is after all a document out of a simpler age, a different culture. It may even be our duty to construct for ourselves another ethic, based on our own impasse or insights or ego. And go from there, with whatever assurance we can muster amid the encircling gloom.

Or on the other hand, we can bow our heads before a few truths, crude, exigent, obscure as they are. The outcome of obedience we cannot know, the outcome of disobedience we can deceive ourselves about, indefinitely and sweetly. Thou shalt not kill. Love one another as I have loved you. If your enemy strike you on the right cheek, turn to him the other. Practically everyone in the world, citizens and believers alike, consign such words to the images on church walls, or the embroideries in front parlors.

We really are stuck. Christians are stuck with this Christ, the impossible, unteachable, irreformable loser. Revolutionaries must correct him, set him aright. That absurd form, shivering under the crosswinds of power, must be made acceptable, relevant. So a gun is painted into his empty hands. Now he is human! Now he is like us.

Does it all have a familiar ring? In the old empires, the ragged rabbi must be cleaned up, invested in Byzantine robes of state, raised in glittering splendor to the dome of heaven. Correction! correction! we cry to those ignorant gospel scribes, Matthew and the rest. He was not like that, he was not helpless, he was not gentle, he was under no one's heel, no one pushed him around! He would have taken up a gun if one had been at hand, he would have taken up arms, "solely for one reason; on account of his love for the kingdom of God." Did he not have fantasies like ours, in hours out of the public glare, when he too itched for the quick solution, his eyes narrowed like gun sights?

How tricky it all gets! We look around at our culture: an uneasy mix of men: gun makers, gun hucksters, gun researchers, gun runners, guards with guns, property owners with guns. A culture in which the guns put out contracts on the people, the guns own the people, the guns buy and sell the people, the guns practice targets on the people, the guns kill the people. The guns are our second nature, and the first nature is all but obliterated; it is gunned down.

And who will raise it up, that corpse with the neat hole in its temple, ourselves? It is impossible, it is against nature.

Christ asks the literally impossible. And then, our radical helplessness confessed, he confers what was impossible.

Dear brother Ernesto, when I was underground in 1970 with J. Edgar Hoover's hounds on my tail, I had long hours to think of these things. At that time I wrote: "The death of a single human is too heavy a price to pay for the vindication of any principle, however sacred." I should add that at the time, many among the anti-war Left were playing around with bombings, in disarray and despair.

I am grateful that I wrote those words. I find no reason eight years later to amend or deny them. Indeed, in this bloody century, religion has little to offer, little that is not contaminated or broken or in bad faith. But one thing we have: our refusal to take up bombs or guns, aimed at the flesh of brothers and sisters, whom we persist in defining as such, refusing the enmities pushed at us by war-making state or war-blessing church.

This is a long loneliness, and a thankless one. One says "no" when every ache of the heart would say "yes." We, too, long for a community on the land, heartening liturgies, our own turf, the arts, a place where sane ecology can heal us. And the big boot comes down. It destroys everything we have built. And we recoil. Perhaps in shock, perhaps in a change of heart, we begin to savor on our tongues a language that is current all around us: phrases like "legitimate violence," "limited retaliation," "killing for love of the kingdom." And the phrases make sense – we have crossed over. We are now an army, like the pope's army, or Luther's, or the crusaders, or the Muslims. We have disappeared into this world, into bloody, secular history. We cannot adroitly handle both gospel and gun; so we drop the gospel, an impediment in any case.

And our weapons?

They are contaminated in what they do, and condemned in what they cannot do. There is blood on them, as on our hands. And like our hands, they cannot heal injustice or succor the homeless.

How can they signal the advent of the kingdom of God? How can we, who hold them? We announce only another bloody victory for the emperor of necessity, whose name in the Bible is Death.

Shall he have dominion?

Brother, I think of you so often. And pray with you. And hope against hope.

– Daniel

ELIZABETH MCALISTER

Elizabeth McAlister was born in Montclair, New Jersey on November 17, 1939 and had a traditional Catholic education. She entered the Order of the Sacred Heart of Mary in 1959. She met Philip Berrigan in New York City in 1966. Their friendship eventually developed into a shared opposition to the war in Vietnam. It was McAlister's letters sent to Philip then in Lewisburg Penitentiary that were intercepted by the FBI and that led to Daniel Berrigan's discovery underground and arrest in August 1970. The correspondence was also to be the foundation of the prosecution's case in the Harrisburg Seven conspiracy case. After the Harrisburg trial had proven the defendants not guilty and the government's case to be nothing more than a (successful) attempt to disrupt the radical Catholic peace movement, McAlister rejoined her religious community and taught college part-time. She and Philip Berrigan were married on Memorial Day 1973. Excommunicated from the Catholic Church – since both were clerics when they married – they brought together other peace activists in June 1973 to found Jonah House in Baltimore. Describing this as a community of resistance, McAlister and Berrigan went on to raise three children of their own and to organize Jonah House along the lines of the Catholic Worker movement.

Since its founding Jonah House has been the focus of dozens of "acts of resistance" to the arms race, including the spread of nuclear weapons, the growing disparity between the wealthy industrialized world and the impoverished Third, and North America's growing culture of violence. Arrested over twenty times by the mid-1980s, McAlister gained nationwide attention again for her participation in the Griffiss Air Force Base action in 1983, for which McAlister served two years in prison. She and Philip Berrigan have recorded their lives' work at Jonah House into the 1990s in *The Time's Discipline: The Beatitudes and Nuclear Resistance.*

The following is excerpted from Elizabeth McAlister. "For Love of the Children," in Daniel Berrigan, ed., *For Swords into Plowshares, The Hammer Has to Fall,* Piscataway, NJ: Plowshares Press, n.d. (1984), pp. 32-36.

383. Elizabeth McAlister, For Love of the Children

As I was sitting in the Public Safety Building in Syracuse (a euphemism for jail in those quarters), some of the reality of what I and my friends had done began to well up in me. It was accompanied, as reality usually is, by terror....

I was in the Public Safety Building because, with 6 friends, I had entered Griffiss Air Force Base in Rome, New York, in the early hours of Thanksgiving morning (1983) and entered what they call Building 101. The building housed, among other things, a B-52 bomber which they were in the process of outfitting to carry a full complement of Cruise missiles. We hammered on the bomb-bay doors of the B-52; poured our own blood on the fuselage of the plane; spray painted the phrases "320 Hiroshimas" and "Thou Shalt Not Kill" and "If I Had a Hammer" on the plane; taped to it photos of our children and children with whom we work, as well as a "People's Indictment" of Griffiss Air Force Base that we had drawn up. Meanwhile, the other half of our group did similar work in a storage area nearby dealing especially with the engines for the B-52 and one engine for the fighter bomber. They painted "Omnicide" and "Stop Cruise" in strategic locations.

The government responded to these acts of ours by indicting us for sabotage, for destruction of government property, for conspiracy. And I was sitting in jail looking at the possibility of spending 25 years there.

That much reality can be frightening, especially when the one facing it has three young children (aged 9, 8, and 2) whom she loves deeply.

Into this atmosphere and these ruminations, a friend sent a cartoon. It depicted two children talking. The first asked if the second had seen *The Day After* on T.V. [the widely viewed and discussed drama about a nuclear war and its aftermath]. "No! My parents wouldn't let me. They thought it would be too scary! Did you see it?" "Yes," responded the first. "Did you find it scary?" "Not as scary as my parents did," said the first. "Oh!" asked the second, "What did they find the scariest part?" "The very end," said the first. "When I asked them what they were going to do to stop it."

So I sent the cartoon to my older children, Frida and Jerome, along with the letter I was writing them that day. *The Day After* was televised on November 20th; our action was November 24th. Their dad and I watched the film with the children (as well as with other members of our community) and we had sat down with them afterwards and talked about the meaning of the film. We talked too about the action I was about to undertake....

Both children said that they understood, in a new way, why resistance was so necessary. They were willing to accept the personal sacrifice of my absence as their part in trying to stop a nuclear war from happening; as their part in trying to avoid the suffering that the movie displayed – in an understated but nonetheless very clear way. They committed themselves to assume more responsibility around the house and especially to be helpful in dealing with the questions and fears of their little sister who was not able to understand as they were. It was a moment of extreme closeness for the four of us; a moment accepting together whatever might come down; and we concluded our conversation with prayer and big, big hugs.

We all back down from moments like that. They remain(ed) querulous, somewhat selfish, lazy; they remain(ed), in short, young children. But we don't back down completely. Something of the clarity of a moment like that stays with us, enlightening a dark time. While they fear prolonged separation, they are proud of their mom and themselves for offering something, for sharing something of the suffering of children in less privileged environments. They are, as we are wont to tell them, first-world children; but they have some consciousness of third-world children which, we hope, will affect their lives and the choices they make in them....

To nurture such innocent life and know, as I do, the threat to [their] life, to know, as many have sought to tell us, the threat to all life on this planet means to make some choices. They are few and clear:

(1) To choose to seek to hide somewhere, anywhere, with my children, to remain protective, isolated. But I know there is nowhere we can go. I guess I also know that it would not be possible for me for very long to choose a "security" for my children that cannot be an option for other (for all) parents.

(2) To pretend that the threat is not there at all; to live without seeing or hearing or thinking about it. It is all too possible of doing. But that means adding my own body and soul, and those of our children, to being part of the problem – to the numbness, indifference, and resultant selfishness that enables the machinery of war to mushroom out of all control by anyone. It also means surrendering the few clues I have arrived at through my life, about what it means to be a decent, responsible, caring human being.

(3) To ask how I can best love my children and to answer by working to provide for them and the millions like them, a hope for a future. And I cannot say that I hope for a future for them, without, at the same time, being willing to do something to make that hope become a reality....

The action we took at Griffiss Air Force Base was the 6th such "plowshares action."... The actions spring from our prayerful reflection on the Biblical mandate out of Isaiah [2:4-5] and Micah [4:3, see 25] to "beat swords into plowshares; spears into pruning hooks." They spring from our shared realization that even as the arms race has been built weapon by weapon, decision by decision, disarmament needs to occur weapon by weapon, decision by decision. Or as one person expressed it, "dent by dent." The hope that the actions bespeak is less that we destroy a particular weapon and more that, in our effort to be obedient to the Spirit, to life, the Spirit might become more present in our world, empowering more and more of us to act in whatever ways we can to say a clear "NO!" to such destructive weaponry; to say a clear "NO!" to policies that call for the use of such weaponry.

The first plowshares action took place at the G.E. facility in King of Prussia, Pennsylvania, in September 1980. Eight men and women damaged two Mark 12A warheads. The group included my husband, Phil

Berrigan, his brother Daniel, two other members of the Jonah House community and four friends. One of the women who acted at King of Prussia is the mother of 6 children. The AVCO Plowshares included four grandmothers; they had collectively 37 children and 25 (or so) grand-children. Many of the men and women who have participated in these actions have done so as parents. Each would articulate differently; all acted so that the children might have some hope of a future. It would be a great service if their voices could be heard more in our days.

It is so clear how torn up people are today. If we try to look squarely at what is happening in our world, we become so full of despair, of hope-lessness, that we cannot live. And so we withdraw into numbness....

Against this ennui, the seven of us at Griffiss (as well as others who have acted for justice and peace before and since our action) felt hope as an urgent imperative calling us to enunciate (albeit in fear and trem-bling) a testimony to life. We seek, above all, to enunciate hope, to an-nounce that, as well as being a time when death appears to reign su-preme, it is a time of hope, a time when the promise of new life is at hand for our world, if people can reach out and grasp for it, if people will in solidarity and with one another, reach out and dismantle the weapons that block our access to life.

Philip Berrigan

The younger brother of Daniel Berrigan [377, 382], Philip was born on October 5, 1923 in Two Harbors, Minnesota. He was raised in Syracuse, New York, and during World War II served in the Army Field Artillery from 1943 to 1946, and then attended Holy Cross College., earning a B.A. under the GI Bill. Upon graduation in 1950 he entered the Josephite Order, an order devoted to serving African Americans, and was ordained in June 1955 and assigned to a parish in Washington, DC. From 1956 to 1963 he taught in the all-black St. Augustine's High School in New Orleans. He published his first work, "A Parish Apostolate," in *Worship* magazine in 1957.

Philip became active in the civil-rights movement of the early 1960s. In 1961 both Berrigan brothers participated in the Freedom Ride led by James Farmer to Mississippi. By the early 1960s the anti-Vietnam war movement had also begun. From 1964 to April 1965 he taught at Epiphany Apostolic College in Newburgh, New York, but resigned after threats were made to the seminary for keeping him on its faculty.

He then moved to Baltimore to serve in another black parish. He continued his involvement in the civil-rights movement, joining the Selma campaign, and actively running the Catholic Peace Fellowship [372] In December 1965 Philip joined Daniel in signing the CPF's "Declaration of Conscience" published in *The Catholic Worker*, pledging a campaign of nonviolent civil disobedience against the Vietnam War. In October 1967, after a series of vigils at the homes of Congressmen to protest the war, Philip and three others – the Baltimore Four – conducted a break-in at Selective Service headquarters in Baltimore and poured blood on files, an act that was to be the forerunner of the Catonsville action [377]. After a series of similar raids, Philip and Elizabeth McAlister were indicted in the famous Harrisburg Seven case that was to tie up both Berrigans – and much of the Catholic peace movement – in a series of court actions that would preoccupy the movement until the end of the war.

During the 1980s Philip Berrigan repeatedly reemerged from Baltimore's Jonah House for new campaigns of active nonviolence. On September 9, 1980, he and seven other entered the General Electric plant in King of Prussia, Pennsylvania and there began the Plowshares campaign. Since then he has spent much of his life in and out of prison, in various acts of nonviolence, and at the Jonah House community. He is the author of many articles and books, including *Widen the Prison Gates* and *Of Beasts and Other Beastly Images: Essays under the Bomb*.

The following is taken from *A Penny a Copy: Readings from The Catholic Worker*, 2nd ed., Thomas C. Cornell, Robert Ellsberg, and Jim Forest, eds, Maryknoll, NY: Orbis Books, 1995, pp. 349-52

384. Philip Berrigan, Help Thou Our Unbelief, from The Catholic Worker, August-September 1994

A year or so ago, in the course of a talk at a university in Maryland, I was questioned by a thoughtful, matronly woman. "How are we to understand the world's mess? What's behind all this war, violence, evil?"

Somehow her question stays with me – perhaps because I gave her only a superficial answer, speaking of economic unrest, neo-nationalism, and so on.

Now that I'm doing jail time, Holy Mother State offers occasion for more serious attention to her question.

I had asked her to explain her word "mess." She did so with a thoughtful vengeance. "War is the biggest business on earth, the nuclear club expands like a black hole, arms are fervently huckstered everywhere (the U.S. sales alone in 1993 being on the order of $31 billion), some forty-five conventional wars are in progress, famine afflicts the third and fourth worlds, the rich/poor gap grows apace, domestic violence surges, the cancer and AIDS epidemics, contamination of air, soil, and water, ozone depletion, greenhouse effect."

She seemed, to say the least, remarkably familiar with our predicament.

And her anguish!

The woman struck me as someone not content merely to catalog doom and gloom. She was groping for light on matters virtually ignored by Washington, the churches, the media, the universities, experts of every stripe. What underlies and impels and multiplies the terror and death? Must the poor of the world be sacrificed to first-world consumers? How to understand the fatal attraction that holds us captive to the Bomb? Are remedies at hand to prevent destruction of ourselves and our planet?

In jail a year later, I'm driven to return to her question. I opened the Bible to the passage in St. Mark 9, the exorcism of the possessed child.

Descending from the Mount of the Transfiguration, Jesus encounters a father and son. The child is desperately afflicted, wordless and deaf. The father anguishes, and the disciples of Jesus, stalemated, can bring neither relief nor healing.

The reaction of Jesus is curious. Rather than addressing the disciples or the father, He turns to the crowd, "What an unbelieving lot you are!" As though to say, "The boy's plight, deaf and mute as he is, stems from the disbelief of you adults! His affliction mirrors your own – your incapacity to hear or speak the truth. It is you who are deaf and mute, and the child pays for it."

Then, "Bring the child to me."

Identified powerfully and unequivocally, its cover revealed, the demonic spirit asserts a kind of last-ditch power over the child, throwing him brutally to the ground in convulsions. In the past, according to the father's sorrowful account, the same spirit "has often cast him into the water and fire to destroy him," parodying sacramental symbols, turning the signs of water and fire to instruments of death.

In jail, we watch as the nation celebrates the fiftieth anniversary of the allied Normandy invasion. Millions of people perished in the war, thousands were butchered in the week of landings. Yet the vast cemeteries, the rows of crosses stretching surreally to the horizon – these seem powerless to remind (literally re-mind, heal, restore). War never again? All week, the nation, the veterans, the politicians neither hear nor speak a word of peace. The churches unlimber their bells – celebrating what?

A deaf and dumb spirit shadows the land. Our spiritual addiction lies heavy on the children of the world, deaf and dumb before their fate. What war next, and where, and against whom? One thing seems certain, if the past is a measure of the future; war upon war will erupt in a bloody trail.

Jesus addresses the boy's father, and understanding dawns. He has failed to protect his son. "I believe, Lord, help my unbelief." But the disciples and the crowd mill about uneasily; they have no clue as to the connection the father has drawn so movingly. Jesus assures the man, "All is possible to the one who has faith." And He proceeds to evict the demonic spirit from the child.

What to make of all this?

Something simple, I venture, and unsettling, as is usual with St. Mark. Which is to say, we Christians are afflicted with "unbelief."

Can we, in any true sense, claim to believe in God, while we hold the world's children hostage with the Bomb? If we believed in God, could we allow the deaths of 40,000 children each day, from hunger and hunger-related diseases? If we believed in God, could the American military slaughter with impunity hundreds of thousands of Iraqis?

If we truly "believed," amazingly constructive events would shortly occur. For a start, the disarming of the nuclear club, a vigorous effort to outlaw war once and for all, a politics in accord with sound ecology, dissolution of corporate capitalism. And, finally, abandoning the lethal divisions of the world into first, second, third, and fourth segments, those bristling frontiers where privilege guards the spoils. And beyond which, the debtors and clients pay up....

I have asked parents whether it is our duty to protect children from such follies. The response is generally enthusiastic, of course. But when it comes down to practicalities, what one might call the whence and how of resistance, there usually follows a stunned silence.

So I ask it here: Whence? What spiritual discipline prepares us to turn an awful situation around? We know something, at least, after all the years. We know that the turn about requires daily prayer. Bible study, Sacrament – the ancient manna of parched desert travelers.

Another angle. Through such discipline undertaken in community, faith takes on its true face. Which is to say, faith opens its heart to social and political reality. It embraces the Cross, in the old phrase; the Cross planted in the world, in time, in human lives. Faith becomes one with the vocation of all the living; indeed, the very form of that vocation – cruciform. A faith that, in such times as we endure, may well imply suffering, imprisonment, loss of good repute, jobs, comforts – life itself.

And what of the "how," the tactic? Here, too, we are not exactly in the dark. Indeed, the tactics, too, have continuity – they are symbolic, they eschew violence and take the legal heat that is sure to follow. Above all (here spirituality and tactic converge) they are not attached to a measurable outcome.

Two verses from St. John have helped me in this quest for an understanding of faith. "The one who believes that Jesus is the Messiah, has passed from death to life" [5:24]. Also, "The one who is marked by love of sisters and brothers, has passed from death to life" [1 John 3:14]. Remarkable how faith in the Messiah, and love of others, converge here. To wit: if love of others is excluded by this or that version of faith, the neighbor to whom the Gospel summons us is reduced to a mere object; indifferently viewed, expendable, a blank or blip on a screen.

Let us put this matter of faith as simply as Scripture does. The truly faithful cling to one Law. "The one who loves the neighbor fulfills the Law" [Rom. 13:9]. This "one law," be it noted, by no means relegates the love of God to second place, or compromises it. The flat statement of St. Paul merely stresses the impossibility of our love of God thriving in a corner – a corner of the heart, or of the world. If there it chooses to dwell, such love can only cower and wither away, out of fear or inanition or both.

St. John and St. Paul, no less than St. Mark, emphasize the primacy of faith. It is as though they were insisting that everything human in our behavior begins there, with faith. Practical and mystical both, world view and view from the heart, one.

UNITED FARM WORKERS

No North American family of the 1960s and 1970s could have been untouched by the work of Cesar Chavez (1927-1993) and Dolores Huerta (1930-), his longtime partner in the United Farm Workers and his co-nominee for the Nobel Peace Prize. Through

strikes, registration campaigns, nonviolent protests, and then the national boycotts of grapes and lettuce, the United Farm Workers accomplished something few in American labor and nonviolent campaigns had ever done: they had involved ordinary, middle-class Americans in a radical campaign to being about basic human rights for farm workers in California and throughout the nation, and had done so through a consistent and principled campaign of nonviolence.

Cesar Estrada Chavez was born on March 31, 1927 near Yuma, Arizona to a family of farmers in exile from the Mexican revolution. When the family lost their farm in 1938 during the Depression, they were forced into a life of migrant labor, enduring the bigotry and segregation meted out to Mexican-Americans on the very lands that used to be theirs before the Anglo invasions of the nineteenth century. During these years of wandering Chavez attended thirty-seven schools, following the whims of the labor market.

From 1944 to 1945, during World War II, Chavez served on a destroyer in the Pacific and returned to California to marry and live in San Jose. In the 1950s he read widely in the social thinking of the Catholic church and worked with the Community Service Organization from 1952 to 1958, serving as its general director from 1958 to 1962. He left San Jose in 1962 to organize, with Dolores Huerta, the National Farm Workers Association, based in Delano. In 1965 the Farm Workers union finally received recognition from large national unions, including the Teamsters and Longshoreman. In 1966 the union merged with the Agricultural Workers Organizing Committee to form the United Farm Workers, which Chavez directed from 1966 to 1973. A series of well-organized and publicized union drives brought them national attention and the volunteer effort of countless supporters. In 1973, for example, Dorothy Day was arrested for the last time during a UFW action. By 1970 the Farm Workers, brought the growers to the negotiating table to sign several contracts with the union: the result of the nationwide grape boycott, intense labor organizing, and a ground swell of popular support.

Chavez served as the UFW's president from 1973 until his death in 1993. For his efforts he was nominated for the Nobel Peace Prize. Toward the end of his life Chavez faced both the declining fashionableness of the Farm Workers with the American public, the ebb-tide of the U.S. labor movement, some bad press, and declining health. He died in Yuma, Arizona in 1993 on the opening day of the trial that awarded a major grower $2.9 million in punitive damages against the UFW for a "secondary boycott" of its non-union lettuce.

The following is excerpted from Cesar Chavez, "Speech Given on Receipt of the Gandhi Peace Award for Promoting Enduring Peace," and was published in *The Catholic Worker* 57.4 (June-July 1990): 1, 4, 7.

385. Cesar Chavez, The Core of Nonviolence

I feel rather ill at ease receiving this award knowing full well that Gandhi would have objected to it very much. So instead, I do want to receive the award, and am accepting the Gandhi Peace Award this evening on behalf of Nan Freeman, a young Jewish woman from New England who was killed on our picket line, our first martyr at a sugar cane field near Belle Glade, Florida, at about two o'clock in the morning on January 25, 1972. She was nineteen years old. Gandhi says, "Those who die unresistantly are likely to steal the fury of violence by their holiness and sacrifice." I also want to accept the award on behalf of our second martyr, Nagi Daifalhh, a young Arab from South Yemen, a farm worker, immigrant, who was beaten to death in the streets of Lamont, California, during our second grape strike on August 15, 1973. Nagi was nineteen years old. And Gandhi says, "He who meets death without striking a blow fulfills his duty one hundred percent. The result is in God's hands." I also want to accept the award on behalf of our third martyr, Juan de la Cruz, 60 years old, from Mexico, a farm worker, who was shot down on the picket line near Irvine, California, two days after Nagi was killed at our second table grape boycott and strike. He was killed around two o'clock in the afternoon by a strike breaker who came with an automatic rifle and shot at the whole picket line. And Gandhi says, "To lay down one's life for what one considers to be right is the very core of nonviolence." I'd also like to accept the award of behalf of our fourth martyr, Rufino Contreras, a lettuce farm worker. He was gunned down by company supervisors during the lettuce strike on February 10, 1979 in Calexico, California, around ten o'clock in the morning. He was twenty-eight years old, married with two children. And Gandhi says, "There is no such thing as defeat or death in nonviolence." Last, I would like to accept this award on behalf of our fifth martyr, Rene Lopez, twenty-one years old, a dairy worker who was killed with a gun, with a shot to the head, when he stepped out of a voting booth having just voted to be represented by our union, near Fresno, California, around ten o'clock in the morning. Rene was twenty-one years old. And Gandhi says, "In non-violence the bravery consists in dying not in killing." We want to receive this award in their memory....

The boycott is working. Across America people are joining together telling the growers that the workers need to be protected from pesticides, that the workers need fair and free elections, and that the growers need to sit down and bargain in good faith with those workers who do want a union and to use collective bargaining as a way to resolve the issues that confront them....

Stricken with Cancer

The central valley in California is one of the richest agricultural areas in the world and in its midst there are clusters of children with cancer – McFarland, Delano, Bakersfield, Fowler, Earlimart, Rosamond. In town after town little children are being stricken with cancer, are being born with physical defects, and are dying. In McFarland, six children have died of cancer and seven more have been diagnosed with cancer and probably will die before the end of the year. The childhood cancer rate is four hundred percent above normal in McFarland. And we are finding more and more sick children in towns all over the valley. Parents fear for the lives of their children, and they ask with fear in their voices, "Where will this deadly plague strike next?"

There is tremendous insecurity among the workers, the families. Farm workers are suffering from nerve disorders, liver and kidney problems, sterility, unexplained illnesses. Farm worker women have high rates of miscarriage; their children often born with deformities....

This is why in July and August of last year I embarked on a thirty-six day, unconditional water-only fast. Some of you here have fasted. You know that some great things happen with fasting. Here's what I learned in my ordeal last summer. When you fast for even a day or two or three, I think you will experience some of the same things. Physically, my fast was torture at first and then it gave way to a great rejuvenation in my body. I felt cleansed when it was all over. Spiritually, my fast worked like a powerful medicine that kept my spirit from sagging. And feelings of fear and doubt and anger that I had were wiped away and I could see things very clearly. I saw the powerful urge that raged within me and drove me to the fast and I saw my self-doubt, and yes, my shame, for not doing enough about this problem. I asked myself, do I share deeply enough the pain of those who work with the poisons? Do I feel their fear, those that lost babies or had miscarriages or died? Do I feel the agony of those who ask, "Where will this deadly plague strike next?" And I began to see other people, the good ones and the bad ones; and I saw the terrible suffering among farm workers and their children. I saw the crushing of farm workers' rights and the death of good-faith collective bargaining and the ever-increasing use of pesticides.

Heart-felt Prayer

The fast proved to me the truth of what I believed when I began. The fast is the heartfelt prayer for purification and strengthening for all of us. The fast is an act of penance for those of us in moral authority. And by that I mean all of us who know the difference between right and wrong. We're in moral authority. The fast is a declaration of noncooperation with those who would put their profits from the sale of California table grapes ahead of tragic human consequences.

During the fast, towards the end, I reached a great clarity where I could see exactly what had to be done. I could see that we needed to build strength to fight the scourge of poisons that threaten our people and our land and our food. I believe fasting is the most powerful way that you can support the boycott. We're urging you to join with us for one day, two days, three days. Join us in the fast and get others to join. We have hundreds, thousands of people fasting all over the country. I believe fasting is the most powerful way we can demonstrate our dislike of what is taking place. We can let them know, those that are empowered to do something, we can let them know that we care. First, by fasting for the boycott, you become involved, not only physically, but also spiritually, with these people. You know, there's a great irony in our country today. The men, women and children whose labor and sweat and sacrifice produce the greatest abundance of food in the history of [human]kind, in the history of the world, often don't have enough to eat themselves....

The times we face truly call for all of us to do more, even more to stop this evil in our midst. It calls for us to do simple, nonviolent deeds for justice. The answer lies with you and me. It is not going to be solved by the government, it is not going to be solved in the halls of Congress; it is not going to be solved by magic; it is not going to be solved by decree.... I've seen nothing done, nothing really substantial, by legislative action or

831

by decree. It has been at the marketplace. And again it will be at the marketplace. Let's win this boycott, ban the poisons. Let's show Congress and everybody else that people can really farm, run large farms, without pesticides.... I hope we will endure until the fields are safe for farm workers, the environment is preserved for future generations, and our food is once again a source of nourishment and life.

CENTRAL AMERICA AND THE USA

THE SANCTUARY MOVEMENT: DARLENE NICGORSKI

As we have already seen in Chapter 6, with the election of Ronald Reagan to the American presidency in 1980, the United States turned to Central America as a convenient proving ground, its "back yard," for ideological war against communism and as a testing ground for new military theories of "low intensity" warfare. In essence the United States turned much of Central America into a huge killing field, as the CIA and U.S. military trained and then funded and supplied rightwing dictatorships in country after country presumably to turn the tide against Cuban-lead infiltration of small democracies, but effectively to protect small oligarchies against both armed insurgencies and nonviolent efforts at reform, including labor organizing, literacy programs, and religious instruction.

The general condition of extreme poverty, war, armed insurrection, and repression combined to send many Central Americans fleeing north, first to Mexico, and then through long-established networks to the United States. Here many found illegal employment, while some found legal sponsors; but Reagan administration policy quickly closed off any legal recourse to such refugees by characterizing them as "economic" and denying them access on humanitarian grounds for those fleeing persecution.

The reaction of the American peace community was rapid. It quickly evolved from isolated instances of individuals aiding refugees to enter the country illegally, or protecting those inside it, into a principled network of church-supported sanctuary. The Sanctuary Movement itself had strong historical roots in the Judeo-Christian tradition and maintained ties to the church-led campaign against U.S. military involvement in Central America.

The movement began in the Southwest, in church communities

along the Mexican border; but by 1984, when the government indicted eleven Sanctuary workers for conspiracy, it had broad-based support among many church communities across the country and drew favorable media coverage for its nonviolent methods and aims. The challenge to the Reagan administration was far too strong for the government to ignore, however. Sanctuary was soon the object of the classic disruptive tactics used against the peace movement of the 1960s: paid informants, agents provocateurs, falsified evidence, the discovery of a great, illegal conspiracy. While a series of government prosecutions in the mid-1980s soon succeeded in disrupting the movement, the fact that their targets were bona-fide and mainstream church groups; and that government methods were far from legitimate, brought as much disrepute upon the Federal prosecution as upon the Sanctuary movement and helped stalemate legal U.S. intervention in Central America.

The following is taken from the special "Sanctuary" issue of *Sojourners* 15.7 (July 1986), and is included in the article by Vicki Kemper, "Convicted of the Gospel: Inside the Tucson Sanctuary Movement," pp. 20-30.

386. *Darlene Nicgorski, No Turning Back: An Interview with Sojourners*

Sojourners: What do you think the Sanctuary trial is about?

Darlene Nicgorski: I don't see this case really dealing with the issues of sanctuary, because of the limitations of the court. I think this is not only an attempt to silence the truth about Central America and to stop the movement, I really think that the government will particularly try to take on what they consider mainline churches – the Catholic Church, the Presbyterian Church, and other Protestant churches. The Quakers have always been into this sort of stuff, so they're not the same kind of threat. But if the government can, they want to make an example and use this trial not only for its impact on sanctuary but also because the churches are beginning to gain momentum on other issues in which the churches feel themselves in conflict with the government, such as South Africa [see 321-322], the Pledge of Resistance [387], Witness for Peace [387], and the peace movement.

The churches' voice on sanctuary and Central America has probably been the clearest voice of any. I think the government has very clearly used this issue as an attempt to intimidate, divide, and separate the churches further for taking a stand that might be opposed to this administration. Doing that with mainline churches is the most effective way to divide administration opponents.

I don't think people realize what's been going on or that this is what this case is about. What the government is trying to do – and this has continued to happen – is discredit us, which is certainly what's happened in history. We know from Martin Luther King Jr. and the anti-Vietnam War movement that one of the things the government is going to try to do is discredit the opposition. And they'll try as much as they can to take away my religious identity and show that this isn't real religion. The government says that Jesus Cruz, the prosecution's main witness, can decide for this country what is religious activity and what is not.

My journey began in Central America. I was in Guatemala, helping to set up a preschool, for only six months when our pastor was shot and killed. After being forced to flee and living in southern Mexico, I came back here and realized I couldn't read the scriptures in the same way anymore. What I had lived made the scriptures live in a new way.

Before, the scriptures were much more a kind of comfort, a consolation. Now whenever I pick them up, there is a challenge – the way of the cross.

Having lived and walked with the people in Central America, having read the scriptures with them, having experienced the fear, the suspicion, needing to flee, and the daily dependence on faith and prayer gave me a sense that when I was back here I could not forget, and I felt compelled to do something. I couldn't go back to being the kind of person I was before; there was somehow a call to give voice to those experiences.

Persecution had followed us into Mexico. The Guatemalan army repeatedly crossed into southern Mexico, looking for subversives or guerrillas in the camps. We took tape recordings of the refugees' stories and then carried the tapes to the United States, not expecting that the same persecution would come here. Right here we found spies and the kind of infiltration of church meetings that was the fear of everybody in Central America. There were searches of houses in Guatemala, so we buried and burned books – anything with the word "liberation" would make you suspect.

I had the same experience at my home in Phoenix. My neighbors told me that more than seven agents of the government, some of them armed, had come to my home and searched my apartment for more than four hours. They made a 20-minute videotape of themselves searching my apartment. You can see a female Salvadoran who was in my apartment. Agents about twice her size were about to break in the door when she opened it. They pointed a gun at her and got her to say on camera that she was there without papers and that she'd been commissioned to be there. Then they went through everything in my apartment. This was the first time that I began to see that what they were going to do in this case was try to negate our religious identity.

One thing they found was an article I had written on being a refugee. I used the phrase "poor and oppressed." They had circled it and written in the column "Marxist Ideology." Well, I didn't know that "poor and oppressed" came from Marx; I knew "poor and oppressed" from the Bible [Lk. 4:1-19, see **30**]. But that's how this investigation came to be viewed through their lens of criminal activity.

One of my concerns is that, while I think it's important to help our government follow good laws – whether international laws or the 1980 Refugee Act – God and patriotism have become one. It is very difficult to get people to respond to a moral imperative, in contrast to one that's legal.

I used to wonder, should we try to raise moral issues in the hope that people can then see that laws can be very wrong? It might mean people going to jail, such as is happening in the peace movement. That was certainly demonstrated in the civil rights days. Rosa Parks did a very small thing, but it was against the law, and her little action is what helped people to see that the laws were bad. What I decided for myself, and what I see happening in the sanctuary movement, is that people need to be led to taking a responsible position from their own moral convictions, as if to say, "I'm going to help this person, and I'm going to do this without anybody stopping me."

Sojourners: Do you think the trial is helping people to get to that decision, or is it muddling the issue?

I don't know. The reason I chose to stay part of this group of 11 is that, because of the greater media attention on a larger group, we are helping to get out more information that I consider important – the truth about what's going on in Central America. What I try to raise whenever I'm speaking in public is the situation of the refugees. It's sad, but the trial has captured the interest of the American public, because now eleven North Americans, mostly church people, face possible prison sentences and not because of the suffering of Central Americans. So if we can use the trial to help raise people's consciousness, I think it has been fruitful.

Sojourners: You and several other defendants have referred to feeling a sense of powerlessness. Can you describe that feeling and also describe the impact this trial has had on your faith?

My faith has gone through a process of clarifying, a kind of cleansing. It's like starting down a road and one choice leads you to the next. I never knew that saying yes to work in Guatemala would lead to experiencing my pastor being killed, or fleeing, or being persecuted, or being in a refugee camp. I think it's faithfulness to prayer and community, coupled with making the choice to walk with the poor and oppressed, that helps these issues come together.

Sometimes you'd like to turn back, but you can't. Then the road gets narrower, and the journey gets sort of lonely. But it also gets clearer in terms of the gospel message.

I don't know where my life will lead me after the trial. But I know that the faith I've experienced in the trial has made me clearer about the sense of powerlessness that a poor person must feel. We defendants are all quite well-educated. Some of us have tried to keep very involved in the process. And yet, it's as if all of a sudden the process gets taken over, and we're left with no alternatives and dare not speak in the courtroom. How much worse it must be for the people without resources.

Sojourners: You spoke about how your work and this trial have affected your faith. What do you think is its effect on the church as a whole?

I see Central American refugees as the new missionaries, missionaries to the North American church. It is time for us to be the listeners. The refugees have so much to teach us, and if we could learn to listen to them, that is the real hope for the North American church.

The sanctuary movement can bring revival to the church. The important thing is for us to listen and see that we have something to learn from Central Americans. By their speaking we can have an opportunity for the conversion of North Americans.

WITNESS FOR PEACE

Like the Sanctuary movement, the Witness for Peace was an innovative response from church-related groups to the Reagan administration's illegal Contra war in Nicaragua. It was launched in 1983. Unlike many mainstream and middle-class movements in the United States, however, the Witness for Peace appealed to the more "athletic" aspect of peacemaking, combining a bit of missionary zeal with backwoods adventure, and the true physical courage that has characterized the early Christian missionaries to the Barbarian West [89-95, 110-113], the peacemakers in the Age of Discovery [224-228, 238-245], or the role of the Maryknoll Order and the four churchwomen slain in El Salvador [347]. The essence of the Witness was to provide and to support teams of individuals who would actually travel to the front lines of the Contra war to interpose themselves as willing hostages to violence, hoping to prevent attacks upon civilian targets, to scale down military confrontations, or to share the fate of the campesinos kidnapped – and often killed – by the Contras, who hoped to spread terror in the countryside and destabilize the fragile Sandinista regime.

Equally as important, the presence of non-CIA North Americans on the front lines raised the attention of the U.S. and world media to events in Nicaragua, made both U.S. and Contra leadership hesitant to escalate the conflict, and brought much public opinion to bear against further U.S. involvement or funding for the Contras. At home the Pledge of Resistance created a network of groups and individuals committed to nonviolent action to prevent a U.S. invasion of Nicaragua.

The work of Witness for Peace was controversial from the start, however. To many – both in North and Latin America – the participants often suffered from the same mind-frame as the U.S. government: heroic North Americans setting out on crusades to save their Latin neighbors from themselves, staying on the scene only long enough to experience vicariously the suffering the people, and then to return to North America self-satisfied and still misunderstanding. To conservative critics in the U.S. and Latin America they represented a clear-cut interference with the efforts of the Contras to restore capitalist "democracy" and were little more than communist dupes or agents.

The following text is taken from Ed Griffin-Nolan, *Witness for Peace: A Story of Resistance,* Louisville, KY: Westminster/John Knox Press, 1991, pp. 235-36.

387. *Witness For Peace, Original Statement of Purpose*

To develop an ever-broadening, prayerful, biblically based community of United States citizens who stand with the Nicaraguan people by acting in continuous nonviolent resistance to U.S. policy. To mobilize public opinion and help change U.S. foreign policy to one which fosters justice, peace and friendship with our Nicaraguan neighbors. To welcome others in this endeavor who vary in spiritual approach, but are one with us in purpose.

The Covenant of Witness For Peace

Together, we make the following Covenant:
- We commit ourselves to a prayerful, biblical approach and unity with one another as the foundation for this project.
- We commit ourselves to nonviolence in word and deed as the essential operating principle of Witness for Peace.
- We commit ourselves to act in solidarity with the people of Nicaragua, respecting their lives, their culture, and their decisions.
- We commit ourselves to maintaining the political independence of Witness for Peace.
- We commit ourselves to honesty, openness and inclusiveness in our relationships with one another.
- We commit significant time and financial resources to Witness for Peace.
- We commit ourselves to circulating our documentation as widely as possible.

The Original Text of the Pledge of Resistance

In the event of a U.S. invasion of Nicaragua, the following will happen:

(1) A signal for action will go out to regional, state and local contact people and groups.

(2) People across the country will gather at a previously designated church in their local community (at least one in every congressional district). These churches will be the gathering points for receiving and sharing information, for prayer and mutual support, for preparing and commissioning one another for action.

(3) A nonviolent vigil will be established at the congressional field offices of each U.S. senator and representative. Each office will be peacefully occupied until that congressperson votes to end the invasion.

(4) A large number of people will come to Washington, DC (in delegations from every area of the country) to engage in nonviolent civil disobedience at the White House to demand an end to the invasion.

(5) The United States citizens who are in active partnership with us (Witness for Peace, Maryknoll, the Committee of U.S. Citizens in Nicaragua, etc.) will launch their own plan of action in Nicaragua in concert with us. Depending on the political situation, the timing of the invasion, and the possibility of getting into Nicaragua before or during an invasion, we will send other people to Nicaragua to join in the actions of the United States citizens already there, if our partners in Nicaragua feel such an action would be advisable.

THE END OF U.S. MILITARY INTERVENTION: SOLIDARITY AMONG THE ELITES

We have already examined the role of liberation theology in Latin America [328-335] and the life and thought of slain Jesuit theologian Ignacio Ellacuría [348]. His murder, along with that of five Jesuit colleagues and their two housekeepers by the Salvadoran military government on November 16, 1989 led to a fire-storm of protest not only among opponents to U.S. involvement in Central America but among the academic and clerical colleagues of the Jesuits. Such protest – from the highest levels of American Catholic thought and opinion-making – not only doomed U.S. government attempts to maintain the status quo in Central America but also demonstrated how deeply the new currents in peacemaking have permeated Catholic thought and life in the United States.

Father Joseph O'Hare, S.J. was educated in the Philippines, where he earned both BA and MA from Berchmans College in Cebu City. From 1955 to 1958 and from 1967 to 1972 he taught on the faculty of Arts and Sciences at the Ateneo de Manila University, and participated in a 1986 fact-finding mission to that country during its "People Power" revolution [325]. In September 1984 O'Hare was named president of the Jesuit-run Fordham University in New York City. He served as chairman of the Association of Jesuit Colleges and Universities from 1989 to 1992, and as chairman of the Association of Catholic Colleges and Universities from 1990 to 1992. In February 1990 he joined four other presidents of Jesuit North American colleges on a journey of

839

solidarity to El Salvador. His homily on the six slain Jesuits was delivered on November 22, 1989 at a memorial Mass at the Jesuit Church of St. Ignatius Loyola in New York. The text here is taken from Jon Sobrino, S.J., *Companions of Jesus: The Jesuit Martyrs of El Salvador,* Maryknoll, NY: Orbis Books, 1990, pp. 174-80.

388. Joseph O'Hare, SJ, Martyrdom in El Salvador

On behalf of the Jesuits of New York Province, I welcome you to this liturgy in which through the words and signs of religious faith we celebrate our solidarity with the people of El Salvador. The occasion for our liturgy is the tragedy of last Thursday when six Jesuits and two of their household family at the Central American University in San Salvador were brutally murdered in the early morning hours. But we mourn not only for them but for all the victims of this wasteful war that for more than ten years has bled a tiny, tortured country.

We mourn for the seventy thousand persons of El Salvador who have died in this war and the hundreds of thousands who have been displaced by the fighting. We remember the martyrs who preceded last Thursday's victims, Father Rutilio Grande, a Jesuit assassinated in 1977, the same year that a right-wing paramilitary group ordered all Jesuits to leave the country or face a sentence of death. We remember Archbishop Oscar Romero [346], struck down by an assassin's bullet in 1980 while celebrating Mass. We remember also the four American women missionaries who were kidnapped, assaulted, and murdered by military forces in December of 1980 [347].

Our celebration today is marked by a deep sense of sorrow at the loss of human life and the cruelty of ten years of fruitless fighting. But our sorrow is based on a strong sense of solidarity with the people and the church of El Salvador. It is a solidarity based on a common faith in a God of justice, on a common mission that all Jesuits share with the Jesuits of El Salvador, and on the common identity that unites a Catholic university in El Salvador with Catholic universities throughout the world. Our sense of solidarity, however, also arises from the more troubling fact that the national policies of our two countries have been, for good or ill, inextricably linked.

And finally, our solidarity with the people of El Salvador is based on fundamental Christian hope, which declares that no matter how dark the signs of death, in the end the radiance of life will prove victorious.

Chapter 7: Catholic Peacemaking in the USA

Our solidarity with the people of El Salvador is based on a shared faith that this world is in the end God's world and that God is the Lord of our history. For this reason, we are committed to the cause for which the Jesuit martyrs of last Thursday died: the dignity of the human person and the kingdom of justice to which the Lord of justice calls us.

This faith in the primacy of the Lord of justice stretches beyond the divisions of race and nations to unite all of us in a common human family. It is a faith that echoes the early call of the prophet Isaiah to work to bring justice to the nations. In the words of Isaiah, the servant of the Lord "brings true justice; he will never waver, nor be crushed until true justice is established on earth.... I, Yahweh, have called you to serve the cause of right; I have taken you by the hand and formed you; I have appointed you as covenant of the people and light of the nations, to open the eyes of the blind, to free captives from prison, and those who live in darkness from the dungeon" [Is. 42:1].

This morning we confirm our commitment to this cause for which the Jesuits of the Central American University in El Salvador gave their lives. They were not men of violence, they were men of peace and reason. Yet they died violently. Like the servant of Yahweh, they did not cry out or shout aloud or break the crushed reed, but neither did they waver nor were they crushed. They did not leave the country in 1977 when right-wing death squads put them under a penalty of death. Nor did they leave earlier this month when government-controlled radio stations broadcast warnings against their safety. Nor will they leave now, when the attorney general of the government blames the unrest in the country on church leaders.

While these six Jesuits were struck down last Thursday, others will rise up to take their place. We pledge ourselves to the covenant with the people that cost them their lives. For us to forget them or to decide that the costs of justice are too high for us to pay would be to betray not only their memory but our faith that this is God's world and that God is the Lord of justice.

For the Jesuits assembled here this morning, our solidarity with last Thursday's martyrs has a more personal foundation as well. Many of us knew some or all of them. Several of them studied here in the United States. For my part, I remember listening to Ignacio Ellacuría during the 33rd General Congregation of the Jesuits in Rome in the fall of 1983, when he spoke with passion of the agony of his people and of the need for a response to the institutionalized violence of massive poverty and repression that crushed the vast majority of the people of El Salvador.

Father Ellacuría's words echoed the common commitment of Jesuits today to serve faith and promote justice, and to see in this twofold mandate the grand intention that should inform all Jesuit works, no matter how varied. "What is it to be a companion of Jesus today? It is to engage, under the standard of the cross, in the crucial struggle of our time: the struggle for faith and that struggle for justice which it includes.... Thus, the way to faith and the way to justice are inseparable ways. It is on this undivided road, this steep road, that the pilgrim church must travel and toil" [*Jesuits Today*, 32nd General Congregation, 1975]....

In eliminating the rector and vice-rector and some of the most distinguished members of the faculty of the University of Central America, the assassins cut out the heart of one of the most respected intellectual institutions in the country. As you know from newspaper accounts, these men were not merely murdered, their brains were spilled out on the ground by their murderers, a chilling symbol of the contempt shown by men of violence for the power of truth.

There are those who have said, and who will say in the days and weeks ahead, that the Jesuits of El Salvador were not disinterested academics, that they had deliberately chosen to insert themselves into the political conflict of their nation. If they had remained within the insulated safety of the library or the classroom, their critics will charge, if they had not "meddled in politics," their lives would not have been threatened.

But such a criticism misunderstands the nature of any university, and most certainly the nature of a Catholic university. No university can be insulated from the agonies of the society in which it lives. No university which identifies itself as Catholic can be indifferent to the call of the church to promote the dignity of the human person.

Pope John Paul II, himself a man from the university world, has often challenged Catholic universities to confront the crucial issues of peace and justice in our world today. On his last visit to this country in September 1987, the pope addressed a meeting of Catholic college and university presidents in New Orleans. On that occasion, he called on Catholic universities to recognize the need for the reform of attitudes and unjust structures in society. He spoke of "the whole dynamic of peace and justice in the world, as it affects East and West, North and South.... The parable of the rich man and the poor man is directed to the conscience of humanity, and today in particular, to the conscience of America. But that conscience often passes through the halls of academe, through nights of study and hours of prayer."...

It was this distinctive mission of a Catholic university that inspired the Jesuits of El Salvador to seek, not only through teaching and writing but also through their personal interventions, a resolution of the terrible conflict that has divided their land. Those of us who carry this mission of faith and justice in the relatively comfortable circumstances of North America can only be humbled by the total commitment to the ministry of truth that stamped the lives of the Jesuit scholars and teachers of El Salvador and in the end cost them their lives....

At a time when our government leaders and our corporate executives hasten to socialize with the leaders of the communist giants elsewhere in the world, why must we assemble our military might to deal with the revolutionary movements in tiny Central American nations? Are our national interests really at stake? Or are we obsessed with the myth of the national security state [see 332-334], a myth that is discredited each day by events elsewhere in the world? After ten years of evasions and equivocations, a tissue of ambiguities, the assassinations of last Thursday pose with brutal clarity, the question that continues to haunt the policy of the United States toward El Salvador: Can we hand weapons to butchers and remain unstained by the blood of their innocent victims?

But the final word of this liturgy cannot be one of anger or denunciation. It must be one of hope. For this too, in the end, is the final ground of our solidarity with the people of El Salvador. If Jesuits are men crucified to the world and to whom the world is crucified, it is only because we believe that out of the crucifixion of our Savior, El Salvador, came life and comes life. With the people of El Salvador we believe in the words of Jesus cited in today's gospel that "unless a wheat grain falls on the ground and dies, it remains only a single grain; but if it dies it yields a rich harvest" [John 12:24].

When Christians celebrate the Eucharist they take the bread, break it and remember him who took his life, broke it and gave it that others might live. With deep hope in the resurrection of the Lord, we pray that the final word in the drama of El Salvador be one of life and hope rather than death and despair. We pray that the irony of that tiny, tortured country's name, El Salvador, the Savior, will be redeemed by the resurrection of its people.

THE BISHOPS AND THE BOMB

THE CHALLENGE OF PEACE

In October 1976 the Detroit Call to Action Conference resulted in progressive positions on disarmament, calling for the condemnation not only of the use or threatened use of nuclear weapons, but also of their production and possession, following this up with a pastoral letter officially recommending these positions. In 1979 the bishops lent their support to the SALT II treaty limiting nuclear weaponry.

By the 1980s individual Catholic bishops had come to the forefront of Catholic witness and prophesy against war. In their 1983 pastoral, *The Challenge of Peace: God's Promise and Our Response* the American bishops formalized these trends toward a theology and practice of peace. The result of three drafts and intense debate inside and outside the church, the pastoral letter promised to produce a revolution in American Catholic thinking on war and peace equal to that of Vatican II and the *Pastoral Constitution.*

Condemned by some as not going far enough for peace, as an affirmation of the church's accommodation to power and to the just-war tradition, and by others as going too far in the direction of "pacifism," the pastoral epitomized the history and scope of the American Catholic dialogue of peacemaking. It presented the first attempt at a new synthesis and compromise between the just-war and pacifist traditions within Catholic history, between the church's recognition of the nation state and the international system and its defense of the rights of individual conscience, between its functions of prophetic denunciation and education and its role as a basic institution in American society. It combined the wisdom of the Gospels, of *Pacem in Terris,* Vatican II, and recent papal teaching, and the experience of recent American history. The synthesis, in fact, was revolutionary, because for the first time in American Catholic history pacifism and "active non-violence" were seen as both evangelical imitations of Christ and legitimate means of serving not only individual conscience and civil society, but more specifically the *political* community. They become means of Christian action as legitimate as military defense in the service of the nation.

Whatever the quibbles of conservatives or progressives over specific passages in the letter, its revolutionary direction is clear: "we fear that our world and nation are headed in the wrong direction.... In the words of our Holy Father, we need a 'moral about-face'." By the end of the twentieth century the American hierarchy had taken on the full prophetic call of peacemaking.

The following is the official "Summary" of the U.S. Catholic Bishops' Pastoral Letter on Nuclear Weapons and War, *The Challenge of Peace and Our Response,* Daughters of St. Paul, ed., Boston: St. Paul Editions, 1983; and various other editions.

389. U.S. Catholic Conference: The Challenge of Peace, Summary

The Second Vatican Council opened its evaluation of modern warfare with the statement: "The whole human race faces a moment of supreme crisis in its advance toward maturity." We agree with the council's assessment; the crisis of the moment is embodied in the threat which nuclear weapons pose for the world and much that we hold dear in the world. We have seen and felt the effects of the crisis of the nuclear age in the lives of people we serve. Nuclear weaponry has drastically changed the nature of warfare, and the arms race poses a threat to human life and human civilization which is without precedent.

We write this letter from the perspective of Catholic faith. Faith does not insulate us from the daily challenges of life but intensifies our desire to address them precisely in light of the gospel which has come to us in the person of the risen Christ. Through the resources of faith and reason we desire in this letter to provide hope for people in our day and direction toward a world freed of the nuclear threat.

As Catholic bishops we write this letter as an exercise of our teaching ministry. The Catholic tradition on war and peace is a long and complex one; it stretches from the Sermon on the Mount to the statements of Pope John Paul II. We wish to explore and explain the resources of the moral-religious teaching and to apply it to specific questions of our day. In doing this we realize, and we want readers of this letter to recognize, that not all statements in this letter have the same moral authority. At times we state universally binding moral principles found in the teaching of the Church; at other times the pastoral letter makes specific applications, observations and recommendations which allow for diversity of opinion on the part of those who assess the factual data of a situations differently. However, we expect Catholics to give our moral judgments serious consideration when they are forming their own views on specific problems.

The experience of preparing this letter has manifested to us the range of strongly held opinion in the Catholic community on questions of fact and judgment concerning issues of war and peace. We urge mutual respect among individuals and groups in the Church as this letter is analyzed and discussed. Obviously, as bishops, we believe that such differences should be expressed within the framework of Catholic moral teaching. We need in the Church not only conviction and commitment but also civility and charity.

While this letter is addressed principally to the Catholic community, we want it to make a contribution to the wider public debate in our country on the dangers and dilemmas of the nuclear age. Our contribution will not be primarily technical or political, but we are convinced that there is no satisfactory answer to the human problems of the nuclear age which fails to consider the moral and religious dimensions of the questions we face.

Although we speak in our own name, as Catholic bishops of the Church in the United States, we have been conscious in the preparation of this letter of the consequences our teaching will have not only for the United States but for other nations as well. One important expression of this awareness has been the consultation we have had, by correspondence and in an important meeting held at the Vatican (January 18-19, 1983), with representatives of European bishops' conferences. This consultation with bishops of other countries, and, of course, with the Holy See, has been very helpful to us.

Catholic teaching has always understood peace in positive terms. In the words of Pope John Paul II: "Peace is not just the absence of war.... Like a cathedral, peace must be constructed patiently and with unshakable faith" (Coventry, England, 1982). Peace is the fruit of order. Order in human society must be shaped on the basis of respect for the transcendence of God and the unique dignity of each person, understood in terms of freedom, justice, truth and love. To avoid war in our day we must be intent on building peace in an increasingly interdependent world. In Part III of this letter we set forth a positive vision of peace and the demands such a vision makes on diplomacy, national policy, and personal choices.

While pursuing peace incessantly, it is also necessary to limit the use of force in a world comprised of nation states, faced with common problems but devoid of an adequate international political authority. Keeping the peace in the nuclear age is a moral and political imperative. In Parts I and II of this letter we set forth both the principles of Catholic teaching on war and a series of judgments, based on these principles, about concrete policies. In making these judgments we speak as moral teachers, not as technical experts.

1. Some Principles, Norms and Premises of Catholic Teaching

A. On War

(1) Catholic teaching begins in every case with a presumption against war and for peaceful settlement of disputes. In exceptional cases, determined by the moral principles of the just-war tradition, some uses of force are permitted.

(2) Every nation has a right and duty to defend itself against unjust aggression.

(3) Offensive war of any kind is not morally justifiable.

(4) It is never permitted to direct nuclear or conventional weapons to "the indiscriminate destruction of whole cities or vast areas with their populations..." [*Gaudium et Spes*, §80]. The intentional killing of innocent civilians or non-combatants is always wrong.

(5) Even defensive response to unjust attack can cause destruction which violates the principle of proportionality, going far beyond the limits of legitimate defense. This judgment is particularly important when assessing planned use of nuclear weapons. No defensive strategy, nuclear or conventional, which exceeds the limits of proportionality is morally permissible.

B. On Deterrence

(1) "In current conditions 'deterrence' based on balance, certainly not as an end in itself but as a step on the way toward a progressive disarmament, may still be judged morally acceptable. Nonetheless, in order to ensure peace, it is indispensable not to be satisfied with this minimum which is always susceptible to the real danger of explosion" [Pope John Paul II, "Message to U.N. Special Session on Disarmament," June 1982, §8].

(2) No *use* of nuclear weapons which would violate the principles of

847

discrimination or proportionality may be *intended* in a strategy of deterrence. The moral demands of Catholic teaching require resolute willingness not to intend or to do moral evil even to save our own lives or the lives of those we love.

(3) Deterrence is not an adequate strategy as a long-term basis for peace; it is a transitional strategy justifiable only in conjunction with resolute determination to pursue arms control and disarmament. We are convinced that "the fundamental principle on which our present peace depends must be replaced by another, which declares that the true and solid peace of nations consists not in equality of arms but in mutual trust alone" [Pope John XXIII, *Pacem in Terris,* §113, see **298**].

C. The Arms Race and Disarmament

(1) The arms race is one of the greatest curses on the human race; it is to be condemned as a danger, an act of aggression against the poor, and a folly which does not provide the security it promises [Cf. *Gaudium et Spes,* §81, **299**; and *Statement of the Holy See to the United Nations,* 1976].

(2) Negotiations must be pursued in every reasonable form possible; they should be governed by the "demand that the arms race should cease; that the stockpiles which exist in various countries should be reduced equally and simultaneously by the parties concerned; that nuclear weapons should be banned; and that a general agreement should eventually be reached about progressive disarmament and an effective method of control" [Pope John XXIII, *Pacem in Terris,* §112].

D. On Personal Conscience

(1) Military Service: "All those who enter the military service in loyalty to their country should look upon themselves as the custodians of the security and freedom of their fellow countrymen; and when they carry out their duty properly, they are contributing to the maintenance of peace" [*Gaudium et Spes,* §79].

(2) Conscientious Objection: "Moreover, it seems just that laws should make humane provision for the case of conscientious objectors who refuse to carry arms, provided they accept some other form of community service" [*Gaudium et Spes,* §79].

(3) Non-violence: "In this same spirit we cannot but express our admiration for all who forego the use of violence to vindicate their rights and resort to other means of defense which are available to weaker par-

ties, provided it can be done without harm to the rights and duties of others and of the community" [*Gaudium et Spes,* §78].

(4) Citizens and Conscience: "Once again we deem it opportune to remind our children of their duty to take an active part in public life, and to contribute towards the attainment of the common good of the entire human family as well as to that of their own political community.... In other words, it is necessary that human beings, in the intimacy of their own consciences, should so live and act in their temporal lives as to create a synthesis between scientific, technical and professional elements on the one hand, and spiritual values on the other" [Pope John XXIII, *Pacem in Terris,* §146, 150].

II. Moral Principles and Policy Choices

As bishops in the United States, assessing the concrete circumstances of our society, we have made a number of observations and recommendations in the process of applying moral principles to specific policy choices.

A. On the Use of Nuclear Weapons

(1) Counter Population Use: Under no circumstances may nuclear weapons or other instruments of mass slaughter be used for the purpose of destroying population centers or other predominantly civilian targets. Retaliatory action which would indiscriminately and disproportionately take many wholly innocent lives, lives of people who are in no way responsible for reckless actions of their government, must also be condemned.

(2) The Initiation of Nuclear War: We do not perceive any situation in which the deliberate initiation of nuclear war, on however restricted a scale, can be morally justified. Non-nuclear attacks by another state must be resisted by other than nuclear means. Therefore, a serious moral obligation exists to develop non-nuclear defensive strategies as rapidly as possible. In this letter we urge NATO to move rapidly toward the adoption of a "no first use" policy, but we recognize this will take time to implement and will require the development of an adequate alternative defense posture.

(3) Limited Nuclear War: Our examination of the various arguments on this question makes us highly skeptical about the real meaning of "limited." One of the criteria of the just-war teaching is that there must be a reasonable hope of success in bringing about justice and peace. We

849

must ask whether such a reasonable hope can exist once nuclear weapons have been exchanged. The burden of proof remains on those who assert that meaningful limitation is possible. In our view the first imperative is to prevent any use of nuclear weapons and we hope that leaders will resist the notion that nuclear conflict can be limited, contained or won in any traditional sense.

B. On Deterrence

In concert with the evaluation provided by Pope John Paul II, we have arrived at a strictly conditional moral acceptance of deterrence. In this letter we have outlined criteria and recommendations which indicate the meaning of conditional acceptance of deterrence policy. We cannot consider such a policy adequate as a long-term basis for peace.

C. On Promoting Peace

(1) We support immediate, bilateral verifiable agreements to halt the testing, production and deployment of new nuclear weapons systems. This recommendation is not to be identified with any specific political initiative.

(2) We support efforts to achieve deep cuts in the arsenals of both superpowers; efforts should concentrate first on systems which threaten the retaliatory forces of either major power.

(3) We support early and successful conclusion of negotiations of a comprehensive test ban treaty.

(4) We urge new efforts to prevent the spread of nuclear weapons in the world, and to control the conventional arms race, particularly the conventional arms trade.

(5) We support, in an increasingly interdependent world, political and economic policies designed to protect human dignity and to promote the human rights of every person, especially the least among us. In this regard, we call for the establishment of some form of global authority adequate to the needs of the international common good.

This letter includes many judgments from the perspective of ethics, politics and strategy needed to speak concretely and correctly to the "moment of supreme crisis" identified by Vatican II. We stress again that readers should be aware, as we have been, of the distinction between our statement of moral principles and of official Church teaching and our application of these to concrete issues. We urge that special care be taken not to use passages out of context; neither should brief portions of this document be cited to support positions it does not intend to convey or which are not truly in accord with the spirit of its teaching.

In concluding this summary we respond to two key questions often asked about this pastoral letter:

Why do we address these matters fraught with such complexity, controversy and passion? We speak as pastors, not politicians. We are teachers, not technicians. We cannot avoid our responsibility to lift up the moral dimensions of the choices before our world and nation. The nuclear age is an era of moral as well as physical danger. We are the first generation since Genesis with the power to threaten the created order. We cannot remain silent in the face of such danger. Why do we address these issues? We are simply trying to live up to the call of Jesus to be peacemakers in our own time and situation.

What are we saying? Fundamentally, we are saying that the decisions about nuclear weapons are among the most pressing moral questions of our age. While these decisions have obvious military and political aspects, they involve fundamental moral choices. In simple terms, we are saying that good ends (defending one's country, protecting freedom, etc.) cannot justify immoral means (the use of weapons which kill indiscriminately and threaten whole societies). We fear that our world and nation are headed in the wrong direction. More weapons with greater destructive potential are produced every day. More and more nations are seeking to become nuclear powers. In our quest for more and more security we fear we are actually becoming less and less secure.

In the words of our Holy Father, we need a "moral about-face." The whole world must summon the moral courage and technical means to say no to nuclear conflict; no to weapons of mass destruction; no to an arms race which robs the poor and the vulnerable; and no to the moral danger of a nuclear age which places before humankind indefensible choices of constant terror or surrender. Peacemaking is not an optional commitment. It is a requirement of our faith. We are called to be peacemakers, not by some movement of the moment, but by our Lord Jesus. The content and context of our peacemaking is set not by some political agenda or ideological program, but by the teaching of his Church.

Ultimately, this letter is intended as an expression of Christian faith, affirming the confidence we have that the risen Lord remains with us precisely in moments of crisis. It is our belief in his presence and power among us which sustain us in confronting the awesome challenge of the nuclear age. We speak from faith to provide hope for all who recognize the challenge and are working to confront it with the resources of faith and reason.

To approach the nuclear issue in faith is to recognize our absolute need for prayer: we urge and invite all to unceasing prayer for peace with justice for all people. In a spirit of prayerful hope we present this message of peace.

BUILDING PEACE

The controversy that surrounded the publication of *The Challenge of Peace* embroiled not only the Catholic community, but the nation as a whole as intellectuals, journalists, politicians, academics, and peace activists came before the American – and world – public to debate the impact, importance, and value of the peace pastoral. So vehement was ciritcism – much of it encouraged by the Reagan administration and its allies among conservative Catholic circles – that the bishops found themselves compelled to justify both their pastoral and political stands on peace. The result was the letter issued on the fifth aniverary of *The Challenge of Peace,* entitled *Building Peace.*

This excerpt is taken from the National Conference of Catholic Bishops (NCCB), *Building Peace: A Pastoral Reflection on the Response to* The Challenge of Peace *and a Report on* The Challenge of Peace *and Policy Developments 1983-1988,* Washington, DC: NCCB, 1988.

390. U.S. Catholic Conference, Building Peace, June 1988

Becoming a Peacemaking Church

…(12) As pastors and believers, we are required by the Gospel to do far more than to develop a pastoral letter and initiate efforts to begin to educate and act on the Church's teaching. We also need to do more than to assess current developments for their moral implications. We must work to broaden, deepen and strengthen the Church's work for peace. The whole Church is called to become a *peacemaking church,* to "form people capable of being true artisans of peace," in the words of Pope John Paul II ["Address to Diplomatic Corps," §12, p. 8]. In this task, we are united with our Holy Father and the Universal Church. It was in Coventry that Pope John Paul said: "Like a cathedral, peace must be constructed patiently and with unshakable faith" [Pope John Paul II, "Homily at Bagington Airport," Conventry, May 30, 1982, *Origins* 12:4 (June 10, 1982): 55, cited in *The Challenge of Peace*, §200]. Five years after the adoption of our letter, we recommit ourselves to that task. We are called to seek practical ways to make the peace and justice of the Kingdom more visible in a world torn by fear, hatred and violence.

(13) A peacemaking church needs to constantly pray for peace. As we share God's word and celebrate the Eucharist, there will be many opportunities to reflect and pray on the biblical basis for peacemaking and church teaching on nuclear arms. Every worshipping community should regularly include the cause of peace in its prayers of petition. It is in prayer that we encounter Jesus who is our peace and learn from him the way to peace. It is in prayer we find the hope and perseverance which sustain us as instruments of Christ's peace in the world. In this Marian year, we call on Mary, the Queen of Peace, to intercede for us and for the people of the world that we may walk in the ways of peace.

(14) A church of peacemaking is also a community which regularly shares the Church's teaching on peace in its schools, religious education efforts and other parish activities. A special effort is necessary in our institutions of higher education where research, teaching and scholarship can be put at the service of peace. Much has been done to integrate fully and faithfully the Church's teaching in our educational efforts. We urge that the teaching of the letter be presented in its totality, including the principles governing a nation's right and obligation of self-defense and an individual's right of conscientious objection.

(15) Much more needs to be done to integrate fully the Church's teaching in our educational efforts. We especially need to work toward a more fully developed theology of peace [see **378**]. As the pastoral letter said: "A theology of peace should ground the task of peacemaking solidly in the biblical vision of the Kingdom of God, then place it centrally in the ministry of the Church" [*The Challenge of Peace*, §25]. We need continued theological reflection in colleges, universities, seminaries and other centers of thought and learning on peacemaking, on the complex question of deterrence and on how the Church can provide clear teaching and strong witness for peace grounded in our Christian faith.

(16) A church of peacemaking is a community which speaks and acts for peace, a community which consistently raises fundamental moral questions about the policies that guide the arsenals of the world. As be-

lievers and citizens, we are called to use our voices and votes to support effective efforts to reverse the arms race and move toward genuine peace with justice. The Deterrence Report focuses on the ethical dimensions of nuclear issues. Our conference will be actively sharing these principles and policy directions with those who shape the policies of our nation as part of our continuing commitment to defend human life whenever it is threatened. The U.S. Catholic Conference and our Department of Social Development and World Peace have a special responsibility in this area, but it is also a task for the whole Church. Each of us is called to participate in the debate over how our nation and world can best move toward mutual disarmament and genuine peace with justice.

(17) We serve a diverse Church with legitimate differences on how best to apply principles to policies. The pastoral and other church teaching are best shared in respectful dialogue. The voice of a *peacemaking church* must reflect the facts, rest on competent analysis and understand that persons of goodwill sometimes differ on specific questions. We cannot just proclaim positions. We must argue our case for peace, not only with conviction and competence, but also with civility and charity. We need to bring special pastoral skill and sensitivity to the important task of helping our people become builders of peace in their own situations. For many of our people, these are personal and professional concerns as well as public issues. They deserve personal support and creative pastoral care as they try to live the values of the Gospel in their own demanding roles and responsibilities and as they wrestle with the ethical dimensions of their own work and citizenship.

(18) Finally, a *peacemaking church* is a community which keeps hope alive. We sometimes find ourselves suspended between hope and fear. Surrounded by weapons of mass destruction, we try to imagine and to bring about a future without them. Our faith does not insulate us from problems; it calls us to confront them and to a constant effort to build a better, more lasting basis for peace, knowing that God's grace will never fail us.

Conclusions

(19) Five years after our letter, we are still at a beginning, not an end. We are grateful for all that has been done to share the message of the letter. We affirm the efforts to act faithfully on its implications. We call for a renewed commitment to pray, educate and work for peace at every level of the Church's life.

(20) We pray that the leaders of our nation and world will find the wisdom, the will and the ways to move toward genuine peace and mutual disarmament. We pray that believers will become more effective witnesses and workers for peace, helping our world say "no" to the violence of war, "no" to nuclear destruction, "no" to an arms race that robs the poor and endangers us all.

(21) As bishops, we recommit ourselves to our pastoral letter of five years ago and to the task of sharing and acting on its message. Our commitment to this task cannot be diminished by the passage of time, the press of other priorities or the frustrations of the moment. Now is a time to build on the activities of the past five years, to renew our efforts to educate and advocate for peace, to help make our Church a truly peacemaking community and to work with all people of goodwill to help shape a world of peace and justice.

(22) In renewing this commitment, we must remember who calls us to this task and why. It was Jesus who said: "Blessed are the peacemakers, for they will be called children of God" [Mt. 5:9, see **31**]. As his followers, we take up again the urgent and continuing priority of "building peace" in the nuclear age. [Pope John Paul II, "Address to Diplomatic Corps," §12, p. 8].

LEROY T. MATTHIESEN

The *Challenge of Peace* marked not only a change in the institutional outlook of the church, but it was also inlarge part the product of a long process of conversion on the part of many individual bishops within the conference. In the following selection Leroy Matthiesen offers some autobiographical reflections on his own path to nonviolence. Matthiesen was born in Olfen, TX on June 11, 1921. He received a BA from Josephinum College in Columbus, OH, an MA from Catholic University in Washington, DC, and a Litt.D. from the Register School of Journalism in 1962. Ordained a priest in 1946, Matthiesen worked as editor of the Amarillo diocese's *West Texas Catholic* from 1948 and began teaching. He became principal of Alamo Catholic High School in 1969 and in 1972 took on the duties of pastor in St. Francis parish in Amarillo. In 1980, as he related below, he was named bishop of Amarillo.

The following texts is taken from *The Catholic Worker* 51.5 (Aug. 1984): 1-2, 8.

391. Leroy T. Matthiesen, Bishop of Amarillo, Texas, The Arms Race: Learning to Speak Out

Let me tell you something about the Pantex nuclear weapons assembly plant in Amarillo. Pantex is the final nuclear weapons assembly plant in the United States – in fact, it's the only one. They make nuclear artillery shells for the U.S. Army, thermonuclear bombs for the Air Force, and atomic depth charges for the U.S. Navy. Plutonium is shipped to Pantex from Georgia, the bomb triggers come from Rocky Flats, Colorado, electronic components come from Kansas and neutron generators come from Florida. These things all come in primarily by trucks – white, unmarked trucks which are always accompanied by security men. Once the weapons are assembled, they go out on the same trucks.

They also bring old weapons to Pantex for refurbishing, because the plutonium and tritium gradually deteriorate. Weapons which are taken off the line are disassembled there. And when there's an accident, like the one in Arkansas where the Titan warhead shot out and landed in the pasture, they bring the weapon to Pantex to be taken apart. There's always the possibilities of crashes and radiation spills with all this activity.

Now the city of Amarillo is basically a conservative place. I think the government decided that Amarillo was a good place to put Pantex because not too many questions would be asked of it there – and that's exactly the way it was from 1954 to 1980. I'm sure they are not very happy with me either because they certainly have been questioned now.

Good ol' Country Boy

If I had come into Amarillo from California or some other state, I couldn't have made the kind of statements that I did because I would have been branded a kook and a radical. What saved the situation and kept it at a level of serious discussion was the fact that I am from Amarillo....

...In 1979, the bishop of Amarillo died of cancer. I was ordained as a bishop on May 30, 1980. I immediately began reorganizing the diocese and starting new programs. Life was very exciting.

In the fall of 1980, the first hearing was held in Amarillo about the possibility of basing the MX missile in the Texas panhandle. Everybody talked against it, but on ecological and economic grounds. See, President Carter had decided to go ahead with the shell game, the multiple basing and moving system with decoys on railroad tracks. When people heard of this they began saying, "We want the missiles for defense but don't put them here. Put them some other place." And that was the first time that I said to myself "That's not right. If we need them, why won't we take them?"

"It's a Contradiction"

At Christmas of 1980, I preached my first sermon on nuclear weapons. I basically said that nuclear weapons were dangerous and that we shouldn't be relying on them. I said, "Here we are at Christmas, honoring the Prince of Peace's birth, but we're building nuclear bombs to destroy. It's a contradiction." The sermon didn't cause any reaction, but people were saying "Yeah, yeah? you're right." But it wasn't personalized. They didn't make the connection between Pantex and what I was saying. And yet I was awakened to the fact that people are really concerned about this. They just weren't saying anything about their fears.

After that, there was a second hearing on the MX and at that point I introduced a written statement. I said, "We don't want the MX missile here. Most people don't want the missile on ecological and economic grounds, but I want to add a third objection – and we don't want it on moral grounds. For that reason we not only don't want it here, we don't want it anywhere." There was something in there that appealed to the local population. I also said, "We cherish our land. It's been good to us and it's important to us. So we don't like somebody else coming in from the outside and destroying what we have built." That also appealed to the people of Amarillo of course, because they don't trust outsiders anyway.

On February 10, 1981, there was a protest demonstration at Pantex....They were arrested and of course that made a big headline. They were charged with trespassing on government property, found guilty and sentenced to about a year in federal prison.

It turned out that three of them were Roman Catholic. While they were in the local jail I went to visit them and discovered that one of the Catholics was a priest named Larry Rosebaugh. Before I saw him, I thought I'd find a weird, anti-American hippie type, but I found just the opposite. He was a very gentle, religious person, very intelligent and not at all anti-American. He said, "I'm doing this because I love my country. If we keep up this insanity, the country's going to be destroyed."

Turning Point

...Then, in April or May of 1981, another major event took place that really…well, it was the second turning point in my awareness. A guy named Robert Gutierrez, who worked at Pantex had been studying to be a deacon in our church; he came to me because those studies had caused him to reflect on what he was doing, working in a plant that was making nuclear weapons. In our Church, clerics are forbidden to bear arms and deacons are clerics [see **96-100**]. So here we had a new dimension, a cleric building nuclear weapons. He had come to the conclusion that what he was doing was wrong, so he and his wife came to me to ask me what I thought.

Well, at that point I pretty well knew what I thought. I told him that I thought it was a situation that was morally suspect, and that he needed to get out of it. I told him he wasn't required to quit his job and be jobless, because that would lead from one bad situation to another, but I did say that he should get another job.

So this was a real turning point for me, along with the protest at Pantex – these two situations forced me to think about nuclear weapons differently.

A Flood of Statements

Then a little later came Archbishop Raymond Hunthausen's statement to the Lutheran Synod in which he strongly condemned the Trident submarine base on Puget Sound. That made a big impression on me. He said that he was thinking seriously of withholding 50 percent of his income tax, because 50 percent of the U.S. budget goes to military spending in on form or another.

I reflected on his statement and thought deeply about his nonviolent response to evil. I think that a lot of bishops were holding personal views that really questioned the arms race, but they weren't saying anything in public until a couple of bishops began to lead the way. As soon as a few more joined Hunthausen, there was a flood of forty to sixty statements and pastoral letters taking positions against the arms race. All these events were adding to my concern about nuclear weapons.

Then in August 1981, Reagan announced that he had decided to go ahead and build the neutron bomb….

I wrote a statement calling Reagan's announcement an anti-life decision. I went on to talk about the vain hope of safety that a nuclear weapon provides. I said that despite its power a nuclear bomb cannot save us – so we've got to trust each other and we've got to trust in God. I called on the government to de-accelerate the arms race and the Department of Defense to use common sense in its defense posture.

Then came the fateful line that attracted national attention: "I urge those who engage in the production, assembly and stockpiling of nuclear bombs to reflect on the moral implications of what they're doing and to consider the possibility of transferring from that kind of work to peaceful pursuits." A reporter interpreted this to say that I was calling on Pantex workers to resign, and there was a real furor in Amarillo.

A Spiritual Leader

The reason I put in the line about workers considering the moral implications of what they do is because of Bob Gutierrez. I had been reading all these statements against the arms race, but no one was asking about the moral responsibility of the people who build the bombs. And I'm convinced that it was a responsible thing to do. There have been times when I've thought, who am I to disturb the consciences of other people? But I didn't set out to disturb them. I was asked for advice. I couldn't say that I didn't know. I'm supposed to be a spiritual leader and guide. I couldn't say, "Do what you think."

As you can imagine, the initial response to my statement resulted in very angry calls and letters. People at Pantex told me that their work was necessary for the defense of our country and that it was patriotic work. I was called a traitor and invited to go to the communist country of my choice and stay there. One Catholic woman wrote to me and said, "How dare you! You should be arrested and tried for treason!"

Of course, there were others who called and thanked me for what I did – especially a lot of young people. That's been an interesting phenomenon. A lot of young people once identified themselves as Catholics but became disenchanted with the Church after they decided that it didn't deal with any real-life issues. These people were happy to hear that someone was finally taking a stand on something they were concerned about. Some of them have decided to come back to the Church because of it, and that has been very consoling.

Thus far I know of only one person who has publicly quit Pantex for moral reasons. His name is Eloy Ramos. He told me that he had decided to resign after thinking it over for two or three years. He said, "This is one of the best jobs I've ever had, but we're building weapons that can kill innocent people and destroy the earth. I can't do this anymore. When you spoke out against it, I knew I had to do it."

Right after I made the statement to Pantex workers, it dawned on me that all the bishops in Texas were going to have their annual meetings in a couple of weeks. Of course they were aware of all the flack my statement had aroused because it had hit the papers. And I was worried, because this is Texas, and some of those bishops are very conservative people. I said to myself, "Here I am, I've been a bishop for little over a year, and I'm coming out with these statements." I thought they were going to tell me not to talk so much.

But then I got a call from a neighboring bishop, Joe Fiorenza, who told me that he supported my statement and he wanted to put it on the meeting agenda for all the bishops to vote on. I said I'd be delighted, but I didn't know what kind of chances it had; so we had our meeting, and when we got to that point on the agenda Fiorenza moved that the group should support my statement. It was immediately seconded. Flores, the Archbishop, asked for any discussion and there was none. I felt that I had to say something so I got up and made the comment that if they voted for the motion they would probably return home to find the media on their doorstep. They voted unanimously to pass my statement.

Later in the meetings another more general statement against nuclear weapons passed unanimously. The group ran off copies of it and called the executive of the Texas Catholic Conference and told him to mail it out. The whole thing was amazing! I mean, they knew what they were getting into and I wouldn't have blamed them for taking a cautionary approach, but they didn't. It really was amazing.

I've found a lot of people in Amarillo who are very concerned about what is going on at Pantex, but who haven't felt free to speak out and who still don't. There's a story in the New Testament about a guy [Nicodemus, in John 3:1-21, 7:50] who came to see Christ at night, under the cover of darkness because it wasn't politically expedient to be seen with Him in the daylight. And that's going on in Amarillo right now. Any number of people have told me, almost in whispers, that they're glad I spoke out. They don't do it themselves because they're afraid that their neighbors will condemn them. And I've gotten letters from people all over the country who seem to feel the same way: "I thought I was the only one concerned about this issue. Thank you for speaking out."

I was like that too. I wanted to speak out, but I didn't for quite a while. It was people like Larry Rosebaugh and Hunthausen who enabled me to speak. In a sense, I felt that if they could speak out, I could do it too....

THOMAS J. GUMBLETON

Thomas Gumbleton was born on January 26, 1930, educated at St. John Provincial Seminary in Michigan and at the Pontifical Lateran University in Rome, and ordained in 1956. By the time he had been named titular bishop of Ululi and then auxiliary bishop of Detroit in 1968 he was already collaborating with the U.S. Bishops' Conference staff on drafting *Human Life* [374]. Gumbleton took a leading role in persuading the U.S. Bishops' Conference to condemn the war in Vietnam; and his steady efforts came to fruition with the bishops' letter of November 1971 [376]. Gumbleton's stand was so clear that he stated at the press conference announcing the *Resolution on Southeast Asia* that anyone agreeing with the bishops "may not participate in the war." Two years later, along with Carroll T. Dozier of Memphis, Gumbleton agreed to act as moderator for the formation of Pax Christi/USA and served in that capacity for many years, along with Dozier persuading over 50 of their fellow bishops to become members. In 1978, along with Pax Christi officers Joe Fahey and Gerald Vanderhaar, Gumbleton rejected the Salt II treaty as too minimal, instead supporting the Hatfield amendment for a nuclear moratorium and the eventual nuclear freeze movement. Gumbleton was one of the key authors of *The Challenge of Peace* [389], infusing the letter with his own commitment to nonviolence. Since the 1980s Thomas Gumbleton has deepened his own commitment to peacemaking by participating in many acts of nonviolence, including the Nevada Desert Experience [365].

The following is taken from Shannon, *War or Peace*, pp. 214-29.

392. Thomas J. Gumbleton, The Role of the Peacemaker

...There is a place deep within us, at the core of our being, where we are called to be the bearers of light and truth and love. And peace. The peace that surpasses all understanding does not just happen. Its seeds are planted in the center of our being. We have to let it grow and develop there; we have to allow it to be born within us. We have to look upon it as something precious beyond measure, something we are willing to nurture along by love and constant attention.

861

If there are violent and spiteful tendencies at our center, then it follows that we have become negligent toward the peace that should flower within us. Maybe we have not been as attentive to its needs as we might be. Maybe we have not recognized it as a pearl of great price. Maybe we have not seen clearly enough the change that has to take place within our hearts before we can become peacemakers. The birth of peace within our own hearts requires a certain amount of dying to ourselves. It is as tragic as it is ironic that the whole world today wants peace, yet there is hardly a spot on earth that is not a witness to brutality and turmoil. Part of the problem is that everyone wants peace on his or her own terms, terms which usually prove to be self-centered and narrow. Pope Paul spoke of peace in terms of justice and truth and harmony. But justice and harmony do not grow and thrive without care and responsiveness on our part....

Peace: A Gift Shared

...Our Lord blessed the peacemakers rather than the peaceful in order to tell us that it isn't enough to be easy within ourselves, to calm the storms raging within our hearts. If we really want to carry out the Father's will we can't stop there, sunning ourselves with inner peace. We have to go about calming the raging storms that put people at odds with one another, that threaten to push them farther apart, that leave them divided, discontented, jealous, cruel, indifferent to each other's needs. Surely this is why the Lord blesses the peacemakers and calls them the children of God. To reconcile enemies, to bring about justice and harmony among all people, to bear witness to truth and goodness: this truly is the work of the Lord, doing through his children what he would do himself. This truly is the will of the Father. This is what has been offered, urged, developed over thousands of years of Scriptures and finally revealed in Christ the Lord. This truly is the work of the peacemaker.

In the course of human history there have arisen men and women who dedicated themselves totally to the betterment of humankind; these people found the peace of the Lord deep within the core of their being. And when they began to externalize what was within them the human family was better for it....

Peace: A Gift Shared through Nonviolence

My own deepening conviction is that the present, intense insecurity in our world is a result of the failure to this point of many peacemakers simply to be sensitive enough to the will of the Father. Too many of us peacemakers have not truly given birth to the peace of the Lord within our hearts, because to do so requires that we die in a real way to ourselves; it involves pain and inconvenience and certainly a measure of selflessness. And because we have not been willing to do so, we have never really brought to life the peace of Jesus deep within ourselves. We have not learned to appreciate true peace as something precious beyond measure, something that we must nurture with love and constant attention. When Jesus, who is our peace, as St. Paul explains [Eph. 2:14], has come to life in the deep core of our being, we must make peace the only way to peace. There is no other way for the one who lives in him. His words, recorded by Matthew, could hardly be more clear. [Quotes Mt. 5:38-45, see 34.]

His example, emphasized to Peter who tried to defend him with force, backs up his words. Insisting that Peter put away his sword, Jesus follows the way of nonviolence even into the ultimate human darkness that is death [Mt. 26:47-56, see 37]. Violence he knew could only beget violence. The way of nonviolence, the way his Father called him, he trusted would lead even through death to life and – to peace! Long hours of prayer in communion with his Father brought him to know that his way was to be the way so beautifully described by the great prophet Isaiah. [Quotes 42:1-3.]

No president, no military commander, not many people at all, given to depend so much on the insights of human wisdom, would agree with him. But "those who believe" as St. Paul declares, join with him in the ever stronger conviction that "God's foolishness is wiser than human wisdom, and God's weakness is stronger than human strength" [1 Cor. 1:25]. This way of nonviolence must be the way of the Christian peacemaker. It is the way in which the peacemaker resists the evil of violence being perpetrated as "an act of aggression against the poor" in the arms race. It is the way of resistance also against that immoral posture of deterrence which is the stated policy of our government.

Will it work? Wrong question. Is it right? Is it the way of Jesus? This can be the only question of the Christian peacemaker.

Resist we must. But only nonviolently. Our resistance must be a witness to the truth, an effort to bring out truth. The work of the Christian peacemaker must start within our own society, to bring about its transformation, to make it a society of peace. Peace will beget peace, as surely as violence begets violence. When we are a peaceful people we will begin to bring peace to other nations and among nations.

But if we do not change our hearts and still harbor most of the old conflicts that have been with us all along, then it will be impossible for us to become peacemakers. What will happen is that we move into constant activity, where, if the interior search for peace becomes tiresome, we can still go through with the exterior motions of pursuing it? It almost seems tempting at times to forget about interior peace because that can prove a hindrance to what we would like to accomplish. And we'd like to accomplish a lot. A nuclear arms protest, for example, can offer a ray of light in a world growing darker with the threat of nuclear war, a war described by Thomas Merton as "a moral evil second only to the Crucifixion." Carried out in a nonviolent way, such a protest should be, as it was for Gandhi, a sign of truth and morality to all who witness the demonstration. But without a genuine commitment to nonviolence such a protest can, in fact, be an attack on those we name enemies. [See Merton, 366-370.]

No one acting in a nonviolent way will provoke anger where it need not be provoked or taunt those against whom a protest is made, or worst of all perhaps, wallow in a kind of proud and condescending self-righteousness that passes for courage and masks the weakness of those who falsely seek to be peacemakers. It becomes tempting to condemn, or at least dismiss as un-Christian and ignorant, anyone not fully appreciative of the demonstrator and all he or she is going through to give witness. To give witness does not mean showing others how wrong they are and letting it go at that. Such a tactic can be received as primarily a personal attack, leaving those responsible for the prevailing situation groping for defense measures or being forced to remain silent, feeling generous just to have put up with the demonstration at all. In fact, such violence will arouse so much antagonism that those enforcing or permitting injustice and violence become more firmly entrenched in what they are doing. This is not to say that ill-will is to be avoided at all cost; at times the price of telling the truth might well arouse terrible antagonism that is also cloaked with justification.

Clearly it is the role of the peacemaker to try to look not for the evil of those threatening the world with violence, with oppression, with nuclear annihilation, but to look for their goodness, their capability, and to begin working with them. Clearly the attitude of the nonviolent peacemaker ought to grow more receptive to possibilities of reconciliation within our own national community. Couldn't our dialogue with those whom we seek to reach express itself in affirmation rather than bitter negation, starting something like this: "Yes, we see eye to eye in that we both want peace, and we both see the need for a strong defense, and we both agree that the military power of the other side is very strong. But then we come to a parting of ways. Maybe your own search for peace, General, Senator, Reverend, would allow you to consider your policy formulations in light of these considerations which have not been taken into account...."

Could we not hope to begin exploring nonviolent ways to achieve national civil defense? Could we not start to put our abundant resources into a Department of Peace rather than continuing to fund a military establishment almost without limit? Could we not start to put forth much more effort into exploring the possible avenues to help reconcile those at odds with one another, finding the ways Einstein pleaded for to change "our modes of thinking?" Could not the Church, the state, the schools, the press, encourage such studies? So many valuable insights could be explored by drawing on the behavioral sciences: psychology, psychiatry, sociology, theology, philosophy, and biology. Could we not begin to disarm now?

Is it too presumptuous, too unrealistic to hope that we might approach a genuine spirit of understanding and reconciliation? I think not. And as we gradually bring this spirit to life and follow entirely new paths to peace in our own country, we could expect our leaders to begin to act in this way with leaders of other nations. Slowly but persistently the true peace of God – which is beyond all understanding – will begin to take firm root in our hearts and the hearts of our brothers and sisters everywhere.

"Blessed are the peacemakers. They shall be called God's children." If any of us wants to be among those called the children of God, our task is clear: nurture that tiny seed of peace within our own hearts. Even die a little to bring it to life. Reach out to a suffering world to bring about human development. *Resist* the immoral demands even of our own government. Challenge ourselves to grow in nonviolence. Seek constantly to find truth and goodness in others – even our "enemies." This is the role, the task, of the peacemaker. This is the call Jesus makes to us in asking us to follow him into the way of peace.

Will I answer this call? Will you? Will we be peacemakers? Our answer might well determine whether the world arrives at the year 2000 in peace or destroys itself before then.

CATHOLICS AND THE DEATH PENALTY

THE 1950S

Catholic opposition to the death penalty has a history as long as Christianity itself. We have already seen it at work among such early Christian writers as Athenagoras [52], Tertullian [55], Lactantius [81], and into the Middle Ages with such figures as Martin of Tours [89], Germanus of Auxerre [92], and Columban [110], and rarely imposed by the medieval penitential system [96-109]. In the Renaissance we have already seen in *Utopia* [214] Thomas More's brilliant satire upon a society that deprives people of every opportunity for a dignified life, pushes them into desperation and crime, and then exacts the death penalty for those very crimes.

Modern opposition to capital punishment stems from many of the same motives and religious impulses: one cannot claim a life of nonviolence if one allows the state to employ the ultimate violence as punishment for crimes. To this one must, of course, add to More's chorus that no evidence exists for the contention that capital punishment acts as a deterrent, and much modern sociological analysis demonstrates that the death penalty is exacted disproportionately upon the poor and people of color. With the abolition of the death penalty by South Africa in May 1995, the United States – along with communist China – became one of the last major nations on earth to impose it.

Anne Taillefer was a major figure at the *Catholic Worker* in New York from the 1950s through the 1960s and contributed many articles, poems, interviews, reviews, and news pieces, often on African and African-American topics, civil rights, and on French religious thought and culture.

The following selection is taken from *The Catholic Worker* 26.11 (June 1960): 3.

393. Anne Taillefer, Picketing Sing-Sing

It is natural for man to expect the color of the day to blend with his state of mind: the temple's veil is constantly torn in our hearts. Thus the radiant spring day that greeted us on May 19th as our minute group met in Grand Central Station, on our way to Sing Sing seemed perfectly alien. Edmund Leites, a student from Columbia, Robert Steed, who had just completed a 46-days fast and picketing for Chessman, and myself were going to picket Sing Sing prison all day to protest the execution of Flakes and Green, two Negroes who had killed the proprietor of a liquor store. The original idea was Edmund's and once before he and Bob had together taken this long walk of 12 hours....

The Law Watches

My companions had warned me that we might be greeted by an important police force at Ossining station; they also urged me to jump quickly from the train as the conductor, seeing their signs, had proved most uncooperative and the train had barely stopped. In my eagerness to comply I nearly jumped off one station ahead, but we arrived normally and inconspicuously at Ossining. That is excepting for a mysterious woman in a car who picked us up and drove us to the prison, as she had done last time it appears, without disclosing her identity or asking any questions. She seemed to be performing an urgent duty.

The twenty or so policemen of the preceding time had been reduced to two and we were allowed to approach the prison entrance which had not been possible previously. Doubtless the non-violence of the pickets had proved reassuring. A quiet street of frame houses inhabited by Negro families, with little children playing on the side-walk led us to our goal. Shady at first our route was later exposed to the blazing sun against which the prudent policemen protected themselves by sitting under one of the trees in the jail yard, some distance from us; only bounding up once to adjure me not to rest one minute – these were his orders – the picket was to march ceaselessly; but at least it was possible to relax within the time it took him to rush upon us. Life Goes On....

Negro Friends

At one we decided to go to lunch and found a clean little restaurant, down the hill, near the station with delicious, simple home-cooking. The warm, comely Negro woman who ran the place knew of our mission though we had left the signs uphill. Later on, in the evening when we came back for some soup she engaged in conversation with us. I wish I could reproduce her tone and her compassionate, simple and wise pronouncements. Her establishment was strategically placed between the station and the prison and the relatives of condemned people usually stopped there. The day before she had seen the young and beautiful wife of Green, a girl of 25. She talked simply of humanity, the inability to judge one's fellow-men's motives, of restoring life once taken; of poverty and all it entails.

More Pickets

The long, hot afternoon unwound itself the hours passing slowly and swiftly at the same time and a certain element of wonder filling us, myself at least, at the power of the body to bear this fatigue so easily as if vanquished by the will's mastery. As evening fell we were joined by other pickets from various groups, War Resisters, Society against Capital Punishment etc., nineteen in all. The Rev. Chinlund who, with Elaine de Koninck, had organized a march of protest for Chessman on April 27 was there. Around 7 o'clock we decided to change our picketing place to another more obvious to the citizens of Ossining and notified the police. Another policeman came down in a car where he sat watching us and we found a big, beefy man in his shirt-sleeves giving him directions literally spluttering with rage. The word rapist was constantly on his lips, nobody knew why, since the crime about to be paid for had nothing to do with it. As he drove away swerving violently I noticed with a sinking feeling that a plastic Sacred Heart wobbled on the bonnet of his car. What deep and murky depths lie in the heart of man, what obsessions. Perhaps capital punishment is nothing else after all than punishing one's own self.

The Time Comes

Night fell silently, deeply velvety, nailed with stars. Our serpentine file meandered back to the prison entrance where we tried to keep a silent vigil but were forbidden by the guards to stay immobile. We walked and walked but whispered to each other that we would pray at the time of the execution. At a quarter to ten somebody began reading the Beatitudes. At ten, wordlessly, Father Chinlund, who is a young Episcopal clergyman, very young and dignified-looking, sank wordlessly to his knees and all but four or five imitated him. The witnesses, the twelve who had the courage to assist to the murder, flashed by our kneeling figures, shielded by our signs. The great night stretched itself out more void, more immense. In terrible unison a despairing shriek, a night-owl doubtless, pierced the opaque silence.

Chapter 7: Catholic Peacemaking in the USA

Official Murder

A great dance of death began to whirl in one's mind, to bob and to fall. The young and the old. The innocent and the guilty, since Abel, joined hands. One thought of Algeria and of Nuremberg, of the Rosenbergs. Of the terrible music in the Dialogue of the Carmelites the whacking sound of every head falling off. And the night owl screeched again to the dreadful understatement of the radio car announcing: "OK, Let's go." The guards, it must be said, left us alone and were silent.

And then as the concrete bit more sharply into our knees the twelve cars flashed out again, some very slowly, reading our signs maybe. And there was nothing left but to go home.

A friend who had followed all this in her heart, being unable to come, said to me two days later: "Your prayers were heard perhaps. These poor men chose to see the Catholic chaplain and kissed his hand just before death. And their death lasted but a few minutes."

Sometimes the Lord does give an answer to our terrible bewilderment. And thus from the third chair came a faint whisper: "Tonight you will be with me...." A voice heard by the separated brethren, reunited in love, the one protesting outside, the other healing inside....

THE 1990s

Born into a middle-class family in Baton Rouge, Louisiana in the early 1940s, Helen Prejean was educated in whites-only Catholic schools, enjoyed the pleasures of foreign travel and the privileges of being white in the old South of segregation and violence against African-Americans.

In 1981 she was assigned by the Sisters of St. Joseph to a ministry in the slums of the St. Thomas section of New Orleans, and there she experienced the inequalities of American life first-hand, just as she deepened her understanding of peacemaking through reading Gandhi, Dorothy Day, and Martin Luther King. Her book is a personal account of her experience in befriending a convicted murderer awaiting execution. She is a frequent guest speaker and lecturer and has appeared on national and international media concerning the death penalty.

The following selection is taken from Helen Prejean, C.S.J., *Dead Man Walking: An Eyewitness Account of the Death Penalty in the United States*, New York: Random House, 1993, pp. 3-22.

394. Helen Prejean, Patrick Sonnier on Death Row

...I also notice that when [African-American] residents of St. Thomas [an impoverished parish in Louisiana] are killed, the newspaper barely takes notice, whereas when white citizens are killed, there is often a front-page story....

...Between 1975 and 1991 Louisiana expanded its adult prisons from three to twelve, with prison populations increasing by 249 percent. Throughout the 1980s Louisiana ranked first, second, or third in the nation as the state incarcerating the greatest number of its residents – at an annual cost per inmate of $15,000, and that doesn't include the cost of prison construction, about $50,000 for the average prison bed. Louisiana's exponential prison expansion is part of a national trend. In 1980 about 500,000 Americans were behind bars; in 1990, 1.1 million – the highest confinement rate in the world. And if parole and probation systems are included, in 1990 the United States had in its criminal justice system 1 of every 43 adults, 1 of every 24 men, and 1 of every 162 women, at the cost of $20 billion a year. Between 1981 and 1991 the federal government cut its contribution to education by 25 percent (in real dollars) and increased its allocation for criminal justice by 29 percent.

Almost every family I meet in St. Thomas has a relative in prison. (In 1989 one in four black men in the twenty-to-twenty-nine age group was under the control of the criminal justice system.) As one woman put it, "our young men leave here either in a police car or a hearse."...

After getting the name of the death-row inmate from Chava, that very night after supper I write my first letter. My new pen pal is a white man, a Cajun from St. Martinville. That's a surprise. I had assumed he would be black. I tell Mr. Sonnier a little about myself and where I work and that if he doesn't want to write back, that's okay, I'll keep writing to him anyway....

We soon become steady correspondents, and I begin to think of him as a fellow human being, though I can't for a moment forget his crime, nor can I reconcile the easygoing Cajun who writes to me with the brutal murderer of two helpless teenagers....

I telephone Chava and ask if I might come to the Coalition office to read the Sonnier files....

I don't know anything about the legal issues in these cases. Once Pat mentioned that he had got a letter from his attorney, but only in passing, and he has never mentioned legal issues. I gather that he has a lot of confidence in his attorney. Since the man offered on his own to take the case, I assume he must be good at what he does.

I look down at the mound of documents.

As Chava leaves he says, "Pull the door behind you when you leave. It'll lock," and he's gone.

There are seven volumes of transcripts. I slide them to one side of the table and open a folder labeled "Correspondence." I find a letter from Eddie Sonnier, Pat's brother, written from parish jail.

"These lawyers we have, I'm not sure what all they're doing for me and my brother because we hardly ever see them. Can you help us?"

I open the top folder full of newspaper clippings.

"Leads are few in murder here," the November 7, 1977, front-page headline of the *New Iberian* announces, and I look down upon the smiling faces of a teenage couple. The young man has laughing eyes and the young woman, a serene half-smile. The article tells how on the Friday evening before the murders, David LeBlanc, age seventeen, and Loretta Bourque, eighteen, had been "just two happy faces in the crowd at Catholic High School's homecoming football game." The couple had each been shot three times at close range in the back of the head with a .22-caliber rifle.

The day after the bodies of the couple are discovered, the *Iberian* runs an editorial, which says in part, "It's hard to imagine that there may be somebody in this fine community of ours who could contemplate, much less carry out, this vilest of vile deeds."

It takes a month to capture the killers. Their sneering faces appear on the front page of the *Iberian* December 2 issue: Elmo Patrick Sonnier, age twenty-seven, and Eddie James Sonnier, age twenty. The article says that the brothers are being held in neighboring parish jails without bond and have been given attorneys to represent them at the court's expense.

In addition to the murder charges, the Sonnier brothers face ten counts of aggravated kidnapping and one charge of aggravated rape. Law enforcement authorities have revealed that a number of teenage couples in the area, six weeks before the murders, had been attacked at the local lovers' lane. Two men, posing as security officers, would handcuff the men and molest the women. Most of the couples were too afraid or too ashamed to come forward, parish deputies said, but now, in the wake of the killings, the young people are revealing what happened to them and identifying the Sonnier brothers as the assailants.

As the trials take place, the horror of David LeBlanc's and Loretta Bourque's last evening of life unfolds: the Sonniers rabbit hunting with .22 rifles, the couple parked in a lovers' lane, the Sonniers posing as security officers, the young people accused of "trespassing" and handcuffed together in the back seat of a car and driven twenty miles down dark, abandoned roads, the car stopping in an abandoned oil field and the girl taken off by herself in the woods and raped, the couple being ordered to lie face down on the ground.

That would be their last physical sensation before the shots were fired: the cold, dew-laden grass. The coroner testifies that they died instantly.

The brothers' confessions are riddled with contradictions. At first, Patrick Sonnier says he shot the young people because he didn't want to go back to Angola [state prison], where he had served time in 1968 for stealing a truck, and he was afraid the couple would identify him to the police. He confesses to the murders not once but two, three, four times over several days. He takes law officers to the scene of the crime and points out the place where he stood as he fired the gun. But then at his trial he says he confessed because he was afraid of the police and that in fact it was his brother who had gone "berserk" and killed the teenagers. But Eddie Sonnier at his brother's trial testifies that it was Patrick who had committed the murders, that he had been afraid of him and had held the flashlight while Patrick shot the youngsters. Both admit to the kidnapping; Patrick denies raping the girl, but Eddie says his brother did have sex with the girl and admits to having sexual intercourse with her himself but claims she was "willing."

At separate trials each brother is found guilty of first-degree murder and sentenced to death, but Eddie Sonnier's death sentence is overturned by the Louisiana Supreme Court, which holds Patrick Sonnier to be the triggerman and Eddie, the younger brother, not as culpable. Patrick Sonnier's death sentence is also overturned by the Louisiana Supreme Court because of the judge's improper jury instruction. At Patrick's second sentencing trial, Eddie, declaring, "I want to tell the truth and get everything off my chest" testifies that it was he who had killed the teenagers, that he had "lost it," because the boy's name was David and shortly before the killings his girlfriend had spurned him for a man named David – not the victim – and something the boy had said had triggered his rage, something had "come over him," and the two Davids had blurred in his mind and the gun was in his hand and he had fired.

872

But the prosecutor discredits this confession of guilt, arguing that Eddie Sonnier, his death sentence now overturned by the court, is transparently trying to save his brother from the electric chair. The jury readily agrees with the prosecutor and resentences Patrick Sonnier to death.

Information about the Bourque and LeBlanc families filters through the news articles.

"The Sonniers exterminated the LeBlanc name," Lloyd LeBlanc tells a reporter. He and his wife, Eula, are older and do not expect other children. David was their only son. The LeBlancs are Catholics who attend Mass regularly and send their children to Catholic schools. They have one other child, Vickie, who is attending college.

Loretta Bourque was the oldest daughter of Godfrey and Goldie Bourque's seven children. The Bourques' youngest child, Hubert, age five, was born with severe brain damage and cannot walk, talk, or feed himself. He lives in a crib in the Bourques' living room and the family calls him God's "special angel." The Bourques are devout Catholics.

The sun is setting and a shaft of orange filters through one of the tall windows. I close the folder and put my head in my hands.

A boy and girl, their young lives budding, unfolding. Snipped.

And their parents, condemned to wonder for the rest of their lives about their children's last tortured hours; sentenced for the rest of their days to fear for their families, their other children; startled out of their sleep at night by dreams of the terror that ripped their children from them.

The details of the depravity stun me. It is like the spinning merry-go-round that I had once tried to climb aboard when I was a child, but it was spinning too fast and it threw me to the ground.

You may take the documents home, Chava had said, but I do not want to take them home. I know enough. More than enough. I leave the documents on the table and walk across the dying sunlight to the door and close it behind me, the words of Jeremiah welling within me:

A voice was heard in Ramah,
sobbing and lamenting:
Rachel weeping for her children,
refusing to be comforted
because they were no more [31:15]....

Louisiana used to hang its criminals until the state legislature in 1940 decided that electrocution would be more humane and efficient. Hanging didn't always work. As the noose was placed around the condemned's neck, the knot had to be positioned exactly right, or the victim died a slow death by strangulation – or worse, decapitation, if the distance of the drop was disproportionate to body weight.

Death by electrocution was introduced in the United States in 1890 at Auburn Prison in upstate New York, when William Kemmler was killed by the state of New York. The *New York Times* described the new method as "euthanasia by electricity," and the U.S. Supreme Court, upholding the state appellate court's decision that death by electricity was not cruel and unusual punishment, had concluded: "It is in easy reach of the electrical science at this day to so generate and apply to the person of the convict a current of electricity of such known and sufficient force as certainly to produce instantaneous and therefore painless death."

A reporter for the *New World* newspaper who witnessed Kemmler's execution reported:

"The current had been passing through his body for 15 seconds when the electrode at the head was removed. Suddenly the breast heaved. There was a straining at the straps which bound him. A purplish foam covered the lips and was spattered over the leather head band. The man was alive.

"Warden, physician, guards...everybody lost their wits. There was a startled cry for the current to be turned on again...An odor of burning flesh and singed hair filled the room, for a moment, a blue flame played about the base of the victim's spine. This time the electricity flowed four minutes...."

That was in 1890.

On October 16, 1985, the electrocution of William Vandiver by the state of Indiana took seventeen minutes, requiring five charges of electricity.

On April 22, 1983, as the state of Alabama electrocuted John Louis Evans, the first electrical charge burned through the electrode on the leg and the electrode fell off. The prison guards repaired it and administered another charge of electricity. Smoke and flame erupted from Evans's temple and leg but the man was still alive. Following the second jolt, Evans's lawyer demanded that Governor George C. Wallace halt the proceedings. The governor refused. Another jolt was administered. It took fourteen minutes for Evans to die.

On May 5, 1990, as the state of Florida killed Jesse Tafero, flames shot six inches from the hood covering his head. The executioner interrupted the standard two-minute 2,000-volt electrical cycle and officials later determined that a sponge on Tafero's head had caught fire.

The only man to walk away from an electric chair alive was seventeen-year-old Willie Francis. On May 2, 1946, he was strapped into Louisiana's portable electric chair in the jail in St. Martin Parish. As the current hit his body, witnesses reported that the youth's "lips puffed out and he groaned and jumped so that the chair came off the floor, and he said, 'Take it off. Let me breathe.' The officials applied several more jolts, but Francis was still alive. They then helped him back to his cell to recuperate from the ordeal.

The U.S. Supreme Court, considering whether it could be considered "cruel and unusual punishment" or "double jeopardy" to subject Francis to electrocution a second time, rendered a split verdict. On May 8, 1947, Louisiana officials once again strapped Willie Francis into the chair, but this time they succeeded in killing him.

Witnesses over the years have rendered graphic descriptions of state electrocutions, which Justice William F. Brennan, in *Glass v. Louisiana,* included in his dissenting opinion:

"The hands turn red, then white, and the cords of the neck stand out like steel bands.... The prisoner's limbs, fingers, toes, and face are severely contorted.... The force of the electric current is so powerful that the prisoner's eyeballs sometimes pop out on his cheeks.... The prisoner often defecates, urinates, and vomits blood and drool.... Sometimes the prisoner catches fire.... There is a sound like bacon frying and the sickly sweet smell of burning flesh...when the post-electrocution autopsy is performed the liver is so hot that doctors said it cannot be touched by the human hand.... The body frequently is badly burned....

It is a common opinion that persons subjected to 2,000 volts of electricity lose consciousness immediately and feel no pain. But Dr. Harold Hillman, director of the Unity Laboratory in Applied Neurology, University of Surrey, England, thinks otherwise. Hillman, who studied autopsies of thirteen men electrocuted in the Florida and Alabama electric chairs from 1983 to 1990, concluded that such executions are "intensely painful" because the prisoner may for some time retain consciousness. For death to be instantaneous, he maintains, the full force of the electrical current would have to reach the brain. Instead, he says, only a small percentage of the current may be reaching the brain because the greater portion travels through and over the skin to reach the other electrode.

The autopsies of electrocuted prisoners which he studied reveal that there was minimal damage to the brain in comparison to massive burns to the skin.

He adds, "The massive electric current stimulates all the muscles to full contraction. Thus, the prisoner cannot react by any further movement, even when the current is turned off for a short period, and the heart is still beating, as has been documented in numerous cases of execution by electrocution. It is usually thought that the failure of the convict to move is a sign that he cannot feel. He cannot move because all his muscles are contracting maximally."

Later, in the months ahead, Patrick Sonnier will confide his terror to me of the death that awaits him, telling me of a recurring nightmare, always the same: the guards coming for him, dragging him screaming toward the chair, strapping him in with the wide leather straps, covering his face with the hood, and he is screaming, "No, no, no...." For him there can never again be restful, unbroken sleep, because the dream can always come. Better, he says, to take short naps and not to sink into deep sleep.

I cannot accept that the state now plans to kill Patrick Sonnier in cold blood. But the thought of the young victims haunts me. Why do I feel guilty when I think of them? Why do I feel as if I have murdered someone myself?

In prayer I sort it out.

I know that if I had been at the scene when the young people were abducted, I would have done all in my power to save them.

I know I feel compassion for their suffering parents and family and would do anything to ease their pain if I knew how. I also know that nothing can ease some pain.

I know I am trying to help people who are desperately poor, and I hope I can prevent some of them from exploding into violence. Here my conscience is clean and light. No heaviness, no guilt.

Then it comes to me. The victims are dead and the killer is alive and I am befriending the killer.

Have I betrayed his victims? Do I have to take sides? I am acutely aware that my beliefs about the death penalty have never been tested by personal loss. Let Mama or my sister, Mary Ann, or my brother, Louie, be brutally murdered and then see how much compassion I have. My magnanimity is gratuitous. No one has shot my loved ones in the back of the head.

If someone I love should be killed, I know I would feel rage, loss, grief, helplessness, perhaps for the rest of my life. It would be arrogant to think I can predict how I would respond to such a disaster. But Jesus Christ, whose way of life I try to follow, refused to meet hate with hate and violence with violence. I pray for the strength to be like him. I cannot believe in a God who metes out hurt for hurt, pain for pain, torture for torture. Nor do I believe that God invests human representatives with such power to torture and kill. The paths of history are stained with the blood of those who have fallen victim to "God's Avengers." Kings and Popes and military generals and heads of state have killed, claiming God's authority and God's blessing. I do not believe in such a God.

In sorting out my feelings and beliefs, there is, however, one piece of moral ground of which I am absolutely certain: if I were to be murdered I would not want my murderer executed. I would not want my death avenged. *Especially by government* – which can't be trusted to control its own bureaucrats or collect taxes equitably or fill a pothole, much less decide which of its citizens to kill.

Albert Camus' "Reflections on the Guillotine" is for me a moral compass on the issue of capital punishment. He wrote this essay in 1957 when the stench of Auschwitz was still in the air, and one of his cardinal points is that no government is ever innocent enough or wise enough or just enough to lay claim to so absolute a power as death.

> Society proceeds sovereignly to eliminate the evil ones from her midst as if she were virtue itself. Like an honorable man killing his wayward son and remarking: "Really, I didn't know what to do with him."... To assert, in any case, that a man must be absolutely cut off from society because he is absolutely evil amounts to saying that society is absolutely good, and no one in his right mind will believe this today....

I am beginning to notice something about Pat Sonnier. In each of his letters he expresses gratitude and appreciation for my care. He makes no demands. He doesn't ask for money. He does not request my phone number (inmates at Angola are allowed to make collect phone calls). He only says how glad he is to have someone to communicate with because he has been so lonely. The sheer weight of his loneliness, his abandonment, draws me. I abhor the evil he has done. But I sense something, some sheer and essential humanness, and that, perhaps, is what draws me most of all.

In my next letter I ask him if anyone ever comes to see him, and he says, no, there is no one. So I ask how I might go about visiting him....

THE PERSIAN GULF WAR

After a full generation of mass movements, peace studies programs, books, workshops, media presentations, films honoring peacemakers, legislative support, peace candidates and the adoption of peace slogans by those in positions of power and influence in the crucial weeks leading up to the Persian Gulf War the American peace movement found itself marginalized and impotent to prevent the high-tech slaughter that would ensue. Why? The following texts present a selection of peacemaking approaches to the Gulf War from within the Catholic tradition that may help resolve this question.

THE U.S. CATHOLIC BISHOPS

The newly emerging positions of Gospel nonviolence that characterize large sections of *The Challenge of Peace* were always understood to have been the result of committee work and of compromise among individuals and groups among the U.S. Conference of Bishops. Cold War – and just-war – arguments and beliefs survived not only the Vietnam era but also the Reagan era of the 1980s at the same time that nonviolence became more and more accepted as a Catholic option. Thus one should not be surprised that a reservoir of just-war thinking remained within leading Catholic circles to provide the Bush administration with its religious justification to go to war against Iraq. Yet what did take many Catholic peacemakers by surprise – and left many in bewildered shock – was the readiness with which most Americans, and most Catholics, accepted the just-war arguments put forward and the vehemence with which they rejected nonviolent solutions.

The new synthesis of traditions – and the differences in Catholic thinking that this could at times produce – is evident in the USCC Letter to the Secretary of State of November 7, 1990 laying out the bishops' concerns and pointing to *several* possible religious approaches to the coming war. In paragraph 1 the bishops identification of "We" clearly with the United States and its political and military objectives revives the old Constantinian alliance of church and state that was so characteristic of the American church in this century. While nonviolent resolution of the crisis is urged – more than once – the unspoken discourse of this letter reduces all Catholic teaching on war and peace to one set of criteria alone: not those of the Gospel but those of the "just war." Thus the bishop's letter appears to concede from the start that the issue here is really one left to the judgment of the government alone. The church here acts merely as an advisor, and the unspoken assumption is that the Catholic hierarchy represents the entire Catholic church in the United States.

The bishops' letter thus appears to reject many of the developments in Catholic thought and action that have taken place during the twentieth century. One might – with only slight exaggeration – compare this statement of principle to a briefing paper to the U.S. government on how best to anticipate and fend off objections to U.S. intervention in the Gulf on superficially religious grounds, inviting the Bush administration to take up their call for a "just" war. Its repeated use of "could" and "would" anticipates the uses put to the letter by the U.S. adminsitration and underscores its presumption of eventual U.S. military action. Gone is any of the prophetic call of the Vietnam years, of the Central American crisis of the 1980s, or indeed of the heroic stance taken in *The Challenge of Peace*.

The following is excerpted from the statement reprinted in *The Reporter for Conscience's Sake* 47.8 (Sept.-Oct. 1990): 1-2.

395. U.S. Catholic Conference of Bishops, Letter to Secretary of State James Baker, November 7, 1990

Dear Mr. Secretary:

I write as Chairman of the International Policy Committee of the U.S. Catholic Conference to share several concerns and criteria regarding possible use of U.S. military force in the Persian Gulf. As Catholic bishops we are deeply concerned about the human consequences of the crisis – the lives already lost or those that could be lost in a war, the freedom denied to hostages, the victims of aggression and the many families divided by the demands of military service. As religious teachers, we are concerned about the moral dimensions of the crisis the need to resist brutal aggression, to protect the innocent, to pursue both justice and peace, as well as the ethical criteria for the use of force. As U.S.

citizens, we are concerned about how our nation can best protect human life and human rights and secure a peaceful and just resolution to the crisis.

Our Conference has thus far emphasized five basic issues in addressing the crisis:

(1) The clear need to resist aggression. We [i.e., the U.S.A.] cannot permit nations [i.e., Iraq] to simply overwhelm others [i.e., Kuwait] by brutal use of force.

(2) The need for broad-based, international solidarity which seeks effective and peaceful means to halt and reverse aggression. We strongly support the United Nations actions and the international pressure which has effectively halted Iraqi aggression and offers hope for the peaceful liberation of Kuwait.

(3) The need to condemn the taking of hostages and the mistreatment and killing of civilians. We deplore the cynical and intolerable actions of the Iraqi government in taking innocent civilians against their will and using them for protection or propaganda, as well as, the brutal treatment of civilians in Kuwait.

(4) The essential need to distinguish between the leaders of Iraq and the civilians of Iraq and Kuwait. In the carrying out of the embargo and other actions we need to take care so that innocent civilians are not deprived of those essentials for the maintenance of life, i.e. food and medicines.

(5) The imperative to seek a peaceful resolution of the crisis and pursue legitimate objectives by nonviolent diplomatic means. We continue to call for effective solidarity, perseverance and patience in the search for a peaceful and just outcome to the crisis.

It is on this last point, the persistent pursuit of a peaceful solution, that I write to you now. As the Administration assesses the military and geopolitical implications of initiating combat, we also ask you to carefully assess the moral consequences of resort to war.

Our country needs an informed and substantive discussion of the human and ethical dimensions of the policy choices under consideration. In the Catholic community, there is a long history of ethical reflection on these issues and diverse points of view. As Chairman of this committee, I share these reflections with you, not to offer a definitive judgment but to suggest some essential values, and raise some key questions which must be considered as the U.S. explores its options. We hope they will contribute to the necessary and growing public debate about whether the use of military force could be morally justified and under what, if any, conditions. We specifically seek to draw attention to the *ethical* dimensions of those choices, so that they are not ignored or neglected in a focus on simply military and geopolitical considerations.

In our tradition, while the use of force is not ruled out absolutely, there is a clear presumption against war. The right to self-defense or to repel aggression is restricted and governed by a series of moral principles, often called the "just war" theory. These criteria spell out the conditions which have to be met for war to be morally permissible.... [Reviews the just-war criteria. See **194-198** and **253**.]

In addition to these criteria, there are others which govern the conduct of war. These principles include proportionality and discrimination, i.e., the military means used must be commensurate with the evil to be overcome and must be directed at the aggressors, not innocent people. For example, the Second Vatican declared:

> any act of war aimed indiscriminately at the destruction of entire cities or of extensive areas along with their population is a crime against God and man himself. It merits unequivocal and unhesitating condemnation.

Military action against Iraq would have to be restrained by these two principles, necessarily ruling out tactics and strategies which could clearly target civilian lives. This means this war would have to be a limited war, raising again the criteria of the probability of success and the price to be paid given the hostile physical environment, the fragility of the anti-Iraq alliance and the volatility of regional and domestic political support.

These considerations lead me to strongly urge that the U.S., in continued cooperation with the United Nations, the Soviet Union, Arab states and other nations, stay the course of persistent, peaceful and determined pressure against Iraq. A resort to war in violation of these criteria would jeopardize many lives, raise serious moral questions and undermine the international solidarity against Iraq. We understand that a strong military presence can give credibility to a vigorous pursuit of non-violent solutions to the crisis. My concern is that the pressure to use military force may grow as the pursuit of non-violent options almost inevitably become difficult, complex and slow. Strength, creativity and persistence are virtues required for a peaceful and just conclusion of this crisis. They may also open the door for a new, broader and more imaginative dialogue concerning the deep-seated and long-standing problems which have contributed to the current situation.

We pray for the safety and welfare of the peoples of that troubled region. We pray for the liberation of the hostages and the people of Kuwait. We pray that the American men and women deployed in the Gulf may by their presence support a peaceful resolution of the crisis and return home safely and soon. And, finally, we pray that our leaders and all other parties concerned will have the persistence, wisdom and skill to resolve the current crisis in peace and with justice.

Sincerely yours,

Most Reverend Roger M. Mahoney

Archbishop of Los Angeles

Chairman, International Policy Committee

PAX CHRISTI/USA

In stark contrast to the U.S. bishops (nearly 100 of whom were members of this organization at the time of *The Challenge of Peace*) Pax Christi condemned the war in no uncertain terms, calling on Catholics and Americans in general to heed the words of the Gospels.

396. Pax Christi, Statement on the Gulf War, January 1991

Pax Christi USA cries out in anguish at the outbreak of war in the Middle East. The tragedy of this terrible violence is unspeakable. Pax Christi has always held that, according to the gospel and Catholic social teaching, attempts to resolve the Persian Gulf crisis militarily are immoral. We especially condemn the decision by the United States to launch air attacks against military targets in Baghdad and other civilian areas, and we remind the US government that putting civilians at risk cannot be tolerated.

The US has put into force a huge array of superior technologies against Iraq. We remind our government that reliance on the technologies of death, no matter how sophisticated, will not bring about peace in the Persian Gulf. We have unleashed forces for destruction and hatred which we cannot begin to imagine.

We call for an immediate halt to the air war against Iraq and a complete cease fire; for the establishment of zones of peace where civilians will be given sanctuary from the ravages of war; for the placing of UN peacekeeping forces between the warring factions; for immediate international aid to be given to all war refugees; and for a diplomatic resolution of this conflict which includes an international conference to address the historical, geographic and political issues that divide the Middle East.

As followers of Jesus, we are compelled to raise our voices and to act in protest. We pledge to resist this war, to join with others in nonviolent demonstrations, vigils and acts of civil disobedience.

Pax Christi believes that if sanctions had been given enough time to take effect, war could have been averted. We voice strong opposition to our government's unyielding attitude which substituted ultimatums for true negotiations.

Time and again in recent months, we have rejected the ominous march toward war. We condemned the Iraqi invasion of Kuwait. We condemned the escalation of conflict occasioned by the United States' massive military buildup in the Persian Gulf. We called "tragic and immoral" the UN Security Council's decision to authorize the use of force in the region. We insisted on the pursuit of honest negotiations to achieve a diplomatic solution.

Pax Christi once again calls on all people of good will to fast and pray. This war is an affront to all humanity, especially the poor. It is an assault on the created order and cries to God for justice.

SOLITARY WITNESS: THE GULF COS

While the draft had long been suspended and the U.S. military depended solely upon an "all-volunteer" system, many in the peace movement had long claimed that the Selective Service draft had been replaced by a system of economic conscription, a "poverty draft." With meaningful work and real wages constantly shrinking through the 1980s many poor Americans saw the military as the only viable way to get work, housing, and whatever job training it promised. Thus many entered the armed forces out of a complex set of motives, many of which had little to do with fighting, killing, or dying for their country. As the passage below will also demonstrate, many young servicepeople had little or no understanding or education in the moral and religious aspects of their military duties.

Not surprisingly, once hostilities seemed likely to begin, the U.S. government had no desire to allow an anti-war movement to develop around the Gulf War. While hundreds of thousands of protesters filled the streets in Washington, DC and other major cities to prevent the coming war, the major media ignored the peacemakers. Learning from its experience during the Vietnam War, the government was also determined to allow very little access to military personnel from peacemakers intent upon offering counseling to possible war objectors within the military. With both the American public and the members of the armed forces cut off from any knowledge of widespread dissent over the war, individuals within the military thus faced a very lonely decision to come forward as conscientious objectors. In the passage below one such objector recounts his own experience and the gradual conversion that led to it.

The following is taken from Margaret Q. Garvey, "Soldier with Courage not to Kill is in Trouble," *National Catholic Reporter* (Dec. 28, 1990): 7.

397. *Gary C. Stiegelmeyer, Conscientious Objection to the Gulf War*

South Bend, Ind. I have just returned from a nine-day visit to the front lines of battle in which American soldiers are waging peace.

At the invitation of the Mennonite Church and with some hastily summoned financial help from generous institutions and individuals, five of us were "rapidly deployed" in locations close to the American military bases of Germany whose personnel are now being poured into the Persian Gulf region and prepared to kill Iraqis on behalf of the United States. Our purpose was and is to counsel and assist men and women among them who cannot, in conscience, agree to do this work. It has been my privilege to spend time with one particularly courageous young man whose ordeal exemplifies what happens when profound Christian convictions encounter the expedience of a nation state.

Gary C. Stiegelmeyer, a Catholic from Cleveland, is in the 123rd Division's Delta Company. Five years ago, at 17, an adolescent impressed by the presentation of a recruiter and desirous of a career as an automobile mechanic, Stiegelmeyer enlisted in the Army. He underwent basic training and attended mechanic school at Fort Jackson, S.C.

On Dec. 16 this year, having refused to accept the weapon he had been issued, he was physically carried aboard a military aircraft bound for Saudi Arabia from Nüremberg, Germany, and has not been heard of since. According to current military directives, his claim of conscientious objection will not be processed until he is in the zone of combat.

Stiegelmeyer is not a remarkably articulate person, but his testimony is animated by an eloquence as old and new as the gospel and well worth quoting at length: "I really believe that I want to leave the Army because I don't want anyone to die, friend or foe," he wrote December 12 as he gave notice of his request for conscientious objector status. "I don't think anyone wants to kill another man, but war makes them do it. My belief is: I choose not to kill another man. In war, even if you are 'victorious,' you still lose because people are wounded in their minds and spirits because they have killed and seen others be killed. I never had anyone who would listen to me and talk about these beliefs, but when I got married last March, I could talk then. My wife, Tina, has given me inspiration and challenge to face my thoughts of right and wrong. I never took time to do that before.

"I haven't been in a family since I was 17. The coming together as family made my beliefs come out. We could talk. My family loves me and I love them. I've never had anyone close listen to my problems. In the Army I never felt comfortable talking to my superiors or peers about any of this. Instead, I'd get drunk. Now that's changed through the support of my family.

"I cannot kill men, because they are created in the image of God.... How can I kill someone who 'my government' makes as the enemy. It is not the man, it is the government's belief you fight in a war.

"Before the [Berlin] wall came down [see **311-319**], I was trained that East Germans and Eastern Bloc Countries were bad. Now that the wall is down...we meet the people we were supposed to kill and we realize that they are the same as you and me. It's just the government that makes them as a threat. How can I kill a person like that? A person just like me.

"...I remember my old ways – I don't want my old ways back.

"In the future I plan to use my beliefs to be a good husband and father to teach my children to stand up for their beliefs. I would teach them right from wrong. I would teach them that it is wrong to kill or to participate in acts of violence. It is courage to fight [for] what you believe in. I know it is wrong to kill."

Every Catholic in the nation, if not every citizen within or without its military forces, must be prepared to make increasingly dreadful and costly moral decisions as the Gulf crisis intensifies. Those who choose, as Gary Stiegelmeyer has chosen, to resist in the name of God the violent enterprise on which their nation is embarked deserve far more than they have yet received of the pastoral attention and institutional support of their church.

Because they are, at the moment, her most faithful witness.

THE GULF WAR AT HOME

In retrospect, the implicit consent to the war by the U.S. bishops, the isolation of Catholic peacemakers by the public at large, and the desperate protests by individual objectors within the military should have been no surprise to those within the Catholic peace movement. Since the Vietnam era the aging of the college generation into middle age, the waning of interest in concerns left behind, the economic and social pressures of the Reagan era on the majority of Americans, and the continued concentration of power and influence by the national media had turned the attention of most Americans away from issues of war, peace, and social justice.

Thus while Catholic peacemakers could point with pride to the growth of Pax Christi or an emerging theology of peacemaking, in many ways they seem to have drifted away from the concerns of the mainstream of their contemporaries who now longed – for good or bad – for some form of "normalcy" more in keeping with former attitudes (real or imagined) toward government and authority. In the end both the sudden onslaught of the war and Catholic peacemakers' inability to prevent it had to be understood in the context of a far more complex Catholic model of attitudes toward war and peace than many had been led to believe existed. One year after the war the journalist David Scott interviewed many Catholics on their attitudes toward war and peace and published his fascinating – and troublesome findings.

The following is excerpted from David Scott, "Fighting Words: Why Catholics Disagree about War," *U.S. Catholic* 57.5 (May 1992): 6-12.

398. David Scott, Who Teaches Peace?

At the height of the U.S.-led war in the Persian Gulf a year ago, a pop-radio station in Erie, Pennsylvania decided to take a poll. Who is the greater monster, the station wondered, Iraqi President Saddam Hussein or the Benedictine sisters who run Pax Christi USA [**380**], the national Catholic peace group based in Erie? It was a tight race, but the nuns won.

Erie is one of those all-American cities where companies test market their products to gauge how well they'll sell in other parts of the country. And since seven out of every ten residents are Catholic, Erie might also be considered a barometer of current Catholic thinking and opinion.

In fact the Erie radio poll was fairly representative of today's Catholic conversation about war. When Catholics talk about war, it's more like an argument than a dialogue – passionate beliefs clash on a battlefield where nobody gives an inch and there's no neutral ground. And in the year since the Persian Gulf War, participants say, the debate has been getting louder and more urgent.…

Even those who never agreed with the militant antimilitarism of the Catholic left regret what they see as a widespread Catholic ignorance of the church's war-and-peace teachings. Like too many other basic Catholic teachings, the church's precepts on warfare are not widely known, [Cardinal Anthony] Bevilacqua [of Philadelphia] acknowledges. "War only becomes an issue when there is a war involving the United States," the cardinal says. "If we don't have warfare, I don't think people are that interested."

A 1990 study by Pax Christi's Center on Conscience and War found that basic terms of the Catholic conversation on war weren't widely recognized by Catholic high-school students and faculty. After years of pastoral work in various parishes, [Sister Christine] Mulready, CSJ says the same is true for people in the pews.

"Most [U.S. citizens] form a moral judgment on war based solely on whether or not legitimate authority has called them to arms," she says.

Some say that indifference or rejection of Catholic moral teaching is most pronounced on military bases and battlefields. Although dozens of Catholics applied for conscientious-objector status during the Gulf War, for most Catholic soldiers and chaplains their religion posed no obstacle to their participating in a war.

Marine Corporal Kevin Kirby spent more than nine months in the Persian Gulf after shipping out of Camp Pendleton, California just after Iraq's invasion of Kuwait in August 1990. He attended Mass each week when the Catholic chaplain made his rounds.

But Kirby says neither he nor the chaplain nor his Catholic comrades ever discussed the morality of the conflict or the church's teachings on war and peace. Moreover he didn't hear anything about the Catholic bishops' debates on the justice of the war or the two letters [Archbishop of Los Angeles Joseph] Ryan wrote to Gulf War chaplains and troops.

He acknowledges that he had never received any formal instruction in the church's war-and-peace teachings while growing up. Nevertheless he sensed that he was engaged in an unjust war.

"I feel it wasn't right for us to be there," he says. "It wasn't our war."

Still he would never have considered conscientious objection, even though it is allowed in the Catholic tradition.

"I signed a contract that says that I was a Marine, and I do what they want," he explains.

The experience of Father Donald Rutherford, a chaplain with the elite 82nd Airborne Division out of Fort Bragg, North Carolina, is similar. He received and read the two letters written by Ryan, the military archbishop, during the war.

But he says he was too busy to initiate discussions on moral issues with troops in his charge. Nor did any Catholic soldiers approach him with moral qualms about the war....

The closer to the center of Catholic efforts to make peace, the more the shock of the Persian Gulf War seemed to have hit home. For weeks and months after the U.S. victory parades had faded away along with the tattered yellow ribbons, members of the Catholic peace community came together in ones and twos, in small groups and large convocations to rehearse the events and lessons of the war and the failure of protest. Reaction in general ranged at first from self-blame for not having done enough quickly enough, to a rejection of American society at large for having ignored the peace movement, to an indictment of the media for having marginalized it. In time, however, blame gave way to more rational – and more faith-based – discourse, to analysis, and to the realization that human efforts, no matter how courageous, must ultimately give way to grace, either to a grace that lifts one up in a triumph not really one's own, or brings one down to a despair not really of one's own making. In this despair, in the darkness of defeat, grace thus works its subtle way to infuse the person of faith with the firm understanding that individuals and human institutions cannot control events and that an openness to grace – to fresh insights and understandings – comes as a free gift.

If the defeat of the Catholic peace movement in the Persian Gulf War had any "lesson," perhaps it was that this human failure was no defeat at all, since it was not the work of the peacemaker to triumph in the first place, but ultimately to be one with neighbors, friends and enemies alike. It may, perhaps, have been a sudden inspiration to many that after great labors one must, last of all, rest and restore vision and the joy of work.

Joan Chittister, OSB was born on April 26, 1936 in Dubois, PA and educated at St. Benedict Abbey and at Maryhurst College, both in Erie. She then went on to Notre Dame and to Pennsylvania State University for higher degrees. From 1955 to 1959 Chittister taught in a Catholic elementary school, from 1959 to 1974 in high school and from 1969 to 1971 at Penn State. In 1978 she was named prioress of the Benedictines of Erie and has served as president of the Conference of American Benedictine Prioresses, as executive director for the Alliance of International Monasticism. Chittister was an early correspondent of Thomas Merton and has contributed dozens of articles to Catholic publications, including a regular column for the *National Catholic Reporter*. She sits on the paper's board of directors. She is the author of several books, including *Women, Ministry and the Church* (1983); *Winds of Change: Women Challenge the Church* (1986); and *Job's Daughters: Women and Power* (1990).

She was among the Catholic leaders who came together to be arrested for nonviolent protest at the White House on January 22, 1991 against the beginning of the Gulf War. She remains active in efforts for peace and justice within American society and the Catholic church.

The following is excerpted from Joan Chittister, OSB, "Viewpoint Woman: When Peace is Unpopular," *Pax Christi USA* 16.1 (Spring 1991): 24, 37.

399. Joan Chittister, When Peace is Unpopular

The trouble with peacemaking is that it takes you more and more into yourself. "While you are proclaiming peace with your lips," Francis of Assisi wrote, "be careful to have it even more fully in your heart."

It is one thing to present a good argument for peace. It is another thing to do it with serenity. But serenity is what it will take.

This country, it seems, is very angry at peacemakers now. Peacemakers, the thinking is, had a right to resist the war before the war but they were supposed to be quiet once the war had started. Peacemakers obstructed the war effort, they said; they were traitors; they were cowards; they were not supporting the troops. A local radio station in Erie, for instance, after hours and even days of mocking the peacemaking efforts of religious in the city, intoned, "They're brave enough to go to Washington to demonstrate against the troops, but they're not brave enough to come on this talk show and say why." Those are all hard words to hear – and unthinking ones.

What the announcer really wanted was what got the nation into war in the first place. He didn't want a discussion of the politics or the theology of peacemaking. He wanted a match. He wanted one side to bloody the other, rather than to listen to the other.

That's what Hussein wanted with Kuwait. That's what George Bush wanted with Hussein when he refused to sustain the boycotts, when he refused to negotiate a cease-fire, when he refused to consider anything but "unconditional surrender." "The time for talking has passed," George Bush said in response to the possibility of a cease-fire and continued to go on destroying what we said we were freeing, and continued to destroy the Iraqi foot soldiers who were as innocent in their warmaking as our soldiers in ours.

The questions now, then, becomes, How do you continue to speak for peace but stay out of the match? How do you support the warriors but reject the war? How do you deal with warmakers and keep peace in your own heart?…

"While you are proclaiming peace with your lips, be careful to have it even more fully in your heart," Francis said. At the rate of one US bomb a minute over the homes and schools and hospitals and mosques of the innocent – 120,000 sorties in all – the deaths from which are still a classified number, it is a great order.

"They make a desert and call it 'peace'," Tacitus noted [see 14] centuries before us. While the country celebrates the collapse of a country that was never a match for us in the first place and who never had a clue that we did anything but support their latest move into Kuwait as we had already applauded their earlier move against Iran, the call to inner peace is clearly an order of high sanctity. But that is surely the only way that we will ever create a real peace movement out of this fiasco.

THE CONVERSION OF NORTH AMERICA

We conclude this study with a subjective sampling of current Catholic thinking on war, peace, and justice, ranging over such issues as technology and economy, community and conversion, nuclear war and its preparation, and the deep spirituality of the peacemaker that comes alive in imagination and vision.

THE CATHOLIC WORKER, AGAIN

The following is taken from *The Catholic Worker* 47.1 (May 1981): 2.

400. Catholic Worker Statement: Justice and Charity

The aim of the Catholic Worker movement is to realize in the individual and in society the expressed and implied teachings of Christ. We see the Sermon on the Mount and the call to solidarity with the poor at the heart of these teachings. Therefore, we must look at the world to see whether we already have a social order that reflects the justice and charity of Christ.

When we examine the society in which we live, we find that it is not in accord with justice and charity:

• The maldistribution of wealth is widespread; the fact that there are hungry and homeless people in the midst of plenty is unjust. Rich and poor suffer increasingly from isolation, madness, and growing individual violence, side by side with a governmental emphasis on implements of war instead of on human well-being.

• The rapid rise of technology, without a fitting development of morality, emphasizes progress based on profit rather than human needs. The triumvirate of military, business, and scientific priorities overwhelms the political process. "Democracy" is reduced to a choice between "brand names" in products and politicians. Bureaucratic structures make accountability, and therefore political change, close to impossible. As a result there is no forum in which to express, effectively, different views of the events shaping our life. The individual suffers as much from these transformations as does the whole social order.

• On a scale unknown to previous generations, the poor throughout the world are systematically robbed of the goods necessary to life. Though we realize the United States is not the sole perpetrator of such immoral conduct, we are North Americans and must first acknowledge our own

891

country's culpability. We deplore U.S. imperialism in its various expressions. Multinational corporations, economic "aid," military intervention, and so forth, have led to the disintegration of communities and the destruction of indigenous cultures – blatant violations of justice and charity.

• The proliferation of nuclear power and weapons stands as a clear sign of the direction of our age. Both are a denial of the very right of people to life and, implicitly, a denial of God. There is a direct economic and moral connection between the arms race and destitution. In the words of Vatican II, "The arms race is an utterly treacherous trap for humanity, and one which injures the poor to an intolerable degree."

To achieve a just society we advocate a complete rejection of the present system and a nonviolent revolution to establish a social order in accord with Christian truth.

The Catholic Worker envisages a social order based on St. Thomas Aquinas' doctrine of the common good, in which the freedom and dignity of the person are fostered, and the good of each person is bound to the good of the whole in the service of God. A person's primary responsibility is to this common good, and not to a political entity.

• The Catholic Worker advocates a society that is decentralized – a society in direct contrast to the present bigness of the state, mass production in industry, in education, in health-care, and agriculture. Specifically, we look forward to a life closer to the land and are encouraged by efforts toward family farms, land trusts (rural and urban), handcrafting, and appropriate technology that fosters a respect for human dignity and the environment. In towns and cities, too, decentralization can be promoted through worker ownership and management of small factories, through food, housing, and other kinds of cooperatives.

• We advocate a personalism in which we take on ourselves the responsibility for changing conditions, to the extent each of us is able. Houses of hospitality have been opened to feed the hungry, clothe the naked, and shelter the homeless. We strive to do this as a family, for hospitality is more than supplying food: it is opening ourselves to others. We see community as a potent remedy to the isolation and spiritual destitution prevalent today. We should not look to the impersonal welfare of the state to provide solutions or to do what we, as Christians, should be doing.

• The Catholic Worker sees voluntary poverty as an implication of Jesus' teaching on the unity of justice and charity. Through voluntary poverty we ask for the grace to abandon ourselves to the will of God, and we cast our lot in solidarity with those whose destitution is not a choice, but a condition of their oppression. We cannot participate in their struggles for justice if we do not recognize that we have both responsibilities and limits in our use of goods. "No one is justified in keeping for their exclusive use what they do not need, when others lack necessities" (Paul VI).

• We believe that the revolution to be pursued in ourselves and in society must be nonviolent and cannot be imposed from above. We condemn all war and the nuclear arms race; and we see oppression in any form as blasphemy against God, Who created all people in His image. When we fight tyranny and injustice, we must do so with the spiritual weapons of prayer and fasting and by noncooperation. Refusal to pay taxes, refusal to register for conscription, nonviolent strikes and boycotts and withdrawal from the system are all methods that can be employed in this struggle for justice.

We see this as an era filled with anxiety and confusion. In response, we, as a lay movement, seek our strength and direction in the beauty of regular prayer and liturgy, in studying and applying the traditions of Scripture and the teachings of the Church to the modern condition. We believe that success, as the world determines it, is not a fit criterion for judgment. We must be prepared and ready to face seeming failure. The most important thing is that we adhere to these beliefs, which transcend time, and for which we will be asked a personal accounting, not as to whether they succeeded (though we should hope that they do), but as to whether we remained true to them.

The following is taken from *A Penny a Copy*, 2nd ed., pp. 316-19.

401. Katharine Temple, Confessions of a Latter Day Luddite, January-February 1987

Latter-Day Luddites, that's how Lawrence O'Neill, president of Riverside Research Institute (RRI), dismisses those who question the military-related work he oversees. Combined with a reference to "pseudo-intellectual, pseudo-moral clutter," this phrase makes it clear that he believes the groups who demonstrate outside his building to be a mob of ridiculous, negative, irresponsible, irrational ne'er-do-wells. To call someone a Luddite seems a worse slur than to call the person an anarchist....

Maybe we should take up the gauntlet and find even more ways to be latter-day Luddites, to recapture their insight, verve, and courage, in a less inflammatory way. Joseph Weizenbaum, who knows "the state of the technological art" probably all too well in the Department of Electrical Engineering and Computer Science at M.I.T., has made one suggestion:

> I think the Luddites have been grievously misrepresented in what outrageously little history is taught in the American schools. Their actions closely parallel those of our people who pound sledge-hammers on the hulls of submarines and missiles. These are actions of last resort, all other attempts to appeal to reason having failed. I think we need a period of detoxification with respect to our science and technology. They have become toxic to our spirit. We need a moratorium on progress. If such thoughts are Luddite, then I am a Luddite, too.

Official reactions to Plowshares Actions (which inflict only symbolic damage) [**382-384**] including prison sentences up to eighteen years, for instance, while not as extreme as in nineteenth-century England, when machine beating was made a capital crime, betray a nervousness not all that far removed. Joseph Weizenbaum also supports the Star Wars refusal campaign, where scientists pledge not to solicit or accept financial support for specific research. Another campaign in direct opposition to unlimited development, it is also not pleasing to the government, but is harder to prosecute.

Then there is tax resistance. This route may not seem as dramatic as smashing the looms that spell unemployment; still, it does strike, nonviolently, at the life-line sustaining the corporate-military mechanism. (Certainly, the State takes it seriously. Consider the lengths they go to collect meager amounts from people who openly withhold money to protest military spending.) Refusing to pay the piper may be the most direct and non-confused way to say "No!" to the forces that enslave.

Most of us don't stop to think how many ways tax resistance can be practiced. At one end of the spectrum is the public and outright refusal to pay, a stance that limits employment possibilities and risks heavy fines or jail. At the other end is the decision, equally fraught with hardship, to live below the taxable limit. In between lie other, less extreme options, such as a partial withholding, working within a lower tax bracket, avoidance of the telephone tax collected for military debts, exchanges of labor without money transactions, rationing (or even giving up!) highly taxed goods, etc. Given that more than half the federal budget goes to military expenses and hardware, every tax avoided through pure means is a moral and political statement of the highest order.

These decisions are not to be taken lightly, for the consequences can bear a heavy price. Any wise builder, we are told, will "first sit down and count the cost whether he has enough to complete it" [Luke 14:28]. Presumably, it is not the best idea to act only in confused, midnight encounters, or to make costly gestures frivolously.

At the same time, if we dismiss tax refusal out of hand, just as when the Luddites have been dismissed, the concern is not always about violence, or the cost, but the futility. Isn't it all doomed to failure? The die is cast, so that neither demonstrations nor symbolic action, nor direct refusals will make the slightest difference. This is what stops us from even the smallest actions. The assessment of failure, though, is always a later one, and we shouldn't give in to historical determinism.

RICHARD MCSORLEY, SJ

Since the 1960s Richard McSorley has remained a constant presence in Catholic peacemaking, as teacher, writer, speaker and participant in many nonviolent actions. He was born in Philadelphia on October 2, 1914, one of fifteen children, seven of whom eventually entered religious life. He became a Jesuit in 1932 and in 1939 went to the Philippines to teach in a Jesuit high school. A prisoner of the Japanese during World War II, upon his return to the USA McSorley attended Woodstock Seminary. He was ordained in 1946 and in 1948 became pastor of St. James Church in St. Mary's City in southern Maryland. There he experienced the first of several conversions and began speaking out vigorously against the racism of his white parishioners, once escaping an assassination plot on his life.

McSorley taught at the University of Scranton from 1952 to 1961, when he earned a Ph.D. in philosophy from Ottawa University. From 1961 to 1985 he taught theology at Georgetown University, where he became central to the lives of a generation, including the children of Robert F. Kennedy. The presidential campaign of 1992 revealed his influence on the young Bill Clinton and his opposition to the Vietnam War. The work of Martin Luther King, Jr. propelled McSorley into the civil-rights movement; and he participated in many nonviolent actions, including those at Selma. From 1965 he became an outspoken critic of the war in

895

Vietnam, ROTC, and the American war culture, began teaching a seminar on war and peace at Georgetown, and eventually founded the Center for Peace Studies there.

McSorley was an early participant in Pax Christi/USA and during the 1970s and 1980s continued a life of active nonviolence, joining the campaigns against apartheid in South Africa and against nuclear weapons, being arrested at both the Soviet consulate in New York and the U.S. Capitol. He has lived in both the Community for Creative Nonviolence and the St. Francis Catholic Worker community. McSorley is the author of many articles and of several books, including *New Testament Basis of Peacemaking, Peace Eyes,* and *Kill? For Peace?*

The following article is perhaps McSorley's best-known work and is included in the collection *It's a Sin to Build a Nuclear Weapon,* ed. John Dear S.J., Baltimore: Fortkamp, 1991, pp. 93-97.

402. Richard McSorley, SJ, It's a Sin to Build a Nuclear Weapon

Does God approve of our intent to use nuclear weapons?

No, I don't believe so. Moreover, I do not believe God approves of even the possession of nuclear weapons.

The danger of world suicide through nuclear war "compels us to undertake an evaluation of war with an entirely new attitude," Vatican II said. Einstein put it this way: "When we released the energy from the atom, everything changed except our way of thinking. Because of that we drift towards unparalleled disaster." Something of what Einstein meant is this: We still look upon war as a conflict between two armies. The armies try to break through each other's front line to reach the civilian population. When they do, the suffering is so great that the war is ended. However, war with nuclear weapons will reach the civilian immediately. Nuclear missiles take only twenty-four minutes to travel between Moscow and Washington. Both the speed and total penetrability are so different from war in the past that the word "war" should not be used. Something like "mutual suicide," "Doomsday," or "Apocalypse" would be more accurate.

What can a nuclear weapon do? In his book, *Nuclear Disaster,* Dr. Tom Stonier of Manhattan College describes what would happen if a 20-megaton nuclear weapon was detonated in the center of New York City....

How many bombs do we really need? If it were not sinful to make a nuclear weapon, how many could we get by with? Between 200 and 400 megatons delivered on an enemy would be enough to destroy the possible enemy as a viable society. Former Secretary of Defense Robert McNamara once argued this before Congress. No one has contested his figures. Delivery of twenty to 400 megatons would destroy seventy-five percent of the industrial capacity of the Soviet Union or any other collection of enemies.

The Soviet Union has roughly 200 cities with a population over 100,000. A bomb or two delivered on these cities would destroy them. McNamara's argument was that we won't need any more than 200 to 400 weapons delivered on target. He was trying to show the Congress and the country that beyond that amount we are not dealing with deterrence but overkill.

How many nuclear weapons do we have in our stockpile today? We have over 30,000 nuclear weapons – 8,000 large (strategic) weapons and 22,000 smaller (tactical) weapons. We are making one new nuclear weapon every eight hours. We have enough weapons in our arsenal to deliver over 615,000 Hiroshima bombs. We can destroy every Soviet city of 100,000 or more forty-five times over. The Soviet Union can destroy every American city of 100,000 or more thirteen times over.

Can the use of these weapons be reconciled with the Gospel? Can even their existence be reconciled with the command "Love your enemies"? The United States policy is that we will retaliate with massive nuclear destruction if we are attacked. This is the very heart of our nuclear-deterrence policy. This is what we mean by deterrence. Is there any way that the Christian conscience can accept this policy of nuclear deterrence?...

Can we go along with the intent to use nuclear weapons? What it is wrong to do, it is wrong to intend to do. If it is wrong for me to kill you, it is wrong for me to plan to do it. If I get my gun and go to your house to retaliate for a wrong done me, then find there are police guarding your house, I have already committed murder in my heart. I have intended it.

Likewise, if I intend to use nuclear weapons in massive retaliation, I have already committed massive murder in my heart.

The taproot of violence in our society today is our intent to use nuclear weapons. Once we have agreed to that, all other evil is minor by comparison. Until we squarely face the question of our consent to use nuclear weapons, any hope of large-scale improvement of public morality is doomed to failure. Even the possession of weapons which cannot be

897

morally used is wrong. They are a threat to peace and might even be the cause of nuclear war. Human history shows that every weapon possessed is finally used. Since use of nuclear weapons is sinful, and possession leads to use, possession itself is sinful. Just as possession of alcohol is wrong for an alcoholic, and possession of drugs is wrong for a drug addict, so possession of morally unusable weapons is wrong for a government addicted to using weapons. The nuclear weapons of communists may destroy our bodies. But our intent to use nuclear weapons destroys our souls. Our possession of them is a proximate occasion of sin.

Technology in the nuclear age teaches us what we should have learned from our faith. As John Kennedy said at the United Nations in 1962: "Because of the nuclear sword of Damocles that hangs over us, we must cooperate together on this planet, or perish together in its flames through the weapons of our own hands."

JIM AND SHELLY DOUGLASS

The appearance of James Douglass' *The Non-Violent Cross* in 1966 was the first time an American Catholic had published a book-length work on Christian nonviolence. That book, and his lobbying efforts with Gordon Zahn and Eileen Egan on behalf on nonviolence at Vatican II earned Douglass wide recognition among Catholic peacemakers in the 1960s. Douglass earned an MA in theology from Bellarmine College in Louisville, KY. While teaching theology there he befriended Thomas Merton, sharing many of the same interests in a new theology of peace. Merton put Douglass in touch with Dorothy Day and the Catholic Worker. While never joining the movement, he did contribute many articles to the paper from 1958 into the 1980s, bringing a radical intellectual critique in the tradition of Furfey [356] and Ludlow [362]. Douglass went on to teach at St. Mary's College at Notre Dame and in 1969 became director of the program in Nonviolence at the University of Notre Dame. In 1971 he published his *Resistance and Contemplation*.

With his divorce and remarriage Douglass left Notre Dame for the University of Hawaii. Here they took up the Berrigans' tactics and destroyed draft files at Hickham Air Force Base. Arrested and convicted for this action, Douglass fled to Canada in violation of parole, an act that alienated many in the mainstream Catholic peace movement, including the leadership of the emerging Pax Christi, whose 1974 assembly was canceled over the controversy spurred by an invitation extended to him to deliver a keynote speech.

By 1975 the Douglass' had become deeply committed to the antinuclear movement, especially involving new U.S. weaponry. In 1977 therefore he and Shelly moved to Bangor, Washington, the home port for the Trident submarine, to begin their Ground Zero campaign of nonviolent protest, persuasion, and conversion. In 1983 Douglass published his *Lightning East to West: Jesus, Gandhi, and the Nuclear Age*, with a foreword by Raymond Hunthausen (New York: Crossroad).

The following is taken from Arthur Dahl, photographer and ed., *Making Peace*, Kansas City, MO: Sheed & Ward, 1990, pp. 156-61.

403. Jim and Shelly Douglass, Ground Zero

Ground Zero was created out of the context of the Trident Campaign, which began as an experiment in Gandhian nonviolence by a group of people who believed and continue to believe in nonviolence as a way of life. As an experiment in the power of nonviolence we began a campaign to explore that power and to, in the course of it, try to stop a submarine and missile system that we had been informed of by its designer, Robert Aldridge.

He had been working sixteen years for Lockheed Missiles and Space Corporation and had designed Polaris, Poseidon and Trident missile systems. In the course of designing Trident, he became aware of its purpose as a first-strike weapon and could not in conscience continue doing that, and in January 1973 he resigned from Lockheed.

He and Janet were both forty-seven when he resigned, and they had ten children. They had to change their whole way of life, and that moved us to a response. We began working on this campaign in January 1975. By 1977 we felt it was an act of violence to come in to the area, hold demonstrations and then retreat to our own residences rather than sharing the situation here with people who are dependent on Trident economically and through social and political pressures. So we decided to try to establish a center for nonviolence near the Trident base....

We began holding these weekly meetings at Ground Zero, and we began to leaflet the workers every Thursday morning in the Trident base. Since then, we've begun to leaflet workers at the Keyport Torpedo Station and the shipyard. Every week we pass out five hundred to a thousand leaflets. We've done that for almost five years in a row now, every week.

We try to develop a relationship of mutual respect and a dialogue through the leaflets....

Unless we can overcome the attitude of alienation and of over or against, the question can't be heard and can't be shared. That's the first thing that has to be built upon. One of the most important parts of this work is building up that relationship.

We hold meetings in houses, house meetings like the [United] farm workers do [385], where we try to talk to people who are most hostile to us. We'll go to a church and ask people in the church if they would have a day of recollection or reflection on Trident nuclear weapons, which often is refused.

But we often meet people who are supportive, one or two or three people, and then we ask if they would hold a meeting in their home. Then we talk to people whom they invite into their homes. It's real hard to get people together, because talking about peace here is like talking about Jewish people next to Auschwitz. It's the same reality. It's very, very threatening in Kitsat County. People realize it's their bread and butter that's at issue.

We tell our own stories. We don't begin by bringing up questions. We begin by sharing our lives. Because there is a sense in which every worker who goes into that base knows the questions. And it's not so much the question – the people know the questions to some extent, but they don't know the hope. They don't know the possibility of change. They don't know the powers of miracles in their lives. They don't know that transformation is possible.

Everybody's for peace, but none of us is willing to recognize the depth of sacrifice necessary to grasp peace. There is a security individually and personally that corresponds to the national security state [see **332-334**]. In order for us to be able to choose a nuclear-free world, we have to choose things like risking or giving up jobs, going to jail, suffering ridicule by our neighbors, losing political office. These are the kinds of sacrifices that should be understood as normal in a situation which is the most serious crisis in the history of humankind. We are on the verge of exterminating life. And unless we can give up all those forms of death that sustain it, which include things very close to us, to all of us. For example, one of the main sources of the nuclear arms race is the family, because of the attitudes of security that are bound up with the nuclear family.

People are for peace, except when it comes to giving up life insurance policies or bank accounts for their children's college educations. We always put it in terms of other people. We don't often put it in terms of ourselves. The most common way of putting it is in terms of my family or my children, the future of my children. If you're blinded by affluence, which we are in this country, and if you don't see any real hope in the power of nonviolence, the attitude becomes one of "I can't give up these things that my children need." That's understood in terms of affluence, and it wouldn't do any good anyhow because...these are forms of death. They're forms of spiritual death. And if we can't believe in the power of nonviolence, then we are accepting a process that's far worse than anything that the Third Reich was involved in. What they were able to do is minuscule next to what we are engaged in doing right now. These boxcars and these shipments that come by our house represent...the White Train that arrived March 22 had at least one hundred hydrogen bombs in it, perhaps two hundred. That goes far beyond the ten million the Third Reich destroyed.

If we continue to be passive cooperators in nuclear extermination than that's what would happen. Noncooperation with evil, as Gandhi taught, is as much a duty as cooperation with good. Which means that we must refuse to pay taxes that go to nuclear war; we must refuse to be silent when these kinds of shipments go by our homes. We must speak up in every way possible against that kind of buildup to a first-strike nuclear war. We must refuse to work in jobs that in any way sustain that kind of operation, no matter what that means to our own futures. We must be prepared to go to jail because of the terrible crime that's being committed in our name and with our cooperation. Those are all things that, unless we can do them and take responsibility for these weapons ourselves, will lead to an inconceivable slaughtering in a relatively short time.

Nuclear weapons are no accident. We need them. If you have 6 percent of the human species in control of approximately 40 percent of the earth's resources, you need nuclear weapons. It's no accident. It's a necessary component of the situation of radical injustices. So a conversion deeper than the kind that we ordinarily understand politically is necessary to do away with nuclear weapons. It requires a transformation of the world, and especially of the attitudes in this country which sustain the arms race more deeply than attitudes anywhere else in the world....

MATTHEW FOX

We conclude our study with one of the most controversial of modern Catholic thinkers and peacemakers: Matthew Fox. Fox was born in Madison, WI on December 21, 1940. He entered the Dominican Order in 1960 in Chicago and completed seminary studies in 1967. In 1968, on the advice of Thomas Merton [366-370], he travelled to Paris to do research on the medieval mystics. The events of Paris in '68 [see 338] politicized his understanding of religious life and set him on a quest to combine the insights of the mystics with the issues of peace and justice on a global scale, a synthesis that has characterized much of Western monasticism since the Middle Ages [see 87-94, 110-113, 128-130]. Fox remained in France, studying under the famed theologian M.-D. Chenu at the Institut Catholique de Paris where he received a doctorate in history and theology of spiritualities in 1970. He did postdoctoral studies under Johannes Metz at the University of Münster. After returning to the United States and teaching at Barat College, a small school for women in Lake Forest, IL, he was sensitized to the need for women's liberation and spirituality. In an effort to combine these directions in his spirituality and political commitment, in 1977 he established the Institute in Culture and Creation Spirituality at Mundelein College in Chicago, and later affiliated it with Holy Names College in Oakland, California, of which he also served as director.

So successful and influential was Fox's "Creation Spirituality" that by 1984 conservative Catholic circles in the United States began picketing his lectures, denouncing him in the press, and sending reports and letters on his activities to Rome. In July of that year Joseph Cardinal Ratzinger, the head of the revived Inquisition, ordered the minister general of the Dominicans to initiate a review of Fox's teachings. In 1987 Ratzinger launched his own investigation, and in April 1988 the cardinal ordered the Dominicans to silence Fox after he had refused to fire his friend and colleague Starhawk, an avowed witch and proponent of the Goddess religion, from the ICCS. Fox complied with the one-year silencing, but upon its termination, he reemerged defying papal authorities, pointing to the popularity his books had enjoyed during his suppression, and stressing his Catholicism. He was finally expelled from the Dominicans and the priesthood in March 1993.

Fox is the author of some of the most important books in creation spirituality, including *A Spirituality Named Compassion* (1979), *Breakthrough: Meister Eckhart's Creation Spirituality in New Translation* (1980), *Original Blessing* (1983), *Meditations with Meister Eckhart* (1982), and Hildegard of Bingen, *Illuminations* (1985). His most recent books are *Sheer Joy: Conversations with Thomas Aquinas on Creation Spirituality* (1992) and *The Reinvention of Work* (1994).

Fox has been and remains so controversial because, like the Hebrew prophets whom we encountered at the beginning of this study, he is himself a mystic and a prophet; and his words are less focused on the present or the past, than on the future: the image of the next millennium, of the renewed image of the universe as a work of God's creation that brings justice and fulfillment, respect for the physical world, including the physical being of men and women, their health, their life of meaningful work and sexuality, respect for differences of tradition, of race, religion, nationality, culture and class, in short a universal *visio pacis* – a vision of peace – as vibrant as any in the ancient and medieval tradition. He brings the imagery of the Apocalypse and its New Jerusalem into the twenty-first century as a contemporary symbol and a very real goal for societies and individuals. Ultimately, this New Jerusalem, the image of the Heavenly City, is a most appropriate text with which to complete this study, for it embraces the most fundamental meaning of peace in the Christian and Catholic tradition. It is the bedrock from which all Christian thought of peace emerges and is the eschatological goal toward which all the work of peacemakers yearns for fulfillment in this world and in the other.

The following selection is from Matthew Fox, *The Coming of the Cosmic Christ*, San Francisco: Harper & Row, 1988, pp. 245-46.

404. Matthew Fox, Vatican III: A Vision of Peace

Since this book began with a dream it seems reasonable to end it with another dream – one that came to me after I thought I had finished writing the book.

The year is 1992. Mother Africa and the so-called Third World has now penetrated Western religion, and the newly elected pope, John XXIV, is the first African pope. Mother Africa, where the human race began, is now represented at the symbolic center of Western faith. Pope John XXIV has called for a new ecumenical council, Vatican III. The purpose of this Council is to define the doctrine of the Cosmic Christ as being intrinsic to faith. The Council will also consider as immediate corollaries to this doctrine the issues of sexuality as mysticism, cosmic worship, deep ecumenism, folk art as a basic means to employ the one billion unemployed adults around the world, and youth and adult relationships. Expected at the Council are not only bishops from around the world but leaders of all the world's religions including representatives of the native religions of Africa, Australia, America, Asia and Europe. The goddess religions are represented as well. Expected also is a large delegation of artists whose interest in the Cosmic Christ and in the renewal of worship in particular is electric. How is it possible that so much creativity and so much hope are coming together in one place in the name of a spiritual awakening of the human race?

Perhaps it has to do with the first action taken by Pope John XXIV, which was to offer a public apology in the name of Western Christianity to native peoples, women, homosexual people, scientists (this action was begun under Pope John Paul II when he removed Galileo from the condemned list) and artists, for the sins of the Church against them. These groups, after considerable debate among their constituencies, have accepted the papal apology and will play a prominent part in the forthcoming, truly ecumenical, Council. All seem interested in celebrating the divine image in all creatures, even human ones. All appear excited about calling forth the Cosmic Christ traditions from their spiritual heritage and offering them as a gift to redeem Mother Earth, as a gift to our children and theirs for generations to come.

Another action taken by Pope John XXIV has been to dismantle entirely the Office of the Inquisition (lately known as the Congregation of the Doctrine of the Faith) and to replace it with a board of grandmothers who will counsel the overall church on implications of doctrine and movements for the young. Still another action taken by this pope has been to gather all the Opus Dei bishops of the world on one island where, it is said, they are undergoing a two-year spiritual retreat that includes a critique of the history of fascism and Christianity on the one hand and an inculcation of creation spirituality on the other. It is said these bishops do body prayer three times daily and art as meditation four hours per day. The native people of the island are the instructors for their art as meditation classes. Women have assumed the office of bishop in their respective diocesan sees.

At the United Nations plans are underway for the great global happening of the year 2000. That happening is, in religious terms, the celebration of the Jubilee Year. The Jubilee Year of 2000 will mark a global switch-over from the current economic and banking system to a new one. It includes the letting go of all debts from so-called Third World countries and the reconstituting of a system of monetary security that includes all nations. The starting point for this economic system is not humanly conceived monetary systems but the shared wealth of the world beginning with the earth's treasures of the waters, forests, soil, animals, birds, fishes, and plants. Preparations for this vast act of global "letting go" and global creativity are occupying the creative minds of all nations. The planet is alive with excitement. To stimulate the countdown for this act of giving and beginning anew there has been, beginning in 1992, a 10 percent *annual* reduction in armaments spending by every nation on the earth. Persons and nations alike are astounded by the amount of available capital and available jobs as a result of this tithing by the military to the defense of Mother Earth. Preparations are underway to convert *all* defense departments of all nations from defending nations against armies to defending Mother Earth against the human species. It is agreed that the changeover in human attitudes required of such a conversion will require a spiritual basis. With this end in sight, spiritual disciplines and traditions are being taught in all educational programs, East and West, from kindergarten through graduate schools. No lawyers, engineers, doctors, or business persons are graduating without knowing the cosmic story of the origins of the universe and of the powers and possibilities of the human species. All are learning both ancient and new ways to praise. The human race is relearning the meaning of reverence: the shared awe about its own existence and responsibilities. Artists are at the forefront – along with native spiritual leaders and regenerated spiritual leaders from West and East – in awakening persons to their own Cosmic Wisdom. In this context a global renaissance seems well underway. And Pope John XXIV, it is widely felt, is lending powerful impetus to this movement. The Third Vatican Council is expected to do the same.

* *
*

905

BIBLIOGRAPHY
OF TEXTS

Agosin, Marjorie. *Scraps of Life: Chilean Arpilleras, Chilean Women and the Pinochet Dictatorship*. Cola Franzen, trans. Toronto: Williams-Wallace, 1987, pp. 93-99.

Alighieri, Dante. *On World Government (De Monarchia)*. Herbert W. Schneider, trans. Dino Bigongiari, intro. Indianapolis and New York: Bobbs-Merrill, 1957.

Anchieta, José de. *Histories*. In Goodpasture, pp. 51-52.

Ángulo, Juan Fernandez de. *Letter to Emperor Charles V,* May 20, 1541. In Las Casas, *Short Account*, pp. 81-83.

Aristide, Jean-Bertrand. *In the Parish of the Poor: Writings from Haiti*. Amy Wilentz, trans. and ed. Maryknoll, NY: Orbis Books, 1990, pp. 3-4, 15-17, 23, 35-37, 52-57, 62-69.

—. "No to Violence." In Jean-Bertrand Aristide, with Christophe Wargny. *An Autobiography.* Linda M. Maloney, trans. Maryknoll, NY: Orbis Books, 1993, pp. 52-53, 56, 164-65.

Baldinger, Franz. "On the Stubbornness of a Martyr." In Zahn. *In Solitary Witness*, pp. 288.

Balduino, Tomas. "The Amazon and the Landworkers, Pastoral Letter dated February 1, 1976." In Lange and Iblacker, pp. 37-46.

Battek, Rudolf. "Spiritual Values, Independent Initiatives and Politics." In Havel et al. *Power of the Powerless*, pp. 97-109.

Benda, Václav. "Catholicism and Politics." In Havel et al. *Power of the Powerless*, pp. 110-24.

Benedict XV. *Encyclical Letter, Pacem Dei Munus Pulcherrimum, on Peace and Reconciliation,* May 23, 1920. In Flannery, pp. 13-18.

—. *Exhortation, Des le Debut, to the Belligerent Peoples and Their Leaders,* August 1, 1917. In Flannery, pp. 10-11.

—. *To the Belligerent Peoples and to Their Leaders (Allorchè Fummo),* July 1915. In Chatfield and Ilukhina, p. 159.

Berrigan, Daniel. "Letter to Ernesto Cardenal: Guns Don't Work." *Na-*

tional Catholic Reporter (May 5, 1978). In Berrigan, *Poetry, Drama, Prose*, pp. 166-70.

—. *Poetry, Drama, Prose*. Michael True, ed. Maryknoll, NY: Orbis Books, 1988.

—. *The Trial of the Catonsville Nine.* In Berrigan, *Poetry, Drama, Prose*, pp. 247-51.

Berrigan, Philip. "Help Thou Our Unbelief." In Cornell et al., *A Penny a Copy*, pp. 349-52.

Boff, Leonardo. "Active Nonviolence: The Political and Moral Power of the Poor." In McManus and Schlabach, pp. vii-xi.

—, and Clodovis Boff. "How to Be Christians in a World of Destitution." In Leonardo Boff and Clodovis Boff, *Introducing Liberation Theology.* Paul Burns, trans. Maryknoll, NY: Orbis Books, 1988, pp. 1-9.

Briand, Aristide. "European Union." In Chatfield and Ilukhina, pp. 220-22.

Burtchaell, James Tunstead, ed. and trans. *A Just War No Longer Exists: The Teaching and Trial of Don Lorenzo Milani.* Notre Dame, IN: University of Notre Dame Press, 1988.

Butterworth, Charles. "Nonviolence in Nevada." *The Catholic Worker* 24.2 (Sept. 1957): 5.

Cabestrero, Teofilo. *Ministers of God, Ministers of the People: Testimonies of Faith from Nicaragua.* Robert R. Barr, trans. Maryknoll, NY: Orbis Books, 1983, pp. 24-30.

Cajetan, Thomas de Vio. *Commentary* on Thomas Aquinas, *Summa Theologiae*, Secunda Secundae, q. *66*, art. 8. In Las Casas, *The Only Way*, p. 67.

Camara, Helder. "Violence the Only Way? A Lecture Given in Paris on 25 April 1968." In Helder Camara. *The Church and Colonialism: The Betrayal of the Third World.* William McSweeney, trans. Denville, NJ: Dimension Books, 1969, pp. 101-11.

Cardenal, Ernesto. "Interview." In Cabestrero, pp. 24-30.

Cardenal, Fernando. "Interview." In Cabestrero, pp. 70-71, 78-79, 84-85, 88-89.

Casaldáliga, Pedro. "On Authentic Voluntary Poverty." In Lange and Iblacker, pp. 46-53.

Catholic Peace Fellowship. "Peace on Earth, Peace in Vietnam." *Commonweal* (Dec. 10, 1965).

Catholic Worker Statement. "Justice and Charity." *The Catholic Worker* 47.1 (May 1981): 2.

Charles V. *Instruction to Hernando Cortés, June 26, 1523.* In Simpson, pp. 58-59.

—. *Instructions to the Second Audiencia of New Spain, July 12, 1530.* In Simpson, p. 85.

—. *The New Laws,* November 1542. In Simpson, pp. 129-32.

Chatfield, Charles, and Ruzanna Ilukhina, eds. *Peace/Mir: An Anthology of Historic Alternatives to War.* Syracuse, NY: Syracuse University Press, 1994.

Chavez, Cesar. "Speech Given on Receipt of the Gandhi Peace Award for Promoting Enduring Peace." *The Catholic Worker* 57.4 (June-July 1990): 1, 4, 7.

Chittister, Joan. "Viewpoint Woman: When Peace is Unpopular." *Pax Christi USA* 16.1 (Spring 1991): 24, 37.

Colet, John. "Sermon to Henry VIII's Army, Good Friday 1513." In Olin, pp. 164-91.

Comblin, José. *The Church and the National Security State.* Maryknoll, NY: Orbis Books, 1979, pp. 64-78.

Cornell, Thomas. "The Catholic Church and Witness Against War." In Shannon, *War or Peace?*, pp. 200-213.

—., Robert Ellsberg, and Jim Forest, eds. *A Penny a Copy: Readings from The Catholic Worker.* 2d ed. Maryknoll, NY: Orbis Books, 1995.

Corrigan, Mairead. "Interview with Richard Deutsch." In Deutsch, pp. 34-46.

Crucé, Emeric. *The New Cyneas.* Thomas W. Balch, trans. and ed. Philadelphia: Allen, Lane & Scott, 1909.

Day, Dorothy. "Editorial: Catholic Worker Stand on the Use of Force." *The Catholic Worker* 6.4 (Sept. 1938): 1, 4, 7.

—. "Our Country Passes from Undeclared War to Declared War; We Continue Our Christian Pacifist Stand." *The Catholic Worker* 9.3 (Jan. 1942): 1, 4.

—. "A Prayer for Peace." In Dorothy Day. *By Little and Little: Selected Writings.* Robert Ellsberg, ed. New York: Alfred A. Knopf, 1983, pp. 331-33.

—. "We Go on Record." *The Catholic Worker* 12.7 (Sept. 1945): 1.

De Bosis, Lauro. "Leaflets Dropped on Rome, October 3, 1931." In Iris Origo. *A Need to Testify: Portraits of Lauro De Bosis, Ruth Draper,*

Gaetano Salvemini, Ignazio Silone. New York: Harcourt Brace Jovanovich, 1984, pp. 244-47.

Delp, Alfred. *Writings.* In Leber, pp. 224-26.

D'Escoto, Miguel. "Interview." In Cabestrero, pp. 96-97, 100-101, 109-13, 117, 126.

Deutsch, Richard. *Mairead Corrigan, Betty Williams,* Woodbury, NY: Barron's, 1977.

Dolci, Danilo. *The Man Who Plays Alone.* Antonia Cowen, trans. New York: Pantheon, 1968, pp. 3, 62-64, 173-76, 290-91.

—. *Outlaws.* R. Munroe, trans. New York: Orion Press, 1961, pp. 216-26, 229-32, 246-50, 254-57.

Donovan, Jean. *Diary.* In Ana Carrigan. *Salvador Witness: The Life and Calling of Jean Donovan.* New York: Ballantine Books, 1984, pp. 161-87.

Douglass, Jim and Shelly. "Ground Zero." In *Making Peace.* Arthur Dahl, photographer and ed. Kansas City, MO: Sheed & Ward, 1990, pp. 156-61.

Dubois, Pierre. *The Recovery of the Holy Land.* Walther I. Brandt, ed. and trans. Records of Civilization, vol. 51. New York: Columbia University Press, 1956, pp. 69-163.

Dussel, Enrique. *Ethics and Community.* Robert R. Barr, trans. Maryknoll, NY: Orbis Books, 1986, pp. 158-80.

Egan, Eileen. "The Right to Refuse to Kill." *Worldview* (Dec. 1974): 19-27.

Éla, Jean-Marc. "An African Reading of Exodus." In Jean-Marc Éla. *African Cry.* Robert R. Barr, trans. Maryknoll, NY: Orbis Books, 1986, pp. 28-38.

Ellacuría, Ignacio. *Freedom Made Flesh: The Mission of Christ and His Church.* John Drury, trans. Maryknoll, NY: Orbis Books, 1976, pp. 217-31.

Erasmus, Desiderius. "Charon."In *Ten Colloquies,* pp. 113-29.

—. *The Complaint of Peace.* In *The Essential Erasmus.* John P. Dolan, ed. New York: New American Library, 1964, pp. 174-204.

—. "Cyclops, or the Gospel Bearer." In *Ten Colloquies,* pp. 120-29.

—. *The Education of a Christian Prince.* Lester K. Born, ed. and trans. New York: W.W. Norton, 1964, pp. 178-80, 204, 224-25, 248-57.

—. *Letter to Paul Volz.* In Olin, pp. 107-33.

—. *The Praise of Folly.* In Dolan, *Essential Erasmus,* pp. 94-173.

—. *Ten Colloquies.* Craig R. Thompson, ed. and trans. Indianapolis and New York: Bobbs-Merrill, 1957.

Fahey, Joseph. "Toward a Theology of Peace." *Catholic World* 213 (May 1971): 64-68.

Feldmann, Attorney. "Letter Dated July 6, 1943, to the Catholic pastor of St. Radegund. " In Zahn, *In Solitary Witness,* pp. pp. 92-93.

Fénelon, François. *The Adventures of Telemachus,* Book 9. Trans. from *Les Aventures de Télémaque.* Jacques Lamaison, ed. Paris: Larousse, 1934, pp. 55-58.

Filipino Voices from the People Power Revolution of 1986. In *People Power: An Eyewitness History. The Philippine Revolution of 1986.* Monina Allarey Mercado, ed. New York: Writers & Readers Publishing, 1986, pp. 17, 54, 77-78, 105, 109-110, 122, 124-26.

Flannery, Harry W., ed. *Pattern for Peace: Catholic Statements on International Order.* Westminster, MD: Newman Press, 1962.

Forest, James H. *The Catholic Conscientious Objector.* New York: Catholic Peace Fellowship, 1965, rev. ed. 1981.

Fox, Matthew. "Vatican III: A Dream." In *The Coming of the Cosmic Christ.* San Francisco: Harper & Row, 1988, pp. 245-46.

Furfey, Paul Hanly. "Christ and the Patriot." *The Catholic Worker* 2:10 (March 1935): 3.

Galen, August Cardinal von. "Statements." In Zahn, *German Catholics,* pp. 84-87; and Leber, p. 188.

Garvey, Margaret Q. "Soldier with Courage not to Kill is in Trouble." *National Catholic Reporter* (Dec. 28, 1990): 7.

Germany's Catholic Bishops. "Statements During World War II." In Guenther Lewy. *The Catholic Church and Nazi Germany.* New York: McGraw-Hill, 1965, pp. 226, 230, 239, 252, 310; and Zahn, *German Catholics,* p. 57.

Goodpasture, H. McKennie, ed. *Cross and Sword: An Eyewitness History of Christianity in Latin America.* Maryknoll, NY: Orbis Books, 1989.

Gremillion, Joseph, ed. *The Gospel of Peace and Justice: Catholic Social Teaching since Pope John.* Maryknoll, NY: Orbis Books, 1976.

Gumbleton, Thomas J. "The Role of the Peacemaker." In Shannon, *War or Peace?,* pp. 214-29.

Gutiérrez, Gustavo. *A Theology of Liberation.* Caridad Inda and John Eagleson, trans. and eds. 15th Anniversary ed. Maryknoll, NY: Orbis Books, 1988, pp. 3-12.

Havel, Václav. "The Power of the Powerless." In Havel et al. *Power of the Powerless*, pp. 23-96.

——. et al. *The Power of the Powerless: Citizen Against the State in Central-Eastern Europe.* John Keane, ed. Armonk, NY: M.E. Sharpe, 1985.

Hennacy, Ammon. *The Book of Ammon Hennacy.* Salt Lake City: n.p., 1964, pp. 262-65, 286-89.

Hespers, Theo. "Selections from *Kameradschaft*." In Leber, pp. 220-23.

Hugo, Victor. "A United States of Europe." In *A Peace Reader: Essential Readings on War, Justice, Non-Violence and World Order.* Joseph J. Fahey and Richard Armstrong, eds. Rev. ed. New York: Paulist Press, 1992, pp. 187-89; and in Chatfield and Ilukhina, pp. 100-102.

Hurley, Denis. "Interview with Hope and Young." In Marjorie Hope and James Young. *The South African Churches in a Revolutionary Situation.* Maryknoll, NY: Orbis Books, 1983, pp. 155-57.

Irish Peace People. "Peace Hymn (from the Londonderry Peace March, Sept. 4, 1976)." In Deutsch, p. 103.

——. "Strategy for Peace, January 5, 1977." In Deutsch, pp. 134-137.

Isabella of Castile. *Codicil to Her Last Will, November 26, 1504.* In Simpson, pp. 14-15.

Italian Priests and Catholic Laity. "Conscientious Objection is not Cowardice." In Burtchaell, pp. 29-33.

Jägerstätter, Franz. *The Nine Commentaries.* In Zahn. *In Solitary Witness*, pp. 212-32.

—— *The Prison Statement*, July 1943. In Zahn, *In Solitary Witness*, pp. 233-38.

John XXIII. *Mater et Magistra.* In Gremillion, pp. 158, 186-87, 193, 197-98.

——. *Pacem in Terris (Peace on Earth).* In Gremillion, pp. 201-39.

John Paul II. "Address at the Peace Memorial (Atomic Bomb Site), Hiroshima, Japan, February 25, 1981." In John Paul II. *The Far East Journey of Peace and Brotherhood.* Daughters of St. Paul, eds. Boston: St. Paul Editions, 1981, pp. 275-81.

——. "Address Delivered at Raj Ghat, India at Memorial Shrine to Mahatma Gandhi, February 1, 1986." In *John Paul II, Pilgrim of Peace: Homilies and Addresses.* New York: Harmony Books, 1987, pp. 147-50.

——. "Address to the Organization of American States, Washington, DC, October 6, 1979." In John Paul II. *U.S.A.: The Message of Justice,*

Peace, and Love. Daughters of St. Paul, eds. Boston: St. Paul Editions, 1979, pp. 223-27.

—. "Homily Delivered at Edmonton, Canada, September 17, 1984." In *John Paul II, Pilgrim of Peace*, pp. 119-22.

"The Kairos Document." In *The Kairos Covenant: Standing with South African Christians.* Willis H. Logan, ed. New York: Friendship Press and Meyer-Stone Books, 1988, pp. 1-43.

Kim Chi Ha. "A Declaration of Conscience." In Kim Chi Ha. *The Gold-Crowned Jesus & Other Writings.* Chong Sun Kim and Shelly Killen, eds. Maryknoll, NY: Orbis Books, 1978, pp. 13-23.

Klausener, Erich. "Address to the Catholic Conference," Berlin, June 1933. In Leber, pp. 190-93.

La Fontaine, Henri. "What Pacifists Ought to Say." In Chatfield and Ilukhina, pp. 152-55.

Lange, Martin, and Reinhold Iblacker, eds. *Witness of Hope: The Persecution of Christians in Latin America.* William E. Jerman, trans. Maryknoll, NY: Orbis Books, 1981

Lanza del Vasto, Joseph Jean. *Make Straight the Way of the Lord.* New York: Knopf, 1974, pp. 85-86, 209-12, 247-54.

Las Casas, Bartolomé de. *Apologetic History.* In *Witness: Writings of Bartolomé de Las Casas.* George Sanderlin and Gustavo Gutiérrez, eds. Maryknoll, NY: Orbis Books, 1992, pp. 99-175.

—. *History of the Indies.* Sanderlin and Gutiérrez, eds., pp. 51-53, 72-79.

—. *The Only Way.* Helen Rand Parish, ed. Francis P. Sullivan, SJ, trans. New York: Paulist Press, 1992, pp. 68-181.

—. *A Short Account of the Destruction of the Indies.* Anthony Pagden, ed. Nigel Griffin trans. New York: Penguin Books, 1992, pp. 3-12, 23, 32-33, 52-54, 125-30.

Leber, Annedore, ed. Rosemary O'Neill, trans. *Conscience in Revolt: Sixty-Four Stories of Resistance in Germany, 1933-45.* Boulder, CO: Westview Press, 1994.

Leo XIII. *Allocution Nostis Errorem to the College of Cardinals,* February 11, 1889. In Flannery, pp. 1-2.

—. *Quod Apostolici Muneris,* December 28, 1878. In *Leo XIII: Social Wellsprings,* Joseph Husslein, ed. Milwaukee: Bruce, 1942, 1:19.

Lichtenberg, Bernhard. *Letters* and Trial Verdict. In Leber, pp. 198-202.

Ludlow, Robert. "The Draft, Christian Anarchism, and the State." *The Catholic Worker* 15.5 (July-August 1948): 7.

Madariaga, Salvador de. "International Organization." In Chatfield and Ilukhina, pp. 211-12.

Marsilio of Padua. *The Defender of Peace: The Defensor Pacis.* Alan Gewirth, ed. and trans. New York: Harper & Row, 1967, pp. 3-8, 89-97, 328-31, 361-63, 431-32

Matthiesen, Leroy T. "The Arms Race: Learning to Speak Out." *The Catholic Worker* 51.5 (Aug. 1984): 1-2, 8.

Maurin, Peter. *Easy Essays.* In Cornell et al., *A Penny a Copy*, pp. 7-8.

McAlister, Elizabeth. "For Love of the Children." In *For Swords into Plowshares, The Hammer Has to Fall.* Daniel Berrigan, ed. Piscataway, NJ: Plowshares Press, n.d. (1984), pp. 32-36.

McKeown, Ciaran. "Interview with Richard Deutsch." In Deutsch, pp. 72-81.

McManus, Philip, and Gerald Schlabach, eds. *Relentless Persistence: Nonviolent Action in Latin America.* Philadelphia and Santa Cruz: New Society Publishers, 1991.

McSorley, Richard. *It's a Sin to Build a Nuclear Weapon.* John Dear, ed. Baltimore: Fortkamp, 1991, pp. 93-97.

Medellín. "Documents on Justice and Peace." In Gremillion, pp. 445-76.

Melchor of Tucumán, *Letter to King Philip IV,* August 11, 1637. In Ruiz de Montoya, pp. 187-89.

Merton, Thomas. "Author's Preface to the Japanese Translation of *The Seven Story Mountain* (Tokyo: Chou Shuppansha, 1966)." In James H. Forest. *Thomas Merton's Struggle with Peacemaking.* Erie, PA: Benet Press, n.d.

—. "Blessed Are the Meek: The Christian Roots of Nonviolence." In Merton, *Nonviolent Alternative,* pp. 208-18.

—. "Man is a Gorilla with a Gun: Reflections on a Best-Seller." In Merton, *Nonviolent Alternative,* pp. 168-71.

—. *The Nonviolent Alternative.* Gordon C. Zahn, ed. New York: Farrar, Straus, Giroux, 1980.

—. "Peace and Revolution: A Footnote from *Ulysses.*" In Merton, *The Nonviolent Alternative,* pp. 70-75.

—. "Peace: A Religious Responsibility." In Merton, *Nonviolent Alternative,* pp. 111-14.

Metzger, Max Josef. "Peace Plan to Rebuild a Democratic Germany." In Leber, pp. 208-11.

Michnik, Adam. "Letter from the Gdansk Prison. "In Adam Michnik. *Letters from Prison and Other Essays,* Czeslaw Milosz and Jonathan Schell, eds. Maya Latynski, trans. Berkeley & Los Angeles: University of California Press, 1987, pp. 76-99.

—. "We Are All Hostages." In Persky and Flam, pp. 247-55.

Milani, Lorenzo. "Letter to the Judges. Dated at Barbiana, 18 October 1965." In Burtchaell, pp. 52-77.

—. "Letter to the Military Chaplains of Tuscany Who Signed the Communiqué of 11 February 1965." In Burtchaell, pp. 18-28.

Montaigne, Michel Eyquem de. *Apology for Raymond Sebond* (Essays, II:12). In *The Complete Works.* Donald M. Frame, trans. and ed. Stanford, CA: Stanford University Press, 1957, pp. 323-50.

Montesinos, Antonio de, December 1511 *Sermon on John 1:23.* In Las Casas, *History of the Indies* III.4-5, pp. 66-68.

Montessori, Maria. "Educate for Peace." In Chatfield and Ilukhina, pp. 236-37.

More, Thomas. *A Dialogue of Comfort Against Tribulation.* Leland Miles, ed. Bloomington, IN: Indiana University Press, 1965, pp. 233-39.

—. *Utopia and Other Writings.* James J. Greene and John P. Dolan, eds. New York: New American Library, 1984, pp. 43-49.

Mothers of the Plaza de Mayo. "Interviews with Marjorie Agosin." In Marjorie Agosin. *The Mothers of the Plaza de Mayo: The Story of Renée Epelbaum.* Janice Molloy, trans. Trenton, NJ: Red Sea Press, 1990, pp. 34-37, 71-73.

National Catholic Welfare Council. "The Pastoral Letter of 1919." In Nolan, pp. 230-33.

Nicgorski, Darlene. "No Turning Back: An Interview." In Vicki Kemper. "Convicted of the Gospel: Inside the Tucson Sanctuary Movement." *Sojourners* 15.7 (July 1986): 20-30.

Nolan, Hugh J., ed. *Pastoral Letters of the American Hierarchy, 1792-1970.* Huntington, IN: Our Sunday Visitor, 1971.

O'Brien, David J., and Thomas A. Shannon, eds. *Renewing the Earth: Catholic Documents on Peace, Justice and Liberation.* Garden City, NY: Doubleday, 1977.

O'Hare, Joseph. "Martyrdom in El Salvador." In Sobrino, *Companions of Jesus,* pp. 174-80.

Olin, John C., ed. and trans. *Christian Humanism and the Reformation: Desiderius Erasmus, Selected Writings.* New York: Harper & Row, 1965.

Pascal, Blaise. *Pensées* 291-304. In Pascal's *Pensées*. W.F. Trotter, trans. T.S. Eliot, intro. New York: E.P. Dutton, 1958, pp. 83-86.

Paul III. Letter to the Archbishop of Toledo (Encyclical, *Pastorale Officium*), 1537. In Parish and Sullivan. *The Only Way,* pp. 156-57.

——. *Sublimis Deus.* In Parish and Sullivan, *The Only Way,* pp. 114-15.

Paul VI. *Populorum Progressio: On the Development of Peoples.* In Gremillion, pp. 387-415.

Pavolini, Luca. "The Fatherland and Don Lorenzo. An Editorial." In Burtchaell, pp. 41-51.

Pax Christi/USA. *Conscience and War.* Cambridge, MA: Pax Christi USA Center on Conscience and War, n.d (1984).

——. *Statement on the Gulf War.* Erie, PA: Pax Christi/USA, 1991.

Pérez Esquivel, Adolfo. "To Discover Our Humanity." In McManus and Schlabach, pp. 238-51.

Persky, Stan, and Henry Flam, eds. *The Solidarity Sourcebook.* Vancouver: New Star, 1982.

Peter of Ghent. *Letter to Emperor Charles V,* October 31, 1532. In Goodpasture, pp. 21-22.

Petrarch, Francesco. *How a Ruler Ought to Govern His State.* In *The Earthly Republic: Italian Humanists on Government and Society.* Benjamin G. Kohl and Ronald G. Witt, eds. Manchester: Manchester University Press, 1978, pp. 38-41.

Philip IV. "Letter Patent to the Viceroy and Government of Peru, April 14, 1633." In Ruiz de Montoya, pp. 192-93.

Pico della Mirandola, Giovanni. *Oration on the Dignity of Man.* Paul Oskar Kristeller, ed. Elizabeth Livermore Forbes, trans. In *The Renaissance Philosophy of Man.* Ernst Cassirer, Paul Oskar Kristeller, and John Herman Randall, eds. Chicago: University of Chicago Press, 1969, pp. 230-32.

Pieris, Aloysius. *An Asian Theology of Liberation.* Maryknoll, NY: Orbis Books, 1988, pp. 120-24.

Pius XI. *Allocution, Benedetto il Natale, to the College of Cardinals,* December 24, 1930. In Flannery, pp. 34-35.

——.*Encyclical, Ubi Arcano Dei, On the Kingdom of Christ,* December 23, 1922. In Flannery, pp. 22-28.

——. *Encyclical Letter, Mit brennender Sorge, to the Archbishops and Bishops of Germany,* March 14, 1937. In Flannery, pp. 38-45.

Pius XII. "An Appeal for Peace, Radio Address to All the Peoples of the

Earth and Their Rulers, November 10, 1956, on the Plight of Hungary." In Flannery, pp. 278-81.

—. "Christmas Message Broadcast to the Whole World. December 23, 1948." In Flannery, pp. 167-72.

—. "Christmas Radio Message. December 24, 1944." In Flannery, pp. 118-31.

—. "Easter Homily, *Quoniam Paschalia Sollemnia,* in Saint Peter's Basilica, April 9, 1939." In Flannery, pp. 73-74.

—. *Encyclical Summi Pontificatus,* October 20, 1939. In Flannery, pp. 77-98.

—. "Nuclear Weapons and Armament Control, Christmas Message Broadcast to the Whole World, December 24, 1955." In Flannery, pp. 269-73.

—. "The Threat of ABC Warfare: Address to the Peoples Assembled in St. Peter's Square, April 18, 1954." In Flannery, pp. 234-35.

Prejean, Helen. *Dead Man Walking: An Eyewitness Account of the Death Penalty in the United States.* New York: Random House, 1993, pp. 3-22.

Puebla. "The Final Document: Evangelization in Latin America's Present and Future." In *Puebla and Beyond.* John Eagleson and Philip Scharper, eds. John Drury, trans. Maryknoll, NY: Orbis Books, 1979, pp. 124-25, 190-98.

Rabelais, François. *The Histories of Gargantua and Pantagruel.* J. M. Cohen, trans. and ed. Baltimore: Penguin Books, 1969, pp. 96-112.

Republic of Italy. "Law of 15 December 1972, no. 772." In Burtchaell, pp. 113-115.

—. Tribunal. The 4th Criminal Division of the Tribunal of Rome. "Decision and Opinion on the Milani Case, 15 February 1966." In Burtchaell, pp. 78-99.

Richard, Pablo. *Death of Christendoms, Birth of the Church: Historical Analysis and Theological Interpretation of the Church in Latin America.* Philip Berryman, trans. Maryknoll, NY: Orbis Books, 1987, pp. 1-16.

Roey, Joseph Cardinal van. "Declaration against Forced Labor." In Semelin, pp. 96-97.

Romero, Oscar. "Final Sermons and Homilies." In James R. Brockman, SJ. *The Word Remains: A Life of Oscar Romero.* Maryknoll, NY: Orbis Books, 1982, pp. 201-23.

Ruiz de Montoya, Antonio. *The Spiritual Conquest: A Personal Account of the Founding and Early Years of the Jesuit Paraguay Reductions.* C. J. McNaspy, SJ, John P. Leonard, SJ, and Martin E. Palmer, SJ, trans. C. J. McNaspy, SJ, ed. St. Louis, MO: Institute of Jesuit Sources, 1993.

Saint-Pierre, Charles François Irenée Castel de. *Project for Everlasting Peace.* M.C. Jacob, ed. and trans. In *Peace Projects of the Eighteenth Century.* New York: Garland, 1974, pp. 1-61.

Salmon, Ben. "Letters." In Torin R.T. Finney. *Unsung Hero of the Great War: The Life and Witness of Ben Salmon.* New York: Paulist Press, 1989, pp. 118-20.

Savanarola, Girolamo. *The Compendium of Revelations.* Trans. and ed. Bernard McGinn, in *Apocalyptic Spirituality.* New York: Paulist Press, 1979, pp. 206-11.

Scholl, Sophie. *Letters and Diary.* In Leber, pp. 16-19.

Scott, David. "Fighting Words: Why Catholics Disagree about War." *U.S. Catholic* 57.5 (May 1992): 6-12.

Segundo, Juan Luis. *The Liberation of Theology.* John Drury, trans. Mary-knoll, NY: Orbis Books, 1976, pp. 3-6, 71-72.

Semelin, Jacques. *Unarmed Against Hitler: Civilian Resistance in Europe, 1939-1943.* Susan Husserl-Kapit, trans. Westport, CT & London: Praeger, 1993.

Servizio Paz y Justicia (SERPAJ). "Preparing for Nonviolence." In McManus and Schlabach, pp. 282-91.

Shannon, Thomas A., ed. *War or Peace? The Search for New Answers.* Maryknoll, NY: Orbis Books, 1980.

Simpson, Lesley Bard, ed. *The Encomienda in New Spain: The Beginning of Spanish Mexico.* Berkeley: University of California Press, 1982.

Sobrino, Jon. *Companions of Jesus: The Jesuit Martyrs of El Salvador.* Maryknoll, NY: Orbis Books, 1990.

—. *The True Church and the Poor.* Matthew J. O'Connell, trans. Maryknoll, NY: Orbis Books, 1984, pp. 160-80.

Solidarity National Congress. "Who We Are and What We Want, October 1981." In Persky and Flam, pp. 205-25.

Taillefer, Anne. "Picketing Sing-Sing." *The Catholic Worker* 26.11 (June 1960): 3.

Temple, Katharine. "Confessions of a Latter Day Luddite." *The Catholic Worker* (January-February 1987). In Cornell et al. *A Penny a Copy,*

2d ed., pp. 316-19.

Thomas à Kempis. *Of the Imitation of Christ.* Justin McCann, ed. and trans. New York: Mentor-Omega, 1962, pp. 26-27, 55-56, 102-6, 123-24.

Toribio da Benevente (Motolinía). *Letter to Charles V,* January 2, 1555. In Simpson, pp. 234-43.

U.S. Catholic Conference. *Between War and Peace.* In Flannery, pp. 346-50.

——. *Building Peace: A Pastoral Reflection on the Response to* The Challenge of Peace *and a Report on* The Challenge of Peace *and Policy Developments 1983-1988.* Washington, DC: NCCB, 1988.

——. *The Challenge of Peace and Our Response.* Daughters of St. Paul, eds. Boston: St. Paul Editions, 1983.

——. *The Crisis of Christianity.* In Flannery, pp. 329-35.

——. *Declaration on Conscientious Objection and Selective Conscientious Objection.* Washington, DC: USCC, 1971.

——. *The Hope of Mankind.* In Flannery, pp. 375-78.

——. *Human Life in Our Day.* In O'Brien and Shannon, *Renewing the Earth,* pp. 451-67.

——. "Letter to Secretary of State James Baker, November 7, 1990." *The Reporter for Conscience's Sake* 47.8 (Sept.-Oct. 1990): 1-2.

——. "Peace and Vietnam." In Nolan, *Pastoral Letters,* pp. 604-7.

——. *Resolution on Southeast Asia.* In U.S. Catholic Conference. *In the Name of Peace: Collective Statements of the United States Bishops on War and Peace, 1919-1980.* Washington, DC: USCC, 1983, pp. 59-62.

Vatican Council II. *Decree on the Apostolate of the Laity.* In *The Documents of Vatican II.* Walter M. Abbott, SJ and Joseph Gallagher, eds. New York: Guild Press, 1966, pp. 491-92.

——. *Gaudium et Spes. The Pastoral Constitution of the Catholic Church in the Modern World.* In Gremillion, pp. 264-65, 313-19.

Velvet Revolution. "Randomly Selected Slogans from the Nonviolent Street Protests, November 1989." In Bernard Wheaton and Zdenek Kavan. *The Velvet Revolution: Czechoslovakia, 1988-1991.* Boulder, CO: Westview Press, 1992, pp. 187-94.

Ventotene Group. "Ventotene Manifesto: For a United Europe." In Chatfield and Ilukhina, pp. 323-24.

Vieira, Antônio. "Lenten Sermon to the Colonists of Maranhão, 1653."

Catholic Peacemakers

In Goodpasture, pp. 74-76.

Vitoria, Francisco de. "On the Laws of War." In *De Indis et de Iure Belli Relectiones*. Ernest Nye, ed., John P. Bale, trans. The Classics of International Law, vol. 7. Washington, DC: Carnegie Endowment, 1917, pp. 163-74.

—. *On the Rights of the Native Americans*. In Simpson, pp. 127-28.

Vives, Juan Luis. *Introduction to Wisdom. A Renaissance Textbook*. Marian Leona Tobriner, SNJM, ed. New York: Teachers College Press, 1968, pp. 128-43.

Walesa, Lech. "Interview with Oriana Fallaci, March 1981." In Persky and Flam, pp. 100-105.

Walsh, Michael J. "Introductory Remarks." In *The Vatican and World Peace. A Boston College Symposium*. Gerrards Cross: Smythe, 1970.

The White Rose. "Four Leaflets, 1942." In Leber, p. x; Chatfield and Ilukhina, pp. 292-94; and *The White Rose: Munich 1942-1943*. Inge Scholl, ed. Arthur R. Schultz, trans. Middletown, CT: Wesleyan University Press, 1983, pp. 85-87.

Witness for Peace. "Original Statement of Purpose." In Ed Griffin-Nolan. *Witness for Peace: A Story of Resistance*. Louisville, KY: Westminster-John Knox Press, 1991, pp. 235-36.

Willams, Betty. "Interview with Richard Deutsch." In Deutsch, pp. 52-60.

Zahn, Gordon C. *Another Part of the War: The Camp Simon Story*. Amherst: University of Massachusetts Press, 1979, pp. v-xiv.

—. *German Catholics and Hitler's Wars: A Study in Social Control*. New York: Sheed & Ward, 1962.

—. *In Solitary Witness. The Life and Death of Franz Jägerstätter*. Collegeville, MN: Liturgical Press, 1964.

Zumárraga, Juan de. *Letter to Charles V,* August 27, 1529. In Simpson, pp. 214-29.

Zverina, Josef. "On Not Living in Hatred." In Havel et al. *Power of the Powerless*, pp. 207-16.

920

INDEX OF
BIBLICAL CITATIONS

923

The Mothers of the Plaza de Mayo. (Photo by Rex Gower)

GENERAL INDEX

Key words generally associated with peace are marked in bold.
Titles of works and the original forms of key words are in italics.

A

Abraham 527
ACCO. *see* Association of
  Catholic Conscientious
  Objectors
American Civil Liberties Union
  (ACLU) 702
activism: Battek 509; Day
  705–707; Gutiérrez 583–
  585, 587; Italy 418; Lanza
  del Vasto 433; Merton 751–
  753, 753–754; post-WWII
  379; South Africa 530
Adela, Maria 641
Adrian of Utrecht *see* Adrian VI
Adrian VI 85; *Sublimis Deus*
  86
African Theology 525, 579
Agosin, Marjorie 640
Agricola, Rudolf 15
Albigensian Crusade 98, 683
Alcuin of York 209
Aldridge, Robert 899
Alexander the Great 24,
  199, 211, 245
Alexander VI 10
Alfaro, Francisco de 163
Alfonsin, Raul 644
Alighieri, Dante *see* Dante
Allende, Salvador 645
Alonso de Ojeda 137

Althusser 581
Alvarus 77
Amnesty International 629
Ancheita, Jose de 153–155, 576
Andrés Pérez, Carlos 654–655
Angell, Norman 435
Ángulo, Juan Fernandez de
  Letter to Emperor Charles V
  137
Antigonus 226
Aphraates 160
Apocalypse: Benda 510,
  511, 514; Berrigans 814–
  815; Dussel 603, 606; Fox
  903–904; Gutiérrez 585;
  Kairos Covenant 533, 535;
  Lanza del Vasto 433;
  McSorley 897–898; medieval
  159, 160; Merton 751–753;
  More 44; Philippines 562;
  apocalyptic peacemaking 2,
  176; Ruiz de Montoya 175,
  178; Savanarola 9–14; visions
  of world peace 235
Apostle, the. *see* St. Paul
Apostles: Day 710; Dubois
  205, 206, 208; Erasmus
  55, 56, 58, 68, 74, 79, 80;
  Jägerstätter 356; Las Casas
  112, 113, 118, 119; Marsilio
  of Padua 188; Thomas à
  Kempis 15; Vatican II 408

G

O

882; legitimizes nonviolence 845; IV, C 605; §25 854–855; §200 853–855; citizens and conscience 849; civil society 845; condemn disrespect for authority 717–718; condemn Vietnam war as immoral 784; conscientious objection 849; "Costliness of War" 700; *Crisis of Christianity* 715–716; *Declaration on Conscientious Objection and Selective Conscientious Objection* 782; deterrence 848, 850; disarmament 854–855; false patriotism 774; "Freedom and Peace" 772–773; freedom has its limitations 718; harmony 773–774; *Hope of Mankind* 727; *Human Life* 776–786; "if you wish peace, prepare for peace" 727; "International Order" 725; Iraq 880–881; just peace in Vietnam 775; just war 845; Kuwait 880–881; *Lessons of War* 697–699; *Letter to Secretary of State James Baker* 879–880; military service 849; "moment of supreme crisis" 851–852; "moral about-face" 852; nation's right & obligation of self-defense 854–855; negotiations 848–849; Non-Proliferation Treaty 777–778; nuclear war 845–852; obedience to state 717–718; *On Personal Conscience*

849; order in human society 847; pacifism 845; Partial Test-Ban Treaty 777–778; *Pastoral Letter of 1919* 698; *Peace and Vietnam* 773; peace not merely absence of war 777–778; peacemaking church 854–855; peacemaking not optional commitment 852; Persian Gulf War 880; *Personal Responsibility* 772–773; presumption against war 847–848; primacy of law & order 728; prophetic call of peacemaking 845; Reagan administration 852–853; Reagan era 879–880; *Resolution on Peace* 776–778; *Resolution on Southeast Asia,* November 1971 267, 784; "Respect for Authority" 717; "Role of Conscience" 779; Rom. 13 716–718; "Russia and Democracy" 726; SALT II Treaty 844–845; serve the nation 699; support nuclear agreements 850–852; teaching ministry 846–847; theological reflection 854–855; theology of peace 854–855; tragedy of Vietnam 785–786; "tribute to military chaplains" 699; Vatican II 773–774; Vietnam 772, 773, 778; vision of peace 847; WW II 715

USA: alternative service 719–720; broad access to power

X

Y

Z

Design and Typesetting of This Book
Were Completed at Italica Press
New York, New York, on
September 12, 1995
Deo Gratias
*   *

*